MATTHEW PRIOR:

A STUDY OF HIS PUBLIC CAREER
AND CORRESPONDENCE

Earl of Jersey.
Master of the Horse to
Queen Mary 1692

EDWARD VILLIERS, 1st EARL OF JERSEY
from the Portrait by HYACINTHE RYGAULT now at Middleton Park

(*By kind permission of the Earl of Jersey*)

MATTHEW PRIOR:
A STUDY OF HIS PUBLIC CAREER
AND CORRESPONDENCE

BY

L. G. WICKHAM LEGG

FELLOW AND TUTOR OF NEW COLLEGE
OXFORD

OCTAGON BOOKS

A DIVISION OF FARRAR, STRAUS AND GIROUX

New York   1972

First published 1921

Reprinted 1972

by permission of the Cambridge University Press

OCTAGON BOOKS

A DIVISION OF FARRAR, STRAUS & GIROUX, INC.

19 Union Square West

New York, N. Y. 10003

Library of Congress Cataloging in Publication Data

Legg, Leopold George Wickham, 1877-
    Matthew Prior.
    Reprint of the 1921 ed.
    Bibliography: p.
    1. Prior, Matthew, 1664-1721.   2. Great Britain—History—
    1689-1714.   3. Great Britain—Foreign relations—France.
    4. France—Foreign relations—Great Britain.

DA497.P7L4   1972   327.20924   [B]   72-5135
ISBN 0-374-94890-9

Manufactured by Braun-Brumfield, Inc.
Ann Arbor, Michigan

Printed in the United States of America

PREFACE

THIS sketch of Matthew Prior's public life has been put together under many difficulties. It owes its existence to a suggestion put forward by Professor Firth, to whom I take this opportunity of tendering my thanks for much advice and encouragement. Arrangements had been made for its publication in a slightly larger form in 1915, but the outbreak of war brought all work upon it to a close, and it is now only possible to put to it a few finishing touches. After so great an interval it is not easy to pick up threads dropped six years ago, and the book must therefore go forth as it stands.

As a writer of light verse, Prior stands second to none in the Augustan age of English literature, but it is only recently that attention has been drawn to him as a writer of prose of unusual excellence. The discoveries made by Mr Waller at Longleat, and the scattered fragments of his voluminous correspondence which have been printed in the Historical MSS. Commission reports and in private collections have brought this aspect of Prior into greater prominence, and the printed material has been fully used by Mr Bickley in his excellent *Life of Matthew Prior*. But in addition to printed sources, there are masses of letters, of varying value, both in the Record Office and in private hands and from these it is possible to reconstruct in detail and to value the work done by Prior in the diplomatic service. It is true that his influence on public affairs may not have been great, and it is probable that his enemies exaggerated it, but his papers enable us to judge some of the matters of hottest dispute in the party politics of the first quarter of the eighteenth century, and to judge the responsibility of the accused in the charges brought by the Whigs against the Tory ministry of Harley and St John. Little therefore will be found in this book by way of criticism of Prior's poetical work. At the same time, in order that the reader may appreciate the poet's skill in prose, it has been thought right to allow Prior's correspondence to speak for itself as far as possible.

The Secretary of the Syndics of the University Press has laid the devotees of Prior under a heavy load of obligation in recent years, and the Syndics might well have been expected to take the view that at their Press, he should have no successor in work relating to Prior. It is therefore no merely formal expression of thanks that I now make to them for their kindness in accepting this work for publication. I have also to thank the officers of the State Archives at The Hague for facilities given to me when working among their records, and more especially to the authorities of the Archives of the French Foreign Office where, with a courtesy worthy of the traditions of French diplomacy, I was allowed to consult the papers dealing with "Mat's Peace" and the attempted Stuart restoration. I have also to express my thanks to the Marquess of Bath, K.G., for allowing me to print the extracts from one of his MSS. which will be found in Appendix C.

Last, but by no means least, I have to thank the Earl of Jersey for the readiness with which he renewed the permission given me by the Earl his father to use and print extracts from the papers now at Middleton Park, as well as for the privilege of reproducing Rygault's portrait of the first Earl, which has only recently been rediscovered. And I should also like to acknowledge the encouragement I have received from the kindly interest taken in the book by the Dowager Countess of Jersey.

L. G. W. L.

Oxford
March 1921

CONTENTS

FRONTISPIECE
EDWARD VILLIERS, 1st EARL OF JERSEY

TITLES OF BOOKS REFERRED TO

[This should not be considered as a full bibliography: the reader who wishes to cover more ground in this period should not omit to consult the standard works of Macaulay, Legrelle, Klopp, Michaels and Felix Salomon.]

A. MANUSCRIPT SOURCES

Cambridge, St John's College, MS. S. 51
Godmanstone, Parish Registers
Longleat, Warminster, MS. xxi
London, British Museum, Add. MSS. 4291, 15,947, 21,508; Harl. 3780; Stowe, 222, 227
London, Public Record Office:
State Papers, Holland, vols. 221–3
S.P. Domestic, King William's Chest, 13
S. P. France, 154, 157–9
Foreign Entry Book, 199
Royal Letters, 7

London, Public Record Office:
F.O. King's Letters, 13, 14
Treaty Papers, 15, 90
Middleton Park, Oxon.: Papers preserved at
Oxford, Bodleian Library (S.C. 25,427), MS. Montagu d. 1
Paris, *Archives du ministère des affaires étrangères*, Angleterre, vols. 233–5, 237–42, 245, 247–9, 253
The Hague, Royal Archives, St Gen. 146, 148–50, 152–3, 155, 2342, 4311, 7339

B. PRINTED SOURCES

Aitken, G. A., article in *Contemporary Review*, May, 1890
A report from the Committee of Secrecy appointed by order of the House of Commons to examine several books and papers, London, 1715
Beeching, H. C., *Francis Atterbury*, Pitmans, 1909
Bickley, Francis, *The Life of Matthew Prior*, Pitmans, 1914
Bolingbroke, *Letters and Correspondence...of...Henry St John, Viscount*, ed. Gilbert Parke, London, 1798
Calendar of State Papers, Domestic, 1694–5
Cole, Christian, *Historical and political Memoirs*, London, 1735
Dobson, Austin, *Selected Poems of Matthew Prior*, London, Kegan Paul, 1889
English Historical Review, July, 1914, pp. 525–32; July, 1915, pp. 501–18

Grimblot, Paul, *Letters of William III and Louis XIV and of their ministers 1697–1700*, London, 1848
Hearne, *Remarks and Collections of Thomas*, vol. vii. Oxford (Oxford Historical Society), 1906
Historical Manuscripts Commission:
Second Report (Papers of W. R. Baker, Esq. and of the Earl of Stair), 1871
Fourth Report, 1874
Seventh Report (Papers of the Earl of Egmont), 1879
Eighth Report (Papers of the Duke of Marlborough), 1881
Ninth Report, pt. ii, Papers of Alfred Morrison, Esq., 1884
The Manuscripts of His Grace the Duke of Rutland, K.G., preserved at Belvoir Castle, vol. ii. (12th Report, App. v.), 1889

Hist. Man. Com. (*cont.*).
　　The Manuscripts of J. Eliot
　　　　Hodgkin, Esq., F.S.A.
　　　　(Fifteenth Report, Appendix,
　　　　pt. II), 1897
　　*The Manuscripts of His Grace the
　　　　Duke of Portland*, vols. IV.
　　　　(Fifteenth Report, Appendix,
　　　　pt. IV.), V. VI. VII. VIII. 1897,
　　　　1899, 1901
　　*Calendar of the Stuart Papers be-
　　　　longing to His Majesty The
　　　　King preserved at Windsor
　　　　Castle*, vol. I. 1902
　　*Report on the Manuscripts of the
　　　　Duke of Buccleuch and Queens-
　　　　berry, K.G., K.T., preserved
　　　　at Montagu House, Whitehall*,
　　　　vol. II. pt. I, 1903
　　*Calendar of the Manuscripts of the
　　　　Marquis of Bath preserved at
　　　　Longleat*, vol. III. (Prior Pa-
　　　　pers), 1908
Hutchins, Joseph, *History of Dorset*,
　　1863
Journals of the House of Commons
Lamberty, G., marquis de, *Mé-
　　moires pour servir à l'histoire
　　du XVIIIᵉ siècle*, Hague and
　　Amsterdam, 1724–40, vol. VI.
Legrelle, A., *La diplomatie française
　　et la succession d'Espagne*,
　　Ghent and Paris, 1888–92
Luttrell, Narcissus, *A brief historical
　　relation of State affairs from
　　September 1678 to April 1714*,
　　Oxford, 1857
Macky, J., *Characters of the Court of
　　Great Britain*, London, 1732
Macpherson, James, *Original Papers:
　　containing the secret history of
　　Great Britain from the Restora-
　　tion to the accession of the house
　　of Hannover*, London, 1775
Manners-Sutton, H., *The Lexington
　　Papers*, London, 1851
Nichols, John, *Literary Anecdotes of
　　the eighteenth century*, Lon-
　　don, 1814
Prior, Matthew, *The works of, with*

*a life by the Rev. John Mit-
　　ford*, Boston, 1854; *Poems on
　　Several Occasions*, ed. A. R.
　　Waller, Cambridge, 1905;
　　*Dialogues of the Dead and
　　other works*, ed. A. R. Waller,
　　Cambridge, 1907
*Private correspondence of Sarah
　　Duchess of Marlborough...and
　　the select correspondence of her
　　husband John, Duke of Marl-
　　borough*, London, 1838
Spence, Joseph, *Anecdotes, observa-
　　tions and characters of Books
　　and Men*, London, J. R.
　　Smith, 1858
Stanhope, James, Earl, *History of
　　England comprising the Reign
　　of Queen Anne until the Peace
　　of Utrecht*, London, 1870;
　　[Lord Mahon] *History of
　　England in the Eighteenth
　　Century*, London, 1836
Strong, S. Arthur, *A catalogue of
　　letters and other historical
　　documents exhibited in the
　　Library at Welbeck*, London,
　　Murray, 1903
Swift, Jonathan, *Works*, ed. Sir
　　Walter Scott, Edinburgh,
　　1814, vol. III.
*The Correspondence of Sir Thomas
　　Hanmer, Bart.*, ed. Sir Henry
　　Bunbury, Bart., London, 1838
*The History of his own time, Compiled
　　from the Original Manuscripts
　　of His late excellency Matthew
　　Prior, Esq.; revised and
　　signed by himself and copied
　　fair for the press by Mr Adrian
　　Drift, his executor*, Dublin,
　　1740
The Works of Alexander Pope, ed.
　　Elwin, W., and Courthope,
　　W. J., London, 1889
Weber, Ottocar, *Der Friede von
　　Utrecht*, Gotha, 1891
Welch, Joseph, *A List of the Scholars
　　of St Peter's College West-
　　minster*, London, 1788

Chapter I

YOUTH AND EDUCATION

"Dorchester, Dorset, 1730 Dec. 7.

Cousin Middleton,

Pursuant to your request I send you here an account of Mr Prior's parentage, from his father's brother's son Christopher Prior. Mr Prior's grandfather lived at Godmanstone, a small village three miles from this town: he had five sons and one daughter called Mary, married to one Hunt of Lighe, a village eight miles hence. Thomas and George, two of the brothers, were bound apprentice to carpenters at Fordington joined east of this town; whence they removed to Wimborne about eighteen miles hence eastward where Thomas lived and died, and where George the father of Mr Prior was married, but how long he lived there I cannot find, only his wife, Mr Prior's mother lies buried at Wimborne or by it, with whom I have heard that Mr Prior desired to be buried before Westminster Abbey was in his eye. That Mr Prior was born at or by Wimborne I find because Christopher says he remembers his cousin Matthew coming over to Godmanstone when a boy and lying with him. George, his father, after his wife's death, I suppose, moved to London encouraged by his brother Arthur who had succeeded in the world and kept the Rummer Tavern by Charing Cross...who took his nephew to wait in the tavern, from which time you know his history...."[1]

[1] The letter is printed in full in Appendix A.

The tradition here set forth by Conyers Place to his cousin Conyers Middleton has the merit of being nearly contemporary with Prior himself and is backed by the authority of a member of the family. Yet, from the first, doubts were entertained as to the place where Matthew Prior was born. On entering St John's College, Cambridge, he was described as of Dorset, which a later hand changed to Middlesex, and as born at "Winburn" in the aforesaid county; the next day he described himself as of Dorset; five years later, on admission as a fellow of the College, he described himself as of Middlesex. Further if it were true that Matthew had been born at Wimborne, it was strange that no trace could be found of his baptism in the registers there, and adherents of the tradition that Wimborne in Dorset was the place consoled themselves with the reflection that Prior's connexions were known to be Nonconformist. Had he not himself written:

> So at pure barn of loud *Non-Con*
> Where with my *Granam* I have gone?

Nor was it unreasonable to suppose that one whose stock came from Godmanstone, the birthplace of Joseph Damer, was other than a nonconformist. This might also explain why there is no trace of the burial of his mother at Wimborne, though it may be observed that Conyers Place is not certain that she was buried in Wimborne itself, for he says "at Wimborne or by it."

On the whole therefore opinion inclined to the view that Prior was born at Wimborne, though Conyers Place's reasons for believing it do not seem convincing; and it was assumed that Prior, being somewhat ashamed of his lowly parentage, tried to hide it by deliberately altering the county of his birth from Dorset to Middlesex. Nevertheless it would seem that Prior was born in

Middlesex, for it has been discovered by the simple method of examining the registers of St Margaret's, Westminster, that Matthew Prior was baptised at St Margaret's on August 2, 1664[1]. This evidence should be considered conclusive; it agrees with the usual date assigned for his birth, viz. July 23, 1664, and in that age the baptismal register may be taken to indicate the immediate neighbourhood of the birth. It is to be feared that Dorset must surrender her claim to Prior as a native son, though his stock was unquestionably drawn from that most captivating county.

(|What then is the explanation of the entries in the registers at St John's College, Cambridge? Here we frankly enter into the realms of conjecture, but it is easy to imagine circumstances which might lead to a *bona fide* misunderstanding by Prior. It is not beyond the realms of possibility to imagine that after Matthew's birth, his father George Prior removed from Westminster to Wimborne round which all Matthew's earliest recollections would turn. Transferred thence to London once more, and finally entered in 1683 at Cambridge, he in ignorance of the true story states he was born at Wimborne Minster. Five years later he has learnt the truth, and enters correctly that he was a Middlesex man. All this of course is guesswork, but it serves to show how easy it is to conceive of circumstances under which the mistake may have arisen.

The stock from which Prior was descended was that of a prolific family of farm-labourers whose home was Godmanstone, and the last local representative of which was apparently Mrs Martha Prior who died in 1889 at the age of 72[2]. His father George was a younger son,

---

[1] See a letter by Mr H. F. Westlake in the *Times Literary Supplement*, March 14, 1918, p. 130, col. 2. "Aug. 2, 1664, Matthew Pryor s. to Geo. by Eliz."

[2] For the whole question of Prior's family see Appendix A.

and he and his brothers Arthur and Thomas under the hard but beneficial rule of primogeniture were thrown upon the wide world to make their way, while Christopher, the eldest son, remained at the "family mansion" at Godmanstone to be the progenitor of yet poorer descendants. Arthur made his fortune as the owner of the "Rhenish Wine Tavern" in Cannon Row, Whitehall. Owing possibly to George Prior's death leaving Matthew destitute, Arthur took young Matthew into his service as a waiter and messenger boy[1]. It seemed as if life would be a hard struggle for the lad, who had at least received some elements of education[2]. His however was not destined to be a career of an able man triumphing by constant perseverance and resource over all difficulties. Prior was throughout his career the sport of fortune, and if the story told by Fleetwood Shephard be true, her most extraordinary stroke in Prior's career was that which opened it.

When still at a tender age[3], Prior was "surprised" with a Horace in his hand by Charles Sackville, Earl

---

[1] Cf. the well-known lines of the "Epistle to Fleetwood Shephard":

> "My uncle, rest his soul! when living,
> Might have contrived me ways of thriving,
> Taught me with cyder to replenish
> My vats, or ebbing tide of Rhenish.
> So when for hock I drew prickt white-wine
> Swear't had the flavour and was right wine,
> Or sent me with ten pounds to Furni-
> val's Inn, to some good rogue attorney;
> Where now by forging deeds and cheating
> I'd found some handsome ways of getting."

(*Dialogues of the Dead and other works*, ed. A. R. Waller, 1907, p. 46.)

[2] Possibly at Wimborne and Westminster, where his career is said to have been cut short by his father's death. But all this is very doubtful.

[3] Bath MSS. III. 32. "The rest is all my own affairs. My Lord Dorset has been pleased to favour them since I was ten year old." This would make the incident occur in 1674; but the words must not be pressed closely.

of Dorset and Middlesex, who came one day into the
Rhenish Wine Tavern to seek for Fleetwood Shephard.
The Earl took the Horace from Matthew

to see what book he had got, he asked him what he did with it.
Young Matthew answered he was looking upon it. How, said
Lord Dorset, do you understand Latin? He replied, a little, upon
saying which, the noble lord tried if he could construe a place or
two, and finding he did, Lord Dorset turned to one of the odes,
and bid him put it into English, which Mat did in English metre,
and brought it up to the company before they broke up, and the
company was so well pleased with the performance and the odd-
ness of the thing that they all liberally rewarded him with money;
and whenever that company met there, it was certainly part of
their entertainment to give Odes out of Horace, and verses out
of Ovid to translate[1].

This lucky incident proved the foundation of Prior's
fortune, for Dorset was so much struck with Matthew's
natural wit that he became his patron and sent him to
Westminster[2], where he made friends with boys who
were later to be influential in the state[3].

Of his contemporaries at Westminster, by far the
most important, and perhaps the closest friend, was
Charles Montagu, famous later as Chancellor of the
Exchequer and Earl of Halifax. Him Prior followed
to Cambridge in 1683, but not to the same College,

[1] Quoted by Mr Austin Dobson from Sir James Montagu's account
contained in the Papers at Longleat. See the Parchment Library *Selected
Poems of Matthew Prior*, ed. A. Dobson, London, Kegan Paul, 1889,
p. 209.

[2] Prior was not admitted as a Scholar at Westminster till 1681, when
he must have been aged 16. His name appears the last in a list of thirteen
for that year. (*A List of the Scholars of St Peter's College, Westminster...*by
Joseph Welch, London, 1788, p. 65.)

[3] In this same year of his meeting with Dorset, he became the
possessor of a Bible and Prayer Book. (See S. Arthur Strong, *A Catalogue of Letters and other historical documents exhibited in the Library at
Welbeck*, London, John Murray, 1903, p. 103.)

for while Montagu went to Trinity, Prior was admitted
as a Scholar at St John's, the Master of which, Dr
Humphrey Gower, was the son of a former rector of
Holy Trinity, Dorchester[1], and had been educated at
Dorchester School.

Prior took his degree of Bachelor of Arts in 1686[2],
and it is during these years at Cambridge that we first
come across the man himself. He had now grown up
into a tall thin man with a long face with hard immove-
able features, which later in life earned for him from
Torcy the appellation of "ce visage de bois." Bright
blue eyes, and a large and commanding nose, imparted
to his face an impression of keenness and intelligence
which his heavy under-lip and hollow highboned cheeks
with their deep hectic flush[3] otherwise belied. But the
moment he opened his mouth, the wit and sparkle of
his conversation amply atoned for any defects in his
appearance.

The first letter of his now extant, dated July 18/28,
1685, is addressed to his uncle, who can be no other
than the prosperous Arthur Prior. Curiously enough,
it strikes the note of financial distress and mendicancy
which was to be characteristic of much of his correspondence all through his life:

> If my necessity, Sir, encourages my boldness, I know your
> goodness sufficient to excuse one and relieve t'other. I am very
> sensible what expenses my education puts you to, and must con-
> fess my repeated petitions might have wearied any charity but
> yours; but since I have no advocate, no patron, no father but
> yourself, pardon that importunity which makes me seek the

[1] See J. Hutchins, *History of Dorset*, Westminster, 1863, II. 376.

[2] He did not proceed to M.A. till 1700, when it was conferred on him
by *mandamus* of the Senate.

[3] It faded in later years and left his cheeks sallow, but Conyers Place,
when visiting Godmanstone in later years, remarks that it was common
to all the Priors.

kindness of all these in you, which throws me at your feet to beg at once your blessing and assistance, and that, since your indulgence has set me safe from shore, you would not let me perish in the ocean[1].

From this letter it is clear that Prior was receiving his education, partially at any rate, from the kindness of his uncle, and this gives colour to the story that by following Charles Montagu to Cambridge and refusing to go to Christ Church, Oxford, he temporarily alienated the sympathies of his patron, Lord Dorset. Though deprived of this powerful support during his years at Cambridge, Prior succeeded in enhancing his own reputation. His facility for making verse, both in English and Latin, became greater, and we find him addressing a Pastoral dialogue[2] to Mrs Katharine Prior, the wife of Arthur Prior, and apologising to her for neglect in writing to her[3]. This apology is accompanied by some more verses, which have been preserved[4]. Various College exercises also have survived, such as the odes at Longleat on the subjects of "Charity never faileth[5]," "There be those that leave their names behind them[6]," "Many daughters have done well, but thou excellest them all[7]," the two latter being effusions in praise of the Lady Margaret, the foundress of St John's. Of the same character is the ode on the coronation of James II[8]. These compositions, however, brought no κῦδος to Prior from the outside world, nor can it honestly be said that they merited much distinction, and it was not until 1687 that the London public began

---

[1] *Hist. MSS. Comm.* Bath Papers, III. 1.

[2] Matthew Prior, *Dialogues of the Dead and other works in Prose and Verse*, ed. A. R. Waller, Cambridge University Press, 1907, p 272.

[3] *Hist. MSS. Comm.* Bath Papers, III. 1. She died on March 21/31, 1698/9. (*Ibid.* III. 330.)

[4] *Dialogues of the Dead*, p. 281.   [5] *Ibid.* p. 274.

[6] *Ibid.* p. 276.   [7] *Ibid.* p. 278

[8] *Ibid.* p. 279.

to hear of him. In that year, jointly with Charles Montagu, he wrote and published a burlesque on Dryden's *Hind and the Panther*, entitled *The Hind and the Panther transvers'd to the story of the Country-mouse and the City-mouse*. This famous parody, which, in pungency of wit and keenness of satire, falls lamentably short of its model, *The Rehearsal*, was judged at the time to have "ruined the reputation of the divine, as the 'Rehearsal' ruined the reputation of the poet[1]," and is reported with no great probability to have so affected Dryden himself that he wept and said it was a shame that an old man should be thus treated. Prior's share in the work has been variously estimated; James Montagu, who was in a very good position to judge, gives the following account of the composition:

The first fruit of this intimacy [between Charles Montagu and Prior] was no less beneficial to the public than to themselves, for about this time came out the celebrated poem of the Hind and Panther, written by Mr Dryden, who had then professed himself of the Romish religion, and that poem being very much cried up for a masterpiece of a great poet, it created great dissatisfaction to all who opposed the bringing in of popery by King James, and it was the wish of many that the same should be answered by an ingenious pen, but it is not certain that either Mr Montagu or Mr Prior at first resolved to undertake the doing of it, but the book which came afterwards out by the name of the City Mouse, and the Country Mouse, which was allowed by all persons to be the most effectual answer to that poem of Mr Dryden's, and which was composed by Mr Montagu and Mr Prior together, happened to owe its birth more to accident than to design: for the Hind and Panther, being at that time in everybody's hands, Mr Prior accidentally came one morning to make Mr Montagu a visit at his brother's chambers in the Middle Temple, London, where the said Mr Montagu lodged when he

---

[1] Preface to the Second Part of "The Reasons of Mr Bayes' changing his Religion."

was in London, and the poem lying upon the table Mr Montagu took it up, and read the first four lines in the poem of the Hind and the Panther, which are these:

> A milk white Hind, immortal and unchanged,
> Fed on the lawns, and o'er the forest ranged,
> Without unspotted, innocent within,
> She feared no danger for she knew no sin.

Where stopping, he took notice how foolish it was to commend a four-footed beast for not being guilty of sin, and said the best way of answering that poem would be to ridicule it by telling Horace's fable of the City Mouse, and the Country Mouse in the same manner, which being agreed to, Mr Prior took the book out of Mr Montagu's hands, and in a short time after repeated the first four lines, which were after printed in the City Mouse, and Country Mouse, viz.

> A milk white mouse, immortal and unchanged,
> Fed on soft cheese, and o'er the dairy ranged,
> Without unspotted, innocent within,
> She feared no danger for she knew no gin.

The repeating of these lines set the company in laughter, and Mr Montagu took up the pen by him, and wrote on a loose piece of paper, and both of them making several essays to transverse, in like manner, other parts of the poem gave a beginning to that work, which was afterwards published to the great satisfaction of many people, and though no name was set to the book, yet it was quickly known who were the authors of it, and as the reputation Mr Montagu got thereby was the foundation of his being taken notice of, so it contributed not less to the credit of Mr Prior, who became thereby reconciled to his first patron, the Earl of Dorset[1].

Peterborough's evidence is to the effect that Prior had a large hand in composing the burlesque, for to an enquirer who asked whether Halifax "'did not write the Country Mouse with Mr Prior,' he replied, 'Yes, just as if I was in a chaise with Mr Cheselden here,

[1] Quoted in A. Dobson's *Selected Poems of Matthew Prior*, p. 214.

drawn by his fine horse, and should say: "Lord, how finely we draw this chaise[1]!" ' ' " But if the *Town Mouse and the Country Mouse* assisted the fortunes of Prior in 1687, the burlesque (if he really did compose most of it) is scarcely of sufficient excellence on which to base a reputation as a wit at the present day. The first four lines which are indisputably his, are by far the best in the whole wearisome compilation.

In another way the year 1687 proved critical to Prior, for his uncle died, and though he left Matthew £100[2], his death was a very serious loss to the young man. So it was fortunate that Matthew's talent in writing verse earned for him that refuge of destitute students, a tutorship, which, Whig though he was, drew him into a society not far removed from the Jacobites. On April 5, 1688, he was admitted a Fellow of his College, and was appointed to write the ode which the College presented every year to one of its benefactors, the Earl of Exeter. *The Country Mouse and the City Mouse*[3], together possibly with this new gift, which has as text, "I am that I am," won him the patronage of Lord Exeter, and his appointment as tutor to Lord Exeter's sons. During the few months that he held this post, he wrote the poems addressed to Lady Exeter; and one, a second epistle to Fleetwood Shephard, dated May 14, 1689, gives us a passing glimpse of his manner of life in the country at Burleigh:

> As soon as *Phoebus'* Rays inspect us,
> First, Sir, I read; and then I Breakfast;
> So on, 'till foresaid God does set,
> I sometimes study, sometimes Eat.

---

[1] Joseph Spence, *Anecdotes*, London, J. R. Smith, 1858, p. 102.

[2] See his will printed below in Appendix A.

[3] *Dialogues of the Dead, ut sup.* p. 386. "The Credit it happened to gain at L.[ondon] was indifferent until my L.[ord] of Ex.[eter] was pleased not to discommend it at Burleigh."

Thus of your Heroes and brave Boys,
With whom old *Homer* makes such Noise,
The greatest Actions I can find,
Are, that They did their Work, and din'd.

The Books of which I'm chiefly fond,
Are such as you have whilom con'd;
That treat of *China's* Civil Law,
And Subjects' Rights in *Golconda*;
Of Highway-Elephants at *Ceylan*,
That rob in Clans, like Men o' th' *Highland*;

Of Apes that storm, or keep a Town,
As well almost, as Count *Lauzun*;
Of Unicorns and Alligators,
Elks, Mermaids, Mummies, Witches, Satyrs,
And twenty other stranger Matters;
Which, tho' they're things I've no Concern in,
Make all our grooms admire my Learning.

Criticks I read on other Men,
And *Hypers* upon Them again;
From whose Remarks I give Opinion
On twenty Books, yet ne'er look in One.

And then for his real diversion:

Sometimes I climb my Mare, and kick her
To bottl'd Ale, and neighb'ring Vicar;
Sometimes at Stamford take a Quart,
'Squire Shephard's Health—With all my heart[1].

This quiet easy life, however, was not for long, for soon after William's accession Lord Exeter broke up his home, and retired abroad. As for Prior, he was by this time known in the literary world, and he enjoyed the friendship of Charles Montagu, who had immediately been taken into William's favour, of Fleetwood Shephard, and also of Lord Dorset, whose high

[1] *Poems upon Several Occasions*, ed. A. R. Waller, p. 14.

estimate of the *Country Mouse and City Mouse*[1] removed the temporary estrangement engendered by Matthew's refusal to go to Christ Church. To Shephard he appealed in another rhyming epistle, which ended with a postscript:

> Our friend Charles Mountague's preferr'd,
> Nor would I have it long observ'd
> That one Mouse eats while t'other's starv'd.

It can be scarcely rash to conjecture that it was through the interest of these powerful friends that Prior was brought to the notice of the King as a promising young man of letters, with the result that in 1690 he was appointed to the post of secretary to Lord Dursley, the English Ambassador at the Congress of The Hague. To have risen in eight years from errand boy to secretary to an embassy is sufficient testimonial to the power of his patrons and their opinion of his ability. With this great advancement, Prior's life begins in earnest.

[1] Cf. his words to William III on introducing Charles Montagu.

Chapter II

APPRENTICESHIP AT THE HAGUE

OF all great European wars, that of the League of Augsburg is undoubtedly the dullest. Battles with stirring scenes which appeal to the imagination are few and far between, and we have to look to the surprise of the French at Steinkirk for an incident which in any way caught the attention of Europe. It is a war of sieges and bombardments, in which the French try to advance over the Netherlands like a rising flood, while the Dutch do their best to check their enemies by a solid dyke of fortresses. On the one side is Louis XIV, face to face with a coalition such as he had never yet encountered, gradually losing his great generals and administrators, relying more and more upon his own favourites, and finding it increasingly difficult to realise his proud mottoes *Sufficit orbi* and *Nec pluribus impar.* On the other side is the Coalition, kept together chiefly by the diplomatic genius of William, but, even when moving most easily, proving itself a machine which creaks and groans at every turn.

It was at the central cogwheel of this cumbrous engine that Prior found himself posted. On November 10, 1690, he announced the fact to the Secretary at Whitehall—so at least we may conjecture, for Prior at this time in unbusinesslike fashion gives no hint of the person to whom his letters are addressed. "I succeed Dr Aglionby," he wrote, "as Secretary to his Exc^{ce} my Ld Dursley; I have sent you the Gazette as usual, and when anything extraordinary occurs I will be sure to advise you of it[1]." It was not a post of great responsibility: the main duty, if we may judge from his somewhat fragmentary correspondence[2], was to pass on to Whitehall the news-letters sent to The Hague from Germany. Twice a week he forwarded these *résumés* of the struggle between Austria and the Turks in the south of Hungary. His humour was tickled by the story of the relief of Esseck, where the Austrian forces were straining every nerve to repel the Turkish advance, and the Grand Vizier with all his army was reported to be preparing to begin a siege[3]:

The siege was begun the 29th of October, the next day about noon the Enemy marched with all forces to post himself conveniently, hoping the Emperor's forces would have abandon'd the Place at his arrival: after most hideous howlings, he began the assault upon the Counterscarp, but perceiving the besieged in a better condition than he expected he retired and began to open the Trenches regularly....

P.S. A Courrier arrived from the D. of Croy with advice that that Prince commanded all the Trumpets and Tambours to sound from the Fortress: that the Enemy thinking some great succour was arrived to the besieged were so surprised that they raised the siege in confusion, leaving all their baggage behind them and 3 pieces of Cannon which was all they brought before the place[4].

But it was very rarely that Prior had such amusing pieces of news to tell. Generally the work was the

1 P.R.O., S.P. Foreign, Holland, vol. 221, fo. 271.

2 We have seventeen letters of Prior in 1690 from Nov. 10 to Dec. 29, 1690, contained in P.R.O., S.P. Foreign, Holland, vol. 221; two of 1691 of Dec. 7 and 14, in *ibid.* 222; three of 1692, in Holland, vol. 222; three of the same year, May 6, Aug. 9/19, Dec. 16/26, in the De la Warr papers (*Hist. MSS. Comm.* IV. 280). From 1693 onwards the Correspondence is fairly complete.

3 On the Drave, about twenty miles from its junction with the Danube.

4 P.R.O., S.P. Foreign, Holland, vol. 221, fo. 277, Prior to Warr, Nov. 21 [1690].

ordinary routine duty of a diplomatic office. He had to
exercise his mind on the characters of the persons to
whom he issued passports, to notify the officials at
Harwich and Westminster should any "disaffected"
persons try to slip over into England without passports; an office which he found difficult to keep free
from abuse, for the number of officers and soldiers,
Dutch and British, and of persons provided with passes
was so great that no effective supervision was possible[1].

But Prior went further than mere complaints and
descriptions of the trouble, for he drew up a "little
scheme" which was designed to remedy the evil, and,

[1] "Concerning my Lord Dursley's giving Passes.

That it is impossible to examine all Dutch, Germans, &c. and particularly French, who come in Companies of 20, 30 or more, as Refugees
who would establish themselves in Ireland and England, or to know if
the attestations or Testimonials they bring be valid.

That the Dutch have no attestations, being Merchants, Burghers, &c.
of several towns, and think it a hardship that they are detained so long
from their affairs, as to be obliged to take a Passport, even at the Brill,
for their sake chiefly it is that such passports are left in Mr Vanderpoole's
hands.

That all officers, soldiers or persons concerned in the King's service,
think themselves sufficiently warranted by their Commissions, orders or
letters, and most of them coming from Flanders would lose at least one
Packet if they come from Helvoetsluys or the Brill to the Hague for a
Passport.

That all English and Scotch who come from England with my Lord
Nottingham's, Sir John Trenchard's or the Scotch Secretaries' pass leave
their passes at Harwich, so that upon such Person's application to my
Lord Dursley for his pass back again, it is impossible for his Lordship to
know if they had such passes from England as they pretended.

That only the Packet-boat and Yachts observe this order of taking on
board only such Persons as have passports, and Multitudes of all sorts of
People come over in every convoy, in all Men of War, Merchant Ships
and small vessels.

(Indorsed):—   Mr. Prior concerning
                               My Lord Dursley's giving Passes."

(S.P. Foreign, Holland, vol. 222, fo. 461.)

he told Adam Cardonnel, had been approved by Secretary Trenchard[1].

Later on indeed, incidents occurred in Holland which Prior thought worth recording. The trial of one Walten for heresy and blasphemy in maintaining "Beckar's opinion concerning the Devil[2]," the whipping publicly of a servant maid for secretly conveying letters to prisoners who are denied all sort of correspondence[3], a fire at Amsterdam arsenal and the blowing up of a frigate at Enkhuysen[4], such is the small beer which Prior chronicles to his masters in England. And whatever other people may have thought of Holland, where the Crown Prince of Denmark "seemed mightily diverted[5]," or of The Hague, which Cresset justly describes as a "sweet place[6]," Prior, to judge from the flatness of his correspondence at this time, found it the reverse of interesting. Persons in subordinate posts, even at the central knot of a great European combination, are apt to find life of less enthralling interest than the general public supposes. Not only this, but the cumbrous alliance was not obtaining even a fair measure of success. In December, 1690, the French went into winter quarters at Mainz; in 1691 they continued, in spite of William's presence, to hold their own in the Netherlands; in 1692 they won the battle of Steinkirk and captured Namur, a feat which was celebrated in a frigid and pompous ode by Boileau, which Prior did

[1] See Bath Papers, III. 7.

[2] P.R.O., S.P. Foreign, Holland, vol. 223, Prior to Vernon, Hague, March 20/30, 1694. Becker's opinion concerning the devil was that there is "but one Devil." (See Bath Papers, III. 22.)

[3] S.P. Foreign, Holland, vol. 223, Prior to Vernon, Mar. 23/Apr. 2, 1693/4.

[4] *Ibid.* Prior to Vernon, June 11/21, 1695.

[5] Bath Papers, III. 6.

[6] *Hist. MSS. Comm.* xiith Report, App. v. 152, Cresset to Lexington, Oct. 13/23, 1693.

not forget. No wonder Prior felt depressed and that he wrote to Dorset in January, 1693:

> 'Tis always my duty to send Your Lordship the news from this side, though at present it is very bad. Furnes and Dixmuyde are lost; the enemy set down before Furnes, the 5th afternoon, opened their trenches in the night, and the next morning summoned the Governor Count Hoorne to render the town, which he did upon capitulation, himself and the garrison marching with two pieces of cannon to Nieuport. This he did, they say, upon letters from the Elector of Bavaria, that in case of extremity he should save the garrison and quit the place....Dixmuyde falls in course: the garrison of that place is likewise retired to Nieuport, whence the Elector is gone to Ostend to give orders concerning the state of that place, in case the French should attack it[1].

In February he writes not much more cheerfully to Vernon:

> When you have done me the favour to write to me, in justice one would think I ought not to answer you when I have little to return besides the impertinence of my thanks; be pleased to excuse me, and be partial to the duty the son owes you where otherwise you would blame the babbling of the Secretary.

> The French lay in such stores and ammunition at Namur and Maubeuge that we fear they design to besiege Charleroi. We have sent a supply to that place under the conduct of Gravenmore with about 3,000 horse, which is safely come thither: if you do not soon finish your parliament matters, and send us our King over, we shall make sorry work in Flanders. We begin to hope well on the Rhine, since Prince Lewis of Baden is to come there, besides what forces the Emperor sends. He asks four regiments of His Majesty: can you spare them? I know not if you have heard that the Elector of Saxe and the Duke of Zell have entered into the alliance made between the King and the States....

> So far politics: now for philosophy, and pray, dear father, are not you a little too serious when you talk of leaving the world at

[1] Bath Papers, III. 2-3.

a time when it could not subsist, *sine fortibus bonisque tuique simillimis*? And why would you leave it without being able to give a good account of it, since you never used to leave anything at that rate? Patience has been a very good recipe ever since Job's time, and you of all mankind (if your modesty does not suffer too much in the advice) should apply the remedy, since you have merit enough to have that patience rewarded in spite of all that fortune can resolve against it[1].

However, in the spring, the outlook of the Netherlands improved, and Prior's spirits rose: in March he was able to tell Dorset that:

In Flanders we are much obliged to the bad weather, which alone has, I believe, saved Charleroi hitherto....The affairs of the Allies are better than we could reasonably expect. The Elector of Brandenburg has informed the States that the 6,000 men which are their appointment, are ready to march, and wait only their orders. The Elector of Saxony is come entirely into the Confederate interest, having signed and exchanged the Treaty upon the same foot with that made between His Majesty and the States General in 1689. He expresses a great desire to do something in this campaign....The Emperor has cunningly enough made this Elector an obliging compliment in sending to Madame Neusch, his mistress, the title of Countess[2]. Sweden has approved the ninth electorate, and Mr Horne, envoy from that Crown at Vienna, has assured the Emperor that his master will not engage with the discontented Party or do anything to the prejudice of the Allies; so that Denmark is not likely to give much disturbance[3].

But dull and gloomy as these months were, they were not unprofitable, for in them Prior was laying the foundations of that reputation for diplomatic skill with which he was credited by so experienced a prince as

[1] Bath Papers, III. 3–4.

[2] Countess of Ratelitz (Prior to Pembroke, April 3, N.S. 1693, Bath Papers, III. 6).

[3] Prior to Dorset, March 3/13, 1692/3, Bath Papers, III. 4–5.

William III. In November, 1692, Dursley left The Hague, presumably on leave of absence, till near the end of April, 1693[1]; and during that time, the Secretary became the channel through which the intentions of the English government were meagrely conveyed to the Dutch States. Several small points of dispute, none of any real difficulty, cropped up between the two Governments. At the end of the year the Dutch announced that six of their ships which had been destined for the Mediterranean would be ready to sail and join the English squadron, but no others, and suggested that reinforcements should go out gradually[2]. How the English government received this we cannot tell; as we know that they were counting on having fifteen Dutch ships there[3], they can scarcely have been satisfied with their allies. Moreover, the Dutch had begun to land in England prisoners captured from the French by their privateers, a practice which was complained of on the ground that the keep of these prisoners entailed extra expense to the English government; while a more discreditable matter was the use that the Dutch made of their ships of war to smuggle goods into England, to the detriment of the English customs. In both these small matters Prior had the satisfaction of conveying to Nottingham the news that the Dutch had yielded to the English representations[4]; and in another matter, Prior

[1] The memoranda of Dursley to the States General bearing dates within this period, from the date of reception would appear to have been written from England.

[2] Prior to Nottingham, Hague, Dec. 30, 1692, N.S., S.P. Foreign, Holland, vol. 222, fo. 435.

[3] S.P. Domestic, King William's Chest, 13, no. 23.

[4] See letters of Prior to Nottingham from The Hague, dated Feb. 24, Feb. 27, Mar. 20, Mar. 31, 1692/3, in S.P. Foreign, Holland, vol. 222, ff. 437, 439, 441 and 443. See also resolutions of the States General, March 26, May 9, 1693. (The Hague, Royal Archives, St. Gen. 146, fo. 372, 605.) But the continuous negotiations on the subject after this date prove that Prior was too optimistic.

gained some success, for he obtained the issue of a
"placard" proclaiming that the Dutch Courts would
not regard the validity of any "insurances for France[1]."
So when Dursley returned in April, 1693, Prior, even
if he relapsed into his former dull routine, might at any
rate console himself with the thought that his services
during the absence of his chief had given him a claim
to the consideration of the government.

The dullness of the year 1694 in public affairs is
even greater than that of 1693, for no feat of arms such
as the battle of Landen illumines its dreary records.
But if it was uneventful in the great world, it brought
considerable gratification to the private ambitions of
Matthew Prior. In October, 1693, Dursley had left
The Hague for good[2], and Prior's fate remained for
some time in doubt. But testimonials to Prior's ability
were not wanting. Cresset at Hamburg wrote the same
month to Lord Lexington, recommending Prior on the
ground that he is "really an ingenious man, and
deserves well[3]." Prior, moreover, was not a man to be
content with letting others work for him. In 1693 he
had reminded Gilbert Burnet and Lord Pembroke of
his existence, and on November 14/24, he wrote a
characteristic letter to Dorset:

We have at present no minister at either of the Northern
Crowns, Vienna, Berlin or Ratisbon. My friend, Mr Stepney,
who is at present negotiating for some Saxon troops at Dresden
may probably be fixed at the same place or sent to Sweden, or
almost choose his post, having had the fortune to be placed in
such a light that His Majesty has known and approved of him.
The other Courts will in all appearance be very soon supplied.
My having had the honour to be bred by Your Lordship, and
trailed a pen here onward of four years, makes some people

[1] S.P. Holland, vol. 222.
[2] Bath Papers, III. 8, Prior to Pembroke, Hague, Oct. 10/20, 1693.
[3] *Hist. MSS. Comm.* xIIth Rep. App. v. p. 152.

flatter me that I may not be forgot in this great harvest with few labourers, since Aglionby, Cresset and Stepney, who are already working, are journeymen as I am, have about the same estates at home, and are sent to preach politics, as the Apostles were on a better errand, without purse or scrip. I take it for granted that Your Lordship will mention me to Mr Secretary Trenchard, if you think anything of this kind proper for me. I wish I may part with these chimeras for the solid blessing of being near my patron and protector in England...[1].

Prior, however, did not obtain any advancement that autumn, for it was not until June 1, 1694, N.S. that Lord Dursley's memorandum taking leave of the States actually reached Holland and formally vacated the post[2]. Then, as luck would have it, Falkland who had been appointed to succeed Dursley, died before taking up the duty, and Prior, once more face to face with unemployment, now addresses himself to Blathwayt:

I know not what change may happen to my affairs upon my Lord Falkland's death, but take it for granted they will prosper in your hands. If I am to reside here any time, I presume either some order to me or letter to the president of the week or to the Pensioner will be necessary: for having taken my leave as my Lord Dursley's Secretary, I know not whose I must say I am, if I give in any memorial or ask any favour. I wish I might call myself Secretary, or Agent, or what you think proper, on better grounds than Kick calls himself Consul: but being at present like Sosia in the comedy—*sumne ego necne?* is a very pertinent question for me to ask myself[3].

The application seems to have been unnecessary in view of the high opinion held of Prior's capacity in government circles. On June 4/14 Blathwayt wrote to Shrewsbury that "His Majesty thinks fit that Mr Prior ...who has been always very careful in that station, may be continued as the English Secretary, with the

[1] Bath Papers, III. 14–15.   [2] *Ibid.* III. 21.
[3] *Ibid.* III. 22.

usual allowance of 20s. *per diem*[1]," and Shrewsbury seems to have come independently to the same conclusion. So Prior was able to write to Dorset that the King "had appointed me to do his business here," which was not really quite satisfactory, for he

had given me the title of his Secretary, which, without advancing me something, is only giving me leave to lay out sometimes eight, sometimes twelve pounds a week for letters, for the payment of which I am to solicit the Treasury a year hence, and get it perhaps in tallies....Patience! but as it is, I hope Sir Fleetwood Shepherd, knight, will ask my Lord Duke of Shrewsbury...if His Grace ever heard of a professed panegyric poet that was able to advance two guineas to the public[2].

A few days later Prior added to the growing list of patrons and protectors the name of one who was to be connected with him at intervals down to the very end of his public career. Charles Talbot, Duke of Shrewsbury, had succeeded Nottingham as secretary for the Northern Department, and Prior began his addresses by offering Shrewsbury some books. Through Vernon he received a gracious reply, and also a "sermon": "You seem to have a mind to write to His Grace. You not only may do it, but in your station you ought to do it[3]," and on July 5 Prior began his correspondence with Shrewsbury with the following elaborate compliment, which is an admirable example how to say nothing in many words:

I do not ask Your Grace's pardon for not having written to you, on your being Secretary of State, Duke or Knight of the Garter: on the contrary I pretend to make a merit of my silence. I really thought it too presumptuous for me to add a letter to the multitude Your Grace has received on these subjects from

---

[1] *Hist. MSS. Comm.* Buccleuch Papers at Montagu House, vol. II. pt. I, p. 77, Blathwayt to Shrewsbury, Hertogenbosch, June 4/14, 1694, and p. 79, Shrewsbury to Blathwayt, Whitehall, June 8/18, 1694.

[2] Bath Papers, III. 25, Prior to Dorset, Hague, June 22, 1694.

[3] *Ibid.* III. 24.

men of the greatest worth and quality, and was afraid to be impertinent since I could only say that I was glad of all this in my own particular, when all the nation is so in general. It is glad, indeed; my Lord, it ought to be so when in that great station where you are it sees a man too good to be tempted by anything but steady virtue and too great to enter into any interest but that of his country. That Your Lordship receives new titles at this time is yet another national good; it is, in the midst of a war with France, to tell our enemies that the English family, their nation most dreaded formerly, is yet in its pristine glory, and it is to add honour to the Order of the Garter to have it given to such a subject of our own as may make our Sovereign's allies ambitious of it. For my own interest indeed, and to act like a barefaced courtier I ought to congratulate Your Lordship's return to the Secretaryship. We young politicians begin to hope well of our future labours when men of your merit and honours condescend to be our masters; and the glory of managing a pen under the Duke of Shrewsbury now will be as great as that of having drawn a sword heretofore under his ancestors. Your Grace will excuse my growing a little florid, and lay the blame upon the grandeur of the subject: it should indeed have been treated in verse, but I despaired of coming up to the height of it: and would rather have Your Grace esteem me an indifferent secretary than know me to be a bad poet[1].

King's secretary though he was, Prior was little better than a starveling[2]. We have seen already how he complained to Dorset that his appointment only meant permission to spend more in postage. The same day that he had written to Dorset, he also wrote on the same subject to Vernon:

You are sure to be again plagued with me, because you obliged me yesterday, as with a common beggar, because you

[1] Bath Papers, III. 27, Prior to Shrewsbury, Hague, July 5, N.S. 1694.
[2] His private fortune was most moderate. Besides his fellowship and the Queen's pension, he cannot have had much more than what represented the legacy of £100 from his uncle Arthur and an additional £50 from Arthur Prior's son, Laurence, who died in 1690.

relieved him the last time you met him in the street....I...pay
sometimes above a hundred gilders a week for letters. So far
all is well, but you remember what Isaac said: *Here is the fire
and the wood, but where is the ram for the offering?* Pray don't
give me Abraham's repartee, but be pleased to advise me if I may
not justly desire some money may be advanced, since in all these
affairs Mr Blathwayt turns me over to you[1].

In spite of the fact that Charles Montagu was
Chancellor of the Exchequer, Prior obtained little
relief: in September he was telling Dorset that his post
had given him "much credit, but as yet not one penny
of money," although, as appears from the following
letter, he had addressed himself to persons very near
the King, and in the person of Portland had added yet
another to his list of protectors:

Whilst the Duke of Shrewsbury is Secretary of State, the
least have access to him, and the meanest are relieved. 'Tis on
this account that I dare write immediately to Your Grace on
so inconsiderable a business as that of my fortune. Whilst the
Court was here I took the boldness to represent to my Lord
Portland and Mr Blathwayt that whenever His Majesty pleased
to supply the ministry here, I had no other pretension than that
of throwing myself in the packet-boat and making the best of
my way for England; that, if I was to be left here, it was no way
proper for me in this post to scramble at ordinaries with Switzers
or French Protestants; that a little house this winter would be
convenient in so cold a country as Holland; that it was not
handsome for me to go to the Pensioner or Secretaries on foot,
whilst they send their clerks back again in coaches, and that
myself and servants could not subsist with any tolerable credit
upon twenty shillings a day, which tallies and the change of
money hardly bring beyond eighteen: that the public Ministers,
owning me with regard to the title I was commanded to take of
the King of England's Secretary, came to visit me, and that
I could not go to them or to Court when I was too dirty. My

[1] Bath Papers, III. 25, Prior to Vernon, Hague, June 12/22, 1694.

Lord Portland was pleased to think my pretensions were rather founded on reason than vanity, and assured as well my Lord Lexington as Mr Blaythwayt and myself that he would move it to His Majesty and get it fixed on this side, so that I hoped to have given Your Grace no trouble in so small a matter at a time when those of the greatest moment are to be formed and guided by your care and conduct: but the King going hence this morning in order to embark, I had no opportunity of seeing my Lord Portland or he of speaking to the King; so I humbly lay my circumstances before Your Grace and desire only to be added to the multitude whom you daily oblige. I ventured to tell my Lord Portland that my requests were in no way irregular, that Mr Foley, who was only called *Gentilhomme Anglais*, had an allowance of three pounds a day, as had likewise Mr Stepney at Vienna with the same character of Secretary which I have here; and that I did not question but that Your Grace would assist my request in England if His Lordship (as has happened) should be hurried hence without an opportunity of representing it[1].

A little more correspondence, and relief came at the end of the year, for on Dec. 21/31 he wrote to his friend the Chancellor of the Exchequer:

I think I never write to you but to ask you to do me some favour, or to thank you for having done it; yet even in these terms you have prevented me one letter, and got me £600 before I had the face to ask it[2].

As he told Lexington the same day Mr Prior was now "secure from starving till April[3]," and although he feared that on the death of the Queen he had lost £100 a year[4], this proved a false alarm, as William promised

[1] Prior to Shrewsbury, Hague, Oct. 30/Nov. 9, 1694 (Bath Papers, III. 34–5). [2] Bath Papers, III. 42.

[3] *Lexington Papers*, ed. H. Manners-Sutton, London, 1851, p. 26.

[4] *Ibid.* p. 47. What post Prior held is difficult to ascertain. Johnson in his life of Prior says he was groom of the chamber to the King, but Prior's name does not appear in the lists of those officials for the years 1692 or 1694 in Chamberlayne's *Angliae Notitia*, nor indeed can I find his name among any of the Court officials for those years.

that all her old servants should continue to draw their salaries[1], which Prior recovered in January, 1696, though in a roundabout way[2].

Satisfaction in obtaining the necessaries of life spurred on Prior's ambitions to move in yet higher diplomatic circles. Even when anxious whether his "extraordinaries" would be paid, and while he was telling himself that he must "e'en arm himself in the Apostle's magazine with the helmet of patience and the sword of faith" he had opened his mind to his old friend George Stepney[3]:

I am well enough affected to a seat in the office, *i.e.*, in case our projects abroad fail, to have it promised, that I may have the offer, rather than, having no provision here if a minister should be sent, to be obliged to make the campaign with Mr B[lathwayt]; but I had much rather have Ratisbon, and consequently be in state to join Lord Lexington *en cas de besoin*; which you know answers to the plan we propose to ourselves of making our forces joined so formidable in the Empire. However, I say, from a seat in the office one may leap abroad after having learnt the routine, and we have precedents of this matter from my Lord Arlington[4] to father Vernon.

Shwinfort is in the right of it to fancy himself fit for an em-

---

[1] Narcissus Luttrell, *Brief Relation*, Jan. 5, 1694–5, III. 422.

[2] See Bath Papers, III. 69, Tucker to Prior, Whitehall, Jan. 17/27, 1695/6: "It was [the Chancellor of the Exchequer's] opinion that you would lose that £100 per annum, if it was not brought into your extraordinaries." See also *Calendar of S. P. Dom.* 1694–95, p. 501.

[3] Stepney died in Sept. 15/26, 1707 and left Prior £50 in his will (Christian Cole, *Memoirs*, Addison to Cole, Whitehall, Sept. 16/27, 1707).

[4] Arlington does not seem a very appropriate instance of a leap abroad from a seat in the office, seeing that he rather leapt from abroad into a seat in the office at home. For, without leave or official notification he took his departure from Madrid for home, and was incontinently made keeper of the privy purse by Charles II. The instance of Vernon, however, is more apposite, for he was employed in the Duke of Monmouth's household and in the *Gazette* office before being sent to Flanders and Zell by Trenchard in 1692.

ployment of which he wants the emoluments. Hughes, you will find, has just the same sentiments; 'tis all a game, Catt, and we that are partners are rather to hold up our cards than blame our adversaries for peeping into our hands, or endeavouring to trump the cards we hope to make our tricks by. I do not find, that we are drawing near a peace, so possibly they will not leave me a year only upon the questions *an?* and *quomodo?* at Ratisbon. You do well to stop interlopers, however, and I see you distinguish my interests no otherwise from your own than by embracing them with more zeal. Pray take your leave of our friends in Channel Row and of Lord Dorset. Maybe, he may send me something to begin house-keeping. See Lady Orrery too, and desire to know if I may be serviceable to her in anything here. Ollinda is miraculously recovered from Folly, and (if one may believe her scrawl) resolves to be *resnabel*. I am perfectly friends with her: how easily we pardon those we love! and count that for certain which we have a mind to hope! and if it were not for the dear deceit, who would desire life and *brigue* foreign employments, when at home one may find twenty ready ways of dying? Or who would be vexed about extraordinaries, whilst arsenic is but ninepence an ounce and a rope costs but three halfpence?[1]

When the £600 came, after thanking Montagu with decent profuseness, he immediately turned to the subject of his own fortune. While quite willing to stay on at The Hague, "as what may place me in a good light and make me known," he nevertheless had heard that the King intended to fill up the post with some one else.

So we must cast about in time. What offers is Ratisbon, where we have no minister, and where if I were I should not be out of the way for *Secrétaire de l'Ambassade* when a peace may come to be treated....If, therefore, anybody is to be a year or two at Ratisbon to see what the Diet does, I may probably be your man. Failing that there is Switzerland, for

I am of no quality and an Englishman, which are two qualifications the Cantons like in a minister from us....I know not

<hr/>

[1] Bath Papers, III. 38, Prior to Stepney, Dec. 11/21, 1694.

if Denmark or Sweden may be supplied...; my last hope, if
these projects fail, is a seat in the next Secretary's office; so, my
Master and Patron, having our plan and our time before us, we
may work with more ease and sureness[1].

The melancholy event of the Queen's death, for a
brief moment drove these thoughts out of Prior's
head, and he expressed his grief as a loyal subject
should:

> *O fallaces nostras spes et brevem fiduciam humanam!* What have
> we to say but our prayers for the preservation of the King's life?
> I have answered His Grace on this sad subject. I hope you have
> or will give me a word of instruction how I must behave myself
> as to the ministers here, if I must give them notice of Her
> Majesty's death (I vow to God I tremble whilst I write the
> word)[2].

And again:

> I have given notice of this cruel change to the States and
> Ministers here in a long trailing cloak and a huge band, the one
> quite dirty with this thaw, the other really slubbered with my
> tears[3];

and on Jan. 25–Feb. 4 he writes to Charles Montagu:
"*Pallida mors aequo*—has struck us all here more than
an earthquake[4]." But by the time he wrote this, he was
recovering from the shock, and was once more casting
about with a view to his future advancement. He told
Charles Montagu that "Her Majesty's death may
hasten a man of quality hither as Plenipotentiary, which
may be Lord Villiers, and from thence we are to take
our measures as we can[5]." In such a case, Prior would
lose his post as King's Secretary. In addition to the four

---

[1] Bath Papers, III. 42–3, Prior to Charles Montagu, Dec. 21/31, 1694.
[2] *Ibid.* III. 46, Prior to Vernon, Hague, Jan. 4/14, 1694/5.
[3] *Lexington Papers*, p. 47, Prior to Lexington, Jan. 14/24, 1694/5.
[4] Bath Papers, III. 47, Prior to Charles Montagu, Jan. 25/Feb. 4, 1694/5.
[5] *Ibid.* III. 47.

places which he had discussed with Montagu in December, two more now came within the field of Prior's vision, namely, Florence and Venice. "*Omne solum forti patria est.* I hope I shall not be left destitute whilst the Duke of Shrewsbury is Secretary and Mr Montagu Chancellor of the Exchequer[1]." For the next six months Prior's correspondence resounds with the word Ratisbon, and his hopes ran high. "God knows how my body is to be disposed of; I believe Ratisbon will yet be my share[2]" he writes in May when he heard that Lord Villiers had been appointed Envoy to the States-General. But he did not rely solely upon letter-writing. The death of the Queen gave him an opportunity of paying attentions to the great in other ways. He designed a medal, copies of which were sent over to England in April, and were distributed by the patient Vernon, one going, as we learn, to the Duke of Devonshire. Of this medal little is known save from Vernon's comment on it:

If you think this will acquit you from the expectations people have of a poem from you, you will be mistaken, for they say you are not to come off with a posey and a shred of Horace; and they further desire, if you write anything in memory of the Queen, that you will take a little more notice of her than you do in her stamp, where she is neither represented by the effigies or the motto[3].

Although in March he had written: "We have had nothing new here for some months but volumes of bad poetry upon a blessed Queen. I have not put my mite into this treasury of nonsense[4]," in May forty-one stanzas, some little else than doggerel, were in Vernon's

[1] Bath Papers, III. 47, Prior to Charles Montagu, Jan. 25/Feb. 4, 1694/5.

[2] *Lexington Papers*, p. 87, Prior to Lexington, May 17/27, 1695.

[3] Bath Papers, III. 50, Vernon to Prior, April 19/29, 1695.

[4] *Ibid.* p. 49, Prior to Dorset, Mar. 8/18, 1694/5.

hands, and a copy was sent not only to Shrewsbury, but also to Devonshire[1]. Fantastic as is the exaggeration contained in them, the simple lines "written on Scheveling Sands with the point of my sword" are worth the whole of the uninspired ode.

> Number the sands extended here;
> So many Mary's virtues were:
> Number the drops that yonder roll;
> So many griefs press William's soul.

Medal and verses however were of no avail, his hopes, which he nourished until the end of July, were dashed to the ground early in August, and the bitterness of his disappointment may be tasted in the affected resignation of his letter to Keppel on August 3:

The siege of Namur gives you toil enough at this time, and the clamours of petitioners allow you little quiet at any time. I should not have dared to appear amongst that number, though your kindness to me at the Hague gave me all the encouragement imaginable, if my Lord Villiers at his return had not told me I might do it without any way offending you. I am extremely obliged to you, Sir, for the kind reception you have been pleased to give me, and I thought to have justified your good opinion of me by showing you I had modesty enough not to importune you; but when all one's fortune lies at stake, one easily forgets good manners. No man would be accused for crying out in a storm, or called a clown for rudely taking hold of his superior to support him if he be just falling. After having hoped, feared, been promised, and (which is worst) congratulated for Ratisbon, the King thinks there is not enough for a minister to do there. 'Tis true His Majesty knows best, for he is as evidently the most experienced man of our age, as he is the best Prince, and if he had been born a private man, he would have made a greater Ambassador than any State ever employed; yet I have one objection that could puzzle him, which is, that though Ratisbon may

---

[1] Bath Papers, iii. p. 54, Prior to Devonshire, Hague, June 14, 1695.

not want a resident, his Secretary at the Hague will soon want a residence; and though His Majesty have small use for a scribbling servant, I have great occasion for the bounty of a Royal Master. Wherever he pleases to send me I am ready to go; where if there be not much business, I shall apply myself to those studies that may make me capable of doing his business when there is any; and when there is nothing to be written for his service in prose, I will write his conquests and glories in verse. A resident or envoy may in some small time be sent to Venice, another to Florence; be it at either of these two places, at Ratisbon, Berlin (where, may be, His Majesty may send rather a resident than an envoy), at Stockholm, Copenhagen, or even Moscow, it is well, provided I may serve my King, my hero and my Master; but it is a sad reflection for me to think of going home as if I were disgraced, after having served here five years with some credit, and spent my little all in order to my being fit for something hereafter; and I take the boldness to protest to you I cannot think of returning to my College, and being useless to my country, to make declamations and theses to doting divines there, having drawn up memorials to the States-General in the name of the greatest king in Europe. You will be pleased to pardon the freedom of this letter, and to help me in this conjuncture of my fortune[1].

For this blow to his fortunes Prior seems to have thought "cold Mr Blathwayt" in some way responsible, but it would appear that it was really the King who decided against establishing a resident at Ratisbon[2]. If he did not get Ratisbon, at any rate he did not, as he had feared, lose his place at The Hague, and have to return to Cambridge: "here I am still, with my twenty shillings a day. Most places are *durante bene placito* except those of a judge or a bishop, and as long as I do

---

[1] Bath Papers, III. 60–61, Prior to Keppel, Hague, Aug. 3, 1695.
[2] *Ibid.* III. 62, 63. "The King will have nobody at Ratisbon out of a principle of good husbandry" (Prior to Lexington, Sept. 2, N.S. 1695).

not starve, I have no reason to complain[1]." He was therefore in fairly good spirits, and William's recovery of Namur in this same September gave him the opportunity of venting them in a retaliatory parody of Boileau's poem of 1692, a performance infinitely more successful than the lifeless lines on the death of the Queen. To modern ears it appeals more than any of Prior's earlier and longer performances, even though, if we would taste the satire, and understand the allusions to Villeroy, Louis and the "Virgin of St Cyr," a knowledge of the original with its classical tropes and mythological trappings is as indispensable as acquaintance with the historical circumstances of the time.

Namur fell on September 5th; on September 23 Prior sent Jacob Tonson the verses[2], and on the 27th Trumbull acknowledged them. For some reason, Prior seems to have been anxious to preserve anonymity; for Trumbull says he enjoined Tonson silence, "though it is not possible to keep it long a secret. I will add but one circumstance to that purpose, which is, that Fleetwood Shephard knows it[3]." But the literary exercises over, his position in the King's service began to give him qualms once more. "I hang like Solomon between heaven and hell[4]," he wrote in October, and he only succeeded in getting his bill of extraordinaries passed by allowing Richard Powys to "make pretty bold with his purse and give Mr Tucker 'three guineas, which is £4. 10s. 0d. to make it slip the better and remove the obstacles he made[5]." But he was still

---

[1] Bath Papers, III. 63. It may have been on his retiring from the Secretaryship on Lord Villiers' arrival that the States-General gave Prior the medal and chain which he pawned in 1696. (See below, p. 64.)

[2] *Hist. MSS. Comm.* II. 71, Baker Papers, Prior to Tonson, Hague, Sept. 13/23, 1695.

[3] Bath Papers, III. 64, Trumbull to Prior, Whitehall, Sept. 17/27, 1695.

[4] S.P. Holland, vol. 223, Hague, Oct. 1/11, 1695.

[5] Bath Papers, III. 65, Powys to Prior, Whitehall, Oct. 11/21, 1695.

complaining that his pay of £1 a day was too little, and he was anxious to have it doubled. His position was indeed very unsatisfactory, for his King's Secretaryship only lasted for six weeks after the arrival of the Envoy, and in strictness therefore Prior had no official position.

My privy seal reaches no longer than six weeks after the arrival of a minister at The Hague; so that we must have a new privy seal passed in order to my continuing here, which point His Majesty has already determined, and not denied the increase of my allowance upon the considerations I mention to Mr Vernon; which point likewise (by our favourite's[1] intercession, to whom *sub rosa* I am much obliged) I hope may be gained, and I become less troublesome to you Lords of the Treasury....If we get our forty shillings per day, for which possibly we have the name of agent, I would not change it for resident and Ratisbon[2].

Neither the one nor the other was he to get;

His Majesty will not be brought to consent to more than 20s. a day, and some consideration in bills of extraordinaries, and those are not to exceed so much more....His Majesty did not think fit to allow you the character of *Secrétaire du Roy*, and if he had, it would not have entitled you to the 40s. a day. Be satisfied, and I am sure you will have no reason to repent it[3].

Hopes held out for the future were but cold comfort to a starving Secretary; but Prior was forced to be patient, although he wrote not uncomplainingly to Montagu:

unless you Lords of the Treasury commiserate my condition, I break....We do what we can to drive Abell over into England... his debts at London make him afraid to venture at the kindness his patrons there offer him, and I have a fellow feeling for the poor

---

[1] Keppel.
[2] Bath Papers, III. 66, Prior to C. Montagu, Hague, Oct. 18/28, 1695.
[3] *Ibid.* 67, Tucker to Prior, Whitehall, Nov. 26/Dec. 6, 1695.

minstrel, because at present I know how damned a thing it is to see faces to whom one owes money[1].

The year 1696, however, was to see the end of this uncertainty. Like the year before, to Prior it began with news that afforded him a subject for his poetical talents, for in March was discovered the Assassination Plot. The invasion which the French prepared at the same time had been duly reported by Prior in January, and on March 2 he was still trying to obtain information as to the exact purpose of the French armaments at Dunkirk[2]. Then on March 9 his indignation blazes out at the news from England. He wrote to Keppel about it in French, a language which he may have thought a better vehicle for his feelings, as well as more intelligible to his correspondent.

Bon Dieu, quel attentat! Mais il y a un ciel qui veille sur la personne du Roy, et il y aura un enfer pour abîmer ses ennemis. Je vous prie, Monsieur, de me pardonner cet emportement. Infâme! traître! assassin! parricide! voilà les seuls termes qui me puissent sortir de la bouche:

and so forth[3]. To the other favourite, Portland, Prior wrote more soberly in English. As to Louis' supposed complicity in the plot, Prior makes no secret of his belief in it. "I hope the King will send a manifesto to

[1] Bath Papers, III. 67, Prior to Montagu, Hague, Dec. 27/Jan. 6, 1695/6. The "poor minstrel" was honoured by Prior giving him an epigram to set to music:

"Reading ends in melancholy,
    Wine breeds vices and diseases,
Wealth is but care, and love but folly,
    Only FRIENDSHIP truly pleases:
My wealth, my books, my flask, my MOLLY,
    Farewell all, if FRIENDSHIP ceases."
                        (*Dialogues of the Dead*, p. 87.)

[2] See his correspondence in P.R.O., S.P. Foreign, Holland, vol. 223, Feb. 10, Mar. 2.

[3] Bath Papers, III. 73.

all Courts in Christendom, that no peace can be made with France till King Lewis be driven like Nebuchadnezzar from the society of all human creatures[1]." This conviction he continued to hold in spite of Louis' repudiation of the accusation, for in May he was greeting the King on his arrival in Holland with the lines:

> O Louis, from this great example know,
> To be at once a Hero, and a Foe[2].

But he soon began expressing his personal anxieties again. In May money matters became pressing owing to the collapse of credit and lack of coin; Powys wrote to him at the beginning of June: "We are here under all the difficulties on account of our coin that can be imagined, all payments stopped and foreign bills protested, nor will anybody so much as touch a tally[3]," and even at the end of the month matters were no better, for although Prior had no difficulty at this time in getting his extraordinaries allowed, the tallies that were sent over could only be discounted at an "extravagant loss[4]." Matters went from bad to worse in the second half of the year; he draws for Montagu's benefit a gloomy picture of his position:

My tallies I cannot sell under thirty per cent. loss; my aunt will not send me one farthing: the chain and medal the States gave me[5] is at pawn; I have but two pistoles in the house or (to say plainly) in the world, and I have every morning a *levée* (God be thanked for the respite of Sunday) of postmen, stationers,

---

[1] Bath Papers, III. 73, Prior to Portland, March 3/13, 1695/6.

[2] *Presented to the King at his arrival in Holland after the discovery of the Conspiracy* (*Poems on Several Occasions*, p. 55).

[3] Bath Papers, III. 79, Powys to Prior, Whitehall, June 2/12, 1696.

[4] *Ibid.* 80.

[5] This chain and medal formed part of the customary present given to the secretary of an embassy on the retirement of the chief, and Prior received a chain and medal, of the value of 300 gilders on Dursley's resignation taking effect, June 5, 1694. (The Hague, Royal Archives, St. Gen. 148, fo. 719.)

tailors, cooks and wine-merchants who have not been paid since last December[1].

On December 7, N.S., he says "tallies at 45 per cent. may make a man mad, especially if he has but 20s. per day, but the wood, I hope, will sell better, and the allowance be augmented in some time."

He had good foundations for his hopes. His begging for promotion, for which some twinges of shame seem to have caught him, as when he told Vernon he was "as unwilling to ask anything with Impudence as to lose it for want of asking[2]," began to bear good fruit. His last rebuff was the post at Lisbon in Methuen's place[3], but when peace grew nearer at hand, he claimed the Secretaryship to the Embassy for the Congress. As we know, he had had his eye on this place some months back, and during the first fortnight of September, Prior had an unrivalled opportunity for pressing his claims to the Secretaryship. He accompanied William III to Loo, when the King went to Cleves on a visit to the Elector of Brandenburg, for the hand of whose ill-favoured daughter it was rumoured the King was going to ask. Prior was able to take a rest in company with young James Vernon: he wrote to the elder Vernon:

You see by the date of my letter I am at a place which affords not much news; the D. of Zell came hither on Saturday: the King and he have been hunting to-day, and no body talks of any thing but dogs, foxes, hares and horses, but Jimmy and I, who content ourselves to walk till we are weary by day, and read Virgil abed together a nights.

The marriage we have been talking of with Brandeburg will (I fancy) come to nothing. My Lord Portland who has been at Cleves gives (I hear) no very favourable account of the Lady as

[1] Bath Papers, III. 86, Prior to Montagu, Sept. 1696.

[2] P.R.O., S.P. Foreign, Holland, vol. 223, Prior to Vernon, Hague, April 17, 1696.

[3] *Ibid*. Prior to Vernon, Hague, July 17, 1696.

to her beauty, and the King has no reason to be contented with a wife without it[1].

Macaulay, it will be remembered, makes great play with the ceremonious manners of the time on the occasion of the Congress at Ryswick, and contrasts the direct business-like character of the proceedings of William III's agent Portland in his meetings with Boufflers in 1697. But surely no love affair was ever marked by such hide-bound etiquette as this courtship —if such it was—of William III. Prior has described the events in the opening pages of his *Journal relating to the Treaty of Ryswick*:

1696, Sept. 5 [15]. The King went to Clèves to pay the Elector of Brandebourg a visit; the Elector met him at Skinkens-kense [Schenkenschanz]; from thence to Clèves, the Elector and the king went in one coach; the Electoral Prince and the Duke of Zell in another; these two last had doubtless very agreeable discourse; for one of them is seven years old and the other seventy-two.

The King played at cards that afternoon with the Electress in her apartment, and with the Duke of Zell, who had an ordinary chair; Mr C[resett] sat in the like chair (as to teach the King and see his hand), and the Princess stood all the while, which was about five hours. The King supped in the same apartment with the Electress, the Electoral Prince, the Princess, the Duke of Zell; the Elector in his own apartment with some of the men.

The King and Elector could not eat together, because the King could not let the Elector have an armed chair, and the Elector could not be treated with less in his own regence. The King's family and the strangers were all treated very greatly at several tables, according to their quality, in the great hall; the meat was good, the wine (all but the Rhenish) bad, and so liberally filled that people were drunk before the desert; but if the guests

[1] S.P. Foreign, Holland, vol. 223, Prior to Vernon, Loo, Aug. 31/Sept. 10, 1696.

lost their understanding, at least they had no occasion for it, for everybody found a servant and a flambeau to convoy them to the gate of the castle, and there a coach to carry them to their own lodging; the same coaches waited for them in the morning[1].

Sunday, the 16th. The King and Elector heard different sermons for the same reason that obliged them to eat at different tables...[2].

This time, Prior's efforts on his own behalf were crowned with success. On the 19th Blathwayt told him that "the King was pleased to answer that he was of my Lord Portland's opinion as to my being proper for" the Secretaryship "and that my pretensions were just and reasonable[3]." He then returned to The Hague (September 22) where he received congratulations, which, though premature as yet, were not this time to be a cause of exasperation to the disappointed recipient. On December 21, Pembroke, Villiers and Sir Joseph Williamson were nominated by William III to be his plenipotentiaries at the peace, and although the Secretaryship was not then filled, Tucker could assure Prior there was no competitor, and that there need be no doubt that Prior would be the person nominated[4]. That forecast was realised, when Prior, who had left Holland on January 23, returned on March 17, after taking leave of the King on Sunday, March 10, "from which day" as he proudly notes, "my privy seal as secretary to the Embassy commences[5]."

[1] It was perhaps this orgy which gave such point to a "passage in Scaligeriana" that Prior turned it into verse:

"When you with High-Dutch HEEREN dine
Expect false Latin and stumm'd wine,
They never Taste who always Drink,
They always Talk who never Think."

(*Dialogues of the Dead*, p. 109.)

[2] Bath Papers, III. 508, 509.   [3] *Ibid.* 509.
[4] *Ibid.* 98.   [5] Prior's Journal (Bath Papers, III. 511).

It was no doubt under the influence of the more cheering prospect with which the year closed that Prior composed the merry lines entitled "The Secretary, written at the Hague in the year 1696." There is a spontaneous brightness about these verses which contrasts pleasantly with the gloomy forebodings of his correspondence, and with the stilted mode of his official verse.

> While with labour assid'ous due pleasure I mix,
> And in one day atone for the bus'ness of six,
> In a little Dutch-chaise on a Saturday night,
> On my left hand my HORACE, a NYMPH on my right.
> No Memoire to compose, no Post-Boy to move,
> That on Sunday may hinder the softness of love;
> For her, neither visits, nor parties of tea,
> Nor the long-winded cant of a dull refugée.
> This night and the next shall be hers, shall be mine,
> To good or ill fortune the third we resign:
> Thus scorning the world, and superior to fate,
> I drive on my car in processional state;
> So with PHIA thro' Athens PYSISTRATUS rode,
> Men thought her MINERVA, and him a new God.
>
> But why should I stories of Athens rehearse,
> Where people knew love, and were partial to verse,
> Since none can with justice my pleasures oppose,
> In Holland half drowned in int'rest and prose:
> By Greece and past ages, what need I be try'd,
> When the Hague and the present, are both on my side,
> And is it enough, for the joys of the day
> To think what ANACREON or SAPPHO would say,
> When good VANDERGOES, and his provident VROUGH,
> As they gaze on my triumph, do freely allow,
> That search all the province, you'll find no man there is
> So blessed as the *Englishen Heer* SECRETARIS[1].

[1] *Dialogues of the Dead and other Works*, ed. A. R. Waller, p. 96.

Chapter III

THE PEACE OF RYSWICK

THE personal war between William of Orange and Louis XIV was decided by the battle of the Hogue in 1692, when Russell defeated the navy of France, and Louis renounced his attempts to retain the sovereignty of the seas. Unless he could profit by moments of confusion such as might occur upon the death of William III, Louis could no longer hope to deliver a blow which could be effective in restoring King James II, while on his side, William III had not the power, nor perhaps, the capacity, to reduce Louis XIV to those straits to which Marlborough was to bring him in the War of the Spanish Succession. That the war was decided the French practically avowed in the winter of 1693–4, for we find Prior reporting home that "France really desires a peace with us, though it chicanes a little in the way of asking it[1]." But the secret negociations which Louis entered upon both in the South of Germany and in Belgium, did not come yet to fruition. The next autumn, the plight of France became serious. If Prior complained of the lack of pay, and if the English government found itself in difficulties over the currency, France was in far direr straits.

Here is a famous *père de l'oratoire*, his name Vasere, just come from France, whether with a design to change his religion, as he pretends, or to be a spy, as some imagine, is yet uncertain....He answers very frankly to any questions put to him in discourse, talks

[1] Bath Papers, III. 17, Prior to Pembroke, Hague, January 19/29, 1693/4; see also P.R.O., S.P. Foreign, Holland, vol. 223, Prior to Vernon, Hague, Mar. 30, 1694.

very particularly of the miseries of France, that more have died in Paris these six last months than have done upon an usual computation in two years: that the premier President de Paris said in his hearing, *Hélas! tout le royaume est devenu un grand hôpital*; and that Monsieur has been forced to break off his table three times this year for want of money to buy daily provisions; that neither the Dauphin or Mons. de Luxembourg are very well in Court, and the Grand Monarch grown so gouty, peevish and superstitious (three excellent qualities) that nobody knows what to do with him[1]

In the winter France suffered yet greater loss by the death of Luxembourg, the only competent general available for the war in the Netherlands. "Luxembourg's lamp," wrote Prior, is "now very near going out. Some letters say that he has been blooded four times for a pleurisy, and is now in the hands of the priests; so probably France may lose a General, and Heaven may gain a Saint[2]." Villeroy, who succeeded him, was to lose Namur in 1695, and in revenge

To bomb the Monks, and scare the Ladies

at Brussels; and he was destined to mark the beginning of the Spanish Succession War by being captured by the Austrians, and end a military career of exceptional incompetence by the wholly unnecessary rout at Ramillies. In the following year, 1696, the talk of peace was yet louder. In May, Louis sent his trusted negociator Caillières into Holland, where his presence was soon discovered in spite of the deep veil of secrecy that was thrown over him.

People will have it that...M. Caillières[3] is somewhere *incognito* in Holland. Some that have formerly known him pretend to have

---

[1] Bath Papers, III. 33, Prior to Vernon, Hague, Sept. 11/21, 1694.

[2] *Ibid.* 45, Prior to Shrewsbury, Hague, Dec. 26/Jan. 5, 1694/5.

[3] The spelling of his name, which appears in various forms, has been modernised.

seen him at Amsterdam: however that may be, it is certain that
Monsieur Dyckveldt has lately made several little journeys out
of the way: which would not be so remarkable if the man loved
either a mese (*sic*) or a mistress, but as it is they think it politics
and argue him wise from his dulness[1].

A fortnight later and the rumours became more
precise:

The talk of negociations towards a peace is almost over.
I believe Monsr Caillières has been in Holland...a gentleman
whom I know here says plainly that about 10 days since he saw
by accident Monsr Dyckvelt and Monsr Borëel with a third
person whom he did not know in a Cabaret at a Village about a
league from the Hague, called Leysendam; this third is concluded
to be Borëel [*sic for* Caillières] since the other two are not used
to go to a brandy-shop together for the Liquor's sake: Dyckvelt's
frequent going to and returning to Bruxelles, and Borëels not
residing at Amsterdam but here, gives us reason to think that
some negociations of this kind have been held, and I believe the
proposals rejected, since as far as I can guess, the French began
to chicane about Luxembourg, and had a mind to spin out another
treaty of Nimègue[2].

Prior's gloomy anticipations were not realised, and
Caillières' remark "We must make a peace, because we
cannot make a war[3]" was nothing less than the truth.
Yet the reefs that beset the ship of peace were many,
and advance was slow and dangerous. In July came the
news of the treaty of Turin. By this act Louis had
succeeded in detaching the Duke of Savoy from the
coalition, and as this event raised the whole question of
the neutralisation of Italy, it was felt that if negociations
were to be undertaken on this point, they might be
undertaken upon all. But the principal importance of

[1] Bath Papers, III. 80, Prior to Dorset, Hague, June 12/22, 1696.
[2] P.R.O., S.P. Foreign, Holland, vol. 223, Prior to Vernon, June 30/
July 10, 1696.
[3] Bath Papers, III. 90, Prior to Trumbull, Sept. 29/Oct. 9, 1696.

the treaty of Turin sprang from the fact that it enabled Louis to face his foes with a firmer front, while it undoubtedly stimulated the desire of the northern powers to end a war which, even with Louis single-handed, had proved so close a struggle. England at any rate, with her financial difficulties, was more than anxious for an end to the war, and as Villiers wrote to Hill at Brussels "Monsieur Caillières is more *fier* since the peace with Savoy; but I rather believe it is our money business that makes him so[1]." Prior's opinion of the treaty may be seen from the following letter:

We know nothing sure of the great affair of Peace or War, though we are every moment talking of it. Dyckvelt is expected here to-night from the Army, but if he speaks as dubiously at his return as he has done in Flanders when he is asked this important question we shall be at a loss to comprehend his answer. The States pretend to have a mind to carry on the war, but are really as weary of it as we can be. France seems really to desire a peace, upon which supposition it.is unreasonable to think that all these negociations should break only on the account of Strasbourg. Spain and the Empire will be hardly brought to accept a neutrality for Italy, so the D. of Savoy's last step will not much retard the general peace. We talk of a French abbé arrived here incognito to assist Caillières[2].

In September, however, the great secret was divulged. On the 4th Prior announced to Vernon that "The Pensioner acquainted yesterday morning the Ministers at the Congress with the negociations Mons. Dyckvelt has had with the French Commissioner, Mons. Caillières, and that the King of France was now willing to establish the Treaties of Westphalia and Nimègue as a foundation to begin a Treaty for a General Peace[3]." That these

---

[1] Middleton Park Papers, Jersey to Hill, Hague, Aug. 2, N.S. 1696.

[2] P.R.O., S.P. Foreign, Holland, vol. 223, Prior to Vernon, Hague, Aug. 7/17, 1696.

[3] S.P. Foreign, Holland, vol. 223, Prior to Vernon, Hague, Sept. 4, 1696.

peaces were to be a "foundation" might be reasonable, but as Lexington and Heemskirk pointed out to the Imperial Ministers, William III and the Dutch had no intention of being satisfied with these two peaces, but they would support the farther demands and claims of their allies with all their power[1]." From the very first, Villiers foresaw the lengthiness of the negociations: "I fear," he wrote on September 4, "this business will drawl out longer than our convenience requires, for every minister thinks to make himself necessary by making difficulties[2]." On both sides there was stiffness. The Emperor put forward the exorbitant demand "first that Aix-la-Chapelle should be the place to treat, so that he takes to himself to have the sole right of naming; secondly, the entire restitution of Lorraine, and thirdly, the ten imperial towns of Alsace to be restored, though the French had them by the treaty of Münster." The Emperor's ministers were informed that such terms could not for a moment be considered, and by the end of October the Imperial Court had been induced to "rebate a little of its stiffness," when another obstacle arose.

"The Imperialists," wrote Villiers on Oct. 26, "are come off some of their difficulties, but they will insist upon having the place of treaty within the Empire. They will have the pleasure to dispute and I believe the disadvantage to yield at last. In the meantime Monsieur Caillières on his side is endeavouring to gain ground, for he now pretends not to have offered Luxembourg as it is, but demolished, which has put the Spaniard in a terrible heat; and it is but reasonable we should stick by them in this point, it concerns us so much....France cannot think that England and Holland will ever consent to such a weakening of the barrier in the Low Countries[3]."

---

[1] Bath Papers, III. 89.
[2] Middleton Park Papers, Villiers to Hill, Sept. 4, N.S. 1696.
[3] Ibid. Oct. 26, N.S. 1696.

The whole Congress, according to Prior, was of opinion that "though the Spaniard's anger was more intelligible than his reasonings, his difficulty was to be taken off before it was possible for any step to be made further[1]." The indignation felt at Caillières' apparent heightening of his demands became even greater at the end of November, when he made difficulties about the recognition of William as King of England, which put both Villiers and Prior in their turn "into a terrible heat." "Caillières," wrote Villiers on November 23, "begins to chicane more than ever, and now refuses to own the King in the preliminaries as at first he declared he would. The ministers resent this change...and resolve to proceed in no other point till this is cleared....I own to you that this behaviour and the preparations at Brest make me fear some ill design like that of last year[2]." It even became a question of a complete rupture of the negociations. To this extreme measure Villiers was opposed.

There is a respite in Caillières' negociation till the King's orders come, relating not only to himself but to that point concerning Luxembourg. In the meantime I will tell you why we do not think it time to send Caillières away, by asking you what we shall do when we have done it? Do you think that the prospect of arming the six circles will take timely effect? or that in case the Emperor should think fit to send those troops upon the Rhine that served in Italy that the circles of Francony and Suabe would ever consent to it? Are they not already armed above their contingent to avoid giving winter quarters to any stranger troops and especially those of the Emperor? Will there not be the same difficulty that there was last year in providing magazines and artillery for an army on the middle Rhine? And do you believe that good correspondence between our German generals that we may expect them to act with consent in any design? And do

---

[1] Bath Papers, III. 92, Prior to Blathwayt, Hague, Oct. 16/26, 1696.
[2] Middleton Park Papers, Villiers to Hill, Hague, Nov. 23, N.S. 1696.

you not likewise think that the French will act upon the Rhine in March and that the Imperialists will scarce be out of quarters by the beginning of June? Besides all this, my opinion is that Kinsky has a mind to break this negociation only to take it up in another place where he may be more master of it and I think the King and States contribute so much to the war to have another interest judge of a peace. I do not mention to you the accidents which may happen in Parliament nor the condition of the nation[1].

The anger of the English negociators, however, was soon deflected from Caillières against the Imperialists whose stubbornness once more became extreme. On December 11, Prior had announced that the great point of the recognition of William III was "like to be adjusted and the negociation to advance[2]." Vernon in reply describes the effect of the news upon the House of Commons.

I received it just before the House went into a Committee upon the state of the nation. I happened to tell my next neighbour the good news it brought, and it ran round the House like fire in stubble, and had a very good influence in restraining people from running into the peevish propositions that some had prepared for that day[3].

As to the question of Luxembourg, Caillières offered the town as it stood, provided Louis XIV had a consideration for the sums he had spent upon its fortification. But the Imperialists objected. "They murmur," wrote Prior, "that it should be rendered in a better condition than Strasbourg, and like the man in the Scriptures take it ill that their neighbours are kindlier treated than themselves[4]." Villiers thought the offer reasonable and was ready to accept it rather than continue a ruinous war: "do you think it is a good economy to be at the vast expense of the war, rather than give a French million and a half which Caillières

[1] Middleton Park Papers, Villiers to Hill, Hague, Nov. 30, 1696, N.S.
[2] Bath Papers, III. 97.   [3] *Ibid.* 97, 98.   [4] *Ibid.* 98.

asks for the fortification of Luxembourg?[1]" What helped to exasperate Villiers and Prior was the irresolution displayed by the Imperialists in the matter of Lorraine. They now insisted the matter should be mentioned in the preliminaries, in spite of the fact that they had themselves proposed that no mention should be made of it. All this deepened Villiers' suspicion that Kinsky had no desire for a peace[2], and the events of the next three months turned the suspicion into a certainty[3]. However, on January 8, 1697, Prior could announce that the preliminary points had been adjusted:

The treaties of Westphalia and Nimègue to be the ground and foundation of this.

Strasburg to be restored in the state the French took it.

Luxemburg in the state the French took it, and means to be thought of for a compensation for the new fortifications.

Dinant as it was taken.

Mons and Charleroy as they now are.

All reunions made since the Treaty of Nimègue to be annulled.

Lorraine to be restored as at the Treaty of Nimègue, which restitution not to hinder the further discussion of that affair in the treaty[4].

Although these points had been adjusted, the procrastinating Imperialists still had opportunities for obstruction. The first was afforded by the question of the place of the Congress. The method of agreement suggested was that the Allies should name three and the French should choose. The Allies named Maestricht,

---

[1] Middleton Park Papers, Villiers to Hill, Hague, Dec. 18, N.S. 1696.
[2] Ibid.
[3] "I hope we shall never be put to force a peace upon our allies: if it is possible we must part friends in order to continue so." Ibid. Villiers to Hill, Hague, Dec. 26, N.S. 1696.
[4] Bath Papers, III. 100, 101, Prior to Vernon, Hague, Dec. 29/Jan. 8, 1696/7.

Nimeguen and Breda[1], but instead of choosing any of these, Caillières revived an earlier suggestion, to hold the Congress at Ryswick, William III's house between Delft and The Hague; the French ministers to live at Delft and the Allies at The Hague. Caillières announced that he "presumed his Master would consent." It need not be said that Prior had to write home that

the Imperialists oppose this, and I think have no other reason for their doing so than *such is Count Kinski's pleasure*: everybody else is for it, and very justly, since they, being already on the place, have nothing to prepare but their equipage[2].

So great was the procrastination that when Prior returned from England on March 17, two months and more after the suggestion had been made, he found that the question of the place was not even then settled.

Sir,

I have the favour of yours of the 9th and 12th to acknowledge: I have not much news to return you, and that which I have is none of the best.

The Courrier is returned from Vienne but has not brought us the Emperor's consent to the place, but on the contrary a chicaning paper by which that court desires an explanation of the sense in which the preliminaries are to be taken and would have them restrained to the Recess of Nuremberg, though they say so in other words than they did 3 months since: so, you see we advance according to the old Austrian pace.

Our French plenipotentiaries are yet at Delft Incognito, their Youth are fluttering here at the Comedies and Assemblies; I wish my Masters were arrived, that we might begin, for if part of the Allies move, t'other must follow, as it was in the case of Hudibras's horse.

We are mightily afraid they have accepted a Neutrality in Catalogne, though we cannot be sure of our fears being well founded 'till this day senight that the Spanish letters come in.

---

[1] Bath Papers, III. 101, Prior to Williamson, Hague, Jan. 5/15, 1696/7.
[2] *Ibid.* 102, Prior to Pembroke, Hague, Jan. 8/18, 1696/7.

We have had a report too of the Flotta's being arrived, but that too we cannot be sure of, so we hope and fear in perfection.

I am ever with respect,

S[r].

Your most obedient and

most humble ser[t]

M. Prior.

Jimmy has his watch[1].

The "chicaning paper" dealt with the other method adopted by the Imperial Court of blocking the advance towards the peace. The Emperor demanded that the preliminaries should be explained by Caillières in a certain sense[2], and that if his demand were not complied with he would have to consult the Diet of the Empire. "This is so very extravagant that it puts me out of all patience, and if this method should be observed we might hope for a peace when we are in our graves[3]." The Emperor also demanded that nothing should be discussed in the Congress before the question of Lorraine was settled, thus giving a prospect of negociations indefinitely prolonged. No wonder Villiers complained on this that the "Imperialists grow worse and worse[4]." Not till May 3, 1697, could Villiers and Prior report that these incidents were over.

The meaning of this conduct on the part of the Imperialists was not far to seek. Not only were they disgusted that the peace was to be concluded at a town outside the Empire, but the news of the serious illness of Charles II of Spain made it entirely to their interest

[1] P.R.O., S.P. Foreign, Holland, vol. 223, Prior to Vernon, Hague, March 16/26, 1696/7.

[2] Caillières was "to declare that he understood the preliminaries according to Mons. d'Avaux's declaration in Swede, and the State's resolution of Sept. 3 past." (Villiers to Hill, March 12, 1697, N.S.)

[3] Middleton Park Papers, Villiers to Hill, March 12, 1697, N.S.

[4] *Ibid.*

to prolong the negociations as much as possible. Should Charles II die, a war over the Spanish Succession would be bound to follow, and the victorious coalition, now on the point of dissolution, would gain fresh life in supporting the claims of the Imperial house to the throne of Spain[1]. When, however, Charles II recovered, the Court of Vienna began to fear that it might be left without allies, and fell into line in the negociations at Ryswick.

Yet for all this irritating procrastination, the situation had its redeeming features. On his return to The Hague, Prior found that some progress had been made during his absence, for the offer of Venice to mediate had been rejected, and the proposal made by the Brandenburg minister, Schmettau, that Sweden should be invited to perform that office had been accepted. On February 4, 1697, Kaunitz, in the name of the Congress, formally asked the Swedish minister Lilienroet to assume, on his master's behalf, the title of Mediator. Though Villiers seems to have thought him as great a dawdler as the Imperialists, Prior's judgement was more favourable, for he wrote that the "Mediator longs to be at work[2]."

If the negociations with the house of Austria were slow, it is just to observe that the movements of the ambassadors nominated by William III were scarcely less dilatory. Although appointed in December, in April Sir Joseph Williamson was "lying very ill with a fever and hath an ill symptom of a great doziness upon him[3]," and eventually he was left behind, and did

---

[1] Middleton Park Papers, Villiers to Hill, February 12, 1697, N.S. "The Court of Vienne think that the King of Spain cannot live above a year, and would be glad to have all Europe in arms to fight their cause. Whenever that happens, it is but right and reasonable that we should act as good allies, but not as principals in the war, as we have done."

[2] Bath Papers, III. 103, Prior to C. Montagu, Hague, March 16/26, 1696/7.

[3] *Ibid.* 108, Vernon to Prior, Whitehall, April 2/12, 1697.

not serve until June 11[1]. Villiers of course was all the time in Holland, and during these months, the whole negociation fell upon him. One question of tremendous import arose. Under what title could Lord Pembroke and Sir Joseph receive passports from France? Although Louis had expressed his intention to recognise William's title, yet he could not do so in the passports before the peace; on the other hand, Lord Villiers told the Mediator that no passports would be accepted which did not speak of William as King of England. The Mediator after consulting Caillières was unable to effect any agreement, as indeed was difficult in a question where the principles were radically opposed, and so "a good convoy is thought the best expedient in this affair[2]."

At length, however, such is the resource of diplomatists, the question was settled on April 3. Every minister was to

have free and secure correspondence with his Master, in order to which blank passports are to be given to each party, the packet-boat to and from England is to be looked upon as a courier: but the merchandises and the passengers which are on board, are not free; if any party desires a passport to go to any other place than the residence of his own Master, it is left to the liberty of the other party to grant or refuse it[3].

When exactly the Imperialists agreed to the place, or when the English plenipotentiaries arrived, the Prior papers do not tell us. In April 1697, as a result perhaps of his heavy work as Secretary, Prior complains of "an ugly defluxion" in his eyes which interfered much with his correspondence. This undoubtedly proved a disappointment to his official friends at home:

[1] Bath Papers, III. 515.
[2] See Villiers' conversation with Lilienroedt, Mar. 5, 1697, N.S. in Bath Papers, III. 510.
[3] Bath Papers, III. 511.

we find Sir William Trumbull writing in such flattering terms as these:

To be free with you in my turn, the accounts my Lord Villiers gives me are very imperfect, and therefore I entreat you to continue to me the satisfaction of letting me know the characters and inclinations of the ministers at the treaty, the progress of affairs there, and what hopes there is of a peace, or the contrary, or what other remarks your station and your talent enable you to make[1].

Unfortunately for us, the replies to this invitation have not survived. It may be that Trumbull committed the most piquant character sketches to the flames, and it is only isolated glimpses of the ambassadors that we can catch in Prior's letters. Don Quiros of Spain, whose anger, we have heard, was "more intelligible than his reasonings," Prior described "as mad as the Catholic religion and a hot temper can make any man[2]." Kaunitz, the Imperial Ambassador, he wrote, "advances very honestly, but is (by the way) a good deal a bigot[3]." Similar strength of mind was also ascribed to the French envoys: "as far as I can inquire into the humour of our French negociators, Harlay and Caillières are (I find) bigots, and Cressy an old chicaner[4]." By the beginning of May, all seemed ready for the Congress, and on May 3 Prior wrote to Charles Montagu as follows:

The steps towards a peace advance as fast as the gravity of the House of Austria will permit. The difficulties which the Emperor made are adjusted, and the only ones that remain to obstruct the opening the treaty are about the reunions which have been made by France in the Spanish Netherlands since Nimègue. The French will not give their answer to the list which the Spaniards

---

1 Bath Papers, III. 109, Trumbull to Prior, April 13/23, 1697.
2 Ibid. 96, Prior to Trumbull, Hague, Dec. 7, N.S. 1696.
3 Ibid. 96, Prior to Trumbull, Hague, Dec. 7, N.S. 1696..
4 Ibid. 106, Prior to Trumbull, Hague, Mar. 30/April 9, 1697.

have made of these reunions till just the beginning of the treaty, because (say they) the Spaniard, not consenting entirely to the answer, may refuse entering into treaty. Chicane (my dear Master) and nonsense, for the French know very well that, let their answer be what it will, the Spaniards are not in a condition to refuse coming to a treaty with the rest of the Allies: and the Spaniards know as well that they shall gain nothing by this little bustle besides the credit of being thought considerable enough to stop the treaty some little time for what they are sure to yield at last. In some days the treaty will open, and things look as if it would succeed[1].

In fact, six days later the Congress opened. It is impossible to describe the tediousness of its proceedings and of its minutes; the same feeling oppressed the diplomatists of the day, and it is not long before Prior's papers give signs of absolute despair. Meeting on May 9 for the first time, the plenipotentiaries did nothing but exchange their powers, and at the subsequent meetings, the viciousness of the arrangements soon became apparent. In a matter which vitally concerned the whole of Western and part of Eastern Europe, two days a week were considered sufficient for the transaction of business, and when business was transacted, it was not to be by word of mouth between the parties interested but by memorandum, solemnly handed by one side to the Mediator and by him to the opposite side, who, at the next meeting might possibly be in a position to return an answer to the Mediator for the consideration of their opponents. By May 24, Prior's summary of what had been done came to this:

the Imperialists gave in Saturday before [May 18] an imperfect paper, and tacitly confessed their having done so by changing it on Wednesday [May 22] and that they made the most ridiculous

---

[1] Bath Papers, III. 113, Prior to Montagu, Hague, May 3, 1697, N.S.

demand imaginable....You see, Sir, how slowly we advance: I hear the French grow impatient at it, and I take this to be a good argument that they are in earnest for a peace[1].

But while the Imperialists and the French were indulging in this war of etiquette, the British embassy was not idle. As at a later treaty, the British and French put their heads together to settle their own accounts independently of the other powers. The principal items in dispute were first and foremost the recognition of William. As regards this delicate point, involving as it did the position of King James, the most subtle play of precedence and "diplomatic" was employed by William. Anything which in the least degree tended even to hint that he was not King of England was rejected with every sign of indignation; and with regard to King James, William was anxious as far as possible to indulge his personal rancour against his father-in-law for the part he had played at the time of the assassination plot. A separate article was drawn up whereby Louis was to be made to promise to expel King James from France and give no protection or support to him or any of King William's enemies. Louis refused to agree to an article which mentioned King James in such terms. "The French," wrote the ambassadors to William, "are very positive that their Master cannot in honour consent to the naming a prince in this manner, with whom he has been in so long and so strict an alliance[2]." Matters that were really more important, but in which William was in fact less vitally interested and which did not need such nice inspection, were the questions of trade and of America: the proposed treaty of Commerce was dropped, "since the balance of trade, as it now stands, is evidently on the English side[3]" and affairs in America, although

[1] Bath Papers, III. 119, Prior to Trumbull, Hague, May 14/24, 1697.
[2] *Ibid.* 128, Lords Ambassadors to William, June 14/24, 1697.
[3] *Ibid.* 127.

they cost Prior many letters, were to be arranged "on the foot they were in at the beginning of the war, which we understand to be Your Majesty's pleasure[1]." Prior, therefore, was fully occupied, and yet nothing was really done. "You see," writes Prior in June, "how near we are to get into the old road of ceremony and nonsense[2]," and on June 28 he thus reported progress to Dorset.

I have hoped that our treaty might long before this have afforded something material enough for me to have troubled your Lordship with, but by what has been written to Your Excellencies in general on that subject, you see, my Lord, that we are advanced but little beyond our Preliminaries, and in fifteen meetings we have hardly agreed to the first article either of the Imperialists or Spaniards, though they contain little more than *pax sit*. I think the mystery of this slowness on the French side is that they have a mind to see the event of what they hope as well from the West Indies as from Barcelona. We are thinking of that part of the treaty which regards us, and then England and Holland will certainly have quicker answers towards making a good peace, or break off those conferences which as yet advance so little towards it. Your Lordship will see by the enclosed protestation in what a posture King James' affairs stand: this is the last entry he is likely to make. The Mediator when he showed it the Congress declared he received and looked upon it as neither valid or of consequence, but read it only as a curiosity[3].

In a letter to Sunderland Prior attributed the slowness of the Congress to the "great love the Germans have to method[4]," but whatever was the cause of this lengthy procedure, the end was in sight. In that same letter, dated July 12, Prior announced the news of an event which was materially to hasten the peace. "My

[1] Bath Papers, III. 127, Lords Ambassadors to William, June 14/24, 1697.

[2] P.R.O., S.P. Foreign, Holland, vol. 223, Prior to Vernon, Hague, June 8/18, 1697.

[3] Bath Papers, III. 130, Prior to Dorset, Hague, June 18/28, 1697.

[4] *Ibid.* 134, Prior to Sunderland, Hague, July 2/12, 1697.

Lord Portland has had an interview with Mons. Boùfflers, which looks as if a suspension of arms were designed[1]." Far more indeed was arranged at this interview than a cessation of the trifling campaign in the Netherlands of 1697, and Prior realized this. To the more confidential friend Vernon he said the interview "we think, may produce more than many meetings at Ryswick[2]." The interest caused at Ryswick by this interview was intense. The Imperialists called to know what it meant, and Prior was instructed to enquire of Blathwayt; but for all reply he received was that "His Majesty is pleased to say that Their Excellencies have already received sufficient informations and instructions in that matter which need no repetition at present[3]." This snub, however, was not followed by information being withheld, for Prior was fully *au courant* with what passed between Portland and Boùfflers. Finally on July 30, he was able to see daylight at last.

His Majesty's business (God be thanked) is done, and France will promise not to assist his enemies etc. in as full terms as words can express; King James not being by name express'd in the article....We shall (in short) have a peace, and that is enough for one post. The enclosed will let you see how dull a way we were trying at Ryswick, but blessed be Heaven, we shall get out of it, and drag these Germans to their own good[4].

So indeed they did, but not without great difficulty. So far as the English, Dutch and Spaniards were concerned, matters went fairly smoothly. In August the English arranged that in Hudson's Bay each party should restore its conquests, and a dispute as to certain

[1] Bath Papers, III. 134, Prior to Sunderland, Hague, July 2/12, 1697.

[2] P.R.O., S.P. Foreign, Holland, vol. 223, Prior to Vernon, Hague, July 2/12, 1697.

[3] Bath Papers, III. 137, Blathwayt to Prior, Camp, July 5/15, 1697.

[4] P.R.O., S.P. Foreign, Holland, vol. 223, Prior to Vernon, Hague, July 20/30, 1697.

forts was left to commissioners. Another matter, which
in the future was to leave one of those indelible stains
of meanness which besmirch William's character, was
the question of the dowry of Mary of Modena. The
French desired that the grants and jointure made to her
should be confirmed in the treaty. Prior was made to
write to England to ask for the contract of marriage and
the acts of Parliament about her, and in return he
received a letter from John Ellis which clearly showed
the Government were trying to shuffle out of giving the
Queen anything. There was a strong temptation indeed
to do so, for, as Prior said, it "in other words is for
King James a pension[1]." Ellis informed Prior that the
contract of marriage was not to be found.

But one thing is to be taken notice of: that the settlement,
properly so-called and that can be accounted such in law, is only
what was made when she was Duchess of York, which does not
amount to £20,000 *per annum*: all the rest was but voluntary
and in the nature of a free gift; and if this be explained to the
French, it is probable they will not insist upon the matter, at
least not so much as if it were what it seems to be, above double
that sum[2].

Such indeed proved to be the case: King William
promised by the treaty that Queen Mary should receive
what she was entitled to by law, and the Ambassadors
on his behalf made a promise at Ryswick that she should
receive

la pension annuelle d'environ cinquante mille livres sterling, ou
de telle somme quelle se trouvera établie par Acte du parlement
et scellée du grand sceau d'Angleterre

on the understanding it was not used against King
William[3]. When a year later no payment of the money

---

[1] Bath Papers, III. 153, Prior to James Cresset, Hague, Aug. 14/24, 1697.
[2] *Ibid.* 156, Ellis to Prior, Whitehall, August 20/30, 1697.
[3] *Ibid.* 532, entry of Sept. 16, N.S. 1697.

had yet been made, Prior was disgusted at such scurvy treatment. He wrote to Charles Montagu:

Do we intend, my dear Master, to give her the fifty thousand pounds *per annum* or no? If we do not, I (or rather my Lord Jersey now) should be furnished with chicaning answers when we are pressed upon that point, for it was fairly promised, that is certain; if we do, the giving it openly and generously would establish the King a reputation in the minds of the French, which if we give twice that money to purchase, would not I think be bought too dear[1].

"Openness and generosity," however, were not William's most prominent characteristics, and so long as he lived, not one penny of the money promised did the exiled Queen at St Germain's receive, nor indeed did she receive anything but fair words from the ministers of Queen Anne.

These and other small matters, such as the claims of the Duchess of Hamilton to the Duchy of Châtelherault and the liberation of French Protestants, were settled by the end of August. But now the Imperialists discovered a great grievance in William's system of equivalents, devised to satisfy the pride of the French, and hasten the peace. He had proposed early in August that the French should retain Luxembourg and give an "equivalent" in its place, such as Ypres, Menin, Condé, Courtray and possibly Tournay, and the Imperialists argued that, if the French retained Luxembourg, they would enslave Western Germany, besides depriving the House of Austria of some of its most ancient patrimony[2]. On this point their firmness was unshakeable, for the present; but they also feared that an equivalent might be proposed for Strassburg[3].

The great business goes on as fast as your unwieldy *corps*

---

[1] Bath Papers, III. 260, Prior to Charles Montagu, Paris, August 30, N.S. 1698.   [2] *Ibid.* 526.

[3] *Ibid.* 147, Prior to Winchester, Hague, Aug. 6/16, 1697.

Germanique will let it. They are all very angry, but they know not why; the Imperialists are exclaiming against an equivalent for Luxembourg, whilst in their hearts they wish one for Strasbourg and talk as high here as if Charles I[1] lived at Vienna, whilst my Lord Lexington writes me word from thence that they have neither money nor credit: but *compellantur ut veniant* will be found as true now as it was in the times of the Apostles, and they must growl on till the day they sign the peace[2].

As August 31, the day on which it was hoped the peace would be signed, approached, the activity of the ministers became more feverish.

We are every day at it at Ryswick, either Imperialists or Spaniards; The former are as stiff as ever, and will only come to because they must; the latter will take an equivalent for Luxembourg, and are at last so bent upon the peace that they stick at nothing but some dependencies and villages; and that I think is only to seem to have something to do till the other part of the *Augustissima Casa* let us know what they would be at[3].

At last the great day arrived, and all was found to be in confusion. The mediator told the Allies that the French were very obstinate, and that they had new conditions to offer the next day, as they had received fresh orders from France. The Imperialists clung to their offers made previously, and at last the mediator took his leave, protesting before God and man that it was not his fault that the negociation broke up. Prior's journal[4] is by no means lucid, but Villiers' account to Hill makes it clear that the "French would not give the Imperialists a time to come in, and we thought we were not to abandon them entirely to the mercy of France, though it was their own positiveness that brought them

---

[1] *I.e.* the Emperor Charles V.
[2] Bath Papers, III. 153, Prior to Cresset, Hague, Aug. 14/24, 1697.
[3] *Ibid.* 154, Prior to Aglionby, Hague, August 17/27, 1697.
[4] *Ibid.* 528–30.

to this[1]." The fact was that Barcelona was on the point of surrendering to the French arms, and the French saw that Barcelona would be an excellent hostage for Strassburg. Hence on September 1, they proposed that Strassburg should remain French at the peace, and on those conditions they would restore Barcelona[2]. The opportunity for a peace having been let slip, everything fell again into dispute, and Villiers became exceedingly pessimistic. September 20, however, was fixed as a term for the signature of the treaty, if agreement could be reached; but meantime the English and Dutch ministers were full of spleen against the French. Still, Prior was hopeful when he wrote to Vernon about Strassburg: "I cannot think that we shall all go together again by the ears for this damned town[3]." Once more the "men of the sword" met to arrange what the men of the pen could not do. On September 5, Portland set off to Brussels to meet Boufflers again, and although the French negociators at Delft did what they could to neutralise this benevolent action, matters were facilitated by the anxiety for peace displayed by all parties among the allies save the Imperialists. On the 13th Villiers said "our affairs are but in a scurvy condition" but yet spoke of William's extreme desire for peace; and on September 17, the Spaniards were ready, the Dutch were ready, and the Imperialists were "coming in for a cessation of arms." The French, however, took advantage of the anxiety for peace shown by the allies, and not only remained obdurate about Strassburg, but stipulated for a recognition of the domination of Roman Catholicism in the town. Firmness met its just reward,

[1] Middleton Park Papers, Villiers to Hill, Hague, September 1, N.S. 1697.

[2] "If they are to give it [Strassburg] up, they will keep Barcelonne." (Middleton Park Papers, Villiers to Hill, Sept. 1, N.S. 1697.)

[3] P.R.O., S.P. Holland, vol. 223, Prior to Vernon, Sept. 6, N.S. 1697.

and on September 20 the meeting for the signature took place. The Imperialists refused to sign, but a period was given to them in which to "come in."

Prior's work on this memorable occasion was to check the French and Latin versions of the treaty, and the language of the Latin version may be regarded to some extent as a specimen of his Latinity. The Dutch and Spanish treaties were signed on the 20th at eleven and twelve o'clock at night: the English, owing to certain alterations having to be made, at three in the morning. Immediately afterwards Prior set out for England and arrived at Lowestoft on the 23rd in the afternoon, arriving at Whitehall twenty-four hours afterwards. His arrival was the signal for immense rejoicings; to use the sober language of Narcissus Luttrell: "the guns at the Tower were discharged, the flag displayed, bells ringing, bonfires and other demonstrations of joy[1]." Prior's own account of it was that the "noble nation... are so overjoyed at the peace that they are all fit for Bedlam[2]." The same day he called on the Lords Justices in town: the Archbishop of Canterbury, the Lord Chancellor, Lords Orford, Romney and Sunderland, and at their meeting the next day but one, Prior received a present of £200, and the *Centurion* was put at his disposal to take him back to Holland. Never again was Prior to receive so much honourable attention from the government at home: but unlike those whom nowadays a government delight to honour, there was no round of feasting in store for him. On the very day that the Lords Justices met and promised him his £200, he left for Holland, and arrived on Saturday the 28th.

Prior stayed on in Holland with Villiers, now Earl of Jersey, till the beginning of November. They stayed so

[1] N. Luttrell, *A brief historical relation of State Affairs from September 1678 to April 1714*, Oxford, 1857, vol. IV. p. 278.

[2] *Lexington Papers*, p. 308.

long because the ratification of the treaty was delayed
by a wrangle as to the use by William III of the title
Rex Franciae; but finally the French said they would

be satisfied provided we declared that we would change it, if it
be found otherwise in the ratification of the Treaty of Breda and
in other treaties made since. Their Excellencies are very willing
to oblige themselves to stand by the example of Breda...but do
not think it proper to consent to such loose terms as *and treaties
made since* import, for that they do not know but that the style
Rex Franciae may possibly have been omitted in those negligent
times when France had but too much influence upon our
negociations[1].

Another difficulty was the language in which the treaty
was cast. The English treaty was in Latin, the French
in their own tongue: and the French tried to insist that
the ratification should be in French only. However,
Vernon reported that Rymer "our historiographer hath
rummaged some of his records of ancient times, for he
hath not yet looked into those of the memory of man,
and he sends you an extract of all sorts when they
treated in Latin, when in French and when in both
languages[2]." Eventually in this matter the French gave
way; and research into the "diplomatic" of the treaty
of Breda resulted in the style of *Rex Franciae* being
tacitly allowed to the King of England by a compromise. In the English ratification William III styled
himself *Angliae, Scotiae, Franciae et Hiberniae Rex,
Fidei Defensor, etc.* and alluded to Louis XIV as *Rex
Christianissimus*, while Louis XIV on his side spoke of
himself as *Roi de France et de Navarre*, and of William
III as *Roi de la Grande Bretagne, etc.* On October 17
Prior exchanged the ratifications with the French
Secretary: "We have nothing left (I thank God) but
to give and receive general passports for ships that may

---

[1] Bath Papers, III. 178, Prior to Blathwayt, Hague, Oct. 4/14, 1697.
[2] *Ibid.* 174, Vernon to Prior, Whitehall, Sept. 28/Oct. 8, 1697.

go out or return on either side[1]." The three weeks that he was yet to stay in Holland were occupied with packing, and watching the Germans sullenly making up their minds to "come in" by November 1. On October 31, between one and two in the morning, the Emperor and the Catholic princes signed, but the Protestants with Brandenburg at their head refused[2]: and it may be noted that, under such circumstances, Prior did not think the peace could last long.

The Germans have their peace, the Imperialists and Palatine have showed themselves too good Catholics to think the Protestants will either heartily forgive them or make a war unanimously with them in some time. These are allowed six weeks to come in, which they will do if it were but six days, but in the meantime six hundred churches in the Palatinate are like to have mass said in them as well after they shall be restored to the Elector Palatine as whilst they were under the French Dominion. The French threaten the Elector of Brandeburg with no less than excluding him the benefit of his article in our treaty, unless he accept the peace. This, Sir, is cavalier enough to us, with whom they have signed and ratified, but I would make such an observation to you alone, and I hope you of the House of Commons will not be foolish enough to depend too much upon our peace, though we ministry have been wise enough to make it for you[3].

On November 7 the King arrived at The Hague in readiness to go to England and in his train Prior crossed over, to undertake at last, as he imagined, duties for which he had received a salary for some six months, but which he had not in the smallest degree performed. On the 8th he sent his formal letter of leave-taking to the States-General, who not merely expressed their formal

[1] P.R.O., S.P. Foreign, Holland, vol. 223, Prior to Vernon, Hague, Oct. 18, N.S. 1697.
[2] Bath Papers, III. 184, Prior to Blathwayt, Hague, Oct. 31, N.S. 1697.
[3] P.R.O., S.P. Foreign, Holland, vol. 223, Prior to Vernon, Hague, Nov. 1, N.S. 1697.

approval of his conduct, but also gave him another chain and medal, this time of the value of 600 gilders, an act which was so unusual that it had to be registered in the Secret Minute book with a special proviso that it was not to be taken as a precedent[1]. Clearly Prior had succeeded in ingratiating himself with the Powers to whom he was accredited, even though we may suspect that William III's influence was not absent[2]. He may have been pardoned any feelings of pride as he sailed homewards if he reflected that by his sojourn in Holland, wearisome and distressful though it undoubtedly had been, he had certainly won his spurs in public life. He was no longer the untried scholar of seven years ago; his worth had been tested, and William III, one of the ablest diplomatists of his age, had not found him wanting; but had even gone out of his way to find a salary whereby Prior might remain in his service. By the age of thirty-three Prior had held a post which, if it was not highly important, at any rate had entailed responsibility in the foreign service of Great Britain, and his reward was that he was to be continued in the service of the King within his own dominions. There was no chance, as he had feared at one time, of being sent back to live in College, and he could look forward with confidence to promotion and advancement in the widest sphere of life that lies open to man.

[1] The Hague, Royal Archives, St. Gen. 2342, fo. 210. "Is naer voorgaande deliberatie ende in agtinge genommen sijnde, dat M. Prior, als Secretaris van Sijne Maj^t van Groot Brittannien een tijtlang bij haar hoog Mogenden is geemploijeert geweest, soo in absentie van de heeren ministers van hoogstged: sijne Maj^t als andersints, ende op huijden affscheijt van haar hoog Mogenden heeft genommen, goetgevonden ende verstaan, dat aan den selven sal worden vereert een goude ketting ende Medaille ter waardije van ses hondert gls. sonder dat dit hiernaar in consequentie sal worden getrocken, ende wert den Goudsmith van Hoecke mit desen gelast, de voorsz ketting ende Medaille ten Spoedigsten te maken."

[2] See a letter from Prior to Blathwayt, dated Hague, Oct. 30, 1697, in B. M. Add. 21508, fo. 17.

Chapter IV

I. THE EMBASSY AT PARIS

THE duties which Prior imagined he would have to undertake were those of Secretary to the Lords Justices in Ireland. In May, Lord Villiers had been appointed a member of that body; and Prior's anxieties about his position had led him to solicit Charles Montagu to obtain for him the office of Secretary[1]. The King had no objection, and on May 21, Prior was able to thank Charles Montagu for his appointment. Henceforth Prior could be free from money cares such as oppressed him during his early years at The Hague. He anticipated that the office would bring him £1000 a year[2]; but in this he was doomed to be disappointed. The fees from which the Chief Secretary derived most profit were the military orders and commissions, and since his return to Ireland as one of the Justices in February, the honest Ruvigny, Earl of Galway, had set himself to reduce the amount of these fees. This unwelcome news reached Prior at the end of July: he wrote to Galway and Winchester:

I entirely submit to any regulation which Your Lordships think proper to be made, and I wish nothing so much as to have been on the place, that the gentlemen of the army (for it is in that part of the list that the regulation is made) might see

---

[1] Bath Papers, III. 114, Hague, May 10 (N.S.), 1697. Villiers obtained for Prior leave of absence from his duties: *Hist. MSS. Comm.* xvth Rep. II. (Eliot Hodgkin Papers), p. 83, letter of Villiers to Blathwayt, Hague, May 25, N.S. 1697.

[2] Bath Papers, *ut sup.* 115.

that I very willingly declined the reception of any fees or per-
quisites which might give any occasion of grievance[1].

But it would seem that to his subordinates, he wrote
protesting, and asking for modifications. Anyhow, on
August 3, Joshua Dawson sent Prior a letter enclosing
the revised tariff of fees in which he expressed his regret
that his representations to Lord Galway had been of no
avail, and said frankly enough that Prior's "yearly
advantage will be far short of what other secretaries
have usually enjoyed[2]." However, in spite of the very
drastic reductions effected by Lord Galway, Prior had
no very serious grounds of complaint. Instead of £1000,
the profits of his office on the first year were £666. 13s.
6d.[3], which was considerably more than he had ever
obtained from the English Treasury in return for his
services in Holland.

But Prior was not destined to go to Ireland. He was
to receive a diplomatic post far more important than
Ratisbon or Lisbon, or the other petty capitals on which
he had so freely speculated while at The Hague. He
had scarcely been in England six weeks, before he
received orders to proceed to France as secretary to
Portland's embassy on the resumption of diplomatic
relations with the Court of Versailles. Galway, who had
been impatient for Prior's arrival in Ireland even before
the signature of the peace, made no secret of his
disappointment[4], but buoyed himself up with confidence
that Prior's mission would be short[5]. The new year

---

[1] Bath Papers, III. 142, Prior to Winchester, July 21/31, 1697.

[2] Ibid. 144, July 24/Aug. 3, 1697.

[3] Ibid. 211, Arthur Podmore to Prior, Dublin, April 16/26, 1698.

[4] "Je suis bien fâché que vous vous éloigniez encore de nous." Bath
Papers, III. 186 (Dec. 7/17, 1697).

[5] "The assurance you give me that your stay in France ought to be
a very short one gives me pleasure." Bath Papers, III. 187 (Jan 4/14,
1697/8).

therefore[1] saw Prior on his way to the capital in which the most important part of his diplomatic life was to be spent. His first experience of the country was not favourable, for he fell seriously ill of a "violent cold" which left him "really at death's door; but not liking much the prospect I made all imaginable haste to return[2]" and by the middle of February he had sufficiently recovered to look about him and to record his observations in a series of letters which more than any others of those that have come down to us reveal his literary genius.

At the Court of France there was much food for Prior's pen, and he spared not. Louis XIV, Madame de Maintenon, the court and the ministers led by Pomponne and Torcy, French society as a whole, and last, but by no means least, King James II, and the Court at St Germains: all these are mordantly described for the entertainment of his great friends in England. For a picture of the court life through the spectacles of a foreigner more than tinged with Philistinism, the letters from Paris are unrivalled. Here is his first letter to Charles Montagu after his arrival in Paris:

(Feby. 18, 1697/8. N.S.)

It is a shame that I have not writ to you, but I have been dying, but as matters stand at present with me, I think I may hold out some years longer, at least I am trying how far patience and posset drink will contribute towards it. I promised to give you some account of the state of things here, and I think it may be done in one word, that the whole money of this nation is at Paris in the hands of the *partizans* and *fermiers*, from whom it must necessarily come into the King's, since they can dispose of their money no otherwise whilst the *louis d'or* is at 14 *livres*; and he will keep it so till he has got all the money he can fright-

---

[1] His commission as Secretary was dated Kensington, Dec. 29/Jan. 8, 1697/8 (P.R.O. Foreign Entry Book, 199).

[2] Bath Papers, III. 189, Prior to Jersey, Feb. 4/14, 1697/8.

ening the people every week with the report of its falling, so that it is better for particular men to trust the government and make what advantage they can of their money, than let it lie dead by them (for all traffic and merchandise is quite lost), whilst they fear they may lose one or two, or indeed three *livres* to bring it to the ancient standard, in 14. The Court, too, having all places and advantages to bestow, and everybody being noted as, according to their condition, they bring in their money, and *bailliages* and intendantships bestowed, whereby those who lend to the King are enabled to recover themselves by robbing the people, every man is obliged to swim with the stream and contribute to ruin the public in his own defence. This in their good humour the most sensible of them do not stick to confess; and even some Maréchals of France, whom I have had the honour to be with, have said openly enough how happy a people we were who were governed by established laws and taxed by our own consent.

The common people of this nation have a strange veneration for their King; it is certain he might have the last penny of them, as well by their inclinations as his power *pour la gloire*: but the people of quality hate him to hell, and (as the French do things always to excess) there is nothing so extravagant as their expressions in this kind in an *auberge* overnight, though they dare as well be hanged as not rise at five the next morning to be at Versailles by eight.

The monarch as to his health is lusty enough, his upper teeth are out, so he speaks a little like old Maynard[1], and picks and shows his under teeth with a good deal of affectation, being the vainest creature alive even as to the least things. His house at Versailles is something the foolishest in the world; he is strutting in every panel and galloping over one's head in every ceiling, and if he turns to spit he must see himself in person or his Viceregent the Sun with *sufficit orbi*, or *nec pluribus impar*. I verily believe that there are of him statues, busts, bas-reliefs and pictures, above two hundred in the house and gardens[2].

[1] Sir John Maynard, the famous lawyer.
[2] Bath Papers, III. 192–3.

It was this style of decoration which drew forth the most famous retort with which Prior is credited. The guide who was taking him over the palace at Versailles, asked him if William III's palaces could show representations of such glorious acts. "The memorials of my master's actions," was the proud answer, "are to be found everywhere but in his own house[1]." And it is clear that Prior's penetrating eye saw beyond the outward glories of Versailles into the real state of affairs of the Court of France. The gloom of the later years of Louis XIV's reign had already settled upon it. "This court," he wrote to Manchester, "is so melancholy and bigot that the news of it is hardly worth sending[2]," while he saw that the lack of success to the French arms during the late war had not escaped the notice of the nation.

Il est certain que la France est bien honteuse de la Paix qu'elle vient de faire: les prêtres et les bigots nous haïssent au dernier point, et c'est assurément avec beaucoup de plaisir que je vois que l'habileté des ministres n'est pas si grande que la malice du peuple. Pontchartrain est universellement décrié comme qui l'entend les finances le moins et qui ruinera le plutôt. Torcy n'a point de génie: tout son mérite est d'être né Colbert, et d'avoir épousé la fille de Pomponne. Ce dernier a la réputation d'honnête homme, et il est reconnu pour le premier ministre après la Maintenon (cela s'entend toujours)[3].

The estimate of Torcy was exceedingly wide of the mark, as Prior was to find out in later days, but the general picture of decay is not unjust.

That Louis did not meditate a fresh war, Prior soon

---

[1] Prior's *History of his own Times*, ed. A. Drift, Dublin, 1740, p. 30. For perhaps more authentic repartees of Matt, the reader should consult Mr Bickley's *Life*, pp. 192–3, and Appendix D.

[2] Bath Papers, III. 203, Apr. 4, N.S. 1697/8.

[3] *Ibid.* 201, Prior to Albemarle, *ca.* Mar. 19, N.S. 1697/8.

became convinced. On April 24 (N.S.) he wrote to Dorset:

> The King particularly has no mind to enter into a new war, and Madame Maintenon (our good friend) increases that pacific humour in him by telling him that all business is destructive to his health. He is so attentive to this doctrine that he has said that, if the King of Spain dies, he leaves the succession to be determined by the Council[1]—whose determination he will not oppose by way of arms, except they give it to the Emperor's second son. In the meantime Madame Maintenon governs him as absolutely as Roxalana did Solyman. He lives at Marly like an Eastern monarch, making waterworks and planting melons, and leaves his bashas to ruin the land, provided they are constant in bringing in their tribute[2].

But whatever the King's intentions may have been as to peace or war, Prior constantly harps on the fact that the French hated us, and that all their protestations of friendship were the hollowest of shams.

> For all the civilities we receive here, they hate us heartily. I heard an oration pronounced on Thursday at the Sorbonne by the Rector of the University which was rather a panegyric upon King James than upon the King of France; so bigoted these people are and so well affectioned to a Prince whom they think has suffered for the good old cause: there were some unmannerly expressions in it of our King, but such as by making him the chief of the united Princes of Europe, the head of the councils and armies of the heretics, etc., did His Majesty more honour than he really intended him[3].

Therefore in dealing with this people, there must be a very strict attention to business, and he constantly advises the application of the *lex talionis*, "an eye for an eye, and a tooth for a tooth is (whatever Mr Stapleton

---

[1] *I.e.* of Castile.
[2] Bath Papers, III. 208, Prior to Dorset, Paris, April 24, N.S. 1698.
[3] *Ibid.* 214, Prior to James Vernon, May 17, N.S. 1698.

may think of it) very good sense, and wholesome, though Jewish doctrine[1]."

Of Louis' family and surroundings, Prior speaks with his usual sarcasm. The Dauphin, he told Keppel, "est à peu près notre Prince George, hormis que l'un ne baise que la Princesse, et l'autre toutes les filles de l'Opéra sans distinction. Monsieur est une petite marionette d'une voix cassée, qui cause beaucoup et ne dit rien[2]." Madame de Maintenon, whom he is never tired of calling "our good friend," is nevertheless a phenomenon that excites his amazement:

'Tis incredible the power that woman has; everything goes through her hands, and Diana made a much less figure at Ephesus. Her niece had t'other day in money and jewels with the Duke of Noailles' son a better fortune than a daughter of France had formerly; and the aunt received the visits of the Court upon it in bed, it being concerted that the Duchess of Burgundy should have a chair set her, and refuse to sit, excusing herself upon the shortness of her visit, and that, the Duchess not sitting, the other ladies and princesses could not pretend to it[3].

Or again on the same theme to Keppel:

C'est prodigieux que le pouvoir de cette vieille gouvernante sur l'esprit de son pupil royal de soixante. Il n'ose rien faire sans elle, ni lui refuser tout ce qu'elle veut. Il y a quelques jours qu'un petit emploi fut donné par l'intercession de Mons. de Torcy à un de ses amis: l'ordre était dépêché, et l'affaire comme faite: un autre s'adressa plus heureusement à la Maintenon: elle envoie sur le champ un valet de chambre seulement au secrétaire, et dans un quart d'heure tout était changé[4].

---

[1] Middleton Park Papers, no. 35, Prior to Jersey, Paris, Aug. 8, N.S. 1699. See also Bath Papers, III. 301, Prior to Vernon, Paris, Dec. 13, N.S. 1698.

[2] Bath Papers, III. 195, Prior to Albemarle, Mar. 1, N.S. 1697/8.

[3] Ibid. 205, Prior to C. Montagu, Apr. 10, N.S. 1698; cf. also p. 208.

[4] Ibid. 201, Prior to Albemarle, ca. Mar. 19, N.S. 1697/8. That she was the wife of Louis XIV Prior never so much as hints, and

Of the grandchildren of Louis we hear little: but in writing to Lord Buckhurst, Dorset's eldest son, Prior says "the King's grandchildren are very good scholars (as I can particularly assure you), and therefore you must take care to show them hereafter that an English nobleman understands Latin as well as a French Prince[1]."

But what was of more interest to Prior as an Englishman and the agent of the government of William III was the Court of St Germain the observations of the doings of which would almost appear to have been assigned to him as a duty. The presence of King James II in the neighbourhood of Versailles was sure to create an exceedingly delicate situation for the Ambassadors of William III, and the hope that the French King would remove King James from the neighbourhood of Paris flashes brightly from Prior's correspondence in the first weeks of his stay in Paris. "There is a talk," he wrote, "that the King of France has a mind to live at St Germains, it being his native air and more proper for him than Versailles. This may be a fair pretext of sending the present inhabitants of St Germains further[2]." Later on Prior eagerly reported the rumour that the exiled family was removing to Chambord[3]. Portland indeed found it impossible to go to any reception or

we may surmise that his information as to secrets of the Court was not as good as it should have been. At any rate, Prior's astonishment at her influence can only be explained by such ignorance.

[1] Bath Papers, III. 306, Prior to Lord Buckhurst, Paris, Dec. 27, N.S. 1698. It is amusing to see how Prior maintains the superiority of the English over the French according to a well-known equation: "Here is no school half so big as Westminster, when the curtain is drawn; everybody learns in a Gazette (sic), without being whipped or fighting with one another, which is a very effeminate way, and I believe is the reason that one English boy can construe or box with three French boys." (Ibid.)

[2] Ibid. 194, Prior to Vernon, Feb. 28, N.S. 1697/8.

[3] Ibid. 282, Prior to Vernon, Paris, Nov. 5, N.S. 1698.

hunt if "the King of England" was to be there. This caused James great satisfaction, and he exultingly said "that the rebels dare not look him in the face, and that he never saw above one or two of Bentinck's crew[1]"; but to the Court of France it was a matter of great embarrassment. Prior was greatly tickled by the situation, which indeed was the creation of Louis XIV's generosity to his unfortunate cousin. "Things continue here in the old train; they are very obliging to us one day, and the same to King James the next[2]." It is unfortunate that Prior seems to have been the first official person who had a sufficiently brazen front to be in the same room as the members of the exiled family. This was on the occasion of a christening at St Cloud.

King James and his Queen were there, and since most of the ministers went thither from Versailles, I went likewise. I saw King James and his Queen (pray do not hang me for so doing), and there was nothing so odd as to see the Duke of Berwick and Lord Middleton traversing the gallery on one side, and I [*sic*] and Lord Reay, of the good Mackay brood, on the other side, each looking on the other with an air of civility mixed with contempt[3]. The gentlemen belonging to the Duke d'Orléans and Chartres were embarassed enough to call him one moment *le Roy d'Angleterre* to them, and speak to me the next of *le Roy Jacques*: it was, as most human things are, a farce ridiculous enough[4].

This extremely awkward scene was entirely of Prior's creation: as if this were not enough, he deliberately

---

[1] Bath Papers, III. 311, Prior to Portland, Paris, January 14/24, 1698/9.

[2] *Ibid.* 215, Prior to C. Montagu, May 21, N.S. 1698.

[3] One cannot help remarking that the ceremonious manners of the age of Louis XIV must have been brought to a high pitch of perfection if it became possible to mingle civility with contempt and display both at once.

[4] *Ibid.* 257, Prior to Vernon, Paris, Aug. 27, N.S. 1698.

went out of his way later in the year to repeat it with the Prince of Wales at Versailles. He shows no compunction for this very undiplomatic tactlessness:

I had the curiosity to see the boy as he passed through the great apartments. My Lord Perth and Melfort were with him; you will imagine how they looked upon an Englishman that let their Prince pass by without taking any notice of him; it was told the boy, I perceived by his looking, who I was; he is not handsome, but he is very lively. I can tell you he is a true papist, for I saw him say his prayers and cross himself before the altar. After all it is a ridiculous figure that the Court of France makes, halting thus between God and Baal. I know not what they will do at Fontainebleau, whither they have already invited King James and his Court, and where also my Lord Jersey will go and expect to be used with all the dignity that an English Ambassador should have; but by twenty things here I perceive they are mightily embarassed about it[1].

The visit of James and his Queen to Fontainebleau gave Louis an opportunity of entertaining them with his usual generosity.

All the court is made to Queen Mary, everybody is at her toilette in the morning, from whence the King of France leads her to chapel: the two Kings and the Queen in the midst sit at the head of the table at dinner with equal marks of distinction and sovereignty, and "*à boire pour le Roi d'Angleterre!*" ou "*pour la Reine*" is spoke as loud and with the same ceremony as "*pour le Roi*" when they mean their own King. It is really not a right figure which we make, being here at Paris whilst all the other ministers are at Court; but on the other side, I know not what we should do there, or how behave ourselves in a place where the two Courts are inseparable[2].

It would seem from the tone of this letter that Jersey's arrival at Paris had been accompanied by a not

[1] Bath Papers, III. 271-2, Prior to J. Vernon, Oct. 1, N.S. 1698.
[2] *Ibid.* 277, Prior to Vernon, Paris, Oct. 18, N.S. 1698.

untimely reminder to Prior how it was fit that a gentleman should behave[1].

So much for the personal and diplomatic position.
In the realm of English domestic politics, Prior con-
tinued to note with savage glee the headlong rush of
James II into a complete breach with the Protestants.
He is

still the very same man we always took him to be....Speaking of
his little daughter: "I intend" says he "to send her to Poissy;
there she shall learn Latin, that is, as much as to make her understand where the priest is when he says the Mass, for it is convenient that a Catholic Child of her quality should be instructed
very soon in her religion." Thus wisely, my Lord, he talks[2].

And Prior saw clearly how all chances of a legitimist
restoration were being thrown away by James: "The
child they call the Prince of Wales they breed up with
all the abhorrence imaginable to heresy[3]"; and again,
"They have ordered that no Protestant servant of any
condition whatsoever shall be about their son[4]." As to
James' attitude to the Protestants that remained loyal
to him, Prior notes with satisfaction as follows:

Poor King James is hardly thought on or mentioned: an
Italian and a Scotch priest govern him and his whole concerns;
he is so directly the same man he ever was, persecuting the few
Protestants that are about him, though they are ruined and

---

[1] Prior's conduct in its way was almost as inexcusable as that of
Mons. Heemskirk which Prior reported, with grave headshaking, to
Portland on Oct. 24, N.S. 1698. "It is with some concern I tell Your
Lordship that Mons. Heemskirk has behaved himself there [at Fontaine-
bleau] unworthy his age or character in coming to the King's supper
after he had drank, and exposing himself by twenty indecencies....Your
Lordship knows these people and the nicety of living with them." (Bath
Papers, III. 280.)

[2] Bath Papers, III. 279, Prior to Portland, Paris, Oct. 20, N.S. 1698.

[3] *Ibid.* 305, Prior to Dorset, Paris, Dec. 26, N.S. 1698.

[4] *Ibid.* 334, Prior to Portland, Paris, Apl. 18, N.S. 1699.

banished for their adhering to him, and rewarding and encouraging any sorry creature that he can make a convert of[1].

In November Sir William Jennings threw up his post at St Germains in disgust; an incident which, according to Prior, was "a good deal the reason of Louis XIV having a bad opinion of" the Court of St Germains[2]. By way of still further conciliating his Protestant subjects, James in March, 1699, disgraced Lord Middleton, the leader of his Protestant party, and restored Lord Melfort, the leader of the extreme Catholics, to complete favour[3].

It was all very well for Prior to assume this cheerful and light-hearted tone in his correspondence[4]. In reality he was animated by a very different feeling towards James II: for he was thoroughly frightened of him. The civilities shown by Louis to King James and Queen Mary were quite incomprehensible to him and Portland, who seem to have considered this characteristic generosity as another signal instance of the French King's duplicity[5]. This suspicion as to Louis XIV's honesty, coupled with the thought of the assassination plot and the presence of the accomplices at St Germains, naturally compelled Prior to maintain a small army of spies to watch that mischief-making court. This intelligence work, as it may now be called, had its usual

[1] Bath Papers, III. 305, Prior to Dorset, Dec. 26, N.S. 1698; cf. also p. 295, Prior to Vernon, Paris, Nov. 16/26, 1698; p. 296, Prior to Portland, Paris, Nov. 29, 1698.

[2] Ibid. 297, Prior to Portland, Paris, Nov. 29, 1698.

[3] Ibid. 319, Prior to Portland, Paris, March 11, N.S. 1699.

[4] We may observe that Prior could mimic the tone of true Roman Catholic unction. In reporting a rumour that the Duke of Berwick was going to Rome to be ordained and receive a red hat, he comments: "Quelle consolation pour des âmes vraiment Catholiques! Et quel honneur pour la véritable Eglise!" (Bath Papers, III. 316, Prior to Portland, Paris, Feb. 28, 1699, N.S.)

[5] See Bath Papers, III. 281, Portland to Prior, Loo, Oct. 28, N.S. 1698, and ibid. 282, Prior to Portland, Paris, Nov. 3, N.S. 1698.

accompaniment of disappointments. Some of his agents proved to be "cheats"; notable among these was one Mark Lynch, "Lieutenant of Foot in the Regiment of Albemarle," who came to France with Lord Jersey bearing a tale that an Irishman named Matthew Wall had informed him of a design to burn the English fleet at Portsmouth and Chatham, and that Pontchartrain, the French minister of the admiralty, had offered them 50,000 *livres* to do it[1]. This led to considerable correspondence between Prior and the English government on one side, and with Torcy and Pomponne on the other. In a month's time from receiving this information (May 24/June 24, 1699) Prior announced "that there is knavery mixed with Lynch's folly" and "one may reasonably conclude him a cheat[2]." The next step followed rapidly. On July 4 he wrote to Jersey that both Wall and Lynch were in the Bastille[3], where they were still languishing when Prior left Paris. Others, however, proved faithful servants[4]. On the eve of leaving Paris, Prior wrote to Jersey an account of them, for the information of his successor.

As to the faithful, here is first Br(aconier), the man that having done service during the war, was suspected here and put into the Bastille, where he remained four years; he addressed himself to my Lord Portland, and was told by him that from me he should know what the King of England designed for him, his affair is only with one correspondent, who has promised, if anything very considerable happens, to give notice of it to Mons. Bra(conier), and for such notice given this correspondent expects a very great

[1] Bath Papers, III. 344, Paper of May 13/23, 1699.

[2] *Ibid.* 359, Prior to Jersey, Paris, June 24, N.S. 1699.

[3] Middleton Park Papers, 20, Prior to Jersey, Paris, July 4, N.S. 1699.

[4] On the whole Prior obtained a lot of information, sometimes of a "spicy" kind, such as was the news that Lady Sandwich and Lady Salisbury had in July and August, 1699, had audiences of Queen Mary. (Middleton Park Papers, 31 and 38, Prior to Jersey, Paris, July 25, N.S., and Aug. 19, N.S. 1699.)

reward....Brocard, as we call him, is Tr(ant), an Irishman encouraged by Mr Vernon; his pretended business is merchandise of English things, as stockings, hats, &c., under which notion he gives our friends at St Germains an account of things in England, he is well with them, and particularly with my Lord Middleton's party. It was this man that amused us all last winter with a story of a fellow sent into England by Frank Stafford; however, though he has not been very useful, he may be so; he costs us between two and three hundred pounds a year....Baily, who is Jo(hnsto)n, and related to the Secretary of that name, has a great mind to be at home, and has written to Mr Alexander Johnson for that purpose, he is a parson disguised, a cunning fellow and a true *débauché*, he is upon the merit of 2 *louis* a week, and picks up what they are doing at St Germains; for the time he will be here, I will turn him over to Stanyan if you think good.

Jannisson as to his ordinary correspondence of who goes and who comes, may he not be given over to Stanyan and paid by my Lord Manchester...?

My widow Langlois and her two daughters Stanyan may have; I think the old woman is a cunning jade as lives, and will pump him in his turn if he is not upon his guard; if he visits her, as he should do, he may know something of most of the rogues and priests about Paris that have any dealings at St Germains...[1].

One spy, indeed, not mentioned in this letter, gave Prior a good deal of interesting information as regards the assassination plot and the notorious view held at St Germains as to the ethics of the design:

I have been enquiring a little into the conduct of our friends at St Germains; one Glover, an engineer, who deserted our service in the beginning of the war, and who has been ever since in King James', let me know privately that he had a mind to speak with me. The man teaches practical mathematics, and under that pretext comes to me, he has a great mind to deserve his pardon by anything he may do. He would attempt the drawing all the sea-ports in France, or anything else he might be ordered,

[1] Bath Papers, III. 359–61, Prior to Jersey, Paris, June 24, 1699.

to show he is sincere, he tells very freely what he knows of everything. He says Hungate is here, and that he saw Brierly the other
day. Amongst other things we fell upon the subject of the conspiracy, he told me particulars which mightily confirms [*sic*] that
King James knew it: viz., that Brierly had actually told him that
King James had said to him (Brierly encouraging him in that
hellish design) that their killing the Prince of Orange (as these
people call His Majesty) at Richmond or Kensington was the
same as if Villeroy had laid an ambuscade for him in Flanders,
and that he, King James, had the opinion of the best doctors upon
that point. You see, my Lord, that the old gentleman is a very
excellent casuist; another thing upon this subject is, Sir William
Ellis t'other day, talking with a gentleman of my friends, was
so angry when the gentleman talked with some suspicion of King
James being in the design, that he, going back to St Germains
at night, actually asked King James if he had ever seen a paper
that was written in vindication of the conspiracy, to which King
James indiscreetly blabbed out that truly he had seen such a paper,
but did not read it; and Sir William Ellis as indiscreetly told
the same gentleman the next day what King James had said upon
this subject. Glover likewise says that he has asked Saunders,
King James' confessor, his opinion upon this point, and that
Saunders did not condemn the assassination as intended.

Another thing is very remarkable: when the thing was discovered, and these hell-hounds returned to St Germains, the
Lord Middleton's party and the honester sort of these people
would not keep these villains company, but called them con-
spirators and assassins; upon which they complained to King
James, who gave order that these names should be no more
heard, that they should all live in friendship together, and be well
with these gentlemen who had had too much zeal for his service.

What makes me so particularly insist upon this is that these
villains go still upon the same principle that King James not
having made a peace with England, though France has, all that
can be done against the King our master by arms, public or private,
is lawful. Brierly particularly says the business is not at an end
yet. Brierly has studied at St Omers, where he learned this good

divinity, and King James received this case of conscience from that university. Ennis, the Scotch priest, I am credibly informed, sustains this doctrine amongst those whom he thinks he may trust.

The reason why I repeat this at present to Your Lordship is that as well Glover as a correspondent, Your Lordship knows, Mr Secretary Vernon employs, agree in this that the whole Court of St Germains are in despair of succeeding any other way than by the horrid one of cutting off His Majesty, and that King James should offer a vast sum of money to the man and his family that should attempt it, or to be divided amongst them that shall undertake it: the Protestants themselves, being now desperate, give in to this[1].

All this shows in what a perpetual state of nerves Prior lived in regard to James II:

Our neighbours at St Germains speak mighty confidently of returning home to England; it seems as if they had some new villainy forging. We have had some advice of that kind, imperfect, some false, but such after all as makes us extremely apprehensive of everything[2].

This apprehension no doubt explains, though it scarcely excuses, the brutally triumphant tone with which he reports the signs of poverty at the Court of St Germains. Of the christening at St Cloud he wrote to Montagu:

I faced old James and all his Court the other day at St Cloud. *Vive Guillaume!* You never saw such a strange figure as the old bully is, lean, worn and riv'led, not unlike Neal the projector; the Queen looks very melancholy, but otherwise well enough; their equipages are all very ragged and contemptible[3].

It is difficult, if not impossible, to defend such unseemly language. Here, as in other departments of life, Prior's taste was deplorable. Whether the baseness

[1] Bath Papers, III. 239–40, Prior to Portland, Paris, July 24, N.S. 1698.
[2] *Ibid.* 208, Prior to Dorset, Apr. 24, N.S. 1698.
[3] *Ibid.* 259, Prior to C. Montagu, Paris, Aug. 30, N.S. 1698.

of his birth or the surroundings of his childhood wove in him a coarse fibre unfitted for a diplomatist it is not easy to say; but this behaviour and these letters have their counterpart in the grossness of his pleasures and the lack of refinement exhibited by his fondness for low company. We may indeed find a palliative for these letters if we consider Prior as a young man on promotion, anxious to please, and in a position where loyalty had to be protested vigorously if it were not to be suspected. Ill-health, too, may have contributed not a little to disturb the balance of his judgement, and in justice to him we may remember that his protests against the failure of the English government to pay Queen Mary's dowry betray a generous feeling towards an unfortunate lady, which contrasts pleasantly with the vindictiveness of his feelings towards the fallen king.

Chapter V

II. IN THE EMBASSY AT PARIS

IN June, 1698, Prior found himself the sole representative of the English government in Paris. At the
beginning of that month Portland went home, and
Jersey, who was to succeed him, was not expected for
three months at least. The immediate result of this
change, so far as Prior was concerned, was to set him
clamouring once more for an increase of pay. In spite
of the Irish secretaryship, the pay of which, to be sure,
seemed uncertain, Prior's position was uncomfortable.
"Dear Horace!" he writes to Montagu after a quota-
tion, "I have a sentence of him upon most occasions,
but I find nothing in him applicable to staying at Paris
upon 40s. a day, where one's coach costs one *louis*, and
one's lodgings another, before I or mine have eat or
drank[1]." And to Albemarle he descanted at length, in
French, on the indecency of a minister of the English
king seeking his dinner in a tavern (which he will have
to do now that he no longer has Portland's table), going
on foot to visit the French ministers, and maintaining
a secretariat with only two lackeys where once there
was an embassy with eighty[2]. The government, however, soon fell in with Prior's views, for, on Montagu's
recommendation, William III gave orders that the

[1] Bath Papers, III. 216, Prior to C. Montagu, Paris, May 21, N.S. 1698.
[2] *Ibid.* 212, Prior to Albemarle, Paris, April 23/May 3, 1698. Prior's
table does not seem to have been very sumptuous, for example:
"St. M(aurice) dined with me yesterday *en philosophe*, and was much
pleased with boiled mutton and custard." (Middleton Park Papers, no. 30,
Prior to Jersey, Paris, July 22, N.S. 1699.)

allowance of the Secretary in Paris should be doubled[1], and a payment of £500 was made to him in September[2].

Of the dignity of his position, Prior was not insensible; but responsible as it might seem to be at first sight, it is impossible to disguise its complete unimportance. Prior himself said, "though I bustle about and pass for a man of business, I am as idle as the best of you[3]," and Portland was at no pains to conceal the fact that Prior had nothing to do. "Je vous prie de me mander un peu des nouvelles de la Cour de temps à autre, car je ne vous crois pas autrement occupé[4]." But the silence of Prior's correspondence on the Spanish Succession is more eloquent than many statements in the letters. There is not a word in his correspondence to show that he had even the ghost of an idea of the momentous discussions that were then passing between William III and Louis XIV through the medium of Tallard, Louis' ambassador in London. Prior's mind is entirely occupied with retailing the gossip of Paris, sending over information as to the doings at St Germain,

[1] Bath Papers, III. 224, R. Powys to Prior, Whitehall, June 14/24, 1698.

[2] Treasury Papers, 1698, Sept. 15/25, 1698. Cf. Bodleian Library (S.C. 25427), MS. Montagu d. 1, fo. 99 b, Prior to Montagu, Paris, Aug. 9, 1698, N.S. "All this time I am fluttering about Paris in a gilt chariot, with 3 footmen in gay coats, so far it goes well, but the galloon man, the tailor, the harness maker, the coachman, begin to grow very troublesome...confess, however, my dear Master, that greatness is very barren, and the glories of this world very empty if Mr. Montagu in all his honours cannot help his friend Matt to 500 pounds on this occasion."

[3] Bath Papers, III. 275, Prior to Charles Boyle, Christopher Codrington and Spencer Compton, Paris, Oct. 15, N.S. 1698.

[4] Ibid. 233, Portland to Prior, Kensington, July 2/12, 1698. In his diary he confesses that he knew nothing of the second partition treaty till October, 1699. "Lord Jersey had communicated to me more plainly what before I knew but imperfectly, that we were making a treaty with France and the States General for the Succession of Spain." (Letters...in the Library at Welbeck, p. 255.)

alarming the home government with news of plots con-
cocted against William III, reporting on the progress
of disputes with the French government about French
réfugiés who had been sent to the galleys, and whose
release the English government demanded, and asking
for compensation for ships which he claimed had been
unlawfully captured by Jean Bart.

With the gossip of Paris, Prior thoroughly enjoyed
himself. His natural wit made him a favourite among
the men of letters, and towards the end of his time we
find him dining with Boileau[1], who seems to have
flattered him to the top of his bent[2]. But his greatest
conquest was the carpet Marshal Villeroy, more puissant
at Versailles and Paris than in the field, who seems to
have pretended to serve Prior as guide, philosopher and
friend. The friendship, if such it can be called, began
soon after Portland's departure:

The Marechal de Villeroy was in town on Sunday; he told
me he had letters from Your Excellency from the frontiers, and
gave me to understand how well you had been treated wherever
you came, which was all so truly French that I could hardly
forbear laughing; he stopped his coach to tell me this in the
Cours de la Reine, and made a hundred other coaches stop likewise whilst he talked with me. This, Your Lordship knows, is

---

[1] "I am going to dine at Hauteoeil with Boileau and the *beaux
Esprits*." Middleton Park Papers, no. 19, Prior to Jersey, Paris, July 1,
1699, N.S. At first, he says, people fought shy of him: "There is some
tolerable satisfaction in the company of some of their men of learning;
but those who expect most preferment from court are a little shy of
being much with me." Bodleian Library MS. Montagu d. 1, fo. 100 *b*,
Prior to Montagu, Paris, Aug. 9, N.S. 1698.

[2] "Patience, I live amongst my savants, and Boileau says I have more
genius than all the Academy—good again." Middleton Park Papers,
no. 28, Prior to Jersey, Paris, July 8/18, 1699. To this Jersey replied in
a postcript, "If you don't come quickly away, Boileau and that flattering
country will spoil you." (Bath Papers, III. 372, Whitehall, July 13/23,
1699.)

so like the man that I cannot forbear telling it to you. I went to wait upon him the next morning; they told me he lay at a little house he has somewhere without Paris, and saw no company in the morning, everybody leaving their name with the porter at his great house, as I likewise did, it not being my business to enquire more exactly where he lay or with whom[1].

Certainly Villeroy's curiosity concerning everything English was sufficient to warn Prior that Villeroy was not searching for knowledge for its own sake. Portland thought it wise to send a warning that Villeroy "was more of a courtier than a friend[2]"; but seeing that in Villeroy Prior saw a subject for lampoons[3], we may conclude the hint was unnecessary, and indeed Prior was under no illusions as to the grounds for Villeroy's friendliness.

"My Governor," for so Prior called Villeroy, "is always with 1255 (Louis XIV), and I dare swear pumps me, to tell half an hour after the effect of his questions; he is an excellent courtier, but if they had no abler heads than he, we might sleep in quiet[4]."

How Prior resisted the process of "pumping" we can only judge from his own accounts: that the application was long and constant is certain, for it began as early as July, 1698, and was first prompted by the doings of the Tory Parliament of William III.

To William's disgust, this Parliament, which had met on December 3/13, 1697, had voted the disbandment of all troops in England, save 8000, and had dragged

---

[1] Bath Papers, III. 225, Prior to Portland, Paris, July 3, N.S. 1698.

[2] *Ibid.* 223, Portland to Prior, London, July 5/15, N.S. 1698.

[3] *Ibid.* 311, Prior to Portland, Paris, January 14/24, 1698/9. "I am afraid my Governor for all his compliments will be paying his court to Queen Mary, and I believe at the bottom he hates us very heartily, which is the reason I am so far from repenting that I have sent Your Lordship the lampoons upon him, that I intend to make one upon the same subject myself."

[4] *Ibid.* 329, Prior to Portland, Paris, April 1, N.S. 1699.

on till July, 1698, while Charles Montagu carried through successfully a scheme for raising £2,000,000 in order to found a new Whig East India Company and wind up the affairs of the old Tory Company. These measures were the subject upon which Prior had to submit to Villeroy's cross-examination:

I waited upon the Marshals Villeroy and Boufflers: the former of these talked with me a good while about the affairs of England, about the bill for raising the two millions, and if we were not to reform our troops? I let him see that as to the two millions it might easily be raised by several imposts which I named, or that more might be raised as the occasions of the nation required. He asked me then what made the session so long? and insisted mightily upon it. I let him understand from passages in their own gazettes that it was that particular affairs were mingled with those of the public, and that the Parliament was rather about the manner how the thing should be done with most ease to the subject, than if it should be done, all parties agreeing in this latter point. I gave our desiring to keep up some troops this turn, that it was rather that we would be grateful to the officers and soldiers that had served so well than that we should have any real necessity for them, that as far as I could judge from England, as everybody was entirely satisfied with the Peace, so my Lord Portland and the English that have been here since the making it might see by everything that His Most Christian Majesty designed absolutely the maintaining it. This pleased him; "*vous parlez avec raison, Monsieur,*" *me dit-il.* But I thought just the contrary[1].

As a matter of fact, the £2,000,000 were to be raised by subscription, and we can imagine the contemptuous satisfaction with which Prior saw the self-opinionated Villeroy taking all Prior's information for truth. Villeroy certainly seems to have thought he had discovered a perfect gold-mine of information, for a few days later, he returned to the charge; and the result

[1] Bath Papers, III. 230, Prior to Portland, Paris, July 9, N.S. 1698.

was an interesting letter on the relation of the militia to the regulars at the end of the seventeenth century:

My tutor Villeroy, who does me the honour sometimes to take me aside, has been mighty inquisitive upon our re-forming and what our militia were. I augmented their number to two hundred thousand, and told him they were stout fellows well fed, and that had for four hundred years past had such a notion of liberty that they would die for their cause, good or bad, provided they thought it good. I said that in the Revolution, these men being generally for the King (then Prince of Orange), we might have expected a battle or two with King James's forces in case they had not forsook him; but by the Lieutenants putting the militia in good order, we should have had no reason to have doubted of the liberty of the nations; and let him know what Cromwell's troops, who were only these a little taught, had done at home, what Morgan's had done before Dunkirk, and what the English new-raised troops, who were actually the same men as the militia, had done this war in Flanders. I know not why he is so very curious; possibly he has been talking with some of our friends at St Germains on the same subject; he ought, however, to have no other notion of that affair[1].

The surprise expressed at Villeroy's curiosity can only be assumed, if we take it in conjunction with the doubt Prior expressed as to the pacific intentions of France at that moment, and the information that he was sending home as to the measures of Louis XIV. The King of Spain, it was thought, was dying; a French squadron "much greater than I sent Your Lordship word[2]" was being fitted for the Mediterranean, and there was great activity at Brest and Toulon.

Their designing this squadron against the Sally men is a jest, six or eight good ships would be sufficient for that service, and they would not send a Vice-Admiral and two Lieutenant-Generals upon an affair of so small consequence. The Marquis

[1] Bath Papers, III. 235, Prior to Portland, Paris, July 15, N.S. 1698.
[2] *Ibid.* 234.

d'Estrées goes into Poitou to keep the new converts in obedience, as they say; but would they employ a Marshal of France in a work which belongs to a captain of dragoons? Your Lordship will judge that the design of his being there is that he is so much nearer Spain and in more readiness to head the troops on that side upon occasion[1].

Corn was being passed "in vast quantities" by the Intendant of Lyons into Provence and Languedoc, while of the troops in Catalonia and Piedmont only some peculiar favourites among the officers were allowed leave of absence, and none beyond October. Further, Harcourt had desired leave for the French vessels and galleys to be received into the ports of Spain. "Why," asks Prior, "should the Spaniards be so difficult in granting it, if they thought it was intended only for their goods?" As for the camp at Compiègne, then the universal topic of conversation, to which the whole Court of France was bidden, including King James and Queen Mary, it "is but an amusement, that by looking at their forces there we may take less notice of what they have dispersed elsewhere[2]." Had Prior known of the negociations between William and Louis as to the Spanish partition, Villeroy's cross-examinations would have given him still further grounds for suspicion: for as long as these had not come to any definite conclusion, it was of vital importance to France to know what forces William could put into the field should the death of the King of Spain and Louis' consequent action be the signal for war between the two countries.

The arrival of Jersey on September 1 put a term to Villeroy's examinations of Prior, but not to the subjects for French inquisitiveness. On September 27, Jersey had his private audience at Versailles, and it was on that occasion that Prior misbehaved himself so

---

[1] Bath Papers, III. 234.
[2] Ibid. 235, ut sup.

signally towards the Prince of Wales. Contrary to
Prior's expectations Jersey did not go to Fontainebleau
so long as James II was there; but, after the departure
of the King who could not be met, Jersey arrived at
Fontainebleau late at night with Prior and demanded
an audience[1]. "Mons. de Torcy said it was utterly
impossible, the King being prepared for his devotions
the next day, which was All Saints', but my Lord afterwards telling Mons. de Torcy the reason, His Excellency had a private audience in the King's cabinet about
10 at night, and the next morning we came away for
Paris[2]." This secret audience, and the immediate return
of Jersey the next day, does not seem to have been
noticed: but his departure to Loo the day following his
return caused unbounded speculation:

My Lord Jersey's voyage to Loo has set these people mightily
upon the enquiry; they will not let a man make a step but it
must be upon some *politique* account; one cannot go to the opera,
but they imagine that it is rather to mind who are in the boxes
than what is done upon the theatre; and if you visit a lady, it
is certainly to meet some spy or minister there[3].

But what was the cause of this sudden visit to
Fontainebleau at which Jersey was able to make
Louis XIV break through his usual rules and do business after having been spiritually tucked up for the
night preparatory to communion the next morning?
and what passed between the King and Jersey? Prior's
account, in his letters to Galway[4] and Winchester[5], is
that it was merely to take leave of the King preparatory
to the journey to Loo. This, in all probability, is the
truth; an audience at which serious business was to be

[1] October 31, 1698.
[2] Bath Papers, III. 282, Prior to Portland, Paris, Nov. 3, 1698.
[3] *Ibid.* 286, Prior to Aglionby, Paris, Nov. 8, N.S. 1698.
[4] *Ibid.* 287, Paris, Nov. 13, N.S. 1698.
[5] *Ibid.* 288–9, Paris, Nov. 14, N.S. 1698.

transacted would under the circumstances have been certainly postponed till after the King received communion. At a merely formal audience, Louis could send a message of compliment to William III without falling into mortal sin; but he did not confine himself to compliments; he professed a resolution to keep the peace, and does not seem to have thought that in such words there was insincerity amounting to mortal sin[1].

Jersey remained away from Paris till the middle of December, and in the meantime Prior continued his routine work, and the chance of promotion once more floated before his eyes. At the end of November he was told that Shrewsbury was at last to be allowed to resign his secretaryship of state and that in all probability Jersey would be his successor. The rumour was confirmed at the end of December[2], after Jersey's return to Paris, and at the same time Prior told Dorset of his penury and his hopes of return.

I have played the minister here in my Lord Jersey's absence, and, now he is returned, we are preparing for his entry, so I am to appear with him as I did with my Lord Portland, in a new gaudy coat and with an expensive equipage. I must own to Your Lordship I am weary of this dancing on the high rope in spangled breeches, and if my Lord Jersey be Secretary of State (as it is thought he may be in some time), I will endeavour to get home and seat myself in a desk in his office, for I had rather be Matt Prior near my dear Lord Dorset...than *Monsieur l'Envoyé* in any Court in Christendom; and I know not how it is, life runs away before one is aware of it, and I shall hardly have time

[1] Bath Papers, III. 282, Prior to Portland, Paris, Nov. 3, 1698. "I am glad the Monarch repeated to Lord Jersey his resolutions to keep the Peace the very night before he took the Sacrament."

[2] *Ibid.* 304, Tucker to Prior, London, Dec. 15/25, 1698. "His Majesty hath been pleased to name Lord Jersey to succeed him [Shrewsbury]."

enough in that part of it which is to come, to testify the obligations I have to Your Lordship for so many years past[1].

But although it was an open secret that Jersey would succeed Shrewsbury, it was not till April that he was formally recalled, or could promise anything to Prior. The close friendship, however, that had sprung up between the two made it certain that Jersey would give him what office he could, and on April 4, N.S. 1699, Prior could write to Dorset: "I think I see it already destined by the higher powers that His Lordship will be Secretary and I his Vernon[2]." But he was told immediately afterwards that he was not to return with Jersey; he was to resume his *interim* ministry, as he called it. "You must not think of removing before my Lord Manchester arrives; how soon you may get away afterwards, I leave to be adjusted between Mr Montagu and yourself[3]." This was a sad blow, for it was not expected that Manchester, who was named to succeed Jersey, would reach Paris before Michaelmas. However, the orders were precise, and all Prior could do was to implore his friends to hasten Lord Manchester's departure.

To us of the twentieth century, Prior's intimacy with Jersey bore other fruit. Whether Prior had exhausted all the stock of gossip about the French court which had filled his correspondence in 1698, or whether Jersey supplied him with information which he had not received before, the fact remains that after Jersey's arrival, Prior's letters become better commentaries on important public affairs than before. The first sign of this is the hint at the negociations for the Spanish business which appears in a letter to Winchester on

[1] *Bath Papers*, III. 306, Prior to Dorset, Paris, Dec. 26, 1698. The original of this letter is at St John's College, Cambridge, MS. S. 51.

[2] *Ibid.* 330, Prior to Dorset, Paris.

[3] *Ibid.* 331, Vernon to Prior, Whitehall, March 27/April 6, 1699.

November 14[1]. That he never was alive to the real significance of the first partition treaty[2], will be seen from his comments on the will of Charles II, signed in November, 1698[3]:

It is beyond contradiction that the King of Spain has made his will, and by it constituted the Electoral Prince of Bavaria his heir, and the Queen to be Regent in case His Majesty dies during the minority of the Prince; thus the lineal right is kept to the younger sister's grandson and heir; the renunciation that France made when the King married the eldest sister is confirmed to be valid; and the Dauphin or (as France was projecting) one of his younger sons, excluded, as well as the Archduke of Austria. The Queen had a great sway in this business, and the reasons that most probably inclined her to this choice were that she might exalt the Palatine family...and that by this contrivance she might hold the government longer (which is not the least of a woman's aim in such cases) the Electoral Prince not being above 8 years old, and as well the Archduke as the Duke of Berry five or six years nearer manhood. The French in general seem to be nettled at this affair, but I think those of them that have best sense are not so really; for all their natural heat and impatience, and the pride they take in the greatness of their monarchy, they begin to see that these notions have impoverished and enslaved them; and the Treaty of Ryswyck has a good deal instructed them, and their own affairs at home convinced them that they have grasped at more than they could secure, and that neither their King nor they are the better for the expense of fortifying and keeping garrisons eight years together in thirty towns which they have been obliged to give back in the ninth. The Monarch himself is old, and, I think, has a good mind to be quiet; to say the truth out he is quite cowed by King William,

[1] Bath Papers, III. 289.

[2] Ratified October 11, 1698.

[3] I am assuming what is generally taken for granted, that this will really did exist, although its text has never been published, and although Charles II denied its existence. (See A. Legrelle, *La diplomatie française et la succession d'Espagne*, vol. II. Paris, 1891, p. 582, *et seqq*.)

and since the taking of Namur he has as fairly wheeled and run as ever any cock did in a pit: with this, the people are far enough from being in an estate of beginning a new war, for they still feel the weight of that which is past very sensibly lying upon them, which is so evident, that as yet they are not in a condition of redressing their money to its intrinsic value, and by consequence cannot open a commerce upon a good foot with their neighbours, so that I hope we may have peace in our time.

This succession of Spain is mostly our King's contrivance and effecting. Some faults he has, or else he would not be a man; as to his character of a Prince, he has carried his reputation to a prodigious height, and this affair must be allowed to be a proof of it beyond denial[1].

Seeing that by the Treaty of October 11, 1698, William had agreed to a Spanish partition, which the will of Charles was expressly intended to prevent, Prior's opinion, though perhaps sound on French affairs, on the diplomatic situation was certainly very wide of the mark.

Nor is there anything to show that Prior was any better informed as to European affairs when, by his death "of a fever and convulsions" on February 6, 1699[2], the Electoral Prince of Bavaria upset all the careful calculations of statesmen. This unfortunate and melancholy event gives us an opportunity of judging Prior's natural political sagacity. The English parliament had passed the famous bill reducing still further the number of troops in England to 7000 native-born troops, thereby compelling William to dismiss his Dutch guards and inflicting upon him bitter personal humiliation. Prior saw the folly of any weakening of English power in the critical situation of Europe, and he wrote vigorously about it:

I wish we were not so very warm in disbanding our army, for we shall hardly hold the balance of Europe (as we call it) whilst

[1] Bath Papers, III. 304–5, Prior to Dorset, Paris, Dec. 26, N.S. 1698.
[2] *Ibid.* 313, Prior to Portland, Paris, Feb. 11, N.S. 1699.

we have not the weight of one armed man to turn the scale on either side; but of this one should write a book and not a letter. We abroad see things ('tis true) in another light than they do at Westminster; and if we do but secure ourselves, I am satisfied; but if we shall or no is the question. Our friends at St Germains are so delighted with what the Parliament is doing in England that they publicly drink their healths: there is no doubt but that France will give them a helping hand whenever there is a bare possibility of succeeding, but

> Prudens futuri temporis exitum
> Caliginosa nocte premit Deus.

This is only to my dear Master and friend, who will burn my letter, which I will take for answering it[1].

These reflexions, which had also occurred to Villeroy, strike a curiously familiar note to the student of modern politics. It must be remembered, however, that in 1699 it was the Tory party which, under Harley's leadership, was thus successfully urging the reduction of armaments. Equally familiar too are the accents in which Prior denounces the party system and charges the opposite party with designs to overturn the constitution. These are to be heard in a letter to Portland which is of more than ordinary interest. In it Prior reviewed the situation in England, and pointed out the great strength of William III's position in a country so monarchical in feeling that it would easily pardon the King for scolding his Parliament and refusing to do as he was told. Not the least interesting part of the letter is his discussion of the Englishman's political views, and his analysis of the power of the Bishops and Clergy, while we may not be rash in surmising that his exaltation of the personal power of the King, and the hit at Gilbert Burnet at the end of the extract, are symptoms of the effect on

[1] Bath Papers, III. 314, Prior to C. Montagu, Paris, Feb. 11, N.S. 1698/9. See also letter to Portland of same date, ibid.

Prior's Whiggery of discussions with the Tory Earl of Jersey:

The address of the House of Commons to the King....I have, and shall make a good use of, by letting the Court of Versailles see that the peevishness of the House is very far from favouring our friends at St Germains, and that, whilst we have such laws against King James and his adherents, and such addresses from our Parliament to put them in force, we are likely enough to preserve our liberties under His Majesty's reign and government without other strength than the united obedience and loyalty of all his subjects. This I say is the turn that must be given to our affairs here; to have them bettered in England, if I were there, I would venture to say at large to Your Lordship what I just set down the *ébauche* of here.

The people of England are wild, at ease, and separate from the commerce and knowledge of the affairs of Europe; some that have a good deal of wit think too speculatively, for want of experience in relation to things abroad; many are personally malicious at the Court because they are not in it; the Ministers therefore should give His Majesty at once a plain direct and honest account how this general bent of the nation is at present, and not tell His Majesty things by halves, letting him see the worst side of them when it is too late; but if some of the Ministers be too deep in their parties' interest to do this, His Majesty's business suffers from their partiality, and as the Scripture says, no man can serve two masters, so no man, I am confident, can serve a King of England, who ought to be master of all parties and persons in the kingdom, who is too much a slave to any party wherein he is engaged.

With this, His Majesty will be pleased to say the kindest things imaginable to the Parliament when he grants a thing, and the most like a king when he refuses; thus did Henry the 7th and Henry the 8th and Elizabeth, who refused more things than any other of our princes, and yet governed us best; and every word and syllable that the King speaks bears a great weight through all Europe, particularly in this Court.

As to this project of an Act to restrain the number of officers in the customs, excise, &c., that shall sit in the House, it will limit the King's power more than any of his predecessors have been, and may have a worse effect in future Parliaments than can be seen at present. Men of good learning and experience should be a little encouraged to take notice and talk of this in their conversations in Westminster Hall, in coffee-houses, &c.; the Ministers and great men about the King should find out such persons for this service.

And it should be intimated that some of these men who are most violent in this matter are breaking into our constitution as much as those who in former reigns were for repealing the penal laws and tests, it being the same thing to the nation if we are hurt by bad subjects or by a bad King, and that we suffered as much by popular rage in '45 as by arbitrary power in '88.

The Archbishop and those Bishops who have power should hint this to the clergy, and this may be said of the Tory clergy preferably to the other, that if they are in the King's interest, they will most heartily espouse his cause. The others, though they have been active for the King, were so because they were against Popery, and thought King James most against them; but they were bred in latitudinarian principles, and are no great friends at bottom to monarchy, though in the hands of the most righteous Prince that ever reigned. This will be found true by all those brought up in Bishop Burnet's sentiments, for my Lord himself, you will find that he will give *tête baissée* into everything that may please the Princess, that he may have the Duke of Gloucester more entirely his own.

I will only observe further on this head that the King's speech as soon almost as he was on the throne, in which he said he would sustain the greatness of the monarchy, did him more service than any speech he has made since, and that the body and commonalty of the people of England love the glory of monarchy in general, and will keep up that of the King in particular who has done such great things for us, if they are rightly managed[1].

[1] Bath Papers, III. 319-20, Prior to Portland, Paris, March 11, N.S. 1699.

A week later and Portland received another instalment of Prior's thoughts on the state of parties:

Your Lordship will have the goodness to pardon my last letter, and take the freedom with which it was written to proceed from its right motive. I would not be ruined or hanged for my sentiments, so I dare only tell them to Your Lordship, and beg you to burn them. His Majesty, upon the many occupations he has, must (according to my wise politics) e'en take one other trouble upon him; he must be his own Minister, and direct his Council, or at least some of them, what he would have done, rather than rely upon their advice as to what he should do. The Whigs have given him good words, and seem to do their best in Parliament for his interest; but if they do their best, or no, or only (as I say) seem to do it is the question, since it is evident that most of those members who have not been in former Parliaments, and who do in this compose that body which they call the country party, are those who have obstructed the King's business, and yet most of them are and have been always Whigs; on t'other side the Tories in these last affairs have voted against their principle, because the chief of their party are peevish, and the multitude of them follow their example, whilst these leading men are against the Court, right or wrong, because they are not of it: the remedy that is to be found of this evil is that in one and the other party some should be gained by His Majesty's goodness and kindness, and others made sensible of his displeasure; this was practised by King Henry the 7th and Queen Elizabeth with success, who, as I observed to Your Lordship, were our best Princes and ruled us best[1].

It is a pity that we have not more of these effusions, for such products of Prior's ruminations would have given us a good idea of his political judgement. All that can be said of these is that, if they are not very original, nor even very lucidly expressed, they are sensible, especially upon the subject of the troops, on

---

[1] Bath Papers, III. 324, Prior to Portland, Paris, March, 18, N.S. 1699.

which he was hard put to it to parry Villeroy's observations[1].

But the spring brought these essays in politics to an end, for Portland quarrelled with William, refused to go to Newmarket, and announced his intention of retiring from the court. On May 20, Prior wrote to Portland expressing his grief at what he had heard, and with the advent of the summer, the abundant stream of Prior's letters to Portland suddenly contracts to the very narrowest trickle[2], and after July runs completely dry. It would be unjust to say that Prior "dropped"

---

[1] Events in England in 1698 and 1699, it may well be imagined, did little to check the torrent of Villeroy's questions, which became a subject for contemptuous jest between Prior and Jersey. Thus we read: "I was *convié*...to the Mareschal de Villeroy: his meat was good, and his questions very simple, so that I ate more than I talked." (Middleton Park Papers, no. 14, Prior to Jersey, Paris, June 17, N.S. 1699.) On the disbanding of the troops his observations were just: "My Governor and I had yesterday a long discourse of our English affairs; he cannot forbear insulting a little and showing his satisfaction at the breaking our troops. Whatever I thought in my heart, I answered him by an historical account of our Parliament's proceedings in the reigns of those Princes whom we loved and revered most, of the nature of our government and of the laws of our constitution, and insensibly led him to see that no step in the House of Commons was made in favour of the people of St Germains, and that neither they or theirs were so much as thought of in the deliberations or votes of Parliament." (Bath Papers, III. 329, Prior to Portland, Paris, April 1, N.S. 1699.) Villeroy's opinion of the instability of the English Government was that of Prince Kaunitz. When Portland retired he thought "England cannot subsist without him, and expects a revolution by the middle of next month." (Middleton Park Papers, no. 11, Prior to Jersey, Paris, June 10, N.S. 1699.) And in August he expressed himself to a similar effect: "I dined yesterday with the old Marechal, and was catechised after dinner alone: he is mighty whimsical, and full of *Speculatije* of what the Parliament will propose in the winter; how they will cramp the King, how uneasy people are in England, with wise reflections of our kingdom's being *le païs des révolutions*." (Middleton Park Papers, no. 34, Prior to Jersey, Paris, August 5, N.S. 1699.)

[2] There are only two letters to Portland after May 20th in the Bath Papers.

Portland now that he was out of favour with the King[1], though it must be remembered that Prior was not a strikingly chivalrous friend; and the following sentences add terribly to the strength of such a suspicion, even though the meaning of the last words is by no means clear:

My Lord Portland's Entre-deux is a Jest, and will give him all the uneasiness of a cast favourite without the quiet of a country gentleman; this method of retiring will lose him even the merit of doing it: he does me the honour to write me a long agreeable letter in which he desires me to be always on his side though he shall never do me any good for my being so. I confess I do not know anything so reasonable as this proposition, I think I may e'en put Swager amongst the friends I named to you last post[2].

However, it is just to remember that the decline of correspondence with Portland coincides also with Jersey's departure to England to receive the seals as Secretary of State, and it is not unnatural therefore that the closer friend should receive the main charge of Prior's thoughts. The letters to Jersey, nevertheless, models of epistolary style and lively though they be, do not compensate for the loss of the promise held out by the later letters to Portland.

After Jersey's departure Prior had to wait in Paris to carry on the business of what he called his "Interregnum Ministry[3]." This of course was the usual dreary work,

[1] He seems to have been anxious enough that Portland should not retire: cf. "I have letters from private people disinterested enough because no way concerned in the matter which say that our friend (Portland) is insupportable and far from obliging the nation...for God's sake advise him, as well for everybody's sake that loves him as for his own." (Middleton Park Papers, no. 4, Prior to Jersey, Paris, May 20, N.S. 1699.)

[2] Middleton Park Papers, no. 10, Prior to Jersey, June 6, N.S. 1699.

[3] Bath Papers, III. 346, Prior to Jersey, Paris, May 27, N.S. 1699. At this point Prior's correspondence becomes singularly complete, for

it is merely concerned with cases of prizes, the *galériens*, the murder at sea of a Captain Mansel and the arrest of two Irishmen on a charge of murder and piracy, the exchange of two political prisoners, Gerrard Bedford and Peter Perauld, the improvement of the postal arrangements, and an order that no English were to remain in the French sea-ports more than eight days. This last gave the French government an opportunity for a very characteristic piece of chicanery. Rumours of this order had reached the ears of the English government as early as November, 1698[1], under the form that it applied only to the English at Calais. On December 13 Prior denied the existence of such an order[2]. However, in the summer of 1699 the English government got wind that the order applied to all the ports. The existence of an order of this sort could not be denied, and Prior learnt that there was a "sly" reason for it; "as if it were done upon our asking it, and to take off all pretext off the French encouraging what should look like an invasion, a descent or correspondence held by the Jacobites from these places with their friends in England[3]." Finally he obtained an answer from Torcy upon the subject: "this order is general to all nations, and not meant against us in particular. I take the answer to be very imperfect, for who can be forbidden the ports of Picardy, Normandy and Bretagne but the English chiefly? and as to the other side, Marseilles to which the Italians chiefly come is excepted from this prohibition, as being a free port[4]."

in the Bath Papers we have Jersey's replies to Prior and one or two of Prior's letters to Jersey, while nearly all the gaps in the Bath Papers are filled by the letters preserved at Middleton Park. See Appendix C.

[1] Bath Papers, III. 296, Vernon to Prior, Whitehall, Nov. 17/27, 1698.

[2] *Ibid.* 301, Prior to Vernon, Paris, Dec. 13, N.S. 1698.

[3] *Ibid.* 369, Prior to Jersey, Paris, July 15, N.S. 1699.

[4] Middleton Park Papers, no. 34, Prior to Jersey, Paris, Aug. 5, N.S. 1699.

These matters, and the great affair of the impostors Lynch and Wall, were the main topics of negociation with the French government. Judging from the frequency with which Prior mentions them, Jersey's personal affairs, his mirrors, his portrait by Rygault, his seals, all of which had to be brought from Paris by Prior if possible, were the other matters of most importance. On the composition of the portrait Prior's critical faculties had some influence. Thus:

Rygault has first set a great Pendulum clock upon the table before you, and you pointed at it, by which all the world would have taken you for Tompion the watchmaker. I got this folly changed, and I think the man has now committed one worse; he has put a piece of blue velvet in your hand of above a yard, a kind of mantle, and it really gives the picture a little the air of *la rue St Honoré*, and as if you were showing your merchandise. I cannot make him alter it, and if he does I am afraid it will be for the worse[1].

However, we get glimpses of weightier matters. The Darien company was then beginning its disastrous attempts at colonization. On July 15, N.S. 1699, Prior reported to Jersey a skirmish between the Spaniards and the company, doubtless the affair of February 6. Prior shared the view prevalent at the time: "If they (the Scots) go on to act offensively, the French will certainly underhand, if not openly, help the Spaniards. I know not how far we avow the Scotch Enterprize, but if we intend they shall be defended, care should be taken of that business in time[2]." Jersey's reply is not without interest, as it shows clearly the position taken

[1] Middleton Park Papers, no. 13, Paris, June 13, N.S. 1699. See Appendix C. The picture is now at Middleton Park, having recently been purchased by the late Earl. See frontispiece.

[2] *Ibid*. no. 26, Prior to Jersey, Paris. Cf. also *ibid*. no. 31, Prior to Jersey, July 25, N.S. 1699. "I only know that the moment the Scotch are driven out, the 1237 (French) will get in: and laugh at us."

up by the English government, of which as a Lord Justice in the absence of the King he was an important member:

It is to be wished that the Spaniard could beat out the Scotch at Darien, for that colony gives a good deal of trouble here; the English are apprehensive that the Scotch settling in those parts (with the advantages granted them by act of Parliament) will be a prejudice to trade here. Many applications have been made to the King about it; His Majesty was not privy to the design, and is resolved not to protect it; orders are sent to all the governors in those parts not to have any correspondence with the Scotch. This is done both in regard to the trade of England, and to some Treaties made with Spain relating to America; so that in your discourse, though without affectation, you are always to make this interest of the Scotch company to have no relation to England, and what the King does not intend to protect; His Majesty has already signified the same to the Court of Spain[1].

At last, at the end of June, Prior began to have glimmerings of a prospect of returning home, for Abraham Stanyan, his successor as Secretary to the Embassy, appeared as forerunner to Manchester. Prior promptly asked for a letter of revocation, not as might be imagined that he might go home the sooner—that was impossible until the very dilatory Manchester came out—but "that I may have my present assured to me, and (as I have heard) augmented above what is usual to a Secretary[2]." No more convincing proof could be needed of Prior's popularity in France, and if we seek to know the cause, it may be found in the comments upon Stanyan which Prior was careful to retail to Jersey:

I have shown my successor twice at Versailles; they say he is *bien fait; bel homme, ma foy, mais Monsr. Prior a-t-il de l'Esprit?*

[1] Bath Papers, III. 370, Jersey to Prior, Whitehall, July 10/20, 1699.
[2] Middleton Park Papers, no. 19, Prior to Jersey, Paris, July 1, N.S. 1699.

always follows. The man is well enough truly, but he has a quiet lazy genius that will not *brille* enough at Versailles, nor be feared enough at the Coffee-house amongst the bullies of St Germains[1].

However, five weeks later, Manchester himself appeared, and Prior's knowledge of Paris was of no small service to the new Ambassador. "With the help of Mr Prior, all things are made easy," so wrote Manchester to Jersey[2]. But if Prior made a good impression on Manchester, the comments passed by Prior's household upon the Earl were scarcely complimentary:

Jane complains that his Excellence blows his nose in the napkins, spits in the middle of the room, and laughs so loud and like an ordinary body that she does not think him fit for an ambassador[3].

However, Lady Manchester, "in native charms divinely fair" as Addison wrote on the glasses of the Kitcat Club, was likely to retrieve the honours of our race:

Lady Manchester arrived last night, *garde le cœur!* for she is very handsome, she has a sty or little swelling upon her eye, but this does not hinder them from being as fine as any in France[4].

Prior's departure could not be long deferred now. All that remained was to arrange the date of his audience of Louis XIV. On August 18th he took his leave. "Nothing could be so kind as these people when I parted with them, the Grand Monarch said such things to me that if my own King says half as much I shall be satisfied[5]." At last on August 27th, having secured, not

---

[1] Middleton Park Papers, no. 28, Prior to Jersey, Paris, July 18, N.S. 1699.
[2] Drift, *Prior's History of his own time*, p. 72, Manchester to Jersey, Paris, Aug. 8, N.S. 1699.
[3] Middleton Park Papers, no. 35, Prior to Jersey, Paris, Aug. 8, N.S. 1699.
[4] *Ibid.* no. 36, Prior to Jersey, Paris, Aug. 12, N.S. 1699.
[5] *Ibid.* no. 38, Prior to Jersey, Paris, Aug. 19, N.S. 1699.

without difficulty, Jersey's seals, spoons, knife and fork, escritoire and portrait, but leaving the mirrors behind in charge of Madame de Croissi, who undertook to see that those supplied had no specks, Prior departed from Paris:

I have wound up my bottom, I have liquored my boots, and my foot is in the stirrup: that is to say I go from Paris to-morrow. I have ten thousand compliments, *baisemains* and *amitiés* to my Lord and Lady Jersey, I shall not trouble you with them, nor with my own sense of affairs between your Lordship and myself; you are sure of an eternal gratitude on my side for all your favours to me. 'Tis for my own interest I say I will make what haste I can to England; this is a kind of parting and one should be tender, but I shall only say I shall find nothing in that kingdom that I love half so well as my Lord Jersey, nor anything that I shall cultivate during my life so much as the honour of his friendship. Farewell, my Lord, God Almighty bless you and yours[1].

[1] Middleton Park Papers, no. 40, Prior to Jersey, Aug. 26, N.S. 1699.

Chapter VI

THE IRISH SECRETARYSHIP AND PARLIAMENT

PRIOR did not return home to England direct. The last months of his residence in Paris had been enlivened by a vigorous correspondence about his Irish secretaryship, and although the matter was well-nigh settled by the time he left the French capital, he thought it prudent to take advantage of the permission granted to him to return by way of Loo, where William III was then residing and working out the second Partition treaty. Prior travelled leisurely: he slept the first night at Péronne, and his stopping places afterwards were Valenciennes, Brussels, and Antwerp[1]. He only reached Rotterdam on September 2nd[2]; and in crossing over thither he ran some risk of losing his life. "It was with difficulty that I could get anybody to cross with me, at last one fellow did, and in a very little boat; it rained, and before we were in the middle of the river a sudden storm of lightning and thunder liked to have lost us, at last we got in among the ships on the side of Rotterdam the storm abated, and I got the Bomb opened[3]." There he stayed "a day that I may arrive at Loo only when they come home, for else I must be obliged to get out a cock-horse to the review which is made to-day or to-morrow, and it is not every secretary's talent (though it be the Honourable's) to ride without boots, and in a

---

[1] *Letters...at Welbeck*, App. v. p. 258.

[2] Middleton Park Papers, no. 41, Prior to Jersey, Rotterdam, Sept. 3, N.S. 1699. "I came hither last night."

[3] *Letters...at Welbeck*, App. v. p. 259.

long wig." He arrived at Loo on the 5th[1] and found his affairs in excellent train:

The Duke of Zell is here; dogs and horses is the language of the place, the King is in mighty good humour, and our friend[2] is all in all; *tant mieux*. The Elephant[3] is always the same, jocular and ignorant, disguising his want of knowing what is doing by affecting to keep it secret. Everybody else are just as you would fancy them: Ireton and Le tems (or L'Etang) deep in the Politics, as Jack Latin is in prayer, and Sir John in the Cellar.

The first thing with which I was saluted at Loo was your triumph over Baldaric-o-Ruvigny reformer of Ireland. I take that affair to be so well retrieved as that I shall gain the point, or have compensation, for I perceive my friends at Loo understand very perfectly my case and my circumstances, what signifies it for all this to be troubling you with *thank you, thank you*? Let Crop[4] write and my Lord Albemarle speak, and I know who will have the better of it[5].

The trouble here alluded to arose fairly early. Prior had continued in the office of second secretary in Ireland one Henry May, who was to perform the duties of first secretary during Prior's absence. For this he was to receive a share of the profits[6], but what the exact proportion was to be, does not seem to have been settled[7]. On April 16/26, 1698, Arthur Podmore informed Prior that May had the profits of his office in his hands, amounting to £666. 13s. 6d.[8] Then in July there arose

---

[1] Middleton Park Papers, no. 42, Prior to Jersey, Loo, Sept. 8, N.S. 1699. "At my arrival here on Saturday."

[2] Presumably Albemarle.

[3] Somers; the Secretary of State in attendance on William III who made the famous remark that he only knew what negotiations were going on from what he read in the Gazettes.

[4] Lord Galway.

[5] Middleton Park Papers, no. 42, Prior to Jersey, Loo, Sept. 8, N.S. 1699.

[6] Bath Papers, III. 122, Vernon to Prior, Whitehall, May 21/31, 1697.

[7] *Ibid.* 227, Tucker to Prior, June 26/July 6, 1698.

[8] *Ibid.* 211, A. Podmore to Prior, Dublin.

a dispute concerning the amount May was to have: Tucker, who was a friend of both parties, refused at first to arbitrate on so delicate a point. It seems clear that May argued that he had performed all the duties of first secretary, that he had been appointed by the Lords Justices[1], and therefore that he was entitled to the whole of the profits. Naturally Prior complained, and in September he put his own case vigorously to Tucker:

> I cannot enough admire that a man, that by all his letters to me has never mentioned anything in a year and a half of his being employed as first secretary by my consent and kindness, should thus act with me; and that too when by his own letters he has given me account from time to time of what has been received in the office; and not only so, but when he knows that my Lord Galway has in a manner excused to me by letter his having abridged some of the fees, and that the Secretary of State has by the King's own order excused more than once my absence upon account of my being absent on the King's business and by his own order; and that he has seen that the Lords Justices themselves have and will continue to divide the appointment with my Lord Jersey, who is in just the same case with me; and that Mr May knows it was in my power to have nominated anybody else to act in my stead[2].

He ended with a threat to use all his interest to bring Mr May to reason, but promised first to write him a friendly letter, which he did on September 17th[3], but rather stiffly. May, however, proved reasonable, said there had been a misunderstanding, and offered to take the share which Tucker should consider just[4]; but added that this would only apply to the past, as to the

---

[1] Bath Papers, III. 251, H. May to Prior, Dublin Castle, August 11/21, 1698, and cf. 267, Prior to H. May, Paris, Sept. 17, N.S. 1698.
[2] *Ibid.* 262, Prior to Tucker, Paris, Sept. 10, N.S. 1698.
[3] *Ibid.* 266, Prior to H. May, Paris.
[4] *Ibid.* 273, H. May to Prior, Dublin Castle, Sept 27/Oct. 7, 1698.

future he claimed an "indisputable right" to the whole of the profits[1].

This last claim was considered unreasonable even by Tucker, who suggested that May should surrender two-thirds of the profits to Prior[2]. Nine days later, May offered Prior the half of the profits[3], and as Prior had received information that Tucker was going to suggest he was to have two-thirds, he was very angry[4]. But in the meantime, May had received Tucker's proposal, and under vehement protests against being thus under-paid for hard work, gave up his two-thirds, so that Prior obtained £823. 19s. 4d. as the profits of his Secretaryship[5]. With that, Prior's wrath was pacified, and Tucker sensibly advised May to make the best terms he could for the future[6].

This, however, proved to be but the prelude to a more violent storm, in which Prior had need of all the interest he could command. He was fully aware how precarious was his tenure of the Secretaryship in Ireland if he did not go there[7], and on becoming Secretary of State, Jersey, together with Winchester, resigned his place on the Irish commission. They were succeeded by the Duke of Bolton and Lord Berkeley[8], so that

[1] Bath Papers, III. 280, H. May to Tucker, Dublin, Oct. 15/25, 1698.

[2] Ibid. 296, John Ellis to Prior, Whitehall, Nov. 17/27, 1698.

[3] Ibid. 299, May to Prior, Dublin Castle, Nov. 26/Dec. 6, 1698.

[4] Ibid. 303, Prior to Tucker, Paris, Dec. 24, N.S. 1698. "Mr May, I perceive, takes us to be both of a party, and being his own mediator, returns what he believes will be sufficient, which, though it had been so, is not a right way of proceeding; and, as we say in the Civil Law, the form of the act was not good, however the matter of it might be so."

[5] The total profits for 17 months came to £1385. 19s. 0d. (Bath Papers, III. 300, May to Tucker, Dublin Castle, Dec. 3/13, 1698.)

[6] Bath Papers, III. 310, Tucker to May, London, Jan. 7/17, 1698/9.

[7] Ibid. 342, Prior to Montagu, Paris, May 20, 1699.

[8] Formerly Lord Dursley. On his father's death he received from Prior a characteristic epistle of condolence: "I cannot play the Minister

Galway was the only member of the old commission left. But Bolton was likely to be absent for some time[1]; therefore, should Galway have reason to complain of Prior, it was only too probable that his influence would over-ride Berkeley's, in spite of the latter's friendship for the first secretary. "My Lord," wrote Prior to Jersey, "this is giving the whole power to Crop, and setting up at Dublin as absolute a monarch as him to whom I paid my adorations yesterday[2]." Jersey, at any rate, promised to try and retain Prior in his Irish post[3]: and Prior did what he could for himself by writing to Bolton and Berkeley with "a saucy humility" on the assumption that though the Commission was changed, the Secretary would remain[4]. However, Galway thought otherwise, and on June 13/23 informed Prior that his place was to be considered vacant, and that he intended to give it to May[5]. Prior at once raised clamours: he wrote a protest to Galway[6]; to Jersey he sent Galway's

enough to write you a letter of condolence, nor am I very sorry that my answer to a letter subscribed Dursley must be directed to the Earl of Berkeley. I would not however have such revolutions too frequent, and though I wish very well to the present Lord Dursley, I would have him keep that title yet this fifty years, except your Lordship should have a higher, and giving him the wearing of this of Berkeley in your own lifetime." (Bath Papers, III. 285, Nov. 8, N.S. 1698.) He wrote to Aglionby the same day (ibid. III. 286): "I am glad old Methusalem is sleeping with his fathers, and that our Dauphin Dursley reigns in his stead. I never found two letters so hard to write as one of condolence to him for the death of his father, and one to Mr Montague upon the death of his wife." Cf. Luttrell, IV. 407.

[1] Bath Papers, III. 354, Jersey to Prior, Whitehall, June 5/15, 1699.
[2] Middleton Park Papers, no. 14, Prior to Jersey, Paris, June 17, N.S. 1699.
[3] Bath Papers, III. 354, ut sup.
[4] Middleton Park Papers, no. 12, Prior to Jersey, no date: somewhere before June 19, 1699.
[5] Bath Papers, III. 358, Galway to Prior.
[6] Middleton Park Papers, no. 23, Prior to Galway, Paris, July 11, N.S. 1699.

letter, not without a touch of the sour grapes: "If we can defer the evil day till I see you, possibly we might find some way of appeasing Crop's wrath: if not, hang Ireland, 'tis a boggy country, and ruled by a fanatical prince[1]." To Portland, for the last time that we know of, he poured out his soul by letter. In this he appealed to the King, by whose orders he had been sent to Paris and retained there, and by whose appointment he had received the Irish Secretaryship: he flattered Portland when he said that

my Lord Gallway has neither by word or warning said once that this storm was coming, but it is easy to know that he did not think good to endeavour to undo what my Lord Portland thought good to do, whilst my Lord Portland was in the Court; but immediately upon my Lord Portland's retiring, down with Mr Prior; so when the pillar is removed, the ivy that depended upon it falls[2].

Prior even "ventured to write to Loo, that my complaints may prevent Crop's representations[3]." Galway however was inexorable:

nous n'avons jamais conté que Mr May fut votre député. Mr May étoit notre second secrétaire pendant que vous étiez le premier; et exerçoit, pendant votre absence, pour les deux charges...jusques à ce que je reçus une lettre de Mylord Albemarle, du 29 Avril passé, dont voicy les propres mots—

"La charge de Secrétaire des Lords Justices va être vacante par l'employ que l'on destine à Mr Prior dans l'office de Mylord Jersey"...

Je ne croy pas que vous ayez jamais cru pouvoir garder l'un et l'autre. Cela ne me paraît pas praticable, et ne convient point du tout au service du Roy, et par conséquent ne nous peut pas convenir. Je vous prie de n'y pas penser[4].

These last words infuriated Prior, in spite of the

---

1 Middleton Park Papers, no. 22, Prior to Jersey, Paris, July 11, 1699.
2 Bath Papers, III. 367, Prior to Portland, Paris, July 13, N.S. 1699.
3 *Ibid.* 369, Prior to Jersey, Paris, July 15, N.S. 1699.
4 *Ibid.* 371, Galway to Prior, Dublin, July 11/21, 1699.

consolation arising from the thought that Jersey was doing well for him:

> I cannot enough thank you, my Lord, for your favour to me in my Irish affair. It is a triumph to be able to repress the insolence of the French Vice-monarch's last letter—*n'y pensez pas, Monsieur*. He should have added *Voulons et ordonnons &c.*, but your letter will have kept him quiet, and if you have a little time we may possibly teach Mr May that honesty and openness is the best way to make people first secretaries[1].

On August 24, O.S., when Prior was at Rotterdam, Galway wrote to Blathwayt asking for instructions once more, which was the first sign he showed of bending. Meanwhile, Prior nearly ruined himself by notifying to Galway his departure from Paris and his future intentions in the following impertinent letter:

à Loo ce 8me Sept. N.S. 1699.

My Lord

Je me suis defait enfin des honneurs imaginaires à la cour de France et je suis icy fort heureux d'en avoir recu des réeles, m'etant trouvé bien accueillé du Roy nôtre Maître: Il vous a fait scavoir, my Lord, sa volonté à l'egard de mes petits interets en Irelande, de sorte que je conte cette affaire entierement vuidée: et j'espere d'être en êtat de vous rendre les services que vous pourrez esperer du premier Secretaire, êtant à Londres, jusques à ce qu'il plaira a Sa Majesté de m'ordonner de venir à Dublin. Il est arrivé ordinairement, my Lord, que le premier Secretaire de la commission d'Irelande a été pour la plupart à Londres, sollicitant ou agissant les affaires de la Commission, de sorte que Monsr: May ou quelque autre qui prendra la peine de consulter les annales du royaume dont vôtre Excellence est un de trois gouverneurs. Elle trouvera rien de nouveau dans l'affaire dont il s'agit, car je seray toujours à portee de vous rendre mes meilleurs services jusques à ce qu'il plaira à Sa Majesté d'en

---

[1] Middleton Park Papers, no. 36, Prior to Jersey, Paris, Aug. 12, N.S. 1699.

ordonner autrement; en attendant je serois trop injuste si je pretendois de tant ôter du merite de Monsr: May que de proposer à Vos Excellences un autre deputé que lui pour suppleer à ma place; car comme vous connoissez d'un coté son habilité dans le Secretariat, aussi suis-je beaucoup assuré de son desinteressement pour ce que me regarde en cas donc qu'un Secretaire sera suffisant sur le lieu il n'y aura pas (à ce que je crois et espere) le moindre changement dans le Secretariat, mais si les affaires sont telles que de demander deux Secretaires Votre Excellence sera abundamment satisfaite dans ce qui regarde le choix de celuy qui agira pour moy en qualité du Premier Secretaire; car ce choix viendra ou de la part de Vos Excellences avec mon consentement ou sera tel que my lord Jersey, my lord Albemarle, Mr Vernon et Monsr: Blathwayt (ou ceux de ceuxcy que Votre Excellence choisira) scauront proposer. Vous voyez, Mylord, comment j'ose vous parler sans fard, et vous declarer le fond de mes pensées: Je ne doute point de votre bienveillance et m'assure que vous avez trop de justice de n'y pas donner les mains. Je n'ose plus avancer sur ce sujet, sinon de vous dire seulement qu'on a donné à Votre Excellence une mauvaise idee de l'employ que je vay occuper pour quelque tems en Angleterre, car il y a de la difference de trois cent pieces par Annum à douze ou treze, qu'il ne soit si bon que celui d'Irelande, que ce sera pour quelque tem seulement, que je le dois occuper, et que je ne desespere point apres mes corvées de venir me fixer en Irelande ou Sa Majesté a eu la bonté de me donner une place pour y mettre le pied, laquelle la bonté de Vos Excellences me reserveront. Je suis avec beaucoup de respect

   My Lord
    De Votre Excellence
     le tres humble et tres
      obeissant serviteur
      M. Prior[1].

It was now Galway's turn to be angry, and he wrote at once to the King:

[1] Middleton Park Papers, no. 43.

au chateau de dublin le 12 sep. 1699.

Sire

Je n'aurois pas osé importuner encore une fois V. M. sur
les pretensions de Mr Prior, sy je n'auois receu une lettre de luy,
dont le stile m'a fort surpris, je prens la liberté de l'envoyer à
V. M., et de la supplier très humblement de prendre la peine de
la lire, je ne peus pas douter que V. M. ne juge que ce seroit
un affront particulier pour moy, sy elle nous ordonoit de re-
mettre Mr Prior dans la place de nostre secretaire, c'est pourquoy
j'espere qu'elle ne trouuera pas mauvais que Mr may continue
dans le poste de premier secretaire, que le Duc de Bolton et moy
luy auons doné, à moins que V. M. ne nous envoye un ordre
positif de l'en oster, Je suis et seray toute ma uie avec un tres
profond respect et fidelité

Sire

de V. M.

le tres humble tres obeïssant

et tres fidele serviteur et suject

Gallway[1].

Prior was not yet safe in his post, for when the matter
was put before the King on September 19/29 by
Albemarle and Blathwayt, it appeared that the King
"was mightily possessed by the Duke of Bolton and
Lord Galway of their right, and 'twas much we could
bring the matter to bear so far as you find in the enclosed copy of an order I now send to your Lords
Justices. I have shaved close, if not strained a point, in
the framing of it[2]." The order, which, after what
Galway had said, was a personal affront to him, ran as
follows:

His Majesty, being informed of what has been done by Your
Excellencies in reference to Mr Prior, does think fit that everything that may concern him in that office be put into the same
condition in every respect as before Your Excellencies' intentions

---

[1] Middleton Park Papers, no. 46.

[2] Bath Papers, iii. 377, Blathwayt to Prior, Loo, Sept. 19/29, 1699.

to make any change in the said office, and do remain so until
His Majesty shall otherwise determine[1].

After this, the matter was at an end, and there was
nothing more for the Lords Justices to do but to put
their pride in their pockets and obey. Galway smarted
under the rebuff, and he sent in his resignation[2], which,
however, was not accepted; on the other hand, Prior
took up his duties under Jersey, and so, as Albemarle
had said, the first secretaryship became vacant, and May
no doubt succeeded to it.

During his visit to Loo, Prior had had on August
31/September 10 "a very long and a very gracious
audience of His Majesty," "particularities" of which
Prior set down in his journal, and from which it is
satisfactory to note that he and Portland were on
friendly terms, and that Macaulay's reproaches against
Prior are not entirely deserved:

The King sent to me and gave me a Private Audience in his
Bed Chamber. I was with him about an hour and half, He ques-
tioned me very particularly about the State of Affairs in France,
and went leisurely over most things that had passed there, during
the Embassy's of my Lord Portland, my Lord Jersey, and (now)
the beginning of my Lord Manchesters; He did me the Honour
to tell me that he was satisfied with my Services, that I was
obliged to my Lords Portland, Jersey and Albemarle, And upon
this occasion he said I had done well not to enter blindly into
all the sentiments of my Lord Portland as some other People
had done I only said that I was his Majesties secretary That I
had reason to respect my Lord Portland as representing His
Majesty, and that his private sentiments not at all relating to the
Embassy, I had nothing to do with them, In the conclusion His
Majesty said he would take care of me And bid me go to the

---

[1] Bath Papers, III. 378, Blathwayt to the Lords Justices of Ireland,
Loo, Sept. 19/29, 1699.

[2] *Hist. MSS. Comm.*, Buccleuch Papers at Montagu House, vol. II.
pt. 2, p. 628, Galway to Shrewsbury, Dublin, November 11, 1699.

Hague and stay there 'till my Lord Jersey came from England, he bid me see my Lord Portland, and the Pensioner who would tell me what I was to do[1].

Nevertheless, in spite of Royal approbation of his conduct, "Je m'ennuye comme un chien" is the burden of Prior's letters[2], until, in spite of illness[3], Jersey came over, and joined Prior about the middle of September, and together they went to Loo. On October 12 they were sent back to The Hague[4], and Prior remained in Holland until, towards the end of the month, the English court returned to England[5].

Yet the time spent in Holland was important for Prior, for it was then that he was admitted into the great secret of the Second Partition Treaty.

"In this voyage" he writes in his diary, "my Lord Jersey had communicated to me more plainly what before I knew but imperfectly, that we were making a treaty with France and the States general for the Succession of Spain, and on Friday my Lord told me that the treaty not having been signed whilst His Majesty was in Holland, Count Tallard (who at His Majesty's quitting Holland had likewise left that Country having desired the K: his Master to give him leave to return for some time into France upon his own private occasions) might possibly give some ill impressions to the K: of France, as if the treaty would be broke off by the K: of England or that His Majesty would not use his utmost interest that it should be perfected: that for this reason I must go immediately for France and that I was to take my Instructions on this subject from the King: accordingly I had

[1] *Letters...at Welbeck*, App. v. p. 259.

[2] Middleton Park Papers, nos. 47 and 48, Prior to Jersey, The Hague, 5/15 and 12/22 Sept. 1699.

[3] Bath Papers, III. 379, Jersey to Prior, Squerries, Oct. 2/12, 1699.

[4] *Letters etc....at Welbeck*, App. v. p. 259, 260; P. Grimblot, *Letters of William III and Louis XIV*, London, 1848, vol. II. p. 359.

[5] A. Legrelle, *La succession d'Espagne*, III. 193, Tallard to Louis XIV, Oct. 24, 1699. "A peine fut-il sorti que le sieur Prior, qui a été en France, entra, et me demanda où mon lord Jersey me pourrait voir."

an audience that day at 12 before dinner of the K: in his Clossett, nobody being by but His Majesty and my Lord Jersey, the King instructed me very particularly in what I was to do, commanded me to go to my Lord Portland to read the treaty (as it was then concerted) and to make what haste I could to Paris: I did wait on my Lord Portland accordingly that afternoon, and having received my Instructions a second time from my Lord Jersey I went post the next day for Dover[1].

So, in order to smooth Louis' ruffled temper, Prior left on November 1, and under the unimaginative name of Thomas Brown arrived in the French capital on November 3[2].

I came hither with all secrecy imaginable; but my being here was soon known after my arrival; I pretend not to be well, and take that pretence for not stirring out, so I have seen nobody, nor will I till I have done the business for which I was sent. The Jacobites are much alarmed at my coming hither: every man has his conjecture and all wrong[3].

He found Louis XIV suspicious as ever of William, and indeed the French King was at little pains to conceal from Tallard his belief in William's bad faith[4]. On the 15th, Manchester and Prior had their private audience[5], and although Louis expressed his surprise

[1] *Letters...at Welbeck*, App. v. p. 255.

[2] Middleton Park Papers, no. 50, Prior to Jersey, Paris, Nov. 4, N.S. 1699.

[3] *Ibid.* no. 51, Prior to Jersey, Paris, Nov. 6, N.S. 1699. King James' opinion was that Manchester was to be recalled, "which for a time gave him great Satisfaction. It is not agreeable to them to see me live in such a manner, that none of the *English* come to *Paris* but they address themselves to me," Manchester to Montagu, Paris, Dec. 8, N.S. 1699. C. Cole, *Memoirs.*

[4] A. Legrelle, *La succession d'Espagne*, III. 189, Louis XIV to Tallard, Oct. 25, 1699, and p. 201, despatch of Nov. 3, 1699.

[5] It could not be earlier, for Louis was at Marly and refused to break the rule never to receive foreign ministers at that retreat. (Christian Cole, *Historical and Political Memoirs*, London, 1735, p. 69, Manchester to Jersey, Paris, Nov. 6, N.S. 1699.)

that the treaty had not been signed before William left Holland, he received them graciously and professed himself satisfied with the King of England's protestations of good faith[1]: "so the Treaty," as Prior said, "was on foot again[2]"; yet, as the delay continued, the King's anxieties soon revived[3] and were not really appeased until the Dutch signed the treaty on Feb. 21, 1699/Mar. 8, 1700.

The day but one after the audience with Louis in November, Prior left for England again. On the 21st he was received by William:

> I first read to His Majesty what your Lordship said to the King of France, and what the King answer'd thereupon; and then I explained to His Majesty the substance of the whole that had passed during my being in France. His Majesty is satisfied with every step your Excellency made; and, in one word, we did as we ought to do....I contracted a Cold in the Voyage, and wisely increased it, by running about these two last days. I am blooded, and kept my Chamber to-day, which is the reason of my using another Hand, I hope your Excellence will excuse it[4].

On his return to England, Prior disappears into the fogs of our islands. It is only now and again that we can catch a glimpse of his increasingly Bohemian figure. There are no more letters to Jersey or to the under-secretaries which for nine years have kept us informed of his varying moods and activities. Indeed, there is good ground for assuming that in these years, tendencies to a moral break-down asserted themselves

---

[1] C. Cole, *Memoirs*, pp. 73–4.

[2] *Letters...at Welbeck*, App. v. p. 261.

[3] See his despatch to Tallard, Dec. 10, 1699. "Ainsi, je veux savoir les véritables sentiments du roi d'Angleterre, comptant toujours que ceux des Etats-Généraux y seront conformes, lorsqu'il le voudra." (Legrelle, *La succession d'Espagne*, III. 213–4.)

[4] C. Cole, *Memoirs*, p. 76, Prior to Manchester, London, Nov. 3/13 [*sic*], 1699.

more markedly than before, and that influences were at work which were to bring Prior to the melancholy circumstances of his later years. He settled in a house in Duke Street[1], Westminster, and was there in comfortable quarters, having a garden adjoining St James' Park[2]. And it is perhaps not rash to conjecture that during these years of office-work in England, he formed the best-known connexion of his life, his intimacy with "Chloe." Who "Chloe" was, or whether she is always the same person, it is futile to enquire; and perhaps we should do well not to do so, for Prior's tastes were miscellaneous and by no means refined[3]. Even before his return to England, his name had been used in scandalous connexions. The *Postboy* printed a rumour that he had married Lady Falkland, "an old Troy that will not be taken in ten years[4]"; this, however annoying to the lady, was at any rate not discreditable to Prior; but the same cannot be said of his reputed connexion with a Miss Crofts. In a very lewd letter to Montagu he practically confesses to a *liaison* with one of his domestic servants in Paris during the summer of 1698[5]. After his return to England, his character in this respect

---

[1] Later Delahay Street, recently demolished.

[2] "A lease unto *Matthew Prior* Esquire, of a small Piece of Ground between the Wall of *St James' Park* and the House he now lives in, for 45 years, from the Date, at 6s. 8d. *per Annum* Rent: this, in Consideration of £300, paid to *Antony Row* Esquire, the present Fowlkeeper in *St James' Park*, for his Interest in the Premises." (*Journals of the House of Commons*, June, 1701, p. 700, col. 1.) Prior and his friends knew it as "Matthew's Palace in Duke Street."

[3] She is reported variously as a butcher's wife at Cambridge (John Nichols' *Anecdotes*, London, 1814, VIII. 661), or a cook maid (*Pope's Works*, ed. Elwin and Courthope, VI (Letters, 1), 64).

[4] Bath Papers, III. 342, Prior to C. Montagu, Paris, May 20, N.S. 1699. See also N. Luttrell, *Relation*, IV. 511, May 2, 1699; Bath Papers, III. 321, R. Powys to Prior, Whitehall, March 2/12, 1698/9.

[5] Bodleian Library (S.C. 25,427), MS. Montagu, d. 1, fo. 100b, Paris, Aug. 9 N.S. 1698.

may have deteriorated, and after his death Pope passed the following severe judgement upon him: "Prior was not a right good man. He used to bury himself, for whole days and nights together, with a poor mean creature, and often drank hard[1]." In fact it was considered at the time of his death, that he had been lucky to escape from a dreadful fate in having to marry Mrs Elizabeth Cox, the woman with whom he was living[2].

Disreputable manners, however, are but rarely a bar to office, and for some six months Prior performed some of the duties of Under-Secretary of State to Jersey. His share in the work was not great; the cold which he contracted on his way home from France left its effects upon him for some time, and it was not till the middle of January that he could do much relating to public business. During his convalescence he was "employed in looking over and adjusting some Articles of the Treaty, and drawing up Pleinpouvoirs for the Earls of Portland and Jersey to sign it and in going to my Lord Chancellor Somers in order to have the Broad Seal set to the Ratification of it[3]": and at the end of this

---

[1] Joseph Spence, *Anecdotes, observations and characters of books and men*, London, J. R. Smith, 1858, p. 2. His cough, of which he frequently complained in later years, was doubtless the result of his drunkenness.

[2] Arbuthnott wrote to Watkins that Prior had had "a narrow escape by dying." See *The poetical works of Matthew Prior*, with a life by the Reverend John Mitford, Boston, 1854, i. xix.

[3] *Letters...at Welbeck*, App. v. p. 261. It is perhaps worth noting that Prior, no doubt for the purposes of the future and to avoid the trouble that arose on the question at Ryswick, noted carefully the styles and titles of the Kings of Great Britain and of France in the treaty. "We gave the French our ratification, vizt: Three Instruments under the Great Seal of England in which We are named first and the King's title at Length, vizt: *King of England Scotland France and Ireland Defender of the faith &c.* and the King of France is only named His Most Christian Majesty and We took their Ratification under the Great Seal of France in which the King is only named King of Great Britain and the King of France is named King of France and Navarre."

business, his future had been provided for. The under-secretaryship was at best but a temporary post, for "the King was pleased to promise my Lord Jersey that he would take care of me, and ordered me to continue in my Lord's Office and give me an additional allowance upon the foot of 600 pound a year 'till he should please to dispose of me otherwise, which he did about Mid-summer after[1]."

The permanent post which was now promised him was a commissionership of Trade and Plantations. The vacancy occurred immediately after Jersey's trans-ference to be Lord Chamberlain in June. Towards the latter end of the month, John Locke, the philosopher, resigned his post on the commission, and on his coming out from his audience with the King, Prior "was con-gratulated by everybody as his successor[2]." Prior ex-presses some gratitude to Locke, as though he thought him in part responsible for the new appointment[3]. The mysterious words which follow may be explicable by those acquainted with Court formalities; in any case, it is clear that they point to Prior being the subject of much jealous feeling and backbiting.

On Sunday the 28th of June my Lord Jersey told me from the King that I might address myself to Mr Secretary Vernon for a warrant to have a new commission drawn up and my own name inserted in it, and about an hour after as the King came out of his Closet through the apartments at Hampton Court to Chapel my Lord Jersey presented me to kiss his hand for the employment. My Lord Jersey being Lord Chamberlain the Rooms from the Drawing room are under his Direction. This was the reason that I staid till the King came into these rooms because if I had kissed his hand in the Bed Chamber I must have

---

[1] *Letters...at Welbeck*, App. v. pp. 261–2.

[2] *Ibid.* p. 262.

[3] "I know not upon what motive Mr Lock did this, nor how kind his Majesty was to me in the thing." *Ibid.*

been presented by one of the Lords of the Bedchamber, this I mention because of a good deal of talk that arose upon it which is not fit to be committed to writing[1].

Gossip was not to leave Prior after this. A few days later William III set out for Holland, and Jersey and Prior accompanied him to Margate, and in August Jersey followed his master abroad, and talk arose of Prior being ordered out also. "The Comments and discourses on my journey were so various, as that I was to go from my Lord Rochester to my Lord Jersey, that I was to carry over people's opinions here in order to the dissolution of the parliament, and such kind of stories, that I thought it better wholly to break off the journey[2]." Other "comments" than these were perhaps more powerful in stopping Prior from going over. The King, Jersey wrote, gave leave, "but it must be so that the business of the Board must not be neglected[3]," and in a subsequent letter Jersey told Prior plainly that if he came over, people would say he "neglected the business[4]," and finally: "I am wholly of opinion that you are to stay where you are, and I hope this will come time enough to prevent your coming hither, should you have any thoughts of it[5]." Prior therefore remained in England. He spent the second half of August, not apparently in looking after the business of the Board, but seeing to the plans for building and improvements at Squeries, the manor recently purchased by Jersey near Westerham in Kent. But even if he did neglect his duties, in the autumn he was to receive a signal mark of the confidence of the government in his diplomatic ability. On the arrival of the news of the King of Spain's death, it was to Prior that William

[1] *Letters...at Welbeck*, App. v. p. 262.   [2] *Ibid.*
[3] Bath Papers, III. 415, Jersey to Prior, Breda, Sept. 9, N.S. 1700.
[4] *Ibid.* 416, Jersey to Prior, Loo, Sept. 17, N.S. 1700.
[5] *Ibid.* 419, Jersey to Prior, Dieren, Sept. 30, N.S.

turned for an agent. He was ordered to Brussels on a secret errand[1], and was received by William III in audience on November 4th:

I being called in, The King spoke to this Effect. That I needed but very little Instructions from him, having already been acquainted with every step he had made in the Treaty, That the Case of the King of Spain's Death being now arrived in order to the Treaty being preserved, he thought it necessary that I should go to the Elector of Bavaria, that I should let him know the concern His Majesty was in upon the Elector's account for his Catholic Majesty's death; that I should promise him in general terms that His Majesty would do for him whatever in reason he could ask; and when the Elector should come to particulars that I should say that His Majesty would use his utmost interest conjointly with the States that things should remain *in statu quo* till the Emperor's determination upon the treaty should be known; that therefore it was his Majesty's opinion (as to the Elector his friend) that he should continue to act in the government.

That in case the Elector spoke to me concerning the great debt which is due to him from the Crown of Spain (which as his Majesty said was a terrible circumstance to the poor Elector and of which he would infallibly speak to me) I should promise the Elector that the King would stand by him in seeing it paid, and to this end the King ordered me to go by the way of Holland to tell the Pensionaire the whole affair upon which I was sent and to take my measures from him that I might say the same things as from the States, which I said from the King: but I was to take care that I promised no more on the King's part than the Pensionaire thought fit I should do from the States.

I was likewise to show the Elector the Secret article and to assure him from the King and the States (supposing the Pensionaire to consent to the latter, of which the King did not doubt)

---

[1] It may be noted that the rumour spread that Prior was to go abroad, for Luttrell notes it in his diary, but says that Prior is to go to Paris. (Narcissus Luttrell, *Brief historical relation*, Oxford, 1857, IV. 705, Nov. 7, 1700.)

that in case the Emperor did not come into the Treaty in the two months therein proposed, His Electoral Highness should be the Prince whom the King and the States would nominate as King of Spain according to the power which they have by the article. For the rest, I was to hear what the Elector said in general of the present state of things, to write from Brussels, and receive his Majesty's further orders there[1].

The next day, however, November 5, O.S., the news reached London that Louis XIV had accepted the Crown of Spain for the Duke of Anjou, and all the plans laid the day before were upset. After the King had dined at Lord Jersey's, Prior was told he was not to go to Brussels, and although three days later, the King had thoughts of sending Hill as his envoy, this mission also fell through. Prior therefore was enabled to turn his attention to the chief business that occupied him during the months of November and December, namely, his candidature for the representation of the University of Cambridge in Parliament[2]. The idea that Prior should enter the House of Commons had been broached during the last weeks of Prior's stay in France, and he had eagerly entertained it. "When, instead of proroguing your Parliament, you dissolve it, I have mighty overtures made me from the University of Cambridge to stand for their representatif; a Prior! a Prior![3]" One of the sitting burgesses, whom it was desired to unseat, was Anthony Hammond, gentleman-commoner of St John's, poet and writer on economics, who died in the Fleet. The moderation of Prior's Whiggery may be gauged from the fact of his standing

---

[1] *Letters...at Welbeck*, pp. 263, 264.

[2] It was probably during this time that he composed the *Carmen Saeculare for the Year* 1700. (See *Poems on Several Occasions*, ed. Waller, p. 104.)

[3] Middleton Park Papers, no. 30, Prior to Jersey, Paris, July 22, N.S. 1699.'

against a Whig, and it is not at all improbable that we may here detect once more the influence of Lord Jersey. Prior's qualifications for the post were not strong, and he felt that he was handicapped by his constant absence from Cambridge. His offices in France and England, however, gave him a position which was not unfit for a burgess of the University, and he had shown his interest in scholarly studies by endeavouring to procure for the University Press a set of Greek types from the Royal Press in Paris[1]. He had some support from his college, and also from outside; but had no resident agent there, for his chief supporter, Dr Nourse, was as non-resident as Prior himself[2]. But the most serious obstacle in Prior's path was the refusal of his own Master to support him. "From my engagements to Mr Hammond," wrote Dr Gower, "I cannot recede[3]." This, it seems, must have been fatal, for Prior threw up the sponge almost immediately on receipt of this letter[4]. Though defeated upon this occasion, Mr Hammond's opponents succeeded in their designs in the next year without Prior's help. They then obtained the return of a man who was far more distinguished in his province than Prior was in his, for Sir Isaac Newton represented the University in the Parliament of 1701-2.

As for Prior, he was easily consoled for this rebuff

[1] Bath Papers, III. 409, the Duke of Somerset to Prior, Petworth, May 19/30 and May 24/June 4, 1700. It has been pointed out to me, as I perhaps ought to have found for myself, that Prior's negociation for the Greek types broke down owing in part to the somewhat self-advertising conditions laid by the French upon the gift. See *Notices et extraits des manuscrits de la bibliothèque du Roi*, 1787, vol. I. p. xciii. *et seqq.*

[2] *Ibid.* 427, J. Talbot to Prior, Cambridge, Oct. 26/Nov. 6, 1700.

[3] *Ibid.* 430, Humphrey Gower to Prior, Cambridge, Dec. 11/22, 1700.

[4] *Hist. MSS. Comm.* Report XII. App. II. Coke MSS. II. 413, J. Brydges to Thomas Coke in Derbyshire, Dec. 19, 1700. "Mr Hammond hath fixed his interest at Cambridge, and some say Mr Prior desists."

by being transferred from one constituency to another, and on January 7/18, 1700/1 he was returned with John Conyers as junior member for East Grinstead, a pocket borough belonging to Lord Dorset.

Of Prior's career in Parliament we know but little, but one incident is of very great importance in his life. For it was in this Parliament that met in February, 1701, that the question of the Second Partition Treaty was discussed, and the Commons impeached the ministers who had been responsible for it, namely, Portland, Somers, Orford, and, what was from Prior's personal point of view a more serious question, Halifax. Portland was impeached on April 1, 1701, on April 12th, Prior and 55 other members formed a committee to translate the Correspondence between Portland and Vernon relating to the treaty, and on April 14 the other three Lords were also declared guilty of a high crime and misdemeanour. Prior voted in favour of the impeachments, and his votes on these occasions have brought upon him the charge of tergiversation and of black ingratitude to his old friends Montagu and Portland[1]. But the villainy of his action is not so deep as at first sight it would seem. That he disapproved of the second partition treaty is scarcely to the point, for it would have been possible to disapprove of the treaty and at the same time to vote against an impeachment on the ground that it was inexpedient. Prior's explanation was that it was necessary to impeach the ministers in order to prevent an attack being made on the King himself, and that he voted for the impeachments in order to

[1] Cf. J. Macky, *Characters of the Court of Great Britain*, p. 135. "He was chosen a Member of that Parliament which Impeached the *Partition*, to this Treaty he was Secretary, and yet joined in the *Vote* with Those who carried the Impeachment against Those who had established him in the World." The grossness of this misrepresentation may be judged from what is said above.

shield the King. Certain it is that Jersey supported the impeachment and this doubtless had much to do with Prior's attitude. But the importance of the vote lies in this, that it is the critical point in Prior's conversion from Whiggery to Toryism; and he is now from the day of this vote onwards definitely reckoned as a Tory. His relations with the Montagu family were sure to have been strained by this incident; but it is pleasant to observe that in 1706 and later, Prior was still on speaking terms with Halifax, and could think it consistent with his own self-respect, to appeal to him for assistance.

Prior's parliamentary career was short. When, on the death of the exiled king, Louis XIV addressed the son of James II by the style and title of King of Great Britain, William III found in the indignation of his people the opportunity he longed for of ridding himself of this Tory Parliament. Prior was not re-elected for East Grinstead, possibly because Dorset and he had not agreed about the impeachments, and so Prior's parliamentary career came to a not discreditable close, for though his parliamentary ambitions were not entirely sated, and he was not destined to enter the House of Commons again, he had no distractions to keep him from his work at the Commission of Trade and Plantations[1].

---

[1] His work there did not prevent him from "making interest" for the keepership of the records in place of Sir Joseph Williamson. (Narcissus Luttrell, *Brief Historical relation*, Oxford, 1857, v. 98, Oct. 9, 1701.)

Chapter VII

THE COMMISSION OF TRADE AND PLANTATIONS AND THE FEUD WITH THE DUCHESS OF MARLBOROUGH

THE death of William in March, 1702, deprived Prior of a friend to whom he owed much, and it was necessary to take stock of the situation created by the accession of a Stuart princess. And so we find that at this time he entered into closer relations with Harley and St John, and was a recognised member of that intemperate body of "Brothers" who divided their time between politics and hard drinking. But as the ministries of the early years of Queen Anne were mixed, Prior retained his place on the commission; indeed, he had saluted the rising sun, and was on friendly terms with the Duke of Marlborough. In some ways these first years of Queen Anne's reign were the happiest years of his life. His income was assured[1]; residing as he did in London, he had everything that a man of his intellectual and sensual tastes could desire; he belonged to the most brilliant literary *coterie* of the day; and in 1704 he was so intimate with Swift as to be able to show to Atterbury either the proofs or an advanced copy of one of Swift's books[2].

---

[1] It is true that in conjunction with his fellow-commissioners, he complained to the government in 1706 that his salary was six quarters in arrear, but he could enjoy its credit. (See the article in the *Contemporary Review* by Mr G. A. Aitken, May, 1890, p. 719.)

[2] Probably the *Tale of a Tub*. See *Hist. MSS. Comm.* xvth Rep. App. IV. p. 155, Atterbury to Harley, Bridewell, 1704.

It is always easier for people to know when others are happy than to know it of one's self, and Prior was no exception to the rule. He evidently suffered from fits of severe depression, in which his condition was almost morbid in its introspection, and of which his diary bears testimony. Only six months after the King's death we find this entry:

August 20 1702.

I have met with such ingratitude and found so ill returns in the world that makes me have so vile an opinion of Mankind in general that in some humours I persuade myself that my friendship with my Lord Jersey will one day break and I prepare myself as it were for it; though I have no reason for any such thought from any action of my Lord to me: and though in justice I ought to be blamed for the wildness of this imagination.

I have cried twenty times upon forming the imagination of my Lord Jersey dead, while he was yet in good health[1].

The next summer, he notes that on Midsummer-day happened the greatest private affliction to me that ever I was sensible of, though I did not know it till 4 days after: and the next day I had an affliction of the same kind (more domestic) which both made me so melancholy that life was a burden to me for a long time.

*   *   *   *   *   *   *   *   *

Reflecting about this time upon my own life I concluded that however I had mistaken the path of life proper for me I was not born for a courtier being in my temper too passionate and too open in my conversation[2].

This puts us in mind of Macky's description of Prior:

On the Queen's Accession to the Throne, he was continued in his office, is very well at Court with the Ministry, and is an

---

[1] *Letters...at Welbeck*, p. 265.

[2] *Ibid*. The second "affliction" may have been the death of Jersey's second son, George Villiers, who was drowned in the Piave in Friuli, and whom Prior commemorated in a threnode.

entire Creature of my Lord *Jersey's*, whom he supports by his advice. Is one of the best Poets in *England*, but very factious in conversation; a thin hollow-looked Man, turned of forty years old[1]

and of this description Swift agreed that it was "near the truth."

But his relations with his fellow-men doubtless were responsible for much of his melancholy. We read:

The 31 *Decr.* 1704 or New Years Day 1704/5. Mr Sam: Prior told Mr Mason that he had not made any alteration in his Will. Mr Biggs who made that Will told me so some time before.

The 2 *or* 3 *of Jan.* Mr Lan: Burton carryed from me a letter to Mr Sam: Prior, to which Mr Prior promised Mr Burton y[t] he would in a day or 2 return me an answer, but did not.

5th *Jan:* 1704/5. Mr James Montagu went to see Mr Prior, but was denyed[2].

In this case it looks as if Prior had been extremely imprudent. It is perhaps safe to quarrel with a relative[3]; but to fall out with persons of influence is always hazardous, and certainly, from this entry, it does not look as if Prior were attempting to close any breach effected with the Montagus by his vote on the impeachment.

On September 15/26, 1707, he lost his friend George Stepney who left him a legacy of £50[4]. But the darkest cloud of all was his variance with the Duchess of Marlborough; who considered him guilty of having written lampoons against her and the Duke. As soon

[1] J. Macky, *Characters of the Court of Great Britain*, p. 135.

[2] *Letters...at Welbeck*, p. 266.

[3] Presumably Mr Sam: Prior was Matthew's uncle or cousin, perhaps the son of the man who kept the Rummer Tavern near Charing Cross in 1688.

[4] Christian Cole, *Memoirs*, p. 481, Addison to Cole, Whitehall, Sept. 16/27, 1707.

as he heard of the suspicion, Prior had taken steps to have it removed. In January, 1704, he notes in his diary that he went to Godolphin and

alleged (as I very safely and conscientiously might) my Innocence, with which declaration my Lord Treasurer seemed fully satisfied and said he would endeavour to let my Lady Marl: know what I said to him in such a manner as should deface any ill impression which this report might have given her of me: my Lord Marl: about this time told me he had been informed that I was the author of some Libel against him but added (and conjured me to think so) that he did not believe it, and gave me as a reason of his not believing it that he told me of it in so free and open a manner[1].

After the victory of Blenheim, Prior wrote a *Letter to Monsieur Boileau Despreaux* in which praise of Marlborough was mingled with courtly comparisons of Queen Anne with Queen Elizabeth. In acknowledging it, Adam Cardonnel, the Duke's secretary and an old friend of Prior's[2], wrote acknowledging the receipt of the poem, and than alluded to the rumour about the lampoons.

His Grace therefore commands me...to let you know...that, though some people may have endeavoured to give him wrong impressions of you, it has not had the least effect with him, and that he is sure if your heart had not gone hand in hand with the poet, you could not have said so much in his favour beyond his merit, and that he will endeavour to deserve your friendship, and that you may rely entirely on his upon all occasions. Thus much for my Lord Duke, being, as near as I can remember, his own expressions[3].

The Duchess, however, was convinced of Prior's guilt, for when he sent her two copies of the *Letter to Boileau* (one for the Queen and one for the Duchess) she

---

[1] *Letters...at Welbeck*, p. 108.

[2] The friendship went back at least to 1691: see Bath Papers, III. 7.

[3] Bath Papers, III. 434, Cardonnel to Prior, Camp at Treves, Oct. 31, N.S. 1704.

returned the packet by the bearer unopened, "declaring that she should not receive anything of my writing, for that she was persuaded that I could not mean well to her or her family[1]." So in November, 1705, we find Prior making still further efforts to dissipate the ill opinion the Duchess had formed of him. On returning from the war in 1705, Marlborough "received me very kindly," and when Prior complained of the Duchess' usage of him, evidently pooh-poohed it saying that though Prior was not a married man he could but know that women would have their humours, and added reassuringly that the thing should do him "no prejudice[2]."

After Ramillies, Prior received Marlborough's "particular thanks" for the Ode to the Queen, and when the Duke came home, he remarks that he was "particularly kind in his discourse to me[3]." The Queen too, in spite of the hostility of the Duchess of Marlborough, accepted the Ode, and let him know she "took it very kindly" of him[4].

But although he was apparently in the Queen's favour, and although Marlborough was his friend, the weakness of Anne, and the absences of Marlborough left Prior exposed to malevolent attacks; and however great a man Marlborough might be, Godolphin was in a position to affect Prior's career more directly than the Duke. And Prior realised well what the loss of Godolphin's favour would mean. Consequently, while he was

---

[1] *Letters...at Welbeck*, p. 109.   [2] *Ibid.* p. 109.   [3] *Ibid.* p. 110.
[4] *Ibid.* p. 109. We may note here what Prior says as to the reception of this ode, an effusion of thirty-five stanzas of ten lines each. "The Whigs tho' they did not openly censure this poem were no way satisfied that I had writ it; they said the imitation was of a verse now grown obsolete, the style a little hard, &c.; in the meantime none of them writ, at least none of note, except Dennis, and Walsh and Roe who came out about a year after; the Tories on the other side cried up my poem too much." Perhaps Prior thought that this excessive praise from the Tories did him harm in Godolphin's eyes.

basking in the sun of Marlborough's smiles, he noted at the beginning of the year after Ramillies:

I could not but observe all this time that my Lord Treasurer looked more coldly upon me than he used to do, and when I took occasion twice or thrice to speak to him concerning what was of consequence to Her Majesty's service, he gave me but general or ambiguous answers: hence I very plainly perceived my favour with him declined, and I was the more assured of this unhappy truth when being commissioned by my Lord Jersey to carry a message to my Lord Treasurer, having done my errand and received his answer, I told him that I took that opportunity to tell him that I hoped my behaviour was such in an obedient respect and zeal for Her Majesty's service and in a constant study of what might any way be satisfactory to His Lordship that I believed and presumed I had his protection, and would continue to deserve it; to which he answered he would protect me if he could: if he could or no, or how he did may be known from this instance: about March [1707] he sent to me and bid me come to him: he began that he did not doubt but that I had heard there was to be a change in the Commission, I said I had heard so indeed from the common talk, but had less heeded it, not imagining myself concerned in it; that I relied upon his protection, and did not doubt but that if Her Majesty thought proper to remove me, His Lordship's goodness would find something else for me; he said with a little warmth that I might be of the number of those who should be reduced, and that the Queen had a great many to provide for, I said I had read St Paul and Epictetus and must be satisfied with what my superiors thought proper for me; he said care should be taken of me so that I should not fall.

Upon this I spoke to my Ld of Marl. who bid me be quiet, and assured me he would be my friend, that he had spoke to the Queen and to my Lord Treasurer about me, and that I ought to be satisfied. I was ill when His Grace went to Flanders, so I did not take my leave of Him[1].

<hr>

[1] *Letters...at Welbeck*, pp. 110, 111.

From his recording this incident, it may be Prior thought he had slightly offended Marlborough, and that the blow which fell might have been averted if Prior had been in good health. On April 22 he writes:

The Postboy assured me I was no longer of the Commission, and being that morning at the board I and my fellow Comr were informed that there was a new warrant in the Secretary's office for a new Commission for L:d Stamford, L:d Herbert, Mr Muncton and Mr Pulteney instead of Mr Pollexfen, Mr Blathwayt, myself and Mr Cecill. I waited on my Ld Treasurer who told me that I was in Her Maj:ties favour, and that something should be done for me, but that I must have Patience and Discretion[1].

To Prior the stroke was hard to bear; and he never forgave Godolphin. Even in the days of his "greatness" he remembered the treatment he had received, and wrote sneeringly of Godolphin. "As the wise Lord Godolphin told me when he turned Me out for having served Him: Things change, and times change, and men change[2]." And indeed of this truth Prior was in turn to prove an excellent example. Nevertheless, he succeeded in obtaining some compensation, if the Duchess of Marlborough is to be believed, from no other person than the Duke himself. He, whose "bounty" was the subject of stinging epigrams, actually gave Prior a pension of four or five hundred pounds: (Her Grace is not always consistent as to the sum)[3], and that Prior did receive a pension from Marlborough is confirmed by a letter of Cardonnel to Prior: "When I first heard of yours and my master Blathwayt's

[1] *Letters...at Welbeck*, p. 111.
[2] P.R.O. Foreign, France, 158, Prior to Bolingbroke, Paris, March 6/17, 1713/4.
[3] See the *Private correspondence of Sarah, Duchess of Marlborough...and the select correspondence of her husband, John, Duke of Marlborough*, London, 1838, II. 139 and 408.

remove, I took the liberty to tell His Grace in the most friendly manner I could what I thought of your circumstances, and he was pleased to answer me, under an injunction of the greatest secrecy, that he had and would take care of you[1]."

Anyhow Prior was now out of employment, and his pride doubtless forbade him to spend his days as Marlborough's pensioner. He considered momentarily, an offer made him by Sir Jonathan Trelawny, Bishop of Winchester, but on reflection rejected it as we learn from the following letter:

The Bishop of Winchester very kindly offered me the name of secretary to him and his diocese, w[ch] I was told was a kind of sinecure, would be of some value to me, and still left me the entire liberty of life: in a few days the good nature of the town, at least that part of it that wished me no good, carryed a glorious story, that I had a provision of six hundred pounds a year settled on me, was to live at Farnham with the bishop, had abandoned all thoughts of ever serving or depending on the court, had turned my thoughts wholy towards orders, was to have all the ecclesiastical preferment the prelate could heap upon me, and in the mean time was to sett up highchurch, and cut down all the bishop's woods into fagotts to burn dissenters: this civil turn might on one hand very easily have ruined me at court, from whence I had very good reason to expect some present favour, and might have hindered my return into business hereafter: and on the other hand, upon a nearer view of the thing I found it not considerable, and such as neither could or ought to be managed by deputation; it comprehended the business of a whole diocese, and was to be managed by some person who should wholy apply himself to it, and however great my L[d] Bishop's intended kindness and complaisance might be to me, it was pretty reasonable his secretary should always be near him: upon these views and reflexion I declined the offer w[ch] (to tell the truth) I had too suddenly

---

[1] Bath Papers, III. 436, Cardonnel to Prior, Camp at Meldert, July 14 N.S. 1707.

embraced: but I think I have done it in such a manner as letts him know that I have a real obligation to him, and a great zeal for his service, and I think the business will terminate so as that I may keep his friendship, and Mr Skelton be his secretary: wch I think will be very proper for his lordship's affairs, as well as my own:...you cannot imagine, S^r, the noise this thing has made, the various talk and censure that have been raised upon it, and the secret trouble it has given me[1].

The Bishop came to hear of the gossip, and wrote accordingly:

I don't doubt of your having your eye upon the bishopric of Winchester, but I beg you would not expect it these twenty years; after that I wish you may have it at least as many more[2].

Nevertheless, the fact remains that had it not been for Marlborough's pension, Prior at this time would have been reduced to living on his fellowship and the readership in medicine to which he had been appointed in 1706[3]. What qualifications he had for this post we may but conjecture, we do know, however, that his pride and ambition would not be satisfied unless he regained office. On May 28, 1708, he wrote to the Duke asking to be restored[4]. He protested vigorously that he had done nothing worthy of blame: on November 16 he wrote again to Marlborough:

I desire no more of my Lady Duchess than that she would not think me a villain and a libeller. I beg no other *eclaircissement* of what is past than that she would forget it; and with the most solemn protestation I aver, that I have ever esteemed her as one

---

[1] *Correspondence of Sir Thomas Hanmer, Bart.*, ed. by Sir Henry Bunbury, Bart., London, 1838, pp. 109, 110, Prior to Hanmer, Westminster, June 24, 1707.

[2] Bath Papers, III. 436, the Bishop of Winchester to Prior, Aug. 2/13, 1707.

[3] See the St John's College Registers. "6º Julii 1705. Mr Prior electus studiosus medicinae," and "5º Julii 1706. Mr Prior lector medicinae."

[4] *Hist. MSS. Comm.* VIIIth Rep., Marlborough papers, p. 36 *a*.

of the best of women, and would justify that esteem with my life, which at present, is no great compliment, for in truth I grow weary of it[1].

Meantime it was necessary to get a living: he turned to Halifax, and we learn from his diary what dirt he was compelled to eat.

The 2d or 3d of Janry. 1708/9. In a visit to Ld Hallifax in wch I wished him a good new Year and talked to him of Indifferent things I at last spoke to him concerning my own affairs, I told him that for above 2 years before I had spoken to Sr Ja: Montagu and for more than a Year before to himself to desire him to do Me a piece of Justice wch was an occasion to let the Duchess of Marlborough know that I had never writ or been contributing to any Mans writing anything against her Grace or her family which might have given her the least occasion of offence: I asked my Lord if he ever had performed this commission from Me. He was out of countenance and said he had not found a convenient opportunity, at the same time he was repeating to Me his own discontents and saying how We should live at Bushey park, and that if he could but see Me restored he would not care for anything further; is this a great Man?[2]

From this it is clear that Halifax was not so affectionately disposed towards Prior as to put himself out on his behalf or to help to remove a grievance for him. So nothing could be hoped for from the Montagus. Upon one more resource could he fall back. As no success had attended his personal appeals to the generosity of the great, he determined to try and raise money on his own merits. In 1707 an unauthorised collection of his poems had already appeared, and in 1709 there issued for the first time an authorised edition of *Poems on several occasions.* Whether it brought him much money we know not. Probably it did not; the unauthorised edition

---

[1] *Private correspondence of Sarah Duchess of Marlborough,* London, Henry Colburn, 1837, II. 407.   [2] *Letters...at Welbeck,* pp. 265–6.

of 1707 may very well have blanketed the later edition, however well authorised, by destroying the demand. Be that as it may, the end of 1709 finds him approaching the great Duke once more. It was only a compliment[1], but it afforded him an opportunity or an excuse to write in January, 1710, to beg his Grace to use his influence to obtain for Prior the place on the commission of trade vacant by Lord Herbert's death. All was of no avail; Godolphin refused to place him again on the commission, and Prior, seeing that nothing was to be hoped for from that quarter, turned completely over to the opposite faction. Bad health doubtless added to his irritation[2], which seems to have been all the greater, in that he seems to have thought that the chief obstacles to preferment in 1708 and 1709 had been removed, by the subsidence of the Duchess' resentment against him. When presenting a copy of his poems to the Duke, he wrote:

My Lady Duchess has been pleased to receive the book kindly, and has ordered Mr B. to let me know she is satisfied I never did deserve her displeasure, and her Grace's justice is such, that all obstacles on that side are perfectly removed. I am very sure (if there be occasion) she will be so far from opposing my being restored, that she will assist it[3].

The Duchess, however, in her character of Prior, says that "notwithstanding all his submissions and all his protestations, of which he was very free, she continued to think" that he had written that "vile libel[4]." But if

---

[1] *Private correspondence of Sarah, Duchess of Marlborough*, II. 408, Dec. 22, O.S. 1709.

[2] *Correspondence of Sir T. Hanmer*, p. 121, Prior to Hanmer, Westminster, August 4, 1709. "My health—the Bath waters have done a good deal towards the recovery of it, and the great specific *Cape Caballum* will, I think, confirm it."

[3] *Private correspondence of Sarah, Duchess of Marlborough*, II. 410.

[4] *Ibid.* II. 139.

Prior's story be true, he had cleared himself of any attacks on the Duke and Duchess before the appearance of the *Examiner*; and it is clear that the note that the Duchess endorsed on Prior's letter of December 22, 1709, must have been written long after that date[1].

To join the extreme Tories at this moment, was judicious and opportune. In April, 1710, the Queen's growing fondness for Mrs Masham culminated in the final rupture with the Duchess of Marlborough; in June Sunderland fell from office, and in August the revolution in the ministry was completed by the dismissal of Godolphin. Harley became Chancellor of the Exchequer, St John, Secretary of State, and Shrewsbury, Chamberlain. Prior therefore had friends at Court at last, and even before Godolphin's fall, they were influential enough to "make him the first fruits of a Restoration[2]," seeing that at the beginning of July he recovered his place on the commission of trade.

Almost immediately after this fortunate event, there appeared the first number of the *Examiner*. Now, whatever may have been the Duchess of Marlborough's feelings towards Prior at the beginning of 1710, whether she really was at that time "satisfied that he had never deserved her displeasure" or no, it is certain that she considered the *Examiner* an unpardonable sin.

"It was thought with good reason," she writes, "that he wrote some of those vile *Examiners*, in which the Duke and Duchess of Marlborough were so beyond all measure and all example abused";

---

[1] "'Tis certain this man has writ some of the scandalous libels of the Duke of Marlborough and me, though he had a pension of four hundred pounds a year from the Duke of Marlborough, when he pretended to be in his interest." *Private correspondence of Sarah, Duchess of Marlborough*, II. 408.

[2] *Hist. MSS. Comm.* xvth Rep., Portland Papers, IV. 551, Lord Weymouth to Harley, Longleat, July 24, 1710.

and further on, after describing what the Duke had done for him she says:

> He made more submissive court to the Duke and Duchess than almost any other. But when their enemies opened the scene, he immediately joined them, and made the vilest returns to him to whom he had long owed his very subsistence. But it is enough to say, that the first part of his education was in a tavern, and that he had a soul as low as his education, incapable of anything truly great or honourable[1].

In discussing this charge against Prior, we must not lay too much stress on the Duchess' invective, for her evidence, especially in personal cases, is by no means reliable. The question resolves itself into an investigation of the share Prior had in the *Examiner*, and whether he can be held responsible for those numbers in which the Duke and Duchess were attacked. Considering what the Duke had done for him, it certainly would have been unpardonable in Prior to have written any of the *Examiners* which attacked the Duke. If, unfortunately, we cannot positively clear Prior, at the same time the burden of proof falls upon those who charge him with this ingratitude.

It must be remembered that the *Examiner* first appeared on August 3, 1710, and twelve numbers were issued before November 2, 1710. The number which then appeared, the thirteenth, was the first which Swift wrote, and as he says, he "continued it about eight months[2]," *i.e.* till June, 1711, when it fell into other and inferior hands, and when Prior was busy preparing to resume his diplomatic career.

Now for how many of the first twelve was Prior

---

[1] *Private correspondence of Sarah, Duchess of Marlborough*, II. 138–40.

[2] *Memoirs relating to that change which happened in the Queen's ministry in the year* 1710 (Swift's *Works*, ed. Walter Scott, Edinburgh, 1814, III. 246).

responsible? In the *History of his own time*, compiled by
Adrian Drift, Prior's servant, we find the statement:

> Mr PRIOR is supposed to have been the author of many of
> the best *Examiners*, which are not particularly distinguished;
> but the following criticism upon a poem of Dr *Garth's* to the
> Earl of *Godolphin* is universally allowed to be his; as the Answer
> which follows, taken from the *Whig Examiner* is well known to
> be Mr *Addison's*, who sided with the Party in Disgrace[1].

The vagueness of the statement that he was "supposed
to have been the author of many of the best *Examiners*"
contrasts strongly with the clearness of the attribution
of the authorship of No. 6; and the whole sentence
really means nothing but that Prior wrote No. 6.
Further, Swift certainly puts him in a subordinate
position among the writers of the *Examiner*.

> About a dozen of these papers, written with much spirit and
> sharpness, some by Mr Secretary St John, since Lord Boling-
> broke; others by Dr Atterbury, since bishop of Rochester, and
> others again by Mr Prior, Dr Freind, &c. were published with
> great applause[2].

It is surely not an unnatural construction to put upon
these words if we interpret them to mean that of the
writers to the first twelve *Examiners* St John was the
most prolific, then Atterbury, and then among the
crowd of the other writers the most distinguished were
Prior and Freind. And as there are only twelve numbers
to be divided among these writers, if Bolingbroke and
Atterbury are to be credited with more than one apiece,
it greatly diminishes the chance that more than one

---

[1] *The History of his own time. Compiled from the Original Manuscripts
of His late Excellency Matthew Prior, Esq; Revised and Signed by Himself
and Copied fair for the Press by Mr Adrian Drift, His Executor:* Dublin,
1740, p. 218.

[2] *Memoirs relating to that change...in the Queen's ministry, cit. sup.*
p. 245.

number of the remainder was written by Prior. The probability is that No. 6 is Prior's sole contribution to these early *Examiners*. For subsequent numbers, we know Swift was mainly responsible, and it is significant to observe that in the *Journal to Stella*, Swift says that the author of the attacks on the Marlboroughs early in 1711 was "not Prior, but perhaps it may be Atterbury." And surely Swift should know[1].

This being the case, the charge of ingratitude to a benefactor vanishes into thin air, and the verdict must be Not guilty. On the other hand, popular opinion did undoubtedly credit Prior with having written some of Swift's *Examiners*, and he had the uncomfortable experience of being insulted in the streets on that account[2]. This opinion may well have been shared by the Duchess of Marlborough, who was not blessed with a dispassionate and judicial temperament. We may indeed suppose guilt in Prior by accusing him of having supplied Swift privately with information about the Marlboroughs. The only ground for this charge would be that it is clear from the *Journal to Stella* that Swift and Prior frequently dined together during the winter of 1710 and 1711, but that anything detrimental to Prior's honour occurred on these occasions can only be asserted; of evidence or proof there is none.

To Prior the winter of 1710/11 was on the whole uneventful: he dined out, entertained, and drank hard: he often walked with Swift in St James' Park "to make himself fat and I (Swift) to bring myself down: he has generally a cough which he only calls a cold[3]"; and like all the wits, he indulged in the new-fangled art of punning. Swift has preserved one or two of his execrable attempts: "Lord Carteret set down Prior the other day

[1] *Journal to Stella*, Mar. 7, 1710/11.
[2] *Ibid.* Feb. 9, 1710/11.
[3] *Ibid.* Feb. 21, 1710/11.

in his chariot, and Prior thanked him for his charity[1]."
With Swift he was constantly sitting up late talking;
once Swift describes the entertainment as a "debauch[2],"
and in 1712 he notes that he stayed at Prior's till "past
twelve, and could not get a coach, and was alone, and
was afraid enough of the Mohocks[3]."

But the next year had its sorrows for Prior: the most
serious undoubtedly was Jersey's death, which took
place suddenly on August 26, 1711; and caused Prior
real grief, as the following letter shows:

Dear Sir Thomas Hanmer,   West[r]. Aug. 28, 1711.

If you ever knew the tenderness of a true friendship, you will
pitty my present condition, when I tell you that my dear Lord
Jersey went seemingly well to bed on Saturday night, and at five
on Sunday morning dyed—be his spirit for ever happy, and his
memory respected. The only moment of ease w[ch] I have found
since this cruel blow is just now while I complain and write
to you. Time and necessity I know cure all sorrows; but as yet
I feel a load upon my spirits which I conceal from the world,
and which must be too hard for human nature if it lasts. I know
you loved my Lord Jersey, and I hope I trouble you while I give
an account of his death: the Queen, the nation, mankind has
lost a pattern of honour, integrity, and good manners, you, S[r],
have lost a man who understood your merit, and courted your
friendship; after you have wept for him, S[r], as I beg you to do,
I will wish in recompense that those years which he might
reasonably have expected, may be added to yours: in the mean
time I desire you to believe that till I lye extended on the biere

---

[1] *Journal to Stella*, Jany. 4, 1710/11. See also August 29. "My lord
treasurer began a health to my lord privy seal, Prior punned, and said it
was so privy, he knew not who it was." The habit lasted some years, for
Prior writes to Harley in 1717 (Bath Papers, III. 449, Cambridge, Nov.
4/15), "I have made a hundred puns in forty-eight hours, to the joy
and wonder of all my hearers."

[2] *Ibid.* Dec. 7, 1710. Cf. also May 16, 1711.

[3] *Ibid.* Mar. 18, 1711/12.

as I saw my poor lord this morning, I remain most sincerely and inviolably, S^r,

Your obedient and humble servant
MAT. PRIOR[1].

The note is true, and the letter shows how deep was the intimacy between the two men. It was indeed a serious loss for Prior, who owed nearly everything to Jersey. But this was not the only anxiety which the year brought Prior, though it was the greatest; there was the extraordinary incident of the stabbing of Harley by Guiscard early in the year, an event which caused Prior to join in the flow of poetry which that surprising action evoked; while in the first half of the year he had been annoyed by being transferred from the commission of trade to that of customs. First mentioned in June[2], the change was not completed till the end of the year, when Swift says: "Prior hates his commission of the customs, because it spoils his wit. He says he dreams of nothing but cockets, and dockets, and drawbacks, and other jargon, words of the custom house[3]." But before this unfortunate change took place, Prior had passed one of the great landmarks of his life, for at the beginning of July, 1711, the ministry sent him, with great secrecy, to France once more. What events led the ministry to do so, must be reserved for another chapter.

[1] *Correspondence of Sir Thomas Hanmer*, p. 129.
[2] *Journal to Stella*, June 26, 1711.
[3] *Ibid.* March 13, 1711/12.

Chapter VIII

"MAT'S PEACE"

THE desperate straits to which France had been reduced by Marlborough had not been greatly eased by the events of the year 1710. It is true that Marlborough had won no signal victory, for the sum total of his gains that year was four towns, the safety of which had been long threatened, and the loss of which had therefore been long discounted. But Marlborough and Eugene were still at the head of their troops, and there was no telling when the next stroke would be dealt by the redoubtable pair. The efforts to bring about a peace by negociations had failed; nor was this fact surprising, for so far had the arrogance of the allies carried them that the Dutch demanded that Louis XIV was to assist in dethroning his own grandson, and was allowed two months for the task. As if this was not short enough a time for him to carry through an enterprise in which the Allies had met with but little success for the last eight years, he was to be assisted, in case of failure, by a renewal of the war on the part of the Allies. The conference was clearly little but a farce; but the bitter disappointment of the French is clear from the valedictory letter which their plenipotentiaries addressed to the Dutch on July 20.

Yet for all their high words, the position of the Dutch was less favourable than at the beginning of the year. The revolution in the English ministry boded no good to Marlborough, and at the end of the year it seemed almost certain that the Dutch would lose his great

services. The Queen at that time did indeed renew
his command, but there were not wanting reasons to
support the opinion that the near future would witness
his disgrace.

In the first place, the fall of the glorious Marlborough
was a necessity, if the new ministers were to establish
themselves firmly in office; and to secure this, peace
must be made with France. In the second place, the
elections of the autumn, which routed the Whigs, gave
the ministry a majority in the House of Commons, and
the more secure they became, the more they looked
askance on Marlborough. Therefore the Queen's speech
to Parliament on Nov. 27/Dec. 8 not only revealed the
debts incurred by the odious Godolphin, but also spoke
in hopes that when peace should come the country
would once more flourish. In the third place, at the
very end of the year, on December 24, O.S., came the
news of the disaster of Brihuega, which might well make
the supporters of the Archduke despair of seeing him
rule over the whole of Spain. The main object of the
war seemed further than ever from attainment. In spite
of the brave words spoken about France being "pushed
with the greatest vigour in the most sensible part,"
the news merely confirmed the ministry in their peace
policy[1]. Even before the news of Brihuega had been
received, practical steps towards opening a negociation
with France had been taken. On December 23, 1710,
a despatch was sent to Louis' great minister Torcy by
a priest named François Gaultier. This man had been
chaplain to Lady Jersey since the beginning of the war,

[1] *Bolingbroke Correspondence*, i. 33, St John to Drummond, Whitehall,
Dec. 26/Jan. 6, 1710/11. The letter shows St John thought that Spanish
affairs were hopeless. "Our misfortune in Spain is very great....I own
that, since Spain cannot be gained by revolution...there is no reasonable,
sober man who can entertain a thought of conquering and retaining that
wide continent."

and under a variety of pseudonyms had acted as a
secret agent of Louis XIV in England. The despatch
he now sent told Torcy on Jersey's behalf that the
ministry were determined on peace, and would give up
Spain provided security was granted to British trade.
As soon as the two crowns were agreed with the British
the allies would be informed, no matter what they
might say or think[1].

The despatch was immediately followed by the *abbé*
himself, who went over to Paris with verbal instructions
and messages from Jersey, Shrewsbury the Lord
Chamberlain, and Harley the Chancellor of the
Exchequer. In order to end the war, they said, they
would negociate at a conference in Holland, but not in
England, for fear of their heads; and at this conference,
it is important to note, not merely was a general peace
to be made, but, developing William III's policy at
Ryswick, the ministry desired a separate treaty between
France and England to be agreed upon, so that if
the Dutch proved refractory, they could be forced
to sign a peace. To this principle the French King
agreed.

It was now all-important to the British ministry that
the French proposal for peace should appear to be
spontaneous, and to come without any suggestion from
England; and in this sense Gaultier wrote to France
soon after his return to London in February. The
enterprise, however, moved slowly, partly because
contrary winds prevented Gaultier from crossing the
Channel, partly perhaps because of Harley's procrastinating habits, and partly from the refusal of
Torcy to make proposals of such a kind as the British
ministers could accept. The French offers, they insisted, must be not less ample than those of the year

1 Gaultier to Torcy, Dec. 23/Jan. 3, 1710/11, *Aff. Etr. Angl.* 230.
(Quoted in O. Weber, *Der Friede von Utrecht*, p. 18, n. 1.)

1710. But in April matters moved quicker, for St John stepped into Harley's place while the latter was recovering from the wound inflicted by Guiscard, and because Gaultier once more crossed to France. He brought over not merely written instructions, but a verbal message of vast import. This was nothing else than the British conditions of peace, which for obvious reasons could not be committed to writing; but it was to serve as a guide to the French government in drafting those "spontaneous proposals" which the British ministers were so anxious to receive. The terms suggested were security for British trade in the Mediterranean, in Spain and in the Indies: the Dutch were to have a barrier against France, sufficient for them and satisfactory to the British; France was to give an assurance that satisfaction must be given, if possible, to the Allies; but in the matter of the succession to Spain and the Indies it was to be sufficient to offer that the solution of the difficulty would be found according to the wish of England. This Gaultier was to say was in favour of Philip, although at the conferences England would at first press strongly the right of Charles.

Torcy could scarcely believe his ears. So anxious was the British government to hasten on the negociations that they not only abandoned their demand for terms not less favourable than those of 1710, but they actually offered better terms than the French expected to obtain. "Il n'y eut donc nulle difficulté à faire ces offres....Le Roi le jugea nécessaire." So into a Court plunged into deeper gloom than usual owing to the death of the Dauphin on April 3/14, Gaultier brought a ray of light, and on April 11/22 these "spontaneous proposals" were signed by Torcy, and Gaultier carried them to England.

On April 27/May 8 St John gravely sent these "preliminary proposals" to Lord Raby, the British resident at The Hague, with orders that they should be submitted to the Pensionary.

The terms of the several propositions are, as your Excellency will observe, very general; but however, they contain an offer to treat; and though there is an air of complaisance through the whole paper shown to us, and the contrary to those among whom you reside, yet this can have no ill consequence, as long as the Queen and the States take care to understand each other[1].

On May 14/25 and 15/26 the Grand Pensioner, Heinsius, replied through Lord Raby; he said the Dutch wanted a good peace, and agreed with St John that the French proposals were too general[2]. However, this reply showed no open objection to a negociation with the French; indeed, it suggested that France should be asked to explain herself more fully, and so the British ministers determined to continue as they had begun.

They had more justification now for seeking peace than at the beginning of the year. Even before the draft had been sent to Holland, news had reached England of the death of the Emperor Joseph I. In announcing this event, the Queen expressed her resolve to use her utmost endeavours to obtain the election of Charles III, King of Spain, to the Empire. Nevertheless, the prospect of a union of the Spanish crown with the Imperial was no less formidable than that of its union with the French, and Peterborough in urging the claims of the Duke of Savoy to the Spanish throne, on the ground that the Emperor could not also be King of Spain, was giving expression to an apprehension that was universally felt, however absurd the statement might be in the light of history[3].

[1] *Bolingbroke Corr.* I. 107, St John to Raby, April 27/May 8, 1711.

[2] *Report of the Committee of Secrecy*, p. 2.

[3] *Bolingbroke Corr.* I. 104, St John to Drummond, April 27/May 8, 1711. The Imperialists would have nothing to do with such a doctrine.

The question now was what step should next be taken; but anyhow an answer had to be sent to the French proposals of April. The English ministers seem to have been reluctant to trust the matter again to Gaultier, so it was necessary to find an Englishman who was sufficiently master of French to be able to argue with a French minister; and Prior, who from party views not only could be trusted, but who from his earlier experience had a good acquaintance with the French court, was the very man for the purpose. Under veil of the utmost secrecy Prior was sent over to Fontainebleau at the beginning of July. His power was "in three lines" under the Queen's sign-manual, but it was not countersigned by any minister.

Anne R.

Le sieur Prior est pleinement instruit et authorisé de communiquer à la France nos demandes Preliminaires, et de nous en rapporter la reponse. A. R.[1]

These demands began by an emphatic protestation that Great Britain would "make no peace but what should be to the satisfaction of all her allies": the Dutch, the Emperor and the Duke of Savoy were to receive barriers, the last-named Prince was to recover all that the French had taken from him, and "what other addition should be thought proper," while France was also to give a "positive Assurance that the Crowns of

---

"Count Sinzendorf says very freely in conversation that if you tamper much with the Marquis Delborgo, and seem inclined to assure the Duke of Savoy of the Spanish succession, the new Emperor will make his terms with France and soon break all your measures." (Portland Papers, v. 2, Drummond to Oxford, June 1/12, 1711.)

[1] The original of this famous "power" is in P.R.O., Treaty Papers, 15. When Prior was asked before the Committee of Secrecy if the Lord Treasurer had sent him over to France, he replied in the negative, but that the Queen had done so. In the absence of any countersignature of a minister it was difficult to maintain that Prior was saying what was not.

France and Spain should never be united." While
France made these concessions, she was also to give
satisfaction to our allies according to their agreements
and treaties with us, and Dutch trade was to be secured.
For ourselves we demanded the monopoly of the
Asiento, and equal opportunities with the French for
trade in the Spanish colonies. Louis must further
recognise the Protestant succession, demolish Dunkirk,
and cede Newfoundland: Gibraltar and Port Mahon
were to remain in British hands, while "all things in
America should continue in the possession of those they
should be found to be in at the conclusion of the peace[1]"
—a clause of some significance in view of the expedition
under Admiral Walker which had just been sent out
against Quebec, though it must be remembered that the
French had a similar expedition under Duguay-Trouin
destined against Brazil.

These instructions and demands in their form already
betray the plan of securing our interests by a treaty
separate from that of our allies. Prior's discretion, it will
be observed, was allowed little play. He had merely to
hand in the British proposals and receive the French
answer. His interpretation of this, however, was that he
might discuss the proposals with Torcy as long as Torcy
did not get the better of the argument: as soon, however,
as this happened, he would entrench himself behind the
letter of his instructions and protest he had no powers
to negociate. Such at least we may infer from the journal
of his negociations which may be seen in the Portland papers[2], and may to some extent be checked by
Torcy's memorandum to Louis XIV[3]. Curiously

[1] *Report of the Committee of Secrecy*, Appendix, p. 2.
[2] *Hist. MSS. Comm.*, Portland Papers, v. 34–42.
[3] *Arch. Affaires Etrangères, Angleterre*, vol. 233, ff. 43 *et seqq*. The
document may be found printed in full in the *English Historical Review*
for July, 1914, pp. 525–32.

enough, Prior's account seems to be defective at the beginning, while Torcy's is incomplete towards the end. However, there is enough common matter to make the two accounts interesting to compare. It is clear from Torcy that on July 21 Torcy saw Prior after having given an audience to Gaultier who posted up Torcy in the events at the Court of St James' since his return in April. Of this interview Prior does not speak, but the French account is instructive as telling us the hopes that Torcy entertained. He clearly expected that Prior would have power to negociate, and he trusted to his own un-rivalled skill in diplomacy to beat down the English demands. The extreme meagreness of Prior's powers therefore came as a severe blow to his hopes, especially as some of the proposals were not as Gaultier had repre-sented them[1], and Torcy admits that he was unable to get much out of Prior[2]. But Prior stated that the British were prepared to allow a prince of the House of Bourbon to remain on the throne of Spain and pointed out that this was a great concession, and was indeed the corollary of the private propositions which demanded a positive assurance that the Crowns of France and Spain should never be united. This gave an opportunity for discus-sion from which, however, no decisive agreement was reached; both sides took refuge under the shelter of higher authority whom they would not commit and next day the conferences were renewed[3]. The proposals had been laid before the King, and Torcy, beginning with small details, announced that there was strong objection

[1] "L'article de la succession d'Angleterre estoit different de ce que Gautier m'en auoit dit." *Aff. Etr. Angleterre*, vol. 233, fo. 46 (*E.H.R. ut sup.* p. 527).

[2] "Je ne pus tirer de luy aucune explication sur ce que les Anglois pretendoient faire pour le Roy en eschange des grands auantages qu'ils demandoient a Sa Mté." (*ibid.* fo. 46 b).

[3] Prior seems to say two days later: Torcy's memorandum is clear, that it was on July 22.

to the use of the words "preliminary" and "demands" as redolent of the horrors of The Hague and Gertruydenberg, and Prior was at considerable pains to explain that no offence was meant. Proceeding to read the articles proposed, Torcy was enabled to raise an important point; what is France to get in return for these concessions? Prior valiantly replied "Spain for Anjou." Well might Prior urge that, compared with the proposals France had entertained the year before[1], this was a liberal concession on the part of the allies[2]. Nevertheless, Torcy in righteous indignation began to scold Prior: since Brihuega and Villa Viciosa, Philip was secure on his Spanish throne, and therefore this could not be considered a satisfactory basis for negociation. Moreover, Great Britain must not ask too much, she had rivals in the field, with whom France might make quite as good a peace. Thereupon he craftily showed the astonished Prior three letters from Pettkum, the Holstein resident at The Hague, two in cipher[3], one, which had arrived that evening, in plain characters[4]. As Prior, whose journal begins at this point, noted, the fact of

its being writ at length without cipher showed plain enough that the writer did not fear that it should be opened; from whence it is evident that it was writ by the knowledge and order of the government in Holland[5].

The gist was that the Dutch implored Louis XIV to renew the negociations, and that Louis would get better terms from them than from the English. In short, "the

[1] See above, p. 144.

[2] *Arch. Aff. Etr. Angleterre*, vol. 233, fo. 49 (*E.H.R. ut sup.* p. 528).

[3] Dated May 27 and June 11 (*Arch. Aff. Etr. Angl.* vol. 233, fo. 49 *b*; *E.H.R. ut sup.* p. 528).

[4] Dated July 16 (*ibid.*).

[5] Portland Papers, v. 35. In the instructions to Mesnager it is plainly stated that Pettkum writes whatever Heinsius tells him to (*Aff. Etr. Ang.* vol. 233).

Dutch were ready to give the French whatever terms they could ask[1]." As for the English, nothing could be expected from them, for "the Whigs would act in concert with the Dutch, but the Tories were privately concerting measures with the Imperialists and were resolved to continue the war."

"At this passage," says Prior, "I could not forbear laughing, and said that if M. Pettkum were no better apprized of the inclinations of the States towards a peace than he was of desires of the English towards the prolonging the war, I thought his advice would not weigh much with M. Torcy[2]."

Having thus gaily revealed the secret of the Dutch and the ignorance of Pettkum, Torcy turned to business. On certain points he frankly said *non possumus*. As to the English demand of Gibraltar, Port Mahon and four places in America, the English "ask no less than to be masters of the Mediterranean and Spain, to possess themselves of all the Indies and to take away from France all that appertains to that crown in America." In a long dispute, Torcy argued that if the English asked for such advantages, the Dutch would do so too, and if so, why not the French? And how could the King of Spain then call himself Lord of the Indies? The fact was that Philip's presence in Spain made such demands unnecessary, for it would bring to the English greater advantages than ever they could get under the Archduke[3]. To this unconvincing exaggeration, Prior replied that the article was to be kept secret from the Dutch, that Great Britain would not oppose French acquisitions

---

[1] Portland Papers, v. 35. Torcy's account is that Pettkum was very anxious to treat by way of Holland, obviously for his own personal advantage. (*Arch. Aff. Etr. Angl.* vol. 233, fo. 50; *E.H.R. ut sup.* p. 528.)

[2] Cf. Torcy's account. "Prior, irrité de toutes ces lettres, m'asseura que le Roy seroit plus content de la maniere de traitter des Anglois que de celle des Hollandois. (*Ibid.* fo. 50; *E.H.R. ut sup.* p. 528.)

[3] *Ibid.* fo. 52 b (*E.H.R. ut sup.* p. 530).

in Spanish America, and besides the Archduke had actually promised these advantages to them and to them alone. Torcy naturally laughed such treaties to scorn; according to his own account Prior retorted that the British proposals were honestly made; if Gibraltar, Minorca and places in America were demanded it was solely in order to protect our trade: nay, even the Spaniards would thank the English for protecting them from the violence of the English and Dunkirk pirates, the former of whom were the worst of the lot[1]. To this fanciful idea Torcy retorted "You will never make Spain believe that it is for their advantage to take away their country," and when Prior began his protestations that he had not power to discuss but only to receive an answer, passed on to the Asiento clause with the remark that it was "impossible to be granted." At this, Prior, knowing what value was attached to that clause at home, says his "heart ached extremely" and that he was "ready to sink"; but with characteristic obstinacy he relapsed into his mulish position that peace could be made on no other condition[2].

As to Newfoundland, here, said Torcy, was another insuperable difficulty. Prior, however, knew that the possession of this island was not an essential point, seeing that Nova Scotia might be exchanged for it, so he temporised: then he fell back on historical arguments; Newfoundland clearly ought to belong to England because Hudson who settled in that district was an Englishman; the names were English, *Terre Neuve* was merely a translation of Newfoundland, the

---

[1] *Arch. Aff. Etr. Angl.* vol. 233, fo. 53 (*E.H.R. ut sup.* p. 530).

[2] Portland Papers, v. 36. Not so Torcy, who represents Prior as saying that "la traitte des negres estoit une affaire par[ticuli]ere des associez aux deux compagnies d'Affrique dont les affaires estoient fort en desordre et qu'ils se flattoient de les restablir par ce moyen" (*Aff. Etr. Angleterre*, vol. 233, fo. 55; *E.H.R. ut sup.* p. 531).

name given to it by Sebastian Cabot, all of them arguments so convincing that apparently the subject dropped
and Torcy raised the question of the Barrier[1]. On this
point Torcy seemed to give way completely and then
appealed to Prior as a friend to say what really would
content the English. But Prior was sufficiently wily not
to fall into this antediluvian trap. Heedless of the fact
that on matters of Spain and Newfoundland he had been
disputing vigorously with Torcy, he said he had no
powers to negociate; he was there merely to receive the
answer which His Most Christian Majesty might be
pleased to make: in short, the whole question was a
matter for the Congress. After an elaborate compliment
to Louis XIV the conference broke up[2].

At this point, Torcy's account begins to fail us. But
Prior has made it clear that two days afterwards he had
another interview with Torcy at night, though Torcy
does not describe any further interview until July 29th[3].

He was gravely told that Louis XIV maintained that
the British proposals were unacceptable as they stood,
but so anxious was he for peace that, rather than send
Prior home with "an absolute refusal," he had determined to take counsel with persons well versed in
mercantile affairs. He therefore suggested delay, to
which Prior agreed, as although his instructions limited
his powers of action, they did not confine him in point
of time. He took occasion to point out, rather disin-
genuously, that the proposals he brought took nothing
away from France or Spain. We must, however, have
our places of surety for trade.

"Sir," I added, "I see nothing in this demand that concerns
France, nor that forbids France obtaining some collateral ad-

---

[1] Here again Torcy says Prior refused to discuss. Perhaps Prior got
the better of the conversation.

[2] Portland Papers, v. 36, 37. Of this last incident Torcy's memorandum
says nothing.   [3] According to Prior, the 30th.

vantage of the same kind from Spain, but that is no way my affair. France may have other politics and other views. We are a trading nation, and as such must secure our traffic: her Majesty and her ministry judge it absolutely necessary that this branch of our trade be secured[1]."

On July 27, Prior met Torcy once more: this time in the gardens at Fontainebleau: "it was dark enough," says Prior, "to conceal who we were." Here Gaultier joined them. After some remarks about the South Sea Company, Torcy returned to the charge. The French will never be convinced that Prior was right in saying that these proposals would secure a "more equal distribution of traffic," and held out little hope of agreement on the subject of the four towns demanded as sureties in the Spanish West Indies. Once more Prior had to set his teeth; and he doggedly replied "it was the only base and foundation of a negociation,...in a tract of above 700 leagues it was impossible that four places should annoy the Spanish." He repeated the clever arguments of two days previously that what was asked did not hinder France in any way from making what bargain she could with Spain. But Torcy remarked that this was a misapprehension, for France was in no way upon a better foot with Spain than in the time of Charles II; for "the Spaniards were most jealous of the French since a Prince of the House of Bourbon" had been "on the throne[2]."

Meanwhile the proposals had been submitted to the examination of two experts, Nicolas Mesnager and La Lande Magon. The greater of these, Nicolas Mesnager[3],

---

[1] Portland Papers, v. 38. In this point, at any rate, Prior showed himself a clever negociator.

[2] *Ibid.* 39–40.

[3] Nicolas Mesnager, by occupation a merchant of Rouen, had been sent by Louis XIV to the conference at The Hague in 1709 with particular instructions to watch the commercial interests of France.

declared them to be unacceptable, but his opinion corresponded with Gaultier's that it would be rash in the extreme to say so. Negociations must be continued therefore, but in view of the fact that Prior cannot and will not negociate, the seat of them must be transferred to London. So on the night of July 30[1] Torcy spoke to Prior. He begán again in the same "grave and concerted manner" to tell him that the proposals had been considered by the Council; "but the more they laboured, the more difficulties they found." Continuing, he cross-questioned Prior yet more as to the intentions of England. Did she really not intend to ruin other nations' commerce? Did she really not aim at a monopoly of trade? Prior replied that that was so, that he could not see how the cession of a few places could make all the difference apprehended in a country which extended from California to the Straits of Magellan. Torcy replied, commenting on the unsatisfactory state of affairs which did not allow Prior to do anything, but receive the King's reply. Prior replied that that was the case[2]. Failing therefore to shake Prior in the position he had taken up, Torcy came to the important point, that, "though the King could not submit to some terrible articles, he was resolved to send us a plan." Prior asked what this meant? he was there to receive the King's answer to the Queen's proposals. Torcy then told him that a special messenger was to be sent over with Prior together with the French answer. Prior said he would be welcome, but, as the King is going to send an answer, what was the use of such a measure? Torcy made no direct reply, but said Prior should have the answer in a day or two, and in closing the interview showed another letter from Pettkum saying now was the time for France to make a glorious peace with the Dutch as Gallas, the

[1] Torcy says "le 29ᵉ Juillet au soir." (*E.H.R.* p. 531.)
[2] *Aff. Etr. Angleterre*, vol. 233, fo. 57, and 57 *b* (*E.H.R.* p. 532).

Imperial envoy in England, had told the Pensionary all negociations between England and France had been broken off[1].

At last on August 1, N.S., Prior received the anxiously awaited answer. Even then it referred to the allies in general, and said nothing about the proposals "concerning Great Britain in particular," and when Prior pointed this out, Torcy replied that Mesnager was fully instructed on that matter. Incidentally it would appear that Torcy alluded to the discrepancy in the value laid upon Newfoundland by Marlborough at The Hague in 1709 and by the British ministers in 1711.

Have you not heard how the Duke of Marlborough asked "La Terre Neuve au nom de Dieu, faites la grace à la reine ma maîtresse de lui rendre la terre neuve," il me semble que vous la demandiez d'une toute autre manière.

Prior replied that this was

according to the Duke's way, easy and familiar, that it was true I did not ask it "au nom de Dieu pour la reine ma maîtresse, mais au nom de la reine ma maîtresse pour la grande Bretagne"; that the Duke was a great general and unacquainted with the particular ways of a treaty[2].

Two days later, on August 3, Prior was received in audience by Louis XIV. He has left us an account of it, by which we may appraise the readiness of his conversation and the quality of his French.

Monsieur Torcy having the day before delivered me the answer to the memoir, and M. Mesnager being now appointed, and empowered to go with me into England, M. Pecquet[3] came

---

[1] Portland Papers, v. 39, 40; *Aff. Etr. Angl.* vol. 233, fo. 57 *b*, 58. (*E.H.R. ut sup.* p. 532.) Torcy says nothing about the further letter from Pettkum.

[2] *Ibid.* 40, 41. Of course this reflection on Marlborough, though it may have served its purpose at the time, was quite false.

[3] Torcy's secretary.

to me in the morning and told me, the King would see me at six in the evening in his closet. Accordingly at that time M. Pecquet went privately with me through the lodgings, and Monsieur Torcy came out from the King's cabinet, and introduced me to his Majesty. The King was walking, he stood still when I came in, and as I made my obeisance to him he nodded a little, bowed to me at my third bow, and sitting, or leaning his back rather, upon a table behind him, as I came up to him, he began: "*A ça, Monsieur, Je suis bien aise de vous voir, vous parlez Français je sçay.*"

I: "*Sire, pour pouvoir exprimer la joie que je sens de revoir votre Majesté dans une santé si parfaite, je devrais mieux parler Français qu'aucun de vos sujets.*"

He: "*Eh bien, Monsieur, c'est bien honnête, vous savez la réponse que j'ai donnée à votre mémoire, et vous savez la volonté où je suis de convenir et de traiter avec l'Angleterre. J'y envoye un ministre avec vous, qui s'expliquera en mon nom sur l'affaire; vous pouvez assurer ceux qui gouvernent l'Angleterre et qui vous envoient que nous ferons tout ce que nous pouvons, moi et le Roi d'Espagne, pour les contenter. Nous voulons la Paix l'un et l'autre, J'y contribuerai de ma part tout ce qui me sera possible.*"

He having named le Roi d'Espagne; I said,

Sire, la Commission dont S. M. la Reine de la Grande Bretagne m'a honoré, le mémoire que j'ay donné à Monsieur de Torci et les discours que je lui ai tenus là dessus sont des preuves convaincantes que l'Angleterre souhaite la Paix. J'espère, Sire, que votre ministre est muni d'un pouvoir ample et plein.

He: "*Il est, Monsieur[1].*"

I: "*Sire, il trouvera l'Angleterre prête à faire tout pour la Paix, qui puisse consister avec l'honneur de la nation et la sûreté de leur commerce.*"

He: "*J'en ferai de même, sur ce fondement la Paix se fera,*

---

[1] It may not be out of place to note here that Mesnager's instructions describe Prior as "connû en France ou il a desja esté secretaire des ambassades du Comte de Portland et du Comte de Jersey, homme d'esprit, bien intentionné et persecuté par les Wichts (*Aff. Etr. Angleterre*, vol. 233, fo. 100 *b*, 101).

entre deux nations descendues du même sang, et qui ne sont ennemies que par necessité; il ne faut pas perdre du temps."

He recommended me again to Monsieur Torcy who stood at a distance while I spoke to the King, and coming up presented M. Gaultier to his Majesty, upon which I took the liberty to say in that gentleman's behalf what really his behaviour merited.

"Sire, voilà un de vos sujets à qui nous devons que la negotiation est parvenue jusques ici, il a pris beaucoup de peine et surmonté beaucoup de difficultés."

Taking my leave, I said, that I wished his Majesty long life and prosperity, and that wherever my duty called me, I should always retain a great veneration for his person, and acknowledgement of the favours I had received in France[1].

In company with Mesnager, Prior returned to England. If, as Pettkum had said in his letters to Torcy, the Dutch really did believe that negociations between England and France had been broken off, they must have been sadly undeceived when the news that a Mr Mathews, *alias* Matthew Prior, had been recognised at Deal coming from France, had been arrested by some officious people of the customs, and only released upon the express order of the ministry[2]. The secret was out now, and all the world knew that negociations were afoot. At once Swift proceeded to write a "formal grave lie[3]" purporting to be an account of Prior's journey. It was probably not written without Swift having first had

---

[1] *Hist. MSS. Comm.* Portland Papers, v. 41, 42.

[2] I can find no confirmation of the story told in Lamberty (*Mémoires pour servir à l'histoire du XVIIIe siècle*), vi. 679, to the effect that Prior was recognised by a ship's captain, who was therefore arrested by the French on his return to France and not released till after the peace, when he returned to London, recognised Prior once again in St James' Park, and thrashed him soundly. It is far more likely that Prior was recognised by J. Macky. Some stories place the recognition at Dover, others imprison Prior at Canterbury.

[3] *Journal to Stella*, Sept. 11, 1711.

a conversation on Prior's journey with St John[1], and though "a lie" it had its political object, and was no doubt, as Sir Walter Scott suggests[2], a "feeler" whether the ministry could give up Spain to Philip V. However, whatever its purpose, it annoyed Prior who showed Swift the pamphlet and angrily exclaimed "here is our English liberty[3]." Why he should have been indignant it is difficult to see, unless Swift had occasionally sailed rather near the wind of fact[4].

Prior might flatter himself that in his mission he had done good service, if not to the country, at any rate to his friends the ministers. He brought home definite news of the great desire of France for peace, and as may be seen from Torcy's note of August 3 to Bolingbroke he had not exposed any weak spots in the armour of his country[5]. What was of greater importance was the knowledge that the Dutch, if not trying to steal a march on us, were at any rate suspicious of our conduct, and that if we were to obtain those separate advantages we so much desired, we must be quick about it. No more therefore than a week after Mesnager's arrival in town, Oxford, Shrewsbury, Jersey, Dartmouth, St John and, after Jersey's death of an apoplexy on August 26, Prior, were nominated plenipotentiaries for signing the preliminaries. Prior was added

because, he having Personally Treated with Monsieur *de Torcy* is the best witness we can produce of the Sense in which the

[1] *Journal to Stella*, Aug. 27. "I have not yet talked with the Secretary about Prior's journey."

[2] *Swift's Works*, IV. 206. Introduction to "A new journey to Paris."

[3] *Journal to Stella*, Sept. 11, 1711.

[4] That it did so is clear from Mesnager's letter to Torcy, London, Aug. 21/Sept. 1, 1711, in *Aff. Etr. Angl.* vol. 233. "Le voyage de M. Prior est publié, quoyqua la verité avec des circonstances fausses."

[5] *Bolingbroke Corr.* I. 175, "J'aurois bien souhaité qu'il eût plus de liberté d'employer les talens qu'il a, et dont je suis persuadé qu'il auroit fait un bon usage."

General Preliminary Engagements are Enter'd into; besides
which, as he is the best vers'd in Matters of Trade of all Your
Majesties Servants who have been trusted in this Secret[1],

he will be extremely useful on the commercial side of
the treaty. Another reason no doubt was that Mesnager
was lodged secretly in Prior's house, so that steps had
to be taken to instruct my Lord Treasurer how to be
put down at Prior's back door[2].

But the course of the negociations, even though conducted in England, was by no means smooth. Two
documents had to be drawn up; namely the preliminaries
to be settled in the English interests in particular; and
the proposals as regards the allies in general.

Difficulties arose at once, and the plenipotentiaries
were found to be at cross purposes. The English wished
to settle their own particular interests with Louis XIV
acting not only on behalf of France, but also of Spain;
the French demanded that the English should likewise
pledge their allies. It was pointed out that constitution-
ally and diplomatically this was impossible, and when
Mesnager inquired why so, if Louis XIV was able to
bind his ally, the debate became what Mesnager called
"un colloque confus," followed by a number of conferences between Mesnager and Prior, and Mesnager
and St John, ending finally in St John telling Mesnager
roundly of the Queen's surprise at Mesnager's refusal
to discuss the terms of peace on the same ground as the
British. Mesnager replied that he was bound by his
instructions, but suggested that Gaultier should be sent

---

[1] *Report of the Committee of Secrecy*, App. p. 3, St John to the Queen,
Sept. 20, 1711. The Committee point out, p. 4, that the Warrant of
full powers is dated Sept. 17th. The explanation they give is unsatisfactory, for they were unaware that negociations had been conducted
between Mesnager and the ministers before Sept. 17, and the ante-
dating therefore was not sufficient to cover those negociations.

[2] *Hist. MSS. Comm.* ixth Rep. pt. ii. p. 463 (Morrison Collection).

over to Paris to obtain the leave of Louis XIV to post-
pone the discussion of the compensation he was to get
in return for his concessions to Britain until the Congress,
and to entrust his own interests to the good offices of
the British. Nevertheless, he added, the razing of
Dunkirk can only be conditional upon the restoration
of Lille and Tournai to Louis XIV, and this proposal,
says Mesnager, was "not rejected."

At a subsequent conference held by St John and
Prior with Mesnager, this conciliatory offer was at first
refused, as giving Louis XIV too great a tactical advantage, and Mesnager was thereupon told he had under
these circumstances better go back to France, as negociation had become useless, and the only alternative was
to continue a war disastrous to both countries, and ad-
vantageous only to the House of Austria. Mesnager
exclaimed that when they had gone so far in the cause
of peace, such an idea was preposterous, and asked for
a boat to take a despatch to Calais, whence his servant
whom he had left there could take it to Versailles. This
was agreed to, and the peace which seemed to have been
almost strangled in its cradle, obtained a short respite
pending the reply of the French King[1].

A few days later, much the same thing occurred.
Mesnager was informed that the Queen could not de-
part from the principle she had laid down for herself,
which was to treat only of the advantages Great Britain
was to obtain without entering in any way into the
demands her allies might make. He might, however,
remain in England, and a ship would be put at his
disposal to send a messenger across to France for
instructions[2]. Gaultier came again to the help of the

---

[1] *Aff. Etr. Angl.* vol. 233, ff. 208–10, Mesnager to Torcy, London,
Aug. 17/28, 1711, in cipher.

[2] *Aff. Etr. Angl.* vol. 233, fo. 214 *et seqq.* Mesnager to Torcy, London,
Aug. 21/Sept. 1, 1711.

diplomats, for after further debate, he went off to France on Sept. 9 (N.S.).

Meanwhile, among the English plenipotentiaries themselves there had not been complete harmony. On August 27, O.S., Shrewsbury wrote from Heythrop that the preliminaries concerning the allies were very unsatisfactory,

"I remember," he wrote, "to have seen, in a paper delivered in by Monsieur Mesnager some propositions so disadvantageous to the Allies, that I question whether notice should be taken of them"; and later, "Looking over the papers again, I am more of opinion there is something in them looks so like bargaining for yourselves apart and leaving your friends to shift at a general treaty, that I am confirmed the exposing such a paper (as it will be in the power of France to do) may create great jealousy and complaint from the allies[1].

The sequence of events was undoubtedly affected by this attitude of Shrewsbury's when Gaultier returned from Paris.

The French reply showed apparently that British diplomacy had won a signal victory. All the demands for Great Britain in particular were conceded: Louis merely demanded "an equivalent" for the demolished Dunkirk; as regards the allies in common the instructions to Mesnager repeated the reply Prior had brought over, with the addition of certain concessions in favour of the Empire. On October 1 the plenipotentiaries met in Prior's house. Nevertheless, difficulties still arose. The ministry made another effort to extort terms from France as regards England, while, doubtless under Shrewsbury's influence, they also made alterations in the "common propositions" in order to make them "more palateable."

In disconnected sentences St John explained that no peace could be made with a power that sheltered the

[1] *Bolingbroke Correspondence*, i. 206–7.

Pretender[1], which Mesnager skilfully parried by saying that here was no question of a peace, but only of preliminaries. Great was the relief of the ministers; and even Shrewsbury who had seemed anxious and thoughtful, expressed his satisfaction at this escape from a serious difficulty. Mesnager gave a verbal promise to sign the preliminaries, and that night, Sept. 20/Oct. 1, St John drew up the warrant of full power, and dated it Sept. 17. Trouble, however, was not yet over. On Sept. 22/Oct. 3 the Duke of Buckingham, Lord President, Earl Powlett, Lord Steward, and Dr Robinson, Bishop of Bristol and Lord Privy Seal, were apprised of the negociations and informed that they were plenipotentiaries[2], and on Sept. 23/Oct. 4 it was found that there was not complete agreement between English and French about Newfoundland, and the rights of fishing. The consideration of the subject was postponed to the Congress, but the French were given the right to dry their cod. Thus almost thoughtlessly, and under the fear of losing the advantage that would come to them from a peace, did the ministers leave open a sore that has never yet been completely healed. All now seemed ready for the signature of the preliminaries, but on the evening of Sept. 25/Oct. 6 Prior saw Mesnager and suggested a number of further alterations, in the "common" proposals. No mention was to be made of the will of Charles II, all powers which took part in the war must receive satisfaction[3]; the trade of England, Holland and other nations must be secured[4]. As regards the Empire, instead of the barrier being allowed, it was to be made; the article about Savoy was to be relegated

[1] By virtue of a resolution of the House of Lords.

[2] Their names are in the warrant of Sept. 17, 1711. See *Report of Committee of Secrecy*, Appendix, pp. 7, 8.

[3] The original proposal was "reasonable satisfaction."

[4] In the original proposal no nations were mentioned, but "those who had formerly carried on trade."

into a separate and secret document; and doubtless to throw dust into the eyes of the allies and remove any suspicion of a secret treaty with England, Louis in this treaty also was to recognise the Queen and the Protestant succession, and promise to raze Dunkirk.

This attempt to squeeze additional concessions from Mesnager can easily be accounted for. Buys was coming over from Holland, Shrewsbury's warning of August had gone home to his colleagues, and in view of the Dutchman's arrival, they wished to make the common articles more "palateable" abroad. At the same time Buys' promised advent would put pressure on Mesnager to sign before untoward arrival of an envoy from the allies. Mesnager was indeed appalled at this cataract of demands, but he was told the situation did not admit of a moment's delay: if Buys arrived, France would not have her peace. He therefore resigned himself to fate, considered that no vital point was affected by these alterations, took upon himself the responsibility of breaking the letter of his instructions, and the next day, Sept. 27/Oct. 8, signed the three documents, viz. the secret treaty with England, the general treaty for the allies, and the secret article about Savoy. On the English side the preliminaries were signed only by Dartmouth and St John, in virtue of a warrant dated Sept. 25/Oct. 6[1].

[1] *The Report of the Committee of Secrecy* (p. 5) makes great insinuations about this narrowing down of the plenipotentiaries to the two secretaries of state. "What is more strange is, that after Mr *St John* had represented it to the Queen, as the unanimous Opinion of her Ministers, that full Powers must immediately pass the Great Seal to Authorize them to meet and treat with the said Mons. *Mesnager*, these Powers should be laid aside. And the Acceptation of the Preliminaries sign'd by Lord *Dartmouth* and Mr *St John*, by Vertue of a Warrant directed to them two only, sign'd by the Queen at top and bottom, and countersign'd by no Body." It is clear from *Bolingbroke Corr.* I. 230 (St John to the Queen, Whitehall, Sept. 24, 1711) that the signature of one Secretary

Thus was "Mat's peace" consummated; France and Great Britain had settled their dispute, Great Britain's terms were secured, while those of the allies in general were left to be debated in the uncertain wranglings of a general Congress.

of State was all that was necessary. M. Mesnager "barely desires, that at the foot of the paper which he signs, a secretary of state may write, by your Majesty's command, some acceptance of these articles, and some promise to set the general treaty on foot." This may perhaps explain why the more cumbrous method of obtaining the signatures of nine persons was discarded; but disagreement among the ministers was, as we have seen, only too probable, and must be borne in mind.

Chapter IX

PARIS ONCE MORE

AFTER such services as he had rendered, Prior was entitled to signal reward, and he was told that he was to be one of the ambassadors for signing the general peace. He expressed a momentary doubt whether he should have this fortune, on the ground that the preliminaries had not been signed, in the form of a convention, by the Great Officers of State, and by himself. "I should then," he said to Mesnager, "have necessarily been made Plenipotentiary at the general conferences." But now it seemed as though a good Whig like Lord Pembroke would obtain the place. The anxiety seemed to be vain when St John told Mesnager that Prior was to be the third plenipotentiary[1]. The matter came to Swift's ears on November 8. On November 20, he wrote to Stella,

I hear Prior's commission is passed to be ambassador extraordinary and plenipotentiary for the peace; my lord privy seal, who you know is Bishop of Bristol, is the other, and Lord Strafford, already ambassador at the Hague, the third....Prior puns very well. Odso, I must go see his excellency; 'tis a noble advancement; but they could do no less, after sending him to France. Lord Strafford is as proud as Hell[2], and how he will bear one of Prior's mean birth on an equal character with him, I know not.

[1] *Aff. Etr. Angl.* vol. 234, fo. 74, Mesnager to Torcy, London, 30 Sept./ 11 Oct. 1711.

[2] "My lord Strafford qui n'a pas beaucoup d'esprit est fier vain fanfaron et indiscret, il se pique d'etre homme de qualité" (Gaultier to French plenipotentiaries [London, Jan. 1712], *Aff. Etr. Angl.* vol. 237, fo. 42).

Swift's doubts were justified: on December 1st, he wrote: "I fear Prior will not be one of the plenipotentiaries," and in fact, he was not. Strafford flatly refused to have Prior as his colleague, and the ministry could not but submit. They tried to console him by making him first commissioner of customs and the French were told he was indispensable to Oxford[1]; but it must have been a serious blow, not only to his personal ambitions, but also to his financial anticipations, for we learn from a note of Gaultier to Torcy, that he had been promised an annual pension from Louis XIV of £500 sterling as soon as he was nominated plenipotentiary. Prior latterly indeed may have been raising his price, for Gaultier recommended that to make sure of Prior, it would be well to raise his pension to £705. 2s.[2] The winter cannot have brought much joy into Prior's life. He was a commissioner for customs, an office he disliked, as we have seen, and at the beginning of March he suffered some further financial loss through the failure of Stratford the stockbroker. That all this should have made a man of his valetudinarian temperament ill is not surprising, and Swift, in noting the fact, adds: "I thought he looked melancholy. He can ill afford to lose money[3]." No doubt he felt disappointed that nothing had yet been done for him commensurate with his services, and we find him and Swift and Freind sitting "reforming the state and finding fault with the ministry[4]." July, 1712, however, found him in an occupation more congenial than his commissionership of customs, which, however, he did not relinquish. This was a fresh journey to France.

[1] *Aff. Etr. Angl.* vol. 237, fo. 29b, Gaultier to Torcy, London, Jan. 27, N.S. 1712.

[2] *Ibid.* vol. 234, fo. 82, Gaultier to Torcy Oct. 14, 17,11.

[3] *Journal to Stella*, Mar. 6, 1711/12.

[4] *Ibid.* Mar. 13, 1711/12.

Since the signature of "Mat's Peace" events had
been moving on the old double lines of secret and public
negociations. Early in October, Strafford had been sent
to Holland, and Buys on his arrival in England had done
what he could by means of noise to shake the resolution
of the Queen and her ministers, but all in vain. The
States-General indeed refused to enter into the Conferences, but the Queen would not be shaken out of the
proposal. Finally to put an end to this Dutch clamour,
Gaultier made one more journey to Paris in November
and had brought back a memorandum from Torcy,
dated November 7/18, 1711, a masterpiece of diplomatic debate, offering a variety of alternatives for the
various allied powers. At the end of the year matters
had so far advanced that a Congress was generally
agreed upon by all parties, the plenipotentiaries had
been named, and in spite of the Dutch preference for
The Hague, Utrecht, to please Louis XIV, was insisted
upon by the British as the place of meeting. More
momentous were the domestic events of the end of the
year. Marlborough, who at the beginning of August
(N.S.) had performed the most brilliant tactical feat of
his whole career in piercing Villars' lines at Bouchain,
returned to England and resolutely opposed any
attempts at making peace. Nottingham, too, who passed
for being a Tory, very coldly received Oxford's intimation that a peace was being negociated[1], and when
Parliament met, he moved, on December 5th, that no
peace "would be safe and honourable if any part of the
Spain or the West Indies should be allotted to any
branch of the House of Bourbon," and carried it against
the ministry by one vote in the House of Lords[2]. Then

---

[1] Portland Papers, v. 101, Nottingham to Oxford, Burley, Oct. 15,
1711.

[2] It is unnecessary perhaps to remind the reader that the same day a
similar motion was lost in the House of Commons by 232 votes to 106.

came a pause, during which politicians wondered what would happen, and at last, at the very end of December, came the famous *Gazette* declaring the creation of twelve new peers, and the dismissal of the Duke of Marlborough from all his employments[1].

The government were now more secure, having the support of both houses, and if the crowds that followed the Bishop of Bristol on his departure for Holland are any test of feeling in the country, their policy of peace had become popular. But it was one thing to make a congress meet, it was another to make it transact business. Prior's experience at Ryswick had clearly demonstrated the difficulty, and what happened at the earlier congress, happened again at Utrecht. The powers of obstruction possessed by the discontented Dutch and Imperialists were used to the full, and even the British plenipotentiaries, who were not yet in the secret of the British ministry, added to the delay, for in the early conferences they combated vigorously any terms less than those offered at Gertruydenberg[2]. On February 9th, the meeting was entirely occupied by the question of the precedence of Count Zinzendorf, the Imperial ambassador. Finally his rights were recognised and his

[1] The French Government were informed of the intention of the British in this respect. See a note in *Aff. Etr. Angl.* vol. 248, fo. 1, received early in January, 1713, as follows: "Dechiffrez vous même. Nous vous prions avec instances de donner a vos plenipotentiaires des pouvoirs fort amples et estendus affin que la paix puisse être faite a la fin de Mars ou au commencement d'Avril parceque nous auons resolu de faire rendre compte au Duc de Mg de ses malversations de le depouiller de tous ses employs et luy faire couper la teste auant la fin de cette seance ou tout au plus tard de l'Année. Gardez je vous prie le secret." The note is not from Gaultier and was deciphered by Torcy himself.

[2] This was anticipated by Gaultier, who, in January 1712, wrote to the French plenipotentiaries a dispatch, now of considerable interest, warning them that this would be the attitude of the British ambassadors, and that they were not to be alarmed thereat. (*Aff. Etr. Angl.* vol. 237, fo. 44.)

vanity perhaps satisfied by placing him in a chair which was distinguished from the rest by being opposite a mirror. On the 5th March, the embassies handed in their replies to the French proposals, which, presented on Feb. 11th, were a summary of the memorandum of November 18th. "Now," said the angry Heinsius, "we can see what is the use of negociating with France without preliminaries." As for the Emperor, he was so far ignorant of the true state of affairs that he did not consider it ridiculous to demand the whole Spanish monarchy for himself, and the restoration of all that France had gained since 1648. The other powers, Holland and England, demanded, the one a barrier, Upper Gelderland, the razing of Dunkirk without compensation, the old tariff of 1664 and other small points; the other, the complete destruction of Dunkirk, the recognition of the Electorate of Hanover, a clearer recognition of the Protestant succession, and, receding from its demand of October 6th previous, it asked for "just and reasonable satisfaction for the Allies." On the 9th, the French asked for three weeks to hand in their reply to these various demands. At the end of the month, in accordance with the arrangement, the French gave their answer, but refused to put it in writing. This the Allies would not accept, and the debates which followed kept the Congress inactive. Meantime the dissensions between the English and the Dutch became ever greater, and although the English offered to surrender the advantages of a 15 per cent. rebate on English goods in France promised by the draft treaty, and also to settle the Spanish and West Indies trade to the state they were in at the time of King Charles of Spain[1], the Dutch would not rise to the appeals of the English

[1] *Bol. Corr.* 1. 440, St John to Torcy, Whitehall, March 24, O.S. 1711/12. *Ibid.* 1. 458, St John to the Lords Plenipotentiaries, Whitehall, April 8, O.S. 1712.

ministers to come into line with the Queen. Finally in April, the English ministers decided to take their own measures; "if the Queen's goodness does not meet with a suitable return" from the Dutch, "she will think herself tied by no obligation to them and they must stand as well as they can by themselves[1]." That the English could take up this position was due to startling events in France.

On Feb. 22nd, N.S., there fell upon the French Royal family the first of a series of crushing blows, which materially altered the position of European affairs. On that day the Duchess of Burgundy died of the small-pox, on the 28th her husband died of the same disease, on March 8th their eldest son, the Duke of Brittany, followed them to the grave, leaving of their issue only Louis, aged two. This feeble life was the only barrier between Philip of Spain and the French crown, and whereas at the beginning of the year the chances that Philip would succeed to the throne of France were negligible, he was now within measurable distance of it, and the dreaded union of the two crowns might, after all, become an accomplished fact. Under these circum-stances, it was imperative that Philip should renounce the one or the other. The English ministers demanded that Philip should renounce his succession to the throne of France, but Torcy pointed out in a strange memo-randum, dated March 23rd, that any renunciation by the heir of France to the throne was *ipso facto* null and void, as the King of France succeeded in virtue of the law, which God alone can repeal[2].

There were therefore two great problems to be resolved. How were the French to be made to agree to the renunciation, and how were the Allies to be made to agree to a peace? The differences between the English

---

[1] *Bol. Corr.* I. 491, St John to Drummond, Whitehall, May 2/13, 1712.
[2] *Ibid.* pp. 435–7, memorandum of March 23rd, 1712.

and the Dutch prevented the Allies from coercing the French and the problem of the renunciation seemed to prevent any effective understanding between the English and the French. If, however, these two powers could agree upon the question of the renunciation, it would be possible for negociations to proceed. Fortunately for the English ministers, Torcy on April 8th receded from the extreme position he had taken up earlier, and the French took a long step forward when it was proposed that Philip should be told he could not have both crowns, and therefore must make his choice, when he became heir to the French crown[1]. The only difference now was a matter of detail. St John insisted that the choice must be made at once, Torcy desired it should be postponed, but eventually came round to St John's opinion[2]. There was now no reason why the alternative should not be submitted to Philip. Either he must renounce his claim to France, or he must at once give up Spain. In the latter case, he would exchange dominions with the King of Sicily, Duke of Savoy, and await a possible succession to the throne of France. On May 13th Torcy wrote to St John that all difficulties on this score between France and England were at an end, and that the alternatives had been despatched to Madrid. On May 9/20, this great news reached St John, and as the union of the two crowns was now impossible, the English ministers had no longer to dread a breach with France. Action was at once taken by them to punish the allies for their obstinacy. On May 10/21 the famous "restraining orders" were issued to the Duke of Ormonde.

It is therefore the Queen's positive command to your Grace, that you avoid engaging in any siege, or hazarding a battle, till

[1] *Bol. Corr.* I. 449, Torcy to St John, Marly, April 8th, N.S. 1712.
[2] *Ibid.* 468–71, Torcy to St John, Marly, April 26th, N.S. 1712.

you have further orders from Her Majesty. I am, at the same time, directed to let Your Grace know, that the Queen would have you disguise the receipt of this order....P.S. I had almost forgot to tell Your Grace, that communication is given of this order to the Court of France, so that if the Mareschal de Villars takes, in any private way, notice of it to you, Your Grace will answer accordingly.

The sequel is well known. Ormonde refused to join Eugene in an attack upon the French, or even to cover a besieging army, and the ministers continued their work by negociating for an armistice proposed by Queen Anne on Louis XIV's suggestion. Then came the news that Philip preferred a bird in the hand to two in the bush, and announced that he would remain King of Spain, and rejected the offer of becoming King of Sicily and Savoy pending his succession to the crown of France. At last on June 22nd, the armistice was agreed to by the French. It was to last two months with power of prolongation to four. Philip was to renounce the French throne, and the Dukes of Berri and Orleans their succession to the Spanish crown; the French garrison was to evacuate Dunkirk and the British troops were to hold the town and citadel until the States-General consented to give the French an equivalent for the demolition of the fortifications. In this case, the fortifications were to be razed. On June 11/22, strong with a majority of 28 in the Lords and 130 in the Commons[1], the ministry commanded Ormonde to carry out the terms of the armistice; and amid the hisses of the allied troops, and to the shame of his own men, Ormonde led off what troops would follow him to Dunkirk and Ghent. He could only control the British-born troops: the foreign troops in British pay clung to the allies, but how serious was the defection came to light when Villars on July

[1] On May 28th/June 8th, *Bol. Corr.* i. 515, St John to Ormonde, Whitehall, May 28th, O.S. 1712.

24th, N.S., defeated the allied troops at Denain, and won
for the French arms the first substantial victory outside
Spain since the beginning of the war.

Yet the armistice could not be proclaimed, for
Louis XIV, after having given up Dunkirk (occupied
on July 19th), raised difficulties about the Duke of
Savoy's barrier, and demanded that the Elector of
Bavaria should be put in possession of the Low
Countries: the latter an impossible request, seeing that
the only towns he held were Luxemburg, Charleroi,
Namur and Nieuport. The British held Ghent and
Bruges, and could of course cede them, but the rest of
the Low Countries were in the hands of the Dutch,
who certainly would not now give up their conquests to
please the English. Other difficulties also arose, but
such was the desire of Queen Anne for peace, that she
decided to send St John, or as he now had been
created, Viscount Bolingbroke, on a mission to France.
He took Prior as his secretary; and accompanied by
Gaultier, they arrived at Paris on August 17th, N.S.,
where they lodged with Prior's old friend, Madame
Colbert de Croissi. Here Torcy met Bolingbroke, and
discussed the four great points of difference; the barrier
of Savoy, the future of the Elector of Bavaria, the renunciation, and the retreat of the Old Chevalier. On all
these points an agreement was arrived at, even in the
case of the Elector of Bavaria, where the agreement was
merely that discussion should be postponed; and in two
days it was possible to sign the treaty of armistice. This
was done on August 19th, though the instrument was
dated August 18th, and on the 22nd the negotiators
moved to Fontainebleau, whence Bolingbroke was able
to announce to Dartmouth the signature of the armistice. Thereupon Bolingbroke returned alone, by way of
Dunkirk, to England.

Prior therefore was left alone in France; having

parted from Bolingbroke "with more pangs than is proper or possible to tell[1]." He stayed at Paris "till I may have something to do at Court[2];" and he spent his time suffering at first from a severe fit of colic, and, as he recovered, in looking for lodgings and taking stock of his colleagues of the diplomatic circle, and the fruit of these observations has fortunately come down to us. The Duc d'Aumont, who was to go to England is described as

a Man of very great Quality and Estate, of the King's bed-chamber, Gouverneur of the Bolonnois, and in favour, a man hearty and honest, a bon vivant but not debauched, knowing a good many things without being thoroughly a scholar: He has been in England; loves us very well, has never been of those who had their habitudes at St Germains, and expresses a perfect respect to the Queen: so that I think we are so far obliged to his most Christian Majesty that we having had the choice could not have fixed it better; He is at Paris preparing for his Ambassy w[ch] he intends to be *fort en Cavalier mais fort magnifique*[3].

Later on, Bolingbroke was to find this estimate highly erroneous; for never was there more *difficile* a diplomat than the Duc d'Aumont, and his departure from England was a positive relief. As for the other ambassadors in Paris:

the D: d'Ossune is a person whom no mortal man can under-stand or describe: He has a jargon that never will be French, nor ever was Spanish: He is to go to Utrecht to make the peace there as soon as he is sure it is made here: His Confrère the Marq: de Monteleon is by birth a Milanois, he has seen a good deal, and is pretty well versed in the present state of affairs; they have both visited me and beg most heartily that Sicily may remain still to their Monarchy: I dare not write explicitly of

[1] *Bol.Corr.* II. 31, Prior to Bolingbroke, Paris, August 24th/Sept 4th, 1712.
[2] *Letters...at Welbeck*, App. VI. p. 267, Prior to Oxford, Paris, Sept. 5th, N.S. 1712.   [3] *Ibid.*

this and other things wch Monteleon mentioned, and things
d'Ossune meant: not having a Cypher, and fearing lest this
letter may be opened: but will do it when I write directly to
England[1].

Elsewhere he says that Monteleon, having been nominated for England, "will suit better with the Genius of
our nation...than the Punto and Gravidad of a natural
Castilian would have allowed[2]." But Prior was soon
called away to Fontainebleau by serious business. The
ratifications of the armistice arrived on September 4th,
and he immediately set out. Although Bolingbroke had
settled some of the most important questions, Prior had
some delicate matters to handle. His position in 1712
is certainly a great contrast to that which he held
thirteen years earlier; no longer the idle busybody
secretary, he had now to transmit to the French Court,
in word and in writing, the intentions of the British
Government on the most important affairs. This was no
light task for him. He had as yet no secretary, for his
faithful servant Adrian Drift was detained in England,
and so he could not have his letters copied, while his
position was unsatisfactory as he had no diplomatic
character[3]. Comparatively trivial matters occupied him
at first, such as the difference in meaning between *les
mers qui entourent les îles britanniques* and *les mers
britanniques*; the issue of passports to enable commerce

---

[1] *Letters...at Welbeck*, App. vi. pp. 267–8, Prior to Oxford, Paris,
Sept. 5th, N.S. 1712.

[2] P.R.O. France, 154, Prior to Dartmouth, Paris, Oct. 9/Sept. 28,
1712.

[3] *Bol. Corr.* ii. 36, Prior to Bolingbroke, Fontainebleau, Sept. 12th, 1712.
"Pray help me, and despatch your orders, the papers, and Drift; I think
my case is this: I have neither powers, commission, title, instructions,
appointments, or Secretary." He received his powers before Oct. 6/17.
(See P.R.O. France, 154, fo. 180, Prior to Dartmouth; see also *Aff. Etr.
Angl.* vol. 242, fo. 115, where a paper dated Oct. 15 states that Prior
has received his credentials.)

to be renewed between France and England. Such questions as these were not subjects of anxiety. Nevertheless, one misunderstanding did come near to jeopardising the peace, and but for Torcy's tactful reticence, might have caused endless difficulties. It concerned the manner in which Lord Lexington was to behave when he went to Madrid to receive the renunciation. Dartmouth wrote to Prior that Lexington "*will acknowledge him (Philip) King of Spain and the Indies, with an et cetera, which I suppose, are all the titles he either values or desires*[1]." As Prior pointed out to Dartmouth, "the Renunciation wch Philip makes is to France, and as King of Spain, in wch quality he must be supposed invested or the renunciation itself is not good[2]." The blundering suggestion of any "recognition" of Philip as King of Spain created the utmost consternation. Torcy "seemed struck with thunder when I began to discourse wth him about it[3]." The gloomy forebodings that "we are all at sea again[4]" were not, however realised: in oblique reproof Bolingbroke wrote at once:

I was equally surprised and vexed to find that by the uncouth way of explaining the Queen's sense, you had been led to imagine, that it was intended my Lord Lexington should make any difficulty of seeing and complimenting the King of Spain, as such....For God's sake, dear Matt, hide the nakedness of thy country, and give the best turn thy fertile brain will furnish thee with, to the blunders of thy countrymen, who are not much better politicians than the French are poets[5].

The alarm subsided therefore, and Torcy with great

[1] *Bol. Corr.* II. 35, Prior to Bolingbroke, Fontainebleau, Sept. 12th, 1712.
[2] P.R.O. France, 154, Prior to Dartmouth, Fontainebleau, Sept. 1/12, 1712. See also *Aff. Etr. Angl.* vol. 242, fo. 646, where the matter is put differently, but is essentially the same.
[3] *Letters...at Welbeck*, App. VI. p. 272, Prior to Oxford, Fontainebleau, Sept. 1/12, 1712.
[4] *Ibid. ut sup.*
[5] *Bol. Corr.* II. 38, Bolingbroke to Prior, Whitehall, Sept. 10/21, 1712.

prudence never mentioned a word of the temporary difficulty to his friends in Spain[1].

In the matter of Tournay, Prior certainly acted with decision and success. Both the Dutch and Louis insisted upon having the place, but by the beginning of October Prior had heard that "the Dutch...would come into signing the peace, provided Tournay was assured to them." Prior therefore pressed this point vigorously upon Torcy, raising at once considerations of justice to the Dutch, the strength of the Whigs, the promises made by Louis XIV the previous April and the danger of the situation should France prove obdurate for "La paix depend presentement du seul point de Tournay." Torcy professed himself unconvinced, but he did not take up such a *non possumus* attitude on October 26th as he did five days earlier and on November 2nd Louis gave up Tournay[2].

But before this happy consummation had been reached in the great questions of Spain and the Barrier, Prior had once more crossed the Channel. According to Bolingbroke, Louis XIV laid as much importance on the fate of the Elector of Bavaria as on anything else, and he was anxious that some fitting compensation should be given to one who had sacrificed so much on behalf of the house of Bourbon. It had been suggested that he should receive the island of Sardinia as compensation for the loss of his hereditary estates, but in this matter not even Bolingbroke and Torcy had been able to come to an agreement, still less likely was it therefore that Prior, a mere subordinate, could effect an understanding. Consequently, on the same day on which he had first held out hopes that Louis might give way on the subject of Tournay[3], Torcy wrote to Bolingbroke:

[1] *Bol. Corr.* II. 51, Torcy to Bolingbroke, Versailles, Sept. 27, 1712.
[2] *Aff. Etr. Angl.* vol. 240, fo. 56 *et seqq.*
[3] *Bol. Corr.* II. 99, Torcy to Bolingbroke, Versailles, October 26th.

Quoique Matthieu soit l'homme du monde le plus insupportable, je crois, my Lord, qu'il a assez de probité pour travailler de bonne foi, et tout de son mieux à finir notre ouvrage. Nous sommes donc convenus qu'il partiroit pour vous trouver.... Finissez donc, my Lord, comme il dépend de vous de le faire, et renvoyez au plutôt Matthieu, afin que j'aie le plaisir de le faire pendre, comme il s'y est engagé, si la paix n'est pas conclue moyennant la cession de Tournay.

The fact was that the British ministry were bound to be firm on the subject, because although both Bavaria and Sardinia were far removed from England, the Elector, as titular governor of the Spanish Netherlands, was a person of consequence. Prior therefore left for England, and took over a letter from Louis XIV to Queen Anne, expressly recommending the Elector to the favour of the Queen.

On October 25th/November 5th he arrived in England once more, and the stocks rose upon his return[1]; for it was held to be a good augury as to the progress of the peace. Torcy evidently expected he would rapidly return; but unexpected events occurred which prevented his going back till late in the autumn. Even before Prior's home-coming the Duke of Hamilton had been nominated ambassador to the Court of France, but on November 15th, he was killed in a notorious duel with Lord Mohun, and Shrewsbury was appointed in his place. The delay thus caused kept Prior in England, and he took the opportunity of visiting his old College. When Prior went to pay his respects to the Master, the Head of the House did not consider it consistent with his dignity to offer a seat to a Fellow of the College, and kept the Queen's minister in Paris standing during the whole of the interview. Prior wrote an epigram which showed that punctilious sensitiveness to points of

[1] *Journal to Stella*, Oct. 28, 1712.

etiquette inculcated in the diplomatic service had got
the better of his sense of humour:

> I stood, Sir, patient at your feet,
> 　Before your elbow-chair;
> But make a bishop's throne your seat,
> 　I'll KNEEL before you there.

> One only thing can keep you down,
> 　For your great soul too mean;
> You'd not, to mount a bishop's throne,
> 　Pay HOMAGE to the Queen[1].

By the time Prior returned to France, much water had
flowed under London Bridge. Not only had the Tournay
matter been settled, but it had been decided to renew
the hitherto abortive conferences of Utrecht. As for the
Elector of Bavaria, Great Britain and France had decided
that he was to remain governor of the Netherlands,
where the towns were to be garrisoned by Dutch troops.
This, however, did not quite satisfy the French, who
demanded some guarantee that the Elector would be
put into possession of these lands and not turned out
by the Dutch. Such was the situation in the European
problem when Matthew returned to Paris, being received at Calais with much pomp and ceremony[2].

Prior's visit to England was meant to be very short,
and Bolingbroke replying to Torcy's letter brought by
Prior, wrote on November 11/22 that "Matthieu doit
partir à la fin de cette semaine" and excused himself
from the trouble of a long despatch because

j'aurai l'honneur de vous écrire en deux jours d'ici par son
Excellence Matthieu. Je crois que vous le trouverez instruit à
finir toutes choses, et que, malgré sa phisionomie, qui n'est pas
des plus heureuses, il ne sera pas pendu pour le coup[3].

---

[1] *Dialogues of the Dead*, p. 171.
[2] See his own account in App. D.
[3] *Bol. Corr.* II. 104, Bolingbroke to Torcy, Whitehall, Nov. 11/22, 1712.

But as we have seen he was delayed, and he lost more time, when he reached France, for he went

about four leagues out of my way to meet the Duke d'Aumont, who was then on his way to England; I thought my so doing showed respect to a man of his quality, and I hope the conversation I had with him may set him right, as to some company that may probably offer themselves to him upon his arrival at London[1].

Thus it was December 7/18 before Prior reached Paris. Though he was still in a subordinate post, for Shrewsbury as ambassador would completely overshadow him, for four weeks Prior was the only representative of Great Britain in Paris. On December 16/27 he was received in audience by the King, after which he and Torcy went through the remaining points of difference between the courts, and the result of this conversation he sent to Bolingbroke in an immense despatch dated Versailles and Paris, Dec. 28th and 29th[2]. Ten days later, another enormous packet[3] was sent by "Matt" to "Henry" full of discussions about St Pierre, Cape Breton and the fishing rights, and so full of business were Prior's letters, that Bolingbroke wrote to Hanmer at the beginning of the year praying for

some account of Mat's private life. Once I was in the gentleman's secret; but his last despatch contains, in almost a ream of paper, nothing but solemn accounts of business, such as made me expect to find Jo. Werden instead of Mat. Prior, at the bottom of the voluminous epistle. We hear much of a certain eloped nun, who has supplanted the nut-brown maid[4].

---

[1] *Bol. Corr.* II. 141, Prior to Bolingbroke, Versailles, Dec. 17/28, 1712.

[2] *Ibid.* 141–57.

[3] *Ibid.* 159–66, Prior to Bolingbroke, Paris, January, 8th, N.S. 1713.

[4] *Ibid.* 169. The "nut-brown maid" of course is an allusion to Prior's famous poem, which was addressed to Chloe. But who the persons alluded to in this bit of scandal are, I am unable to determine. The eloped nun may have been Madame de Tencin.

But though he bored Bolingbroke, the dissolute
minister was doing his work well. Torcy wrote to
Bolingbroke on December 29th:

Vous nous avez renvoyé, my Lord, sous l'extérieur de Mathieu,
le véritable fils de Monsieur Buys; il ne lui manque que de rem-
plir le verre de son père. Il est d'ailleurs aussi Hollandais, et je
crois beaucoup plus opiniâtre. Il a fallu céder et se conformer
presques à tout ce qu'il a voulu; encore n'était-il pas content;
j'espère cependant que vous le serez, et que toutes les difficultés
qui arrêtent encore la signature du traité vont être levées; mais
je vous avoue, que je m'attends à des reproches terribles de la
part des Plénipotentiaires du Roi, qui disputaient fortement
avec les vôtres sur des articles que Mathieu a obtenus sans
beaucoup de peine, et peut-être avec moins de raison[1].

This of course was diplomatic exaggeration, but matters
in this wearisome and complicated colonial question had
undoubtedly advanced towards a solution during Prior's
residence. Shrewsbury's arrival, however, brought stiffer
demands yet from England.

Your friend Torcy is in the last concern to find the Duke's
instruction so strict in a point which cannot be given up by
France, at a time when we well hoped that difference was
adjusted[2]; pray, my Lord, let us have your distinct and positive
orders hereupon by the first, as likewise, if it be possible for us
to settle our commerce in general with France upon the foot of
the tariff of 1664 mutually, or seek some new epoch of time,
for at present it lies pretty chimerical[3].

Prior, however, was able secretly to suggest a way out
of both these difficulties.

I have heard no more from the Congress of Utrecht than if
it were the Council of Jerusalem;...if you agree with the pro-

---

[1] *Bol. Corr.* II. 167, Torcy to Bolingbroke, Versailles, Dec. 29th, N.S. 1712.

[2] The question of allowing the French to have fishing rights off Newfoundland or only off Cape Breton.

[3] *Letters...at Welbeck*, App. VI. p. 282, Prior to Oxford, Paris, Jan. 8/19,
1712/3.

posal of Newfoundland, which is the same you and I (*N.B.* this is Matt and Harry) laid down; and if we can take 1664 for our plan, in order to reduce the traffic to that era, the peace is made; otherwise I see no shore; not but that I am ready to swim as long as you please *in alto mari* or *super altum mare*, for that you remember was a point of grammar long discussed; as are some other points, *arrogavit*, or *assumpsit*, etc.[1]

In other words, we were to give the French what they asked with regard to Newfoundland, for it was what they had originally been offered by Bolingbroke and Prior themselves. Eventually this was agreed to, though not without some strong observations on Bolingbroke's part as to the conduct of the French ministry[2]. On February 7th, Shrewsbury and Prior had the satisfaction of announcing to the ministers at home that the treaties between England and France were ready for signature.

This Express comes to tell your Lordship that the article of commerce as sent in Latin by Lord Bolingbroke is agreed, the Article of Newfoundland received, and the Isle of Sablé yielded to us, as our boundary on the side of Cape Breton; so that I congratulate your Lordship for that. All we had to do with France is adjusted, and the Queen at liberty to sign her own peace and mediate that of her allies as Her Majesty may judge proper[3].

This arrangement seems to have been very largely the work of Prior himself. In December, as we have seen, he went over the ground with Torcy, but from anxiety to deal fairly with the French he gave them a loophole for "chicanery" of which they were not slow

---

[1] *Bol. Corr.* II. 184, Matt to Henry, Paris, January 12/23, 1712/3.

[2] See *Bol. Corr.* II. 191, Bolingbroke to Shrewsbury, Whitehall, Jan. 19/30, 1712/3. "The Queen looks on this proceeding to be a direct violation of faith"; and cf. P.R.O. Treaty Papers, 90, Bolingbroke to Prior, Jan. 22/Feb. 2, 1712/3. "Make the French ashamed of their sneaking chicane, by heaven they treat like pedlars, or which is worse, like attorneys."

[3] *Letters...at Welbeck*, App. VI. p. 285, Prior to Oxford, Versailles, Feb. 7, N.S. 1713.

to take advantage. However, he repaired this mistake by the suggestions contained in his letter to Bolingbroke of January 8/19 which formed the basis of ultimate agreement. Prior's own account of the matter is as follows:

The article of commerce as agreed here, and returned for the approbation of what my Lord Duke declared upon it, has made all discourse upon that subject useless; however, in answer to yours of the 24th, I cannot but observe, that what is expressed in my memorial of the 7th of January, which they call *remise par le Sieur Prior*, was received from Monsieur de Torcy, and sent, not as conclusive, but as to be redressed, in order to be agreed, or as wholly to be rejected....Now again, I must own that, in civil and general terms, I thought I was to make them as easy as I could consent to the *amicissima gens*, to which you see they have given another colour and turn, having endeavoured, as you see, to embroil and entangle this business, both at Utrecht and London, while they let it sleep without saying one word of it here; nay, not even when, or since, they received the Latin article, which, I thank God! has not received an iota of alteration: but sure, if they had understood I was concerting with them so widely from what that article announces, they would have said so, not only to me, but to the Duke of Shrewsbury; and their silence upon that head is a fairer argument than any I can frame by troubling you longer upon it. I will therefore leave it, when I have confessed the expression is such as is capable to be wrested, if disjoined, from the whole tenour of the negotiation; but the offering to wrest it, and sending it to Utrecht as a thing done, was by no means fair or generous.

Upon another occasion, I have something of the like nature: it has been urged at London that the cession of Tournay was only made reciprocally, the Queen being obliged to procure for the Elector of Bavaria the proprietary possession of the four places to which he pretended, or to get him Limburg instead of Luxemburg; whereas, the memorial with which I charged myself, when I waited on you in England, has a clause in it that particularly specifies her Majesty to be under no obligation, but that of her own generosity; and the matter of Limburg was not so much as proposed to me, nor had I heard of it, otherwise than in the general plan of peace, proposed to be separated from the Pays-Bas and given to the Elector Palatine, as an equivalent for the Upper Palatinate. *Mem. by Gaultier, in Nov.* 1711.

I have troubled you, my dear Lord, too long; I shall be constantly on my guard, and more so than I have been with these people, being very glad that we have finished with them, as to our own affairs, and impatient to hear what her Majesty says to her Parliament on that head[1].

Torcy, in congratulating Bolingbroke on the completion of the negociations, says he is satisfied, "quoiqu'il ait fallu céder à la véhémence de Matthieu[2]," and the "great confidence and prevention[3]" which the Duke of Shrewsbury showed towards Prior, who always assisted at the writing of His Grace's despatches[4] showed that Prior was by no means a cipher during these important weeks. Shrewsbury certainly bore generous witness to Prior's efficiency. "Mr Prior has been in the last degree useful to me, and serviceable to Her Majesty in all this negociation. I wish you would write and encourage him[5]." Indeed, without detracting from Shrewsbury's undoubted ability, we may say that Prior's assistance was indispensable, for he alone, beside Bolingbroke, knew what had passed between the French and English courts during the last six months.

After some slight questions of detail had been raised, peace was at length signed by the Plenipotentiaries at Utrecht on March 31/April 11. The moment the news came that the peace was signed, Shrewsbury and Prior went to Court to congratulate Louis XIV, and "our

---

[1] *Bol. Corr.* II. 239, Prior to Bolingbroke, Paris, Feb. 13, N.S. 1713.
[2] *Ibid.* 273, Torcy to Bolingbroke, Versailles, Feb. 7, N.S. 1713.
[3] *Ibid.* 184, Prior to Bolingbroke, Paris, January 23rd, N.S. 1713.
[4] *Ibid.* 242, Prior to Bolingbroke, Paris, February 16th, N.S. 1713.
[5] *Ibid.* 291, Shrewsbury to Bolingbroke, Versailles, March 8/19, 1712/3.

compliment upon the peace was answered by him with
all the respect and civility imaginable to the Queen[1]."
The next great event was Shrewsbury's "entry" as
ambassador to the French Court, an occasion for much
display by the embassy. Poor Prior, who had foreseen
this contingency, had in February asked Lord Oxford
for instructions how he was to behave on this occasion.
"What I am to do or how to behave myself; pray, my
Lord, one word of direction[2]." But, as was usual with
enquiries made to Lord Oxford, answer came there
none. After the peace Prior wrote:

I have your favourable promise of 17/28 Feb^ry that I should
hear from your Lordship by the very next post: and every post
from that time to this I have troubled you upon my own (or
rather your affair) my expense and figure at my Lord Duke's
entry[3].

Shrewsbury had not been silent, he had said:

When I make my entry, it will look strange if he have not
some sort of handsome equipage, to appear at the same time; as
he lives, he spends a great deal of money, and yet makes no show,
for want of a fund to buy something at first that is creditable[4].

Eventually the entry took place on June 11th, but
whether Prior got his equipage or not, cannot be told.
At any rate, when Shrewsbury took leave of the French
court in July, Prior's position attracted much attention.

We have paid and received all our public visits: in all those to
the Ministers your humble servant has had all the honour of
a third chair placed for him in like manner as for the minister
and the ambassador, which, however you may think nothing in

---

[1] *Letters...at Welbeck*, App. vi. p. 289, Prior to Oxford, Versailles,
April 7/18, 1713.

[2] *Ibid.* p. 286, Prior to Oxford, Paris, 15/26 Feb. 1712/3. See also
p. 287, letter of March 9, N.S.

[3] *Ibid.* p. 290, Prior to Oxford, Paris, April 6, N.S. 1713.

[4] *Bol. Corr.* ii. 291, Shrewsbury to Bolingbroke, Versailles, March 8/19,
1712/3.

England, makes a mighty noise here, as a particular favour to Her Majesty's minister[1].

At last Great Britain and France were at peace. While the great negociations were being carried on, Prior reported to Oxford that

Monsieur de Torcy constantly drinks your health, and Madame de Torcy, who has a great deal of good humour and wit, drinks to Robin et to Harry, mais "Je croy" dit elle, "que Robin est trop serieux pour nous[2]."

Well indeed might Torcy drink the health of the Tory ministers. The withdrawal of Britain from the alliance had given the French such terms of peace as three years earlier they could not have dared to ask; and enabled the setting sun of Louis XIV to illumine the history of Europe with one fitful gleam through the rift before it ended its long and once brilliant course below the clouds of the Spanish Succession War. Nor can posterity withhold a word of thanks to these much abused ministers. However dishonourable their methods, they obtained all unwittingly a stable frontier between France and the Netherlands, which, except at such a cataclysm as the French Revolution, has never varied since, and here the work done at Utrecht may not unjustly be held up for the guidance of statesmen and contrasted with the more ephemeral results of harsher terms imposed on the vanquished at Pressburg, at Tilsit and at Frankfurt-am-Main.

[1] P.R.O. France, 157, fo. 219, Prior to E. Lewis, Paris, July 31, N.S. 1713. Possibly this was done as a sop to Prior's feelings when he did not apparently get at the "entry" everything that he claimed. See in *Aff. Etr. Angl.* vol. 249, fo. 186, a memorandum from Breteuil to Torcy on the ceremonial to be observed at Shrewsbury's entry. Prior made claims based on what he alleged took place at Jersey's entry, but Breteuil seems to have been satisfied they could not be substantiated. Shrewsbury then stated he would make them a basis for a claim when he took leave.

[2] *Letters...at Welbeck*, App. vi. p. 271, Prior to Oxford, Fontainebleau, Aug. 29/Sept. 9, 1712.

Chapter X

THE LAST YEAR OF QUEEN ANNE

WITH the departure of Shrewsbury in August, 1713, the great business of the treaty of Utrecht was closed. Prior could now devote himself entirely to the wearisome routine work of the office, such as the various discussions about prizes captured during the last days of the war, complaints of merchants, supplications of British subjects who had got into trouble in France, the everlasting question of the French protestants, and so forth. He expected to return soon to England, but in the meantime he enjoyed a position of great magnificence. His health indeed seems to have left much to be desired: in September, 1712, he had "a distemper cruel to bear as unmannerly to name[1]"; and in May, 1713, one of those recurring attacks which always brought him to death's door and which he used to call cholera-morbus, when he told Oxford that

after strange efforts of a Cholera-morbus, and pleuritic pangs, (Dr Arbuthnott shall have the case) I had an Imposthume in the lungs broke, which has been so watched and guarded by a good Scotch physician that I believe it is all(most) come away: I am at present as well in health as I have been some Years past[2].

Nevertheless, his health was very uncertain. This did not prevent him from taking his place as the repre-

---

[1] *Letters...at Welbeck*, App. VI. p. 275, Prior to Oxford, Versailles, Sept. 16/27, 1712.

[2] *Ibid.* p. 292, Prior to Oxford, Paris, May 2/13, 1713.

sentative of Great Britain at the Court functions, and following the Court to Fontainebleau in September;

> We are in huntings, comedies, feasts and all that the generality of the world calls pleasure. I am mightily *en odeur*, as we call it; but it is a strange fancy I have, I had rather hear once a month from my Lord Treasurer than be talked to once a day by the Grand Monarch[1].

Busy as Prior was with important work, he nevertheless did not lose the faculty of writing those letters about people which threw such charm over his correspondence from Paris during his less busy secretaryship. Louis XIV he found the same as ever, showing to Prior marked friendship, extremely gracious when Shrewsbury presented his credentials, so much so that Prior reported to Oxford that he had "never seen the monarch so blithe since I have been here[2]." All the same, the old heartlessness was still a trait of Louis' character. When in the beginning of May, 1714, the Duke of Berry, the sole grandson remaining at Versailles, died of the smallpox, the King continued "to plant and shoot, unconcerned for the Duke of Berry as if that Prince were still alive, or had never been born[3]." In the autumn it is the same:

> We go on here *sicut olim*: the King hunting, shooting or walking every day and at night eating with a great appetite and an easy mind; talking last night as pleasantly with the Duchess of Berry in the deepest mourning of a widow as he did last year when he saw her covered with brocard and diamonds and her husband his grandson in health on tother side the table[4].

This insensibility of Louis XIV no doubt made the

---

[1] *Letters...at Welbeck*, App. vi. p. 294, Prior to Oxford, Fontainebleau, Sept. 18/29, 1713.
[2] *Ibid.* p. 282, Prior to Oxford, Paris, Jan. 19, 1713.
[3] P.R.O. France, 158, Prior to Bolingbroke, Paris, May 9, 1714.
[4] *Ibid.* 159, Prior to Bolingbroke, Fontainebleau, Sept. 11,1714.

void round him tolerable. Madame de Maintenon indeed was still alive, but we hear next to nothing of her,
the grand Dauphin his son, and the Duke of Burgundy
his grandson were dead, the Duke of Anjou was now
King Philip of Spain, and now the Duke of Berry was
taken. Thus only the future Louis XV[1] was left; and
the Grand Monarch realised one of the dearest wishes
of his life when he decreed that the *Légitimés* were
capable of succession to the Crown. This ceremony
Prior mentioned, and adds words which show the feeling that was aroused by the act.

Most of the nobility congratulate the Duke of Maine and
the Count of Toulouse upon this occasion; some few there are
that refuse or at least defer to pay so extraordinary a compliment[2].

Of his old friend, Villeroy, we hear but little. After
Ramillies, though not unkindly received, he had fallen
into disgrace, and was only now beginning to return
to Court. At any rate he was not commissioned as in
former days to ply Prior with questions. Pontchartrain
the Chancellor, Prior cordially hated, and when in July,
he resigned, Prior cannot but have been pleased.

The new Chancellor's elevation is the subject of our discourse
here; the reasons alleged for Monsieur Pontchartrain's resignation, besides his desire of repose, is his being averse to the Père
le Tellier's conduct, and the reception and registring the Constitution[3] and other acts which in all probability are and must be
consequential to it. The Secretary of War[4] by his new dignity
taking place of all the Presidents and chief men of the Robe has
given as much distaste to them as people are permitted to take

---

[1] *Bol. Corr.* ii. 157, Prior to Bolingbroke, Paris, Dec. 29, 1712. "I saw
the Dauphin yesterday; he was brought to the King at table; the child
looks very well, a little pale; he is handsome and seems to have a good
deal of spirit."

[2] P.R.O. France, 159, Prior to Bolingbroke, Paris, August 4, 1714.

[3] *Unigenitus.*   [4] Voisin.

here. The Court is at Marly, and the old gentleman like Gallio careth not for these things[1].

In fact, the constitution *Unigenitus* came near to bringing about the resignation or disgrace of a greater man than Pontchartrain, namely Torcy himself. In 1714 the French world was all agog on the subject.

A kind of Council of Cardinals and some Doctors meet at the Cardinal d'Estrées' in order to find some temperament by which the refusing Bishops may yet admit this precept....The Archbishop of Paris in the meantime does not relent in the least, the Bishop of Metz has gone further, having taken upon himself to explain the manner in which he would have the constitution understood, and that explanation having been rejected by the Court of Rome. Our friend the Bishop of Montpellier[2] having received the King's order by Monsieur de Vrilliere for receiving the constitution in his diocese, omitted for some months to return any answer to that letter, and upon a second letter writ requiring the reason of his silence, he has answered in short that it was because either as a Doctor of the Sorbonne, a Bishop of the Gallican Church, or a faithful subject to the King, he could not obey the contents of the letter. This makes a good deal of noise here[3].

And it rebounded on Torcy. In November Prior reported in cipher to Townshend;

Our friend Torcy has suffered a little mortification in the affairs of Rome, which were in his province, being *pro hac vice* given to the care of Mr Voisin. The true reason is because Torcy's brother, bishop of Montpellier has appeared one of the most vigorous against the constitution, and that all the family are rather Roman Catholics than Papists[4].

The English in Paris occupied much of Prior's time. If the most remarkable of these was the Earl of Peter-

---

[1] P.R.O. France, 158, fo. 199, Prior to Bolingbroke, Paris, July 6, 1714.
[2] Torcy's brother.
[3] P.R.O. France, 159, Prior to Bolingbroke, Paris, July 27, 1714.
[4] *Ibid.* Prior to Townshend, Paris, November 16, 1714.

borough, the most troublesome was the widow of Prior's old friend and patron Jersey. Prior's relations with her gave rise to a series of scenes which Prior described in his best style. On October 19, 1713, it came to Prior's ears that Lady Jersey was "in France, and either at or in her way to Paris. Your Lordship will judge I was surprised at this piece of news, not having had any previous notice of it[1]." A week later he writes on the subject:

Little Dowager Jersey is shot hither like "the brisk Lightning, I" in the *Rehearsal*[2]: who knew of her coming, or what she intends to do here, God knows; I have seen her twice, but in company, I perceive she acts mightily upon the reserve towards me, and I easily see she has her lesson on that head from her priests. Her little son is with her. I suppose I shall have your sentiments upon this adventure, and, by your canal, my Lord Treasurer's, who has been always even to a fatherly kindness charitable to the child. The matter stands in the mean time as I have told it to your Lordship. She went on Tuesday to the King's supper. I would not be there, for [on] one hand as I do not know if she has the Queen's leave for coming: on the other, I am acquainted well enough with this court to know the difference she will find between Madame de Jersey and Madame l'Ambassadrice d'Angleterre[3].

The matter proved to be really serious, for she had left without the Queen's leave.

I have been frequently to visit her. She was not at home; she was at table and twenty follies of this kind, and when I did see her, she was *en compagnie*, which spoke all plain enough her

---

[1] P.R.O. France, 157, Prior to Bolingbroke, Versailles, Oct. 20, 1713. Torcy got to hear of her approach by an undated letter of Lady Jersey, saying she was coming for the salvation of her son, which he docketed with the date Sept. 26, 1713. (*Aff. Etr. Angl.* no. 249, fo. 370.)

[2] Cf. the *Rehearsal*, Act I. *Thunder*: I am the bold Thunder. *Lightning*: The brisk Lightning, I.

[3] P.R.O. France, 157, fo. 327, Prior to Bolingbroke, Paris, Oct. 27, 1713.

ladyship did not care to converse with me alone. I broke through that, told her I must speak with her privately; I did so, and laid before her what my duty to Her Majesty and my observance of your commands required, and mingled it with all the concern that my long and real friendship to her family could dictate. I found her prepared to combat an enemy rather than to answer a friend, and fortified with all the chicane which her lawyers in England (with whom she confessed she had advised) or her priests here could give her. She answered me as if she had been upon her trial, denied at first that the Duc d'Aumont knew of her coming, and having fended and proved upon that point till she was beaten out of it, she returned to her frequent answer, that she would accuse nobody, was sorry the Queen was angry with her, did not imagine that such a poor woman as herself was worth all this bustle, et cetera. In short, according to all appearance she intends to throw herself upon this court, thinks she has secured her jointure in England, and designs to keep her son with her, to make him a Roman Catholic and probably a priest. This I say I take to be her meaning[1].

It was therefore incumbent on Prior to rescue the boy, Henry Villiers, from his mother's religious designs. Torcy had to be spoken to, and was told by Prior that "the child I saw baptized in the Church of England: the late King, the late Earl of Rochester and the Duchess of Somerset stood witnesses to it"; he was educated and confirmed in the religion of his country, and brought up at Westminster, a school founded by a Queen of England: "reflect how it will look if any attempt here should be made upon his religion, and what consequences it may produce to those of your religion in England[2]." Although Torcy said it was *une affaire embarassante*, Prior did not anticipate that the French

---

[1] P.R.O. France, 157, fo. 333, Prior to Bolingbroke, Paris, Nov. 1, 1714. She made no secret of her intentions to Torcy; see her letters in *Aff. Etr. Angl.* no. 249, where she describes Prior as "mon plus grand ennemy."
[2] *Ibid.*

government would give much trouble; and as Prior foresaw: "I find her very much neglected here; the whole Croissy family are only barely civil to her[1]." Prior therefore set himself to the odious task of trying to undermine the boy's affection for his mother. "I have often invited the child to dine with me, to take the air with me, etc., and she as constantly finds some excuses to refuse it[2]." Peterborough, who at this time was in Paris, was called in to help, and offered to take the boy with him to Sicily, and bring him back to Lady Jersey in the spring, but "this proposition, however generous and good-natured it may look, met with a cold and scarce a civil return[3]." Prior, however, did not desist from his negociations with the Lady, and with Torcy.

Our Lady Jersey is broke out into an open war with me, and sustains it with all the stratagems that her priests and confederates can teach her. As well the Duke d'Aumont as herself had given out that it was a thing in which Her Majesty did not at all interest herself, and that it was I only that inflamed it, upon I know not what former prejudices I might have conceived to her....Knowing our good Lady's play for many years past, to show Monsieur de Torcy that I was not altogether that *Boutefeu* that I was represented, I drew out your Lordship's letters to me upon that subject....I was prepared too by a letter I had from Gaultier, which was very honestly writ in answer to one in which I almost accused him of being conscious to the lady's flight....Monsieur Torcy seemed to laugh this matter off, but I find he is most heartily alarmed at it. He promises to come to Paris to see the Lady, and if the child is resolved to go back he will order matters so that his going shall be effected.

[1] P.R.O. France, 157, fo. 376, Prior to Bolingbroke, Paris, Dec. 6, 1713. Torcy, without actually committing himself one way or the other, certainly wrote letters to Lady Jersey which could have had no other result than to encourage her.

[2] *Ibid.*

[3] *Ibid.* fo. 384, Dec. 14, 1713.

I have told your Lordship that the Lady will not let the child stir out of her sight, except with those of one family. I saw her on Tuesday, found the child with her, and as the Boy has a good deal of sense, I said before her and him everything I could from his baptism to this day. I never saw anything of his age armed with such a resolution, though with great deference to his mother. The particulars of this set battle which lasted about three hours, I must reserve till I have the honour to see you, for it is impossible for me to write it. I think it was the most Tragi-comical encounter I ever sustained. I left her in a flood of tears, rather terrified than convinced by what I had said.

I have since writ secretly to the child by Hunter the very words in which he shall answer Monsieur de Torcy, the Archbishop of Paris, or anybody else that may speak to him, and from everything I can learn I believe our little Church of England man will act his part gallantly. He is to say he thinks France a very fine place, but he will go to no school but Westminster, that he loves the Lady Jersey as his mother, but that he has a higher duty to the Queen who is the mother of his country, and that in short he will go home[1].

After this matters came to a standstill: Lady Jersey remained obstinate, and the boy, Prior thought, would tell all "that have the curiosity to ask him, that he is and will continue a Protestant[2]." At the end of February Prior joyfully announced that his formula had been successful[3]. Louis XIV had ordered Torcy to see the boy, and the boy replied as Prior had told him, "having answered him in a manner that became a young English nobleman, and a kinsman of my Lord Bolingbroke." Thereupon Lady Jersey surrendered: "I am no longer

[1] P.R.O. France, 157, Prior to Bolingbroke, Paris, Dec. 14, 1713.

[2] *Ibid.* fo. 402, Dec. 25, 1713.

[3] The affair caused some stir in England, and that a solution favourable to Prior was found must be attributed also to Gaultier, who wrote to Torcy in considerable alarm as to the consequences of delay in sending the boy back (*Aff. Etr. Angl.* no. 253, fo. 271, Gaultier to Torcy, Feb. 8, 1714).

her enemy, and the child is no longer a prisoner," while Torcy's behaviour is described as that which "became a gentleman, a minister and a Christian." For the future Prior would "have the Child to converse with him, and to show him Paris." With a "Common Prayer Book in French, a Latin Bible and a Mons Testament," his panoply as a Protestant was complete against all the assaults of his mother who confessed that her design had been to educate her son as a Roman Catholic. Now all that was abandoned, and the only thing that remained to be done was to convey the boy back to England[1]. Peace was finally made on March 7th, when Lady Jersey, the Princesse d'Espinay, Madame de Croissy and the Duchess of Portsmouth dined with Prior: "and since she knows again to obey the Queen, I would have these people see that the Queen's minister knows to behave towards her[2]." *O si sic omnia!*

In the European drama then being enacted, there was much to occupy Prior's attention. The treaty of Utrecht could only be called an universal peace by the most outrageous of fictions, for neither the Empire, nor, to put small along with the great, the Catalans, had accepted it. To the efforts of the Princes on the Rhine who were extremely anxious for peace as likely to be the chief sufferers by a war, Queen Anne added her own in trying to persuade the Emperor to give up war; and she sent an envoy to Vienna for that purpose. The Emperor himself soon saw the folly of attempting single-handed to resist France, and on his side Louis XIV himself was anxious to restore as far as possible the shattered finances of France, and resume his beloved building operations. The autumn therefore saw a perfunctory campaign on the Rhine which degenerated

[1] P.R.O. France, 158, fo. 35, Prior to Bolingbroke, Paris, February, 27, N.S. 1714.
[2] *Ibid.* fo. 43, March 7, N.S. 1714.

into a conference between the generals, Eugene and Villars, at Rastadt. Prior duly notified the home government of these conferences, but it was not until the next year that he could say the preliminaries were settled. According to Prior, this delay was not due to any fault on the French side. Prior had warned the French ministers in November that he hoped

the King would not stand rigorously upon the advantages which this last campaign may have seemed to give to France, but by treating generously with the Emperor show the real desire which the ministers here always said they had to the peace (and indeed, though I did not say it to Monsieur Torcy, it is evidence enough that their own wants plead more for a peace than their words could have expressed it)[1]:

Had it not been for this strong desire for peace, the conferences at Rastadt might well have broken up, for in December, the Emperor, in accordance with his usual discernment, sent demands

as much more extravagant now, as his power is diminished since Her Majesty withdrew her assistance from him. He seems to add derision to what has hitherto been thought but pride; what secret views he may have, God knows; but to judge by human appearances he is sacrificing those people whom he ought to protect, and justifying France in ruining the Empire[2].

This phase did not last long:

"Prince Eugene recedes much from the *hauteur* of the late demands....The substance of the propositions which he now makes, and with which (a little more or less) France will most certainly close, are the Treaties of Nimegue and Ryswick to be the basis of this: the French to keep Landau and some of the forts undemolished shall remain as the equivalent for Fribourg[3]; the Elector of Bavaria to be established in his rank, dignity and

[1] P.R.O. France, 157, fo. 365, Prior to Bolingbroke, Paris, Nov. 23, 1713.
[2] *Ibid.* fo. 384, Dec. 14, 1713.
[3] Freiburg surrendered to the French on November 17, N.S. 1713.

dominions as before the war, upon which consideration he is to renounce his pretensions to Sardinia....At present," adds Prior, the Elector "seems averse to it, but what is free will if necessity constrains[1]?"

The other points to be settled were that the Emperor, like Great Britain and France, should guarantee to the Duke of Savoy the possession of the throne of Sicily, and secure him the fortress of Vigevenasco; and the fate of the unhappy Catalans of which nothing had yet been said. But the complaisance of the court of France doubtless tempted the Emperor to raise his demands, for at the beginning of the year, the French court was surprised to find that Eugene's offers, mentioned above, had been modified. The Emperor insisted on the cession to him of Porto Longone, and that the Catalans should enjoy their "ancient" liberties. To this France replied that both these questions were beyond her control: Porto Longone belonged to the King of Spain, and as for the Catalans, France and Great Britain had interposed "their best offices from which it was to be hoped these people should have received all the immunities and privileges that it was reasonable for them to expect[2]." Nor was this enough; on January 24th, Torcy showed Prior a project forwarded by Prince Eugene: "a convention upon which a future treaty shall be founded"; but the "tenour of it is extraordinary and extravagant. ...The first and greatest absurdity is that the Emperor styles himself Imperial and *Catholic* Majesty." The claims put forward in December are of course maintained; but there was also a demand that the King of France shall not assist Philip in reducing the Catalans, but that the Emperor shall be able to send them what assistance he thinks proper. All persons who had supported the cause of the house of Austria in Spain,

[1] P.R.O. France, 157, fo. 402, Prior to Bolingbroke, Paris, Dec. 25, N.S. 1713.   [2] *Ibid.* fo. 420, January 5, N.S. 1714.

Italy and the Low Countries were to have a complete immunity and maintenance in their estates and honours.

It is very saucy for me to make any comment while it is only my duty to send you plain fact. But as I have the zeal of an Englishman, nay, though I had only the phlegm of a Dutchman, I cannot without indignation remark how our Imperial Ally dare use the nation that has fought his battles, and the Queen that has given him kingdoms. He goes on to declare peremptorily that he will not hold himself obliged to make any renunciations or to regard either treaty or guaranty entered into by any other prince on that account; and whatever obligation of this kind France may have already entered into, he insists shall be deemed null and void[1].

As to the question of Italy, nothing definite was said, though later the Emperor claimed "Naples and its dependencies." The French reply was an ultimatum based on Eugene's proposals of November[2], and to prepare for a campaign in the spring[3]. Certainly the conduct of the Emperor was sufficiently exasperating, and marked by the usual inability of the House of Austria to look facts in the face. At last, however, he was brought to recede from his impossible demands[4]. He consented to hold in Italy whatever he possessed at that moment, an arrangement which safeguarded the interests of the Duke of Savoy and of the Duke of Parma; and the complicated affairs of Italy were to be settled by a congress at Baden, while the exiled Electors of Cologne and Bavaria were to return to their lawful

[1] P.R.O. France, 158, Jan. 26, 1714.
[2] *Ibid.* Jan. 26, N.S. 1714.
[3] *Ibid.* fo. 31, Feb. 16, N.S. 1714.
[4] *Ibid.* fo. 43, March 7, N.S. 1714. "The Emperor having dropt the great point hitherto insisted, that His Most Christian Majesty should renounce to any obligation he lay under from the Treaty signed at Utrecht last year."

dominions[1]. The peace of Europe was now practically assured, and no one was more relieved than Louis XIV who replied to Prior when offering his congratulations on the auspicious occasion: "I have done what I could to obtain it, and you, Sir, who have been here, know it very well[2]."

The Elector of Bavaria, who was now allowed to return to Munich, had been during the war one of the numerous guests of misfortune maintained by the generous French King. At the congress of Utrecht his claims for compensation had not been overlooked, and by the treaty drawn up there he was to have received the Kingdom of Sicily (or as was arranged later, Sardinia) in lieu of his German territories. During his stay in Paris, Prior contrived to see much of the unfortunate Elector, who made no secret of his anxiety for the future. He doubted whether he would obtain even the pittance allotted to him at Utrecht, and uttered piteous entreaties to Queen Anne not to forget him:

"He assures her Majesty," says Prior, "that he has the greatest sense imaginable of her goodness to him, and (as he expresses it) to the most distressed family at present in Europe. What I find uppermost in his heart is the Kingdom of Sardinia and the means of being invested soon in it. He repeated his great disappointment as to Sicily which had been promised him: that now the Duke of Savoy was to possess that kingdom, and he was all the while as it were left out. He left it to Her Majesty to consider if France assisting him in the possession of Sardinia would not be a proper means to hasten the general peace: that the princes of Germany would more easily be induced to rehabilitate a man who had already the title of King and the favour of the monarchs of Great Britain and of France, than one who had no other name than of a prince under the ban of the empire, and that if the Emperor should die now, he was in the most unhappy circum-

---

[1] P.R.O. France, 158, fo. 73; Prior to Bolingbroke, Versailles, March 13, 1714.   [2] *Ibid.*

stances imaginable. Still I saw he deferred to Her Majesty's pleasure with all good manners and complaisance[1].

When it was clear that by arrangement with the Emperor, he would be restored to his own dominions, he did not seem best satisfied. Prior wrote to Bolingbroke:

I made a visit some days since to the Elector of Bavaria who is in private here at Monsr Monastrolles' house (as indeed the Elector himself had desired). He reflected with a good deal of melancholy on his own circumstances, that at one time he was to be King of Sicily, another time of Sardinia, and that he was as he expressed it *le jouet de la fortune.* He had likewise spoke, I know, in very high terms upon the same subject to Monsieur de Torcy. He came at last to this, that his yielding up his right to the Low Countries was purely conditional, and if what was promised to him upon that account could not be made good, he hoped the renunciation itself should be returned to him, and be looked upon as void, and not made; for 'twould be very hard that he should be the only prince that should be tied down whilst, as he understood it, the pretentions of every body else concerned were to be left open, and their claims at least undetermined, and he desired I would write of this to Your Lordship. I represented to him (as well as I could) that the present advantages which France was stipulating of having him restored to the Dignity and Dominion which his family had already possessed might possibly upon a more mature reflexion be found preferable to any other equivalent, which at best would be new, untried and uncertain; that I was not indeed able to judge or even to advise in a point of this weight, but since His Electoral Highness was pleased to speak so openly to me upon it, as Monsieur Monastrole had likewise done by his order, I desired His Highness to remember that though this Court might not possibly do all for him that he did either expect or deserve from them, yet it was certainly his interest to make the best that he could of their friendship, and act in concert with them; that the very mention of the recalling the Renunciation would certainly alarm the Emperor to the

[1] P.R.O. France, 157, fo. 284, Prior to Bolingbroke, F'bleau, Sept. 22, 1713.

greatest degree imaginable, and might be a means of breaking off the conferences. That France (His Electoral Highness plainly saw) was determined at any rate to have a Peace, and that if the Emperor flew off, they might purchase it upon terms yet severer to His Electoral Highness. I asked him if it was not advisable that he should see a little the whole of what France intended for his interest before he made a further step any way in so nice a conjuncture. He has since discoursed with Monsieur de Torcy, as I have done with Count Monastrole: From what Monsieur de Torcy has told me and from what I observed in Monastrole, the Elector is a good deal better satisfied. In one word, a very round sum of money must be the peace-offering[1].

Even when the treaty was signed, the poor Elector was not much happier:

I went yesterday to St Cloud, where the Elector of Bavaria has a house, to pay my compliment to him upon the peace, as all the foreign ministers here have likewise done. He received me with a very distinguishing civility and showed me more particular marks of honour than (to say the truth out) I think he ought to have done. The effect of a long discourse I had with him after his complaints for not having the Low Countries nor Sardinia was that peace would give him at least liberty and occasion of showing that he was perfectly sensible of Her Majesty's goodness and that he would always endeavour to merit her *protection* and *friendship*: I assured him I had already informed Her Majesty as much: he answered that I could not do him a greater favour than to repeat it, and in an easier style he said that before the war he hoped he had a great many English friends, so now he hoped the war being done, they would all be reconciled to him again. He walked me about an hour in his garden, and in discourse about the goodness of the air of St Cloud, I told him that of Munich was much better. He said he was of my opinion and should be very glad to see me there. I had a great deal of speculative talk with him, which I would not remark to your Lordship as a thing of immediate significancy, but as what may possibly

[1] P.R.O. France, 157, fo. 420, Paris, Jan. 5, N.S. 1714.

hereafter have its effect.... *Elector of Bavaria is by no means satisfied with the King of France*[1].

The abandonment of the Catalans is generally considered to be one of the most shameful features of the treaty of Utrecht. Certainly neither Great Britain nor the Emperor have much cause for pride in the part they played in this business. Nothing certain had been settled about their fate when Shrewsbury left Paris, and although the French court undertook to intercede for them, that their lives should be spared, their property secured, and be put on an equality with the other Spaniards[2], Torcy was constantly reminding Prior, that Louis XIV had but little influence at the Spanish Court. In November, Philip V sent back his answer, that he would spare the Catalans, provided they immediately laid down their arms. But to this "those turbulent but wretched people" would by no means consent: they demanded the restoration of their "old privileges," which

are said by the Duke de Noailles, Marshal de Tessé, and others, who should know the thing, to be so extravagant and against all the rules of reason and justice as that neither the Queen of Great Britain nor the King could insist upon them if they were explained to Their Majesties[3]." And again "They were inconsistent with the safety of Spain in general, and tended only to the mutual destruction of the very people that required them, and in fine to anarchy, murder and rebellion[4].

At Rastadt, indeed, the Emperor made one effort to save these "old privileges[5]," but single-handed he could

---

[1] P.R.O. France, 158, fo. 79, Prior to Bolingbroke, Paris, March 6/17, 1713/4. The last sentence is in cipher.

[2] *Ibid.* 157, fo. 315, Prior to Bolingbroke, Versailles, Oct. 20, 1713.

[3] *Ibid.* 157, fo. 376, Prior to Bolingbroke, Paris, Dec. 6, 1713.

[4] *Ibid.* 159, Prior to Bolingbroke, Paris, Aug. 28, 1714.

[5] *Ibid.* 157, fo. 420, Prior to Bolingbroke, Paris, Jan. 5, N.S. 1714, and *ibid.* 158, Prior to Bolingbroke, Paris, Jan. 26, 1714.

do little, and in the final treaty they were forgotten. After the signature of the treaty they were at the mercy of the two Bourbons, for the Emperor failed even to carry his point that Louis XIV should not assist in the reduction of the unhappy people. All now turned upon whether the Catalans would submit to the terms offered by Philip. These were

in case they should lay down their arms, a full and perpetual amnesty and pardon, together with the possession of their estates and honours and all privileges *which his other subjects enjoyed.*

This did not satisfy the Catalans, and though the help they expected in virtue of the promises of Great Britain was not forthcoming; Great Britain was not prepared to reopen the war for their sake; for seventeen months they rejected Philip's offers, and Philip, with French help, pressed forward the siege of Barcelona. On the pretext that the Catalans had seized a richly laden vessel bound for England, a British squadron was sent to "chastise the Catalans," and after a heroic struggle the town surrendered in September, 1714. The Catalans lost those privileges which they had till then enjoyed, and the British had promised by treaty to maintain, but which, in the end, they helped to destroy.

The chief argument which the Tories had used against the Whig war policy was that advanced cogently but not convincingly by Swift in his *Conduct of the Allies*. The war, he urged, should have been carried on by this country in the interests mainly of her commerce and her colonies, and the Tory ministry had urged the desirability of safeguarding our commerce, and of not sacrificing our interests to those of the Dutch, as, it was professed, had been done by Townshend in the Barrier Treaty of 1709. The complement of the political treaty of Utrecht in Bolingbroke's opinion would be a commercial treaty which should justify the arguments and realise the promises of the Tory party. Abortive though it proved to be, this commercial treaty was the most important work which engaged Prior during these months. On the signature of the armistice, commerce between the two countries was resumed, but only through passports issued to merchants who wished to trade. Strictly speaking, trade with France was still illegal to Englishmen, and matters were in what Prior would call "a good deal of *brouillon*." Therefore at Utrecht a draft treaty was signed, arranging for the commercial relations between England and France. Three main questions, however, arose with a view to the settlement of the details of this treaty. Commissioners were to be appointed on both sides, and Prior had much ado to secure that the French commissioners, Anisson and the Marquis de Fénelon, obtained instructions which would make the conclusion of the treaty possible. Two clauses, the eighth and the ninth, were the source of much difficulty. The British intended and demanded urgently, that they should be considered reciprocal, but though Torcy saw from the first that this was a perfectly reasonable demand, it was not till the beginning of 1714 that Prior could obtain this concession from the French government. The fact was that in this matter he had to deal not so much with Torcy as with Desmaretz and his superior, the Anglophobe Pontchartrain, who to Prior was a *bête noire*, "a quiver, whence we shall never find any arrow pointed with justice or winged with honour[1]." Desmaretz was afraid that these clauses constituted no economic bargain for France, and there was much in the fear: but the cards which Prior played successfully against this were that the clauses were not necessary to the treaty, which could well be passed without them, but that they were essential to the confirmation not

[1] P.R.O. France, 157, fo. 292, Prior to Bolingbroke, Fontainebleau, Sept. 29, 1713.

merely of peace, but also of an *entente* between the two nations. It was this argument which overbore Torcy's objections, and brought him definitely on to Prior's side. This was the greatest matter of all: subsidiary questions arose, such as the position of the provinces of France which were not subject to the determining tariff of 1664; what exactly was the meaning of British goods, that is, how far might it be understood to include stuffs from the East Indies, which were not dreamt of in 1664; what was to be the exact manner of the removal of the prohibitive duties imposed by each nation on each other's products in time of war. As to the first two questions, they were naturally referred to the commissioners, the third fell to Prior's lot to determine. Who was to take off the prohibitive duty first, the King of France or the Queen of Great Britain?

I explained to him with how much better grace it would look towards the opening the Commerce and how effectual a means it might prove to that end if the Queen could say to her people at the beginning of the Parliament that France had complied with what Her Majesty was already enabled by Act of Parliament to do in that behalf....Monsieur Desmaretz comes up to this, that the King shall begin on this side to take off the duty at any certain day that shall be appointed (and the sooner the better); in case that this court has an assurance from Her Majesty that she shall be pleased on her side to take it off in some reasonable time after, Her Majesty shall be master of that time....By Monsieur Desmaretz receding thus far the reciprocity of the article is quite taken away, and the point of honour remains to the English nation, the French taking off the duty first and we only following upon the consideration that they had already done so[1].

It looks as if a great deal of pother were being made about a very small point. Certainly, the matter "found more difficulties with Monsieur Desmaretz than I

[1] P.R.O. France, 157, fo. 371, Prior to Bolingbroke, Paris, Nov. 29, 1713.

could have apprehended," says Prior, but at last on January 5th, N.S. he informed Bolingbroke that the "difficulties were now past," and an edict was issued abolishing the French duties from the 15th of January and the British duties naturally followed suit[1]. However, the breath and the ink used in these negociations were entirely wasted. The treaty did indeed pass the commissioners, but when submitted to the House of Commons, it was considered to be injurious to the national trade, and to Bolingbroke's intense disappointment, it was rejected. If this treaty was the most important affair which engaged Prior's attention, the most vexatious and the most interminable question was, undoubtedly, that of Dunkirk. The treaty of peace provided that the fortifications of the town "*diruantur, ac solo aequentur*," and the harbour was to be filled up (*compleatur*). The work began in September, 1713[2]; but the French did all they could to hinder the process of destruction. Fair words were given to Prior when he made representations—the treaty would be literally executed[3], the ships were paid off and removed and the work on the fortifications carried on "with all diligence imaginable[4]." Soon, however, difficulties of interpretation arose. Did the words *diruantur, ac solo aequentur* mean that the very foundations of the works were to be removed, or did they mean only that the fortifications should be razed to the level of the ground[5]? Prior, stoutly maintaining the former view, said the "destruction must be entire, and that the least stone left within the whole circuit of the place would be heavy enough to knock out any Englishman's brains concerned in that

[1] P.R.O. France, 157, fo. 420, Prior to Bolingbroke, Paris, January 5, N.S. 1714.

[2] *Ibid.* fo. 284, Fontainebleau, Sept. 22, 1713, fo. 292, Fontainebleau, Sept. 18/29, 1713.   [3] *Ibid.* fo. 315, Versailles, Oct. 20, 1713.

[4] *Ibid.* fo. 333, Paris, Nov. 1, 1713.   [5] *Ibid.* fo. 365, Nov. 23, 1713.

affair[1]." It was well perhaps to leave to Iberville, who was leaving as ambassador for England, the task of settling the question, if Prior was going to talk like this. Hardly was this question settled, than trouble arose over the sluices. The French wanted to keep three sluices, on the ground that they were not wanted for the harbour, but to prevent the surrounding country from being "drowned[2]." Much correspondence followed on this; Colonel Armstrong, one of the English commissioners, said that an old canal should be re-opened, and then the sluices could be destroyed[3]. Some such plan apparently was found feasible by the French engineers, and they began to construct a canal which was to do the work of the sluice at Bergue.

"They do not intend," wrote Prior in view of an obvious objection to a canal, "to make the canal navigable for great ships, or keep the harbour open; no more than I believe we did ever intend to drown the country by the immediate destruction of the sluice[4]."

All seemed settled, and Prior on May 4/15 announced triumphantly that the end was in sight.

The King has set nineteen battalions upon this work, and to comply with the Queen's *commands* (as the King gallantly always expresses himself). He is at a very excessive charge upon this account, but he repeats to the Queen that he hastens this work as much as possible, and assures Her Majesty that the demolition shall be perfected by the end of June, N.S.[5]

But Prior was reckoning without that "chicane" which was characteristic of the French court. A month later he had the mortification to write that the French

1 P.R.O. France, 157, Prior to Bolingbroke, Paris, Nov. 23, 1713.

2 *Ibid.* fo. 402, Dec. 25, 1713.

3 P.R.O. France, 159, Prior to Bolingbroke, Paris, Jan. 18, 1714. (This letter is misplaced in the Record Office, being bound up with the letters of January 1715.)

4 *Ibid.* 158, fo. 99, Prior to Bolingbroke, Paris, April 2/13, 1714.

5 *Ibid.* fo. 139, May 4/15, 1714.

said that the demolition promised by the end of June was not that of the fortifications, but only of the sluices[1]. "To cut off all excuse here, and all pretence of clamour in England," Prior drew up a convention, and by it Torcy promised on behalf of the French government that the fortifications should be pulled down, and the harbour filled by the end of July. Early in July there were still complaints as to delays in demolishing the sluices[2], and as the end of the month drew nigh, the French raised another difficulty. Was it necessary to pull up the fascines of the jetties[3]? They were not mentioned in the article of the treaty, and it would be useless to endeavour to destroy them[4]. It was at this point that Queen Anne died, and with the dismissal of Bolingbroke, who continued to tell Prior the fascines must be pulled up[5], the controversy entered upon a new stage.

The new government had no propensity to deal tenderly with the French. They were the leaders of those "malcontents" who had raised doubts about the canal of Mardyck. Stanhope succeeded Bolingbroke in office, and as soon as his instructions reached Prior, the minister plenipotentiary's tone altered. Torcy had blandly said that the Mardyck canal was made in accordance with Armstrong's suggestion, because the English engineers refused to allow the sluices to remain. Prior's retort was easy. "A canal, or rather harbour of four hundred and fifty foot broad and twenty-one foot deep capable of receiving ships of the third rate" was excessive, and "the breadth and depth of the sluices and canal were not only superfluous, but extravagant" if they were merely designed for purposes of drainage[6].

---

[1] P.R.O. France, 158, fo. 159, Prior to Bolingbroke, Paris, June 5, 1714.
[2] *Ibid.* 159, Prior to Bolingbroke, Paris, July 6/17, 1714.
[3] *Ibid.* Aug. 4, 1714.   [4] *Ibid.* Aug. 12/23, 1714.
[5] *Ibid.* Aug. 9/20, 1714.
[6] *Ibid.* Prior to Stanhope, Fontainebleau, Oct. 16, 1714.

Here however the matter remained: both sides refusing to recede, and when Prior left Paris, it was still the most important question at issue. That the Mardyck canal was a discreditable subterfuge, the English were convinced, and posterity has upheld their opinion; but it did not fall to Prior's lot to finish the quarrel.

Last of all there was the question of the Pretender and his family. After Bolingbroke's visit to Paris, when Bolingbroke and the Prince had sat opposite each other at the opera, the Prince was ordered, in accordance with the terms of the armistice, to withdraw from France. This he did by retiring to Lorraine, which the government of Queen Anne seem at first to have considered sufficient[1]. Although not nearly such a bugbear to Prior as was his father, observation of the unfortunate prince and his relatives could not be neglected. But before addresses had been voted on the subject in both houses[2], the government felt that the Chevalier had not retired sufficiently far; Prior therefore, in accordance with orders received, told the Minister of Lorraine that the residence of the Pretender in Lorraine was "inconsistent with the friendship between Her Majesty and the Duke[3]." Prior seems to have thought that these remonstrances would bear fruit, for in announcing the news of the dismissal of Lord Middleton, he says, "the Pretender, it is said, is going to reside at Berne[4]." Three months later, the Prince had not yet gone, and Prior made strong representations on the matter to the Lorraine envoy[5]: he also went to Marly and spoke upon

---

[1] *Bol. Corr.* II. 12, Bolingbroke to Dartmouth, Fontainebleau, August 22, N.S. 1712.

[2] Lords, April 1714; Commons, Mar. 17/27, 1713/4.

[3] P.R.O. France, 157, fo. 371, Prior to Bolingbroke, Paris, Nov. 29, 1713.

[4] *Ibid.* fo. 402, Dec. 25, 1713, in postscript.

[5] *Ibid.* 158, fo. 119, Prior to Bolingbroke, Paris, April 9/20, 1714.

the same subject to Torcy. Torcy consulted Louis XIV, and drew a characteristic reply.

> The King having acknowledged the succession to the Crown of Great Britain in the Protestant line of Hanover and the Person mentioned in the 4th article of the Peace being actually out of His Majesty's dominions, as he was at the signing of the treaty, and no cause of complaint or even of suspicion on His Majesty's part having been given since, he looks upon himself to have performed all that is incumbent upon himself by the article, which he will continue most strictly to observe[1].

Nevertheless, Torcy added that the French court would try and expedite the Chevalier's removal out of Lorraine. In May Prior was still having disagreeable interviews with the envoy of Lorraine[2], and at the end of that month became thoroughly angry, for the abuse of enlisting Irishmen for the Pretender's service still continued, in spite of the protests of the English. In May the Lorrainer replied to the observations of Prior that "though with a very great regret for fear of displeasing Her Majesty," his Master

> found himself under a necessity of permitting a care residence only in his dominions to the Chevalier de St George or person so calling himself, having already received him upon passports from the Emperor especially worded and designed for that purpose[3].

Finally, however, Prior's repeated exorcisms seemed to be having some effect when it was announced that the Emperor had invited the Pretender to his dominions[4]. A little patience and perhaps the evil spirit would be cast out of Lorraine.

As to the great question of the dowry of Mary of Modena, all was fair words on the British side; but little cash passed. At the end of December, 1713, we

---

[1] P.R.O. France, 158, Prior to Bolingbroke, Paris, April 9/20, 1714.
[2] *Ibid.* fo. 139, May 4/15, 1714.   [3] *Ibid.* fo. 151, May 18/29, 1714.
[4] *Ibid.* fo. 171, June 8, N.S. 1714, in postscript.

learn that Oxford promised that "this very week shall not pass before he hands me over six months of Queen Mary's dowry." To which Gaultier, knowing his Earl of Oxford, adds: "God grant nothing may happen to make him fail in his word[1]." As we know something must have happened, for the dowry was never paid.

At last the event occurred which was to involve the Pretender, the English Ministry and Prior in irretrievable ruin. On August 13th he wrote to Bolingbroke:

> After the news which Monsieur de Torcy's express has brought of the Queen's illness, and the state of matters on your side, if I could write common sense I ought to be hanged, and yet I can't let Lord Peterborough part without sending you something, but what to say till I hear from you, God knows. My Lord Treasurer being dismissed would at any other time be the subject of a great deal of reflexion to me, but all is swallowed in the cruel contemplation of the Queen's death[2].

Four days later he was

> "still in the sad incertitude or rather mortal apprehension of what has happened....Upon the best inquiry," he adds in cipher, "I cannot find that anything is acting for the Pretender, an express is gone to Lorraine from his mother to acquaint him with the present case of the Queen of Great Britain as signified by d'Iberville's express to this Court. At the distance I am from you, and the light in which I see matters from hence, you will easily judge, my Lord, how much I am astonished at what has passed within this three weeks at London; what may pass there in three weeks more, God above only knows. It is in such extraordinary conjectures that one either requires or needs one's friends. Whilst you continue to act as you have hitherto done, for the safety and honour of your country, I will abandon you and life at the same time[3]."

[1] *Aff. Etr. Angl.* vol. 247, fo. 156, Gaultier to Torcy, London, Dec. 19, N.S. 1713.

[2] P.R.O. France, 159, Prior to Bolingbroke, Paris, August 13, 1714.

[3] *Ibid.* August 17, 1714.

In his next letter he added in cipher a postscript saying the Pretender had been to Paris *incognito*, and had been sent back without having seen Louis XIV[1], who, he learnt afterwards, had sent "a very severe message[2]." Another alarm occurred in January, when a Baron Buleau informed Prior of a plot, hatched in Lorraine, to murder George I and raise a rebellion in England[3]. A little investigation convinced Prior that Buleau was "one of those Knights of Industry, who design no more by their plots than to get money by them[4]."

Was Prior at any time guilty of treasonable communications with the Jacobites? This is a question which no one can fail to ask. His close relations with the Tory ministers and his position in Paris were such as to establish a *prima facie* case against his innocence, and we shall see later on that the Whigs in their hour of triumph thought that Prior's papers would contain full evidence against Lord Oxford[5]. In such a case it is generally easier to establish guilt than innocence, and if we turn from the vapourings of the Whigs to such documentary evidence as we possess, we find in the Stuart papers a number of entries, going back as far as September, 1712. In these the persons about Queen Mary of Modena were corresponding with Prior on a subject the nature of which does not appear[6]. On November 25th Marshal Berwick wrote to James III that they would "be in the dark" until Prior returned from England, and on February 24th he again wrote a letter which more than hints at secret communications.

I have desired M. Torcy to tell P[rior] not to speak with

---

[1] P.R.O. France, 159, Prior to Bolingbroke, Paris, Aug. 20, 1714.

[2] *Ibid.* Aug. 23, 1714. The Pretender did not, as a matter of fact, reach Paris, though he entered France and came as far as Claye.

[3] *Ibid.* Prior to Townshend, Paris, Jan. 4, 1715.

[4] *Ibid.* Prior to Stanhope, Paris, Jan. 29, 1715.   [5] See below, p. 231.

[6] *Hist. MSS. Comm.* Stuart Papers, I. 247, Sept. 22, Oct. 1, 1712.

anybody; and he has assured me he would, and that he was very sure P. would willingly comply with your commands, for he is very shy; so for the future I think you may depend upon it all will pass through M. de Torcy's hands[1].

We may observe that there is nothing to show what it is all about; it is quite possible it concerns Queen Mary's dowry. In April, 1714, there is a reference to Prior which suggests double dealing. At the time when he was vehemently urging on old Monsieur de Barrois, the Lorraine envoy, that the Pretender must no longer be permitted to remain at Bar, we learn from Berwick:

M. Talon (Torcy) also told me...that M. Pecour (Prior) had writ a note to him telling him there was now no more necessity for M. Robinson's (James III) parting with M. Laumaire (Lorraine); but M. Pecour did not explain the reasons; he will I suppose tell him when he sees him next[2].

Moreover in Torcy's correspondence in the Archives of the Ministry of Foreign Affairs in Paris, there is evidence that even as early as 1711, Prior had informed the Jacobites of the "good intentions[3]" of the Tory ministry, and we may reasonably presume that in the many conversations which he had with Berwick, he continued to do so. He seems to have been consulted occasionally by Gaultier as to the wisdom of certain proposed lines of action; for example, we find Gaultier writing to Torcy during one of his visits to Paris that

Mr Prior does not think it fit that I should inform the Treasurer of what Montgoulin [i.e. James III] has done in consequence of the memorandum I sent him on my arrival two months ago, nor of the orders which he sent to Scotland[4].

---

[1] *Hist. MSS. Comm.* Stuart Papers, I. 256.   [2] *Ibid.* 318.

[3] *Aff. Etr. Angl.* vol. 248, fo. 35, James III to Torcy, Châlons, Jan. 5, 1713. "...L'année 1711 Richard d'Hamilton me dit qu'il auoit uüe Mr Prior pendant l'esté...que Mr Prior luy auoit fait scauoir les bonnes Intentions du ministere." Cf. *E.H.R.* July, 1915, p. 502.

[4] *Ibid.* vol. 246, fo. 39*b*, July 12, 1713.   Cf. *E.H.R.* July, 1915, p. 505.

But this is not to say that Prior knows of any intrigue to restore the Stuarts.

As against these doubts we must remember that in a letter to Halifax after the Queen's death he vehemently protested that all suspicions were unfounded; and although this does not amount to much, for it is what any man might be expected to do in like circumstances, it is supported by the fact that Berwick, even when Prior was smarting under his dismissal from office by the Hanoverian government, stigmatised his Jacobitism as very lukewarm.

I had a long discourse with M. Pecour, but he insisted so much upon M. Robinson's making up with M. Pery (? Protestantism) that I could bring him to no conclusion favourable for this present time[1].

But far clearer evidence of Prior's innocence of anything but the vaguest professions of good intentions is provided by Gaultier's correspondence with Torcy. At the very beginning of the intrigue we find Gaultier writing: "Il ne faut pas sil vous plaist que M. Prior sache rien de tout cecy, car il me semble que M. de Bolingbroke luy en ueut faire un mistere[2]," and at the very height of the business when transmitting to the French minister Oxford's advice to James III in February, 1714, Gaultier adds: "Mathieu doit absolument ignorer tout cecy[3]." This and the silence of his official papers make it reasonable to suppose that the ministers did not take Prior into their confidence in this important matter. Thus we can explain at once the lack of results ensuing on the transference of Prior's papers to Lord Stair and

---

[1] *Hist. MSS. Comm.* Stuart Papers, I. 342, Berwick to James III, St Germain, Jan. 6, 1715.

[2] *Aff. Etr. Angl.* vol. 240, fo. 82, Gaultier to Torcy, London, Oct. 12, 1712; cf. *E.H.R.* July, 1915, I. 502.

[3] *Ibid.* vol. 253, fo. 268, Gaultier to Torcy, Feb. 5, 1714; cf. *E.H.R.* July, 1915, 507.

the confidence that Prior showed when the Queen died. The evidence is all in favour of Prior's innocence of taking part in a conspiracy to break the laws of his country, and it also might be taken to indicate what has been already suggested that Prior's political position was of no very great importance. In spite of close personal friendship, similarity of political opinions, and fellowship in the work of peace, neither Bolingbroke nor Oxford seems to have been prepared to entrust him with knowledge of their more important schemes[1]. Prior seems to be little better than a hack doing the routine work of the office; the important personage is Gaultier. It may be so, but we must remember that ministers had to take measures to cover up their tracks in the event of failure. Had they employed Prior, there would have been available in London, not merely the drafts of his instructions, but also the evidence of clerks who had written them out; there would further have been found in the Embassy in Paris, the fatal originals themselves. The method of negociating through Gaultier had this great advantage, that he would transmit to James III or Torcy the messages given to him verbally by Oxford or Bolingbroke, and thus the compromising documents would be filed in Jacobite and French archives to which the British government had no access. When therefore the Whigs came into power and appointed a Committee to enquire into what was a matter of common gossip, no documentary evidence could be produced either from the offices in London, nor from the Embassy in Paris, and it was not until a hundred years later that any view based on other than guesswork became known to the world. For these reasons we should do well to avoid jumping at the conclusion that in the days of his "greatness," Prior's position was little better than a hollow sham, because he knew nothing of this most dangerous affair of state.

[1] *E.g.* he knew very little of the proposed alliance with France in 1714.

Chapter XI

THE YEARS OF TROUBLE

PRIOR had no desire to continue as minister in Paris, and even in the lifetime of the Queen preparations had been made for his recall by appointing General Charles Ross as ambassador[1]. But as Ross did not undertake the mission, Prior was kept on in Paris, and he did not receive his final letters of revocation till the next year[2].

The fall of Oxford had removed his best friend from the ministry; but the loss was not so serious as might at first sight appear, for Shrewsbury, who succeeded Oxford as Lord Treasurer, was a good friend to the man who had so ably seconded him in Paris. However, on the accession of George I, Prior's old boon companion, Bolingbroke, was driven from office, and although Bolingbroke had not been too friendly disposed towards Prior during the last few weeks, Prior now had need for all the help he could possibly obtain from his friends.

On receiving the news of the Queen's death, he immediately wrote a letter of congratulation and loyalty to the new King, and so long as George I was separated from his ministers, continued to correspond directly with him[3]. Although certain persons were offended at

[1] P.R.O. Royal Letters, 7. The date is St James', April 23/May 4, 1714; and F.O. King's Letters, 13. Date, St James', April 23,/May 4, 1714.

[2] P.R.O.; F.O. King's Letters, 14. Dated, St James', Dec. 31/Jan. 11, 1714/15; cf. also Shrewsbury's letter (obviously to Prior), dated Sept. 29, 1713, in *Hist. MSS. Comm.* Portland Papers, v. 341.

[3] P.R.O. France, 159, Letters of Aug. 20, Aug. 23, Sept. 21, and Sept. 28, 1714.

this proceeding, because they thought the despatches should have been first sent to London[1], the King seems to have received the letters graciously, and not to have taken offence[2]. To those about the King he was not unknown. The young Earl of Dorset might prove a protector in these difficult times, and Prior wrote to him assuring "My dear Lord Dorset...of my continued and inviolable respects[3]." When the ministry was changed, Prior wrote letters of congratulation to his new chiefs. From one, James Stanhope, he received a friendly reply: "if you will let me know wherein I can be serviceable to you, I shall gladly embrace the occasion of showing that I am not forgetful of my old acquaintance[4]."

If words could be relied on, Prior might perhaps have been satisfied. But he knew that he needed more than words, for he was now heavily encumbered with debts, and without Oxford he could not rely on their being paid. Shrewsbury could not pay anything out without a sign manual from the Lords Justices, and they "reasonably declined any distribution of money but what directly tended to the preserving the peace[5]."

It was therefore necessary to obtain as much influence as he could, and fortunately, he could write to Halifax without loss of self respect. The attempts of Oxford to persuade Halifax to join in support of the ministry, had borne fruit perhaps in Halifax writing to Prior at the beginning of 1714 to ask for some trees

[1] *Hist. MSS. Comm.* Portland Papers, v. 493, News letter, Sept. 4, 1714.

[2] Cf. P.R.O. France, 159, Prior to the King, Fontainebleau, Sept. 21, 1714. "Sire, La Manière gracieuse et benigne dont il a plu à Votre Majesté de répondre à la liberté que j'ai prise de lui écrire en droiture."

[3] *Ibid.* Prior to Dorset, Versailles, Aug. 20, 1714.

[4] *Ibid.* Stanhope to Prior, Cockpit, Oct. 7/18, 1714.

[5] *Hist. MSS. Comm.* Portland Papers, v. 497, Shrewsbury to Prior, London, Oct. 4, 1714.

and seeds for his garden. Prior sent the trees, and some melon seed, and was asked in return for "some seed of the herbs commonly used for 'salating' and was offered some 'malt drink[1]'." Encouraged by Halifax's friendly tone, Prior wrote him two letters, of which the second has survived:

My Lord,   Paris the 12/23 Oct. 1714.

The answering my last letter is a point referable only to your own Goodness. Friendship can no more be forced than Love, and those persons sometimes are the objects of both Indulgence in this kind who may least have deserved our favour. I have however the satisfaction to believe that you think me an honest Man and an Englishman: for my having acted as the Queen's orders given Me by her ministers enjoined, my dispatch sent to the Court of England, the copies of my letters here, (I may add) the testimony of the D: of Shrewsb[ury] and all I have had to do with, and my own *Mens conscia recti* will abundantly justify me; for the pride of my mind, pass; there may be some defects and faults in it on that side, but for the Integrity of it, and as to any underhand doings, before God, Angels and Man, I shall stand cleared: and you, my Lord, may pass your word and honour upon that account. I will only add that few men alive have more merit in this regard than my Self, and as long as the 4th article either of Ryswick or of Utrecht remain legible I may as well be thought a Mahometan as a Jacobite: but as these are little reflexions raised by the underlings who had a mind to justify some of their masters' being angry with me, so they will all fall half an hour after you are pleased to be my friend. Pray let that be within half an hour after you receive this letter, and now at the same time that I congratulate your being again first Commissioner of the Treasury, I must implore the immediate succour of your Justice and Humanity: I will complain as little as I can and just as much as is absolutely necessary to let your Lordship see the present state of my affairs, and I believe in this the D. of Shrewsbury's goodness has prevented Me: since my

[1] Bath Papers, III. 443–445.

first being sent to this Country I neither have had advance money extraordinary allowance or payment stated by privy seal, but upon a verbal power I always drew, as my occasions in the service required, upon the Lord Treasurer who accordingly answered Cantillon's bills drawn upon Arthur: In this state a bill bearing date the 15th July for 2,000 pd: was accepted by my Lord: and the payment thereof was ordered: and upon what my Lord of Oxford said upon that affair, Cantillon as well as myself thought it entirely satisfied: somebody or other (for by God I know not who) wrests the staff from my Lord of Oxford's hand as it seems to reign in his stead: how much any of these persons were my friends will appear from the very first act of their Power in that they prevailed with the Queen to defer the giving out or satis-fying those orders; till a little while after, her death put this sum which I expected was paid, amongst her Majesty's debts: and I have since that time run on upon the same foot, expecting every day the D: of Shrewsbury's assistance, and presuming to hear that this sum was paid, and that I might send another bill which has been contracting since June last and which in its course might have the like acceptance and discharge: and which I must send finding Cantillon very scrupulous since the retardment which this bill already sent has met with: though the Treasurer does not as yet refuse to supply me, which you may find by my being still alive: but (as I have said) I hope the D: of Shrewsbury has found remedy to this evil; as you will do by receiving this other bill which I must send you, and by putting me upon such a foot as you may judge proper as long as His Majesty's commands enjoin my stay here. Give me leave in the meantime, my Lord, to represent to you that having been 6 weeks at Fountainebleau, the most expensive place upon Earth except Paris itself, I returned hither 2 days since with Eleven horses, thirteen servants, etc. in a Pomp of Woe that put me in mind of Patroclus' funeral, myself melancholy enough though the Horses did not weep; but maybe, they did not reflect that their provender was not paid for: in short, this whole affair is left to the D: of Shrewsbury and your Lordship and after all, my Lord, pray do your part to let me see that I can have no better friends than you two, and that you both judged it reasonable, however the Treasury was changed, that the Plenipotentiary of England should not be left for Debt in the Chatelet at Paris.

I have two other things to desire both which I believe you will think just: first that our old Fellow Collegiate and my *fidus Achates* Mr Richard Shelton, whom my Lord of Oxford after 4 years importunity on my part, made a Commissioner of the Stamp office some Months since, may by your favour be retained still in his employment: second, that Mr Drift who has been with me these 15 year, and is now my secretary here with leave from his then superiors (and my lord of Oxford in particular) for his so being may be safe in his place of first Clerk or under-secretary in the plantation office, where he has served for 14 years past and received from myself as well whilst I was in as when I had the misfortune to be put out of that Commission, all the instruction I have been able to give him in the understanding and discharge of his business. Your command to Mr Popple upon this account will be sufficient, and I will stand bound as well for him as for 'Squire Shelton that their acknowledgements and gratitude to your Lordship shall be faithful and lasting. I have troubled you with a book rather than a letter but you must remember I have the silence of a great many years to atone for: and a good many things, as you see, to ask.

I am with great respect
My Lord
Your Lordships most obt. and most humble servant
M. Prior[1].

In reply to the first letter, he received from Sir James Montagu the intimation of

Lord Halifax's kind intentions to renew his friendship....He expressed more concern than I care to represent in this paper, to find there had no better care been taken of you. He is likewise a good deal uneasy to find people here so little disposed to do anything in your favour....The chief thing at present he desires to be informed of is how matters stand[2].

[1] B.M. Add. MS. 15,947, fo. 1.
[2] Bath Papers, III. 445, Sir J. Montagu to Prior, Oct. 17/28, 1714.

This did not sound very promising; but worse was to follow, for the second letter drew a stern reply from Halifax himself, and must have come as a bitter disappointment to Prior.

I have received the favour of two letters from you, to which I was uneasy to give an answer. In those you was pleased to speak of some points about which our notions are very different. I shall always avoid to say disagreeable things to anyone, especially to those one wishes well. Nor would I willingly seem to be misled and imposed upon. Therefore, if you please, let all those matters be passed over, and not mentioned any more.

As to your affairs in the Treasury, I send you the account of what you have received and of the bills you have drawn. I mentioned it to Mr Shelton, who was surprised at the sum, and seemed not to believe it was so. If you think fit, you will explain it.

The commission in the customs is renewed, in which you are omitted. I doubt in that you will think you might have been favoured, but, if I may have credit with you, it was impossible[1].

Thus, not merely was he not receiving the pay for his office at the Court of France, but the ministry at home, bearing him no good will, had deprived him of the salary and fees he derived from his commissionership of customs. And this time, there was no allowance of £500 from the Duke of Marlborough to compensate for the loss. Thus, deeply involved in Paris, the only means he had whereby to meet his liabilities, were the emoluments of his Fellowship at St John's. Bitterly chagrined, he must have poured out his soul to Paul Methuen, who explained how affairs stood.

It does not appear that you ever had any Privy Seal or settled allowance, as all other ministers who go abroad have, and consequently those who are in the Treasury have no authority for paying you anything. Besides which they say you have drawn bills for more money since your being in France than would

---

[1] Bath Papers, III. 445–6, Halifax to Prior, Nov. 4/15, 1714.

have been due to you if you had had the character of ambassador extraordinary, which I do not believe....Upon the whole matter, I must do my Lord Halifax the justice to say that I think he is disposed to serve you, and I hope will somehow or other bring it about[1].

Meantime, Prior had to make up his mind to tell Halifax how matters stood.

[No address: to Halifax]

My Lord.   Paris, the 12/23 Nov. 1714.

Since my very Subsistance and Being depend upon the favour of your answers Your Lordship will easily judge your letter of the 4th was very welcome to me: as you therein command, my Lord, I have drawn up the fairest explanation I can of the particulars of those Sums which I have been obliged to expend in the service here, and which remain unsatisfied. As to the 2,000 pd. for which a bill was drawn, and a warrant signed by the Queen, I wrote thereupon a little after her death to the Duke of Shrewsbury and upon the King's arrival in England, the Duke represented to his Majesty the difficulties and hardships I lay under, his Majesty was pleased to enter very graciously and favourably into them, I make no doubt that his Justice and Goodness has already, or will soon (upon your Lordship's kind Intercession) satisfy both this and the Sums since due. The Extraordinaries including the two festivals and two distinct Mournings with my journey to Fountainebleau which is really an Expence very particular (the price of everything there being monstrous) amount to above 1,000 pd: the Monthly expence here, at Versailles and Marli amounts to above 350 pd. Sterl. so that even upon that Calculation the Expence of 8 months will amount to 2,400 pd. Ster(l.) added to the forementioned

$$\frac{1000}{3400}$$

I acknowledge, my lord, that I have lived here like an Ambassador: I have had the respect and honour from this Court very

[1] Bath Papers, III. 446, P. Methuen to Prior, London, Nov. 27/Dec. 8, 1714.

near to that of an Ambassador: and my table has been as open and handsome as that of an Ambassador: this as well the French as British Nobility and All the Gentlemen of our country that have been here can testify: this, I say, my lord, was allowed and I thought judged necessary for the honour and dignity of the Nation; and Moment I received your Commands or that I understand your pleasure to be that I should live in less Compass, I am selling some of my horses and putting off some of my servants: as to my own part, God knows I am so far having taken pleasure in this noise and magnificence that I have been incumbered with it: but so it was, my Lord and Patron, I was minister from a great Monarch to the most Expensive Court in Europe, as every man who has been here and had an Estate, my lords Jersey, Manchester and Shrewsbury can testify, and as I, who have no estate, must testify by lying in Jail except your candour[1].

The Treasury officials therefore drew up the following *résumé* of the situation:

Mr Prior went for France the 1st of Aug. 1712 from whence to the 1st of Aug. 1714 is two years and a quarter in which time there hath been paid on

	li.	s.	d.
his Bills	11810	.	.
And he hath drawn Bills which are yet unpaid for	4458	.	.
	16268	.	.

The pay of an Ambr. for that time on his Ordinary and Bills of Extray. would amount to 15300 . .

So that he hath exceeded that of Ambr. by 968 . .

The pay of a Plenipo: for that time would be only 7918: and his Exceedings, (reckoning that way) would be 8350

Mr Prior in his letter seems to give an Accot. only of eight months, as tho' these Bills for 4458

---

[1] Here the MS. breaks off. (B.M. Add. 15,947, fo. 7.)

were drawn for that time, and if it should be
lookt upon, that the sum of 11810. li.
paid by warrants of the late Lord Treasurer
the Earl of Oxford was accounted for to him,

	li.	s.	d.
Then the Accot. as Ambr. for those 8 months would be	4533	6	8
And those Bills being	4458	.	.
Is less than the Pay of an Ambr. by	75	6	8

But the Pay of a Plenipo. for that time would be
only 2346. li. 13s. 4d.⎫
so that he hath exceeded that of Plenipo. by ⎬ 2112 6 0

Mr Prior in excuse for this large demand lays before your Lordship Several Extraordinary expences within the said eight months,
amounting to 16135 Livres, Vizt.

	Livres.
Celebrating her late Majesty's Coronation Day	3100
Mourning for the Duke of Berry . . .	1935
Do. for her late Majesty . . .	3300
Expences at Fontainebleau	4400
Celebrating his Majesty's Coronation . .	3400
	16135 Livres,

which is about 942 li. sterling[1].

Payments made to Mr Prior or on Bills drawn by him from
France, Vizt.

	Livres.		
Paid by Warrant dated 28th Aug. 1712	400	.	.
29	660	.	.
22 October . .	500	.	.
4 November .	200	.	.
28	1000	.	.
20 January . .	550	.	.
3 March 1712/3	1200	.	.[2]

[1] B.M. Add. MS. 15,947, fo. 16. (*Endorsed:*—State of Mr Prior's
Demands:—1 Dec. 1714. The King will give him the allowance of a
Plenipo. from the 1st of August to be paid immediately.)
[2] "Gilligen" struck through here.

		Livres.		
16	500	.	.	
14 April 1713	600	.	.	
8 May . . .	600	.	.	
30 June . .	800	.	.	
7 August . .	600	.	.	
9 Sept. . .	800	.	.	
20 October . .	1300	.	.	
5 January . .	1000	.	.	
25 March 1714	1100	.	.	
25 April . .	1200	.	. 11,810	

Other Sums drawn and advised of which are not
yet satisfied, vizt.

24th July 1714 a Bill drawn and a Warrant⎫
Signed but not satisfied   .   .   .   .⎭   2000 . .

Advice brought of other Bills drawn by Mr Prior
amounting to   .   .   .   . 2458 . .

16268 . .[1]

The accountants who drew up this document certainly did their best to paint Prior's conduct in the
blackest colours. It is quite clear from the detailed account of the Payments from the Treasury that his
"salary" up to April 25, 1714, had been paid. On
July 24, just before Oxford's fall, a "bill had been
drawn and a warrant signed but not satisfied" for a
further payment of £2000, since when further bills had
been drawn of £2458[2]. The result of the action of the
Treasury was not at all satisfactory to Prior. On December 2/13 Halifax wrote:

I read your letters to the King, and did not omit doing you
all the good I could. The King has therefore ordered you should
be paid the allowance of a plenipotentiary from the 1st August
to the 1st December, together with a bill of extraordinaries

[1] B.M. Add. MS. 15,947, fo. 18.   [2] *Ibid.* fo. 13, 14.

amounting in the whole to £1,176, and the bills which were
due to you in the Queen's time will be paid in course out of the
Queen's arrears. I hope this will be to your satisfaction: I do
assure you, if I could have contrived a rule more favourable to
you, I would have offered it[1].

Now, the pay of a plenipotentiary was £293. 6s. 8d.
a month. Prior was to be allowed this for four months,
and this sum amounts to £1173. 6s. 8d. With extraordinaries the sum sent him was £1176, so that the bill
of extraordinaries, so loudly trumpeted by Halifax,
amounts to the generous sum of £2. 13s. 4d. As Prior
was already in debt to the sum of £4458, this did not
go very far to relieve him, but "*in course*" there was to
be paid him the arrears of the Queen. Presumably the
bill drawn on July 24, amounting to £2000 was included in this and a week's pay as plenipotentiary from
July 24 to August 1, amounting to £74. 6s. 8d. If all
these sums be added together, the result is that we find
Prior with liabilities £4458, and assets £3247. 13s. 4d.
or £1110 to the bad. The result could easily be foreseen.
Although his letters of revocation were dated Dec.
31/Jan. 11, 1714/15, Prior could not leave Paris till the
end of March, because of his creditors. In February he
was still corresponding with Stanhope on what sums
should be included in the Queen's arrears[2]. But at last
the government relented, and on February 7/18 both
Stanhope and Halifax wrote to Prior to tell him that
his debts were to be paid.

"I represented to His Majesty in Council," says Stanhope,
"that it would be impossible for you to return home, unless you
were enabled to pay your debts[3]." "The King," says Halifax,
"has directed us to pay you £2,408 for the two bills of extra-

[1] Bath Papers, III. 447, Halifax to Prior, Dec. 2/13, 1714.
[2] P.R.O. France, 159, Prior to Stanhope, Paris, Feb. 12, 1715.
[3] Bath Papers, III. 447, Stanhope to Prior, Whitehall, Feb. 7/18, 1714.

ordinaries which you demanded, which together with what is due to you yet on your ordinary allowance shall be despatched with all the favour and civility we can show you[1]."

At last therefore Prior was enabled to think of setting out homewards, and he lost no time in his preparations. On March 5, he was received in audience by Louis XIV and took leave, but except that Prior begged that the Mardyck question might be settled to the satisfaction of Great Britain nothing remarkable passed. After taking leave of the King, he went the usual official round of waiting upon the Princes and Princesses. The day after the interview with Louis, Torcy presented him with

the King's picture set round with diamonds. The Jewel is very rich, the value as I am told amounts to £900 sterling, and to it he added a great compliment of the pains I had taken in the course of the negociation[2].

Prior therefore asked and obtained permission to accept the gift. In acknowledging this kindness, Prior reflected whimsically upon the unpopularity of the negociations in which he had had any part.

After our first visit, Sir, came the partition treaty, with which the nation were little satisfied; and to my second visit succeeds a treaty in which I think they are as little satisfied[3].

On March 25 he left Paris in the evening, and had a miserable journey.

I set out...not having been in any state of health for some time before. I was taken here [Boulogne] very ill with a violent colic, vomiting and something worse. This, Sir, is strange stuff to entertain of a secretary of state with—I wish I had better[4].

[1] Bath Papers, III. 447, Stanhope to Prior, Whitehall, Feb. 7/18, 1714.
[2] P.R.O. France, 159, Prior to Stanhope, Paris, March 9, 1714/15.
[3] *Ibid*. Prior to (Stanhope), Paris, March 21, 1715.
[4] *Ibid*. Prior to Stanhope, Boulogne, March 29, 1715.

Thus ill at ease in body, Prior crept home to England. He had grounds to be also ill at ease in mind, for he could have had little doubt of the disposition of the Whig ministry to the *employés* and friends of their predecessors. Already he had been superseded by Lord Stair in the ministry in Paris, and had been roughly commanded to yield up all his papers to the Earl[1]. This he probably had done without compunction or difficulty, for he knew there was little in them that could compromise his position or that of his friends. He therefore obeyed the command at once, to the intense jubilation of the Whigs, who thought hereby to obtain the fullest evidence against Lord Oxford[2]. But he did not anticipate the treatment he was to receive. Not only was there no joyful welcome as in 1697, but on June 9 at the demand of the Secret Committee, the Speaker granted a warrant for his arrest, and he was taken into nominal custody in order to be examined by the Committee[3]. He lived apparently in his own house in Duke Street, under the supervision of a messenger. On June 16 he was examined by the Committee, but as he has left a most diverting account of this examination, he must be left to tell it in his own words:

In outward Appearance, they were all very civil; set me a Chair equal to the Table where they sat, and next to Secretary *Stanhope*, who had the Books and Papers of the Secretary's Office before him. Mr. *Walpole* the Chairman said little more than mere Compliment. Mr. *Lechmere*, with great Industry, hid from me, and often himself looked into Papers in Folio, unbound, and covered with a blue Sheet. I did not then know what they were, but during the Examination, I perceived it was the Report then

[1] *Hist. MSS. Comm.* Stair Papers, Report ii. p. 188.
[2] *Ibid.* vii. 247a, Earl of Egmont Papers, Daniel Dering to Lord Percival, London, July 19, 1715.
[3] *Ibid.* Portland Papers, v. 510, Letter to W. Hayley, June 11, 1715.

printed, and in some few Days after published. He began with an affected Eloquence, that as I had served in a very high Employment, and with very great Applause, the Committee relied upon my Candour and Probity: That as what they asked me was for the King's Service, so what I answered would be for my own Honour. After this some of them began with several vague Questions: What I knew of the Negotiation? How long I had been acquainted with the Abbe *Gaultier?* If the Propositions came first from *France,* or if we sent them? And desired me to give them an account of whatever I could of that whole Matter; which, it seems, they thought I was so ready to do, that some of them took their Pens and Paper, as if I were to begin a Sermon, and they to take short Notes.

I said, That as I had always acted abroad by the Authority of the Crown of *England,* and had, in Obedience to the King's Commands, given up all the Memorials and Papers which related to that Part of the Peace in which I had a Share, I was desirous to answer the Honourable Committee (before whom I understood such Papers were) in every thing that might help to explain them: That my Books were already before them: and, as I had already written to Mr. Secretary *Stanhope,* those Books must even speak for themselves. The Committee seemed to acquiesce in my Answer. Lord *Con.** whispered the Chairman, and said, No, we will begin with the Money.

The Committee then desired to know what Money I drew from the Treasury in 1711, when I went into *France.* I answered, Two hundred Pounds; and, as I remembered, that was the Sum. I had either Credit from Mr. *Clifford,* on his Correspondent, or from Monsieur *Cantillon:* I could not well remember which, it being now four Years since. Had you these Bills, some of them said, from my Lord Treasurer? I replied, No. They asked me, Was it by his Order? I said, I hoped there was no Occasion for a Reply to that Question. I presumed it would be found, as other Money expended on the like Occasion, by Direction of the Sovereign. I found they were not pleased with this Answer. *Wal.* said, Will you think a little of the Method in which this

* Coningsby.

Examination is to proceed? And Mr. PRIOR will be pleased in the mean Time to retire a little.

When I was called in again, the same Question was asked me, and the same Answer returned. I added, That I well hoped those Sums, and several others of much greater Importance, were paid: That otherwise, for want of Knowledge in the Crown Laws, I should find my self a Beggar; and from an Hotel at *Paris*, might spend the rest of my Days in the Counter: And here I addressed myself to Mr. *Stanhope*, as to what I had writ to him concerning my Debts. He said, That nothing of all this concerned me. *P.* I must apply myself to you upon another Head. I must own myself unexperienced in the Method of Parliament; I have no Papers by me; I have no Council; for want of Memory or Judgment I may err; and tho', Gentlemen, I am accused of nothing, I know not but that I may accuse myself through Inadvertency or Mistake.

Here Mr. *Stanhope* rose up, and told the Committee, That he had the King's particular Direction, that whatever I said to them, or they to the House of Commons, should not be of any Prejudice to myself. I took a Sheet of Paper, which lay before me, and wrote this down, as I did what they had already said to me. Here, after they had whispered, and some even separated themselves from the Table to confer in a Corner of the Room, the Chairman told me I might withdraw; which I did, leaving the Notes I had taken upon the Table.

When I was called in again, I found their Civility much abated, and the Battery quite changed. The most confused Questions were put to me, upon several Heads, backward and forward, by *Lech.* and *Bosc.* and *Con.* (the two first of whom I think understood not one Word of what they were saying). *Con.* at length prevailed. Mr. PRIOR, you were sent out that you might have Time to recollect more particularly upon whom you had Credit, when my Lord of *Oxford* sent you into *France*. *P.* I have great Respect to the Earl of *Oxford*; but he never sent me into *France*. And turning to Mr. Secretary *Stanhope*, who had the Books of the Office of 1711 in his Hand, I said, That as I had the Honour to be sent into *France* by the Queen's especial

Appointment and immediate Direction, I presumed the Copy of my Powers were to be found in the Books before him*. He turning to it, Mr. PRIOR, is this the Copy of your Instructions? *P.* I believe it is; but to give the Committee no further Trouble on this Head, I am ready either now, or any other Time, to produce the Original, as I think it may tend to my Service. Being asked of whom I received Money in *France?* I answered of Monsieur *Cantillon. Bosc.* Was he not a Papist? *P.* Else, Sir, he could not have been a Banker at *Paris,* which he had been for several Years before I knew him. In one Word, he was the common Banker to whom the *English* addressed themselves, and I think *Clifford* of *Amsterdam* was his Correspondent. *Stan.* and *Wal.* I found frowning and nodding at each other, and extremely ashamed at this vile Stuff.

Being sent out, and called in again, I found the Thunder broke out. *Wal.* referred it to *Stan.* to speak. *Stan.* The Committee are not satisfied with your Behaviour to them. I have already told you, that the Lords above, and the Committee here, have taken Notice, that they find a constant Correspondence on your Side to Lord Treasurer, but no Answers from him; whereas all your Letters from Lord *Bolingbroke* are entire, and commonly in their right Order. Some of those indeed are missing. The whole Committee ecchoed the same Thing. *P.* I was told some Hours since, by this Honourable Committee, that I should be asked nothing that might prejudice myself. I am a good deal confused; I have no Council; and with great Respect, I look upon this to be a downright Accusation of myself, as if I should have held any Correspondence I was unwilling to declare. I must refer my self to you in this Point, Mr. *Stanhope.* The Letters that we receive, when abroad, from the Secretaries of State, we keep, copying our Answers to them, both which justify our acting according to our Orders sent us; and I presume it will be found that my Letters, which you have in your own Keeping, answer those written to me by the Secretaries of State under whose Departments I acted; which Letters you have likewise. You have also the Letters I have wrote to the Lord Treasurer in my

* Vide the Report, Folio 3.

Books, at least those of them that related to the public Affair, and consequently were worth keeping. I did not, nor could I expect a constant Correspondence from him. What I wrote was for his Information; what Use his Lordship made of that Information, I had reason to presume was for the Queen's Service; and the Answers and Directions to me were to come by the Secretary of State. *Commit.* It is very strange, that not above two or three Letters should appear from my Lord Treasurer. Did he not write more to you? *P.* He writ to me several Times, and I obeyed his Commands intimated to me therein. Those Commands performed, the Letters were of no Use, and I no more kept them, than I did Letters received from other Noblemen, the Duke of *Buckingham*, the Lord *Halifax*, Lord *Harcourt*, then Lord Chancellor, &c. They related no otherwise to the Negotiation, than in commending me, assuring me that he represented my Services to the Queen in a right Light, and wishing a speedy End to the Negotiation, that I might come home to him.

I was sent out again, and recalled; was asked how many Letters I might in all have received from my Lord Treasurer, and what was the Substance of any of them. *P.* As to the Number, I cannot particularly tell; I received a Letter from him sometimes of five, sometimes of ten or twelve Lines, ordering me to pay Sums of Money to Persons who had the Queen's Pension, and were then in *France*, or recommending some of his particular Friends to my Acquaintance, or, which I thought much better, telling me he had ordered the Payment of my Bills; but I might very safely affirm, that I had no Letter that could possibly concern the Committee, or any body else. I have one Letter that as Lord Treasurer he writ to me, which related to the Payment of the Dowry of King *James*'s Queen *Mary*; a Thing publickly transacted, and known here in *England*: But as no Progress was made in that Affair during my Stay in *France*, and that it did not belong to the Negotiation of the Peace, I had not indeed given up that Letter, but, as I thought, I could find it, or the Copy of it, if it should have been thought of any Use. In the mean time, I thought proper, in case any Thing had been done in that matter, to keep that Letter for my own Justification; as indeed it would have been my Order. *Bosc.* Sir, you say you do not know how many Letters you had; Might you have ten? *P.* I believe I might, *Bosc.* Might you have fourteen? *P.* I believe I might. *Bosc.* Might you have sixteen? *P.* Indeed, Mr. *Bosc.* I have told you that I cannot answer you to any indefinite number. It was still urged with great Vehemence, that I kept a constant Correspondence with my Lord Treasurer. *P.* I am very far from denying it; but he did not keep a constant Correspondence with me. It was my Duty to write to him, and he was to make what Use he pleased of my Letters. I complained sometimes of the Objections I met with at the Court of *France* in the Execution of my Orders; and was very glad when by the Letters from the Secretary of State, I found my Difficulty made easier: But, Gentlemen, since we are upon this Subject, throughout the whole Course of my Letters to my Lord Treasurer, and even in those I wrote to the Duke of *Shrewsbury*, after his Grace's Return, both in *England* and *Ireland*, I still complained that my Lord Treasurer did not write to me. And here indeed, being very much teized and vexed, my Lord *Con.* raving and threatening that these Letters must be produced; I said, If there be such Letters in the World, that contain the Secrets of the Negotiation written by my Lord Treasurer, it might be very well presumed, his Lordship kept Copies of them, and he must produce them: For, said I, by the eternal God I know of no such Letters; and you know, my Lord, that your Countryman is no very exact Correspondent. This I said, having known that my Lord *Con* had troubled great Men, if not my Lord Treasurer particularly, with Letters, who had never taken Care to answer him. I grant this was very foolishly said; for one should never provoke a Hedge-Hog. *Con.* breaking out into a great Passion, This is imposing upon the Committee! *P.* Imposing, my Lord, is a very hard Word. He lifted up his Voice in Anger, and was going on: But *Stan.* yet louder than he, swore, that he could produce every individual Scrip of Paper that had been written to him by any Man alive, or that he had written to any Man during his being a Minister abroad. *P.* Mr. *Stanhope*, I am sorry I cannot do the like; if it be so, you are the most careful Minister that ever yet were sent abroad. They proceeded in asking me to give an Account of what, they said, I must needs know of the Meeting of the Lords at my House, with *Mesnager* and *Gaultier*. I had already heard, that they had consulted their Friends of the Law upon that Point, and had determined to fix upon that Meeting, wherein the Preliminaries were signed, as an Accusation of Treason. How justly I leave to the Judgment of all disinterested and honest Men; since first, in the Nature of the Thing, it is impossible for any two Nations in War to come ever to an Accommodation, or begin any Plan, upon which a future Peace may be founded, without some Overture and Intervention of this Kind. All Treaties, from that of *Vervens* down to this Day, have been thus mediated. *Calieres* was in *Holland*, and discoursed and conferred privately with Monsieur *Dyckvelt*, on the Part of the States, above two Years before he took a public Character, and signed the Treaty of *Ryswick*. Monsieur *de Torcy* was publickly in *Holland*, 1709, conferred with the Pensioner, and the Deputies of the States; and our own Plenipotentiaries the Duke of *Marlborough* and Lord *Townshend*, reported from those Deputies to Her Majesty, what the *French* Minister either proposed or granted. *Mesnager* had as full Powers as *France* could give, had owned the Queen's Authority, and seen her Person; and had, by Her Majesty's Directions, several Times conferred with the Lords of a Committee of Cabinet; all the World seeing the Man, and knowing the Fact: So that any Meeting after this could not be secret, dangerous, or treasonable. Mr. *St. John's* Letter of the 25th of *September*, 1711, to Her Majesty, informs Her immediately of this Meeting, and her Majesty approves of what is there done, by Her especial Warrant for signing the Preliminaries, containing, The Demands made by her Order*.

It may be observed that Mr. *St. John* writes to the Queen thus,

"The Committee of Council met this Morning at the *Cockpit*, "and directed the Earl of *Dartmouth* and myself to confer with "Monsieur *Mesnager:* We saw him accordingly this Evening, "at Mr. Prior's House, where my Lord Treasurer and Lord

* Appendix to the Report, Page 8.

"Chamberlain were likewise present." The Treason therefore, if there were any, was committed in the Morning by the Committee of Council, and at the *Cockpit*, and not at Mr. P RIOR's House in the Evening. It may properly here be added, the Queen had signed a Warrant the 17th of *September*, 1711, to the Lord Keeper, for full Powers*; in which my Lord *Harcourt*, then Lord Chancellor, the Earl of *Oxford*, Lord Treasurer, the Duke of *Buckingham*, President of the Council, the Bishop of *Bristol*, Lord Privy Seal, the Duke of *Shrewsbury*, Lord Chamberlain, the Earl *Poulett*, Lord Steward of the Houshold, and the Earl of *Dartmouth*, and Mr. *St. John*, Secretaries of State, and MATTHEW PRIOR, Esq; were nominated and empowered to meet with the Sieur *Mesnager*, provided with sufficient Authority to settle an eventual or conditional Convention between Her Majesty and the most Christian King; and that this Warrant was not made use of, for Reasons given, being very natural, because they were Offers only on the *French* Side, and did not oblige Her Majesty to any Thing: So they were only signed *Mesnager*, and *Dartmouth* and *St. John* are only Witnesses that these Articles are to be looked upon as Conditions which his most Christian Majesty agrees to grant and which are afterwards to be reduced into Form, and explained to the common Satisfaction of *Great Britain* and *France*. Though this Procedure will, without doubt, hereafter appear consonant to common Sense, conducive to the Safety and Good of *Great Britain*, and justifiable by the universal Custom and Law of Nations, *Nunc non erat his locus.* I said, Monsieur *Mesnager* had often been at my House; that the Secretary of State had seen him there; that I had eat and drank, and been abroad with him several Times. They took great hold of this. *Bosc.* expressed himself with great Joy, This is more than we knew before! And from thence they ran wildly back, When I knew *Gaultier?* Where I had been with *Mesnager?* I answered to this in as general Terms as I could. The Chairman perceived that they would lose their Point in this Multiplicity of Questions, and, checking their Speed, restrained it to this one Demand. *Chairm.*

* Appendix to the Report, Page 7.

What Lords were present at your House, at the Meeting when the preliminary Articles were talked of, or signed? I answer'd, The two Secretaries of State; for it is certain they were so, their Names appearing in the Instrument. *Chairm.* Was my Lord of *Oxford* there? *P.* I cannot recollect it: One of the Lords were absent; whether the Duke of *Shrewsbury*, or the Earl of *Oxford*, I cannot tell. In all Sincerity and Honour this is Truth. They grew extremely anger'd upon it, and sent me out to recollect if both these Lords were not present.

I came in, and assured them again, That as well as I could remember a Transaction, of which I took no Notes, and which was now above three Years past, and of which I was so far from expecting to be called to any Account, that I thought it was an Honour to me, I could not determine which of the two were absent. I said again, That this was Fact, that I do not remember it: I have only an Idea that one of them was absent. The Answer indeed had this Effect, that it was the same Thing as if they were both absent, since they could not determine which of them was present. But upon this Meeting no less Accusation than an Article of High Treason was to be founded. Was any Thing more difficult ever put upon a Man, than to endeavour to extort an Evidence from me, in order to bring those to the Scaffold who were Friends and Patrons, under whose Orders formerly, and with whom jointly now, I had the Honour to act, by the Queen's Directions, and in a Matter not only innocent, but laudable! Or could any thing be more absurd, or more inhuman, than to propose to me a Question, by the answering of which I might (according to them) prove myself a Traytor! Since, as I had heard, every Man who is a Partner, is a Principal in Treason: And notwithstanding their solemn Promise, that nothing which I could say should hurt myself, I had no Reason to trust them; for they violated that Promise about five Hours after (as I shall say anon). However, I owned I was there present. Whether this was wisely done or no, I leave to my Friends to determine.

From my being taken up by Order of the House of Commons, this Examination was just a Week. They now, after I had been turned out, and returned again, interrogated me: If since my

being taken into Custody, I had not seen my Lord of *Oxford*, or
any of his Relations? I said, I had seen my Lord of *Oxford* the
last *Sunday* at Mr. *Thomas Harley's* House; and was going on to
explain that Mr. *Thomas Harley* and I, who were taken up at
the same Time, (living within three Doors of each other) commonly dined together at one or the other of our Houses, our
respective Messengers guarding us. That on *Sunday* going to
dine with Mr. *Harley*, I saw my Lord of *Oxford* at the Stair-
head, going out; that I asked him if he dined with us: He told
me, he was to dine in better Company: That this was all that
passed between us; the Messenger at the Bottom of the Stairs
heard every Word I said to him. As I was telling this, they
answered it was sufficient, I had seen my Lord of *Oxford*, and
his near Relation; which was the Question ask'd.

I here was ordered to retire, and when I was called in again,
the Chairman, from amongst many Books and Papers, which he
had before him, (and the Secretary of State had on the other Side
as many; and I perceived many of them were my own) the
Chairman, I say, abruptly enough threw one Half-sheet of the
large Demy Paper, written very foul, and razed in several Places,
which, indeed, when he gave into my Hand, I hardly knew what
it was, so far as to give any reasonable Account of it, it being
without Date or Title, and, as I say, very imperfect as to the
very Words and Stile. He asked me dryly, and without any other
previous Word, If I knew that Hand? *P.* There are two Hands
in it, one is very like the Hand I write when first I make any
Brouillon. *One or two of the Committee.* Sir, What do you mean
by a Brouillon? *P.* When I write any Thing at first only for my
own Memory, as to what I would draw up after in a more
perfect Manner. I perused this Piece of Paper, and, upon a little
Reflection, directing myself to Mr. *Stanhope*, said, I believed this
Paper contained some Notes upon a Letter I received from his
Predecessor, my Lord *Bolingbroke*. He was apprised of this before:
for he readily turned to the Letter which was registered in the
Office-Book. I added, that I thought there were some Notes
I had taken in the *French* Language, to enable me to speak more
particularly to Monsieur *de Torcy* of the Matters mentioned in

the said Secretary's Letter. As that Letter was written four Years before, and I was not in Possession of my own Letters, the Secretary himself and the Committee could best inform themselves of the Substance thereof. There was written, *My Lord, Tr. ne doute point que la Cour de France n' y trouve de remede.* Now whatever Lord that might mean, they had already printed it my Lord Treasurer*: and in so doing had given that Sentence the wrongest Construction imaginable, as proving that my Lord Treasurer would give up *Tournay* to *France*; whereas the whole Hint was meant to renew to the Ministers at that Court, that *Tournay* was to be given to the Allies; and it was to keep the Court of *France* from endeavouring to hope the contrary. As what was in this Brouillon was sometimes an Abridgment, and sometimes a verbal Translation of my Lord *Bolingbroke*'s Letter, which Mr. *Stanhope* still held close, and as I read the *French* into *English*, I asked him if the same Sense was in the Letter. He did not deny it. *Con.* grew extremely angry, and on a sudden broke out into some Expressions, which neither he should have utter'd, nor will I repeat; and so I was ordered to withdraw again; which was into the next Room, where not only a Messenger of the House of Commons, but a Door-Keeper of the Secretary's Office, waited all Day, and were still ready to receive me.

Being called in again, I was interrogated without Method or Connection, as any Member of the Committee pleased, and indeed with Confusion and Disorder enough among themselves; for they sometimes stopped each other's Question, and proposed new ones of their own. At last it came to this. *Chairm.* Mr. PRIOR, we cannot doubt but that you are apprised of the whole Affair of *Tournay*. Did my Lord ever write about *Tournay?* *P.* I cannot readily answer, as not understanding the Force of the Question: I believe my Lord Treasurer may have writ to me concerning *Tournay* at the Beginning of the Negotiation: I am sure he has spoke to me about *Tournay:* I may be mistaken as to the Time; but I think in 1711 the *French* insisted upon their having *Tournay:* But I very well remember, †that the Queen's

* Vide the Report, Page 34.
† Vide Answer to the Memorial, dated *Nov.* 18, 1711. Append. to

Instructions to her Ambassadors for the general Peace, were positive that the *Dutch* should have it: I understood the Negotiation to continue always upon that Foot. I added, that as the Affair of the Barrier was transacted at *Utrecht*, I had nothing in my Instructions relating to that whole Matter, otherwise than as it might relate in general to the Peace. What I have of the whole Negotiation is before you. Here *Wal.* and *Stan.* grew mightily perplexed; one in a sullen, and t'other in an unbounded Passion. *Con.* raved outright. I may justly protest that I could not conceive the Cause of this Disorder; for I did not know that they had already founded their High Treason upon the Articles of *Tournay*, against my Lord Treasurer; nor can I since comprehend why they did. To shew the Justice, as well as the good Judgment of these Men, it must certainly appear not only extravagant, but ridiculous to all who think righter than the Committee, that is, to all Men living, that an Article of High Treason should be founded against an *English* Minister upon *Tournay*, which was not given up to the *French*, and no mention ever made of *Lisle*, which actually was given up. This by the way. It may be further observed, that at that Time not one third Part of the Committee themselves did know upon what Point the Accusations either against the Earl of *Oxford*, or any Man else, were to be grounded; several of them having since told me themselves, that they never drew up or read the Report; but that those Things came to them, as they merrily expressed it, ready cut and dried.

But to return to my Journal; this various and incoherent manner of Examination having now lasted above nine Hours. Two of my Masters (by the way) Mr. *Onslow* and Mr. *Erle*, had left the Committee almost at the Beginning of the Day; for to give them their Due, they asked me very few Questions while there, and by going away seemed ashamed of the Proceeding: And now *Wal.* himself grew weary of it, and was going, but hindered, and, as it were, kept in the Chair by Mr. *Stan.* who said openly, they could not go on without the Chairman. I was ordered to withdraw, and during about half an Hour's

the Report, Page 14. the Queen's Instructions to Her Plenipotentiaries, *ibid.* Page 20.

Recess into the next Room, or rather Passage, as the Door was by chance opened, I heard them extremely warm and loud with one another. Whilst I was in this little Room, in which the Messenger under whose Custody I was, and a Door-Keeper of the Secretary's Office, as I have already said, were waiting, *Con.* came out by a back Way, as *Bosc.* did by the fore Door. In this Room was a Trunk, and in it several Papers and Memorials, to which the Committee had Recourse during the Examination. The Trunk was open, and I could not but perceive by the Indorsements, that many of the Papers were my own. *Con.* whispered the Officers to take care that I should not come nigh the Trunk, and really looked on me more like a Fury than a Man; though certainly I had all the Right imaginable to see every Paper that related to me in my Examination, which was pretended to be made upon no other Foot, than that the King should be informed of what I had done for his Service in the Negotiation of the Peace; and if the Committee themselves had really a Mind to be apprized of the Truth as to Fact, the hindering a Man whom they intended should become an Evidence from seeing his own Papers, was but an ill Method towards his giving them a clearer Intelligence.

I was now called in for the last Time, and I found that they had collected several Heads of what they thought proper I should set my Hand to. I read them, and made some Objections thereunto, but to no Purpose. I said, that to many Questions I had not, nor could answer, in the positive manner that was there set down: That as to divers Facts, I could not take Things upon my Memory: That as to others, I had indeed said I believed, I thought, I had heard, or understood they were so: That the Omission of these Words made me say positively, and as an Evidence, what I should not be able to maintain, having only answered them as my Memory served me, and as much as I knew of the Heads upon which I had been interrogated; knowing that they themselves had blamed my Answers, for being very imperfect; and I had more than once told them, I was sorry I could not answer them more fully. I objected against these Words: *He confesses that since his Confinement he has conversed with the*

Earl of Oxford, *and his nearest Relations.* I did not, I said, confess. Confession supposes a Crime, I was told, I was accused of none. I said I had seen the Earl of *Oxford* at Mr. *Thomas Harley*'s; and as I was going to tell the Thing again, Jesus! said *Con.* how perjur'd is this Man? *P.* My Lord, have a care of ——. *Con.* No, Sir, 'tis you that must have a care. Seeing now the Face of the Committee against me, knowing and presuming that if ever the Duke of *Shrewsbury*, the Earl of *Oxford*, or Lord *Bolingbroke* himself, should be brought to Trial, I must be sure before the Lords have an Opportunity of explaining what I had said, and declaring what Usage I had found from the Committee, I signed the Paper. I cannot here omit a ridiculous Instance of my *Middlesex* Justice's Skill in the Law: He was just going to set his Name on the Left Hand of the Paper, where I was to have set mine; and if he had not been timely cautioned by the Chairman, it would have been the Deposition of *Hugh Boscawen, jurat, coram me, Matt. Prior.*

When I had thus signed the Paper, the Chairman told me, that the Committee were not at all satisfied with my Behaviour, nor could give such an Account of it to the House that might merit their Favour in my Behalf: That at present they thought fit to lay me under a stricter Confinement than that of my own House. Here *Bosc.* played the Moralist, and *Con.* the Christian; but both very aukwardly. *Bosc.* said, that he had often heard Mr. *Stepney* (who was a wise Man) and our old friend, repeat this Proverb, *Near is my Shirt, but nearer my Skin*; and told me, if I had remembered that Saying, and acted according to it, it would have been better for me. And *Con.* said, he had known me a long Time, and was heartily sorry for my Condition; but all this proceeded from my own Fault. Now this kind Commiseration did not last above a Minute; for the Messenger to whose House they intended to confine me, being called, *Con.**

* Lord *Coningsby's* Behaviour, during this Examination, seems to have been the Ground of that Resentment express'd against him by Mr. PRIOR in his Ballads of *Down-Hall* and the *Viceroy*; the first of which is in the Third Volume of his former Works, and the other in the Second of these posthumous Volumes.

asked him if his House were secured by Bolts and Bars. The Messenger*, who is by Birth a Gentleman, and a very good-natur'd Man, was astonished at the Question; and answered, that he never had any in his Custody but Parliament Prisoners, (as he expressed it) and there were neither Bolts nor Bars in his House. At which *Con.* very angrily said, Sir, you must secure this Prisoner; it is for the Safety of the Nation; if he escapes, you shall answer for it. And now I met with another Hardship, which indeed, I could not have expected, as I had all Day taken Notes of the Heads of their Examination, and my Answers, and particularly that Mr. *Stanhope* had, by his Majesty's Order, informed the Committee, that from whatever I should say in this Examination, nothing should or ought to redound to my own Prejudice: Nor indeed could it be imagined I should answer upon any other Foot; for without the King's Consent, I doubt if I ought at all to have answered to the Committee.

M. P.[1]

It is not surprising that the Whigs were furious at being baffled by the want of documentary evidence. That there had been a plot to alter the succession they were convinced, for it was the subject of ordinary conversation before the Queen died, and yet evidence that could be used was not forthcoming. That the evidence was in Paris they seem to have suspected, and therefore they assumed that Prior's papers would reveal it. They were right in their suspicions, but wrong as to the place where it was to be found. The evidence was beyond their reach, for it had been carefully filed by Torcy, through whose hands the negociation between James III and the Tory ministers had passed. It is a matter for surprise that anything like a full extract from the correspondence has never been published, and that Lord Stanhope, who had access to the papers and realised their importance, was content that they and his transcripts should remain in manuscript, while for the

---

* Mr. *Hollingshead.*　　　[1] *History of his own time*, pp. 286–302.

period subsequent to the treaty, in which the negociations were most fully developed, he never seems to
have attempted to supplement what he had written in
his earlier work[1], where he had to rely on the very
slight quotations given in an article in the *Edinburgh
Review* from the transcripts made by Sir James
Mackintosh in 1814[2].

The negociation, which, as we have already seen,
was kept secret from Prior, grew hot towards the end of
the year 1712, when Gaultier wrote that Bolingbroke
was beginning to work seriously in the cause of James[3].
He insisted on knowing what offers the Whigs had
made a year and a half before, and that the ministers
would have no communication with James save through
the medium of Torcy. On receiving an assurance from
James that he had not had any such offer from the
Whigs[4], the ministry halted for some six months. Then
on the eve of the signature of the treaty, Oxford sent
for Gaultier, and began a somewhat vague opening on
the subject of James, to whom he would render services
as soon as peace was signed. Queen Anne was to be
kept informed of the negociation, for she had the same
sentiments as he; meanwhile James must make up his
mind not to stay in Lorraine, but must go and travel
somewhere, Italy, Switzerland, Bavaria, or even Spain,
anywhere rather than rouse suspicions that he is constantly on the watch for trouble in England[5]. The
Chevalier replied in a letter to Torcy, which from the
terms used about Oxford's "consummate wisdom"
and the "love of his country" was clearly meant for
the Lord Treasurer's eye, accepting the overtures in

---

[1] *Reign of Queen Anne*, pp. vi, vii. *History of England*, I. 43.
[2] *Edinburgh Review*, vol. LXII. no. cxxv., Article on Bolingbroke. Some
of the documents have since been published in the *English Historical
Review* for July, 1915, pp. 501-518.   [3] *E.H.R.* July, 1915, no. I. p. 502.
[4] *Ibid*. no. II. p. 502.   [5] *Ibid*. no. v. p. 503.

general terms[1], and now the intrigue began in earnest. Gaultier, who in this month of April, 1713, was in Paris, apparently paid a visit to the Chevalier, and brought back a memorandum of points mentioned by James for use in conversation with Oxford. What if Queen Anne were to die suddenly? Again, Oxford need not say more at present about what he proposes to do to please the Chevalier. Further, provided the Chevalier is far from France and in a place where Marlborough is not likely to see him, it does not matter where he passes the winter. Nor must he fail immediately to make his intentions known to the Non-Juring and Roman Catholic Lords[2]. Finally the *mot d'ordre* apparently went forth that James must not be impatient[3]: time and his enemies were on his side, for there was more to be hoped from the folly of the Whigs than from any active measures on the part of the ministry. Patience was the refrain of Gaultier during the latter part of the summer and early autumn, but at the end of November, a fresh request that James would go to Venice for the Carnival was sent from England[4], and from Venice he was to go to Cologne. To this Torcy replied in terms of vigorous remonstrance: such a demand could not possibly be accepted[5], and Torcy evidently considered it a ruse to get the Chevalier further from England than ever. Yet there was subtlety in the proposal, as Gaultier explained a fortnight later[6]. If the Chevalier would go to Venice in the spring, he would see many more English than he ever would at Nancy, for it would be impossible to refuse passports to the English to go to a place so much frequented as Venice, whereas to issue passports to Nancy was tantamount to giving

[1] *E.H.R.* no. VI. p. 504.   [2] *Ibid.* no. VII. p. 504.
[3] *Ibid.* nos. VII. and X. pp. 504 and 505.   [4] *Ibid.* no. XI. p. 505.
[5] *Aff. Etr. Angl.* vol. 247, fo. 75, Torcy to Gaultier, Nov. 25, N.S. 1713.   [6] *E.H.R.* July, 1915, no. XIII. p. 506.

a passport to visit the Pretender. As to Cologne, the ministers would be glad to see him there when peace with the Empire was signed, and his uncle Charles II was there when he was recalled to England. Then without apparently any sense of the ludicrousness of the proposal, Oxford urged that if the Chevalier intended to return to England, he must behave as his uncle Charles II did at the end of his exile, and "in all ways must follow the means used by that Prince to recover the affections of his people." "Quil laisse faire aux Wights et a la maison d'Hanover tout ce qu'ils uoudront, plus ils trauailleront a luy faire du mal et plus il luy fairont du bien[1]." But a few lines later he harps again on the need of imitating his uncle. To make such a suggestion argues a complete misapprehension of the Chevalier's character; true, it was rumoured in England at the beginning of 1713 that he had taken a couple of mistresses[2]. But the precariousness of the situation was too strongly felt by Oxford and Gaultier not to mention it. "Pray God the Queen lives for some years, for if she were to die immediately and suddenly, all those who serve her will be lost, and the Chevalier would be in no better case, so his friends tell me; and in such an event, they can give him no advice." As to the House of Hanover, said Oxford, "so long as he lived he would never consent to England being governed by a German," and the next Parliament was so to manage affairs that the Chevalier would of necessity return on the Queen's death, provided always that he imitated the conduct of Charles II. Moreover, lest he should imagine that the House of Hanover is his only rival, it was strange but true that the King of Sicily was offering that his second son should be brought up as a Protestant and should succeed on the death of Queen Anne[3].

[1] *E.H.R.* no. xiii. p. 506.   [2] *Ibid.* no. iv. p. 503.
[3] *Ibid.* no. xiii. p. 506.

This important overture, the most detailed that had
yet been made, was followed by a number of despatches,
filled with very sound advice given by one who knew
the English well, one of which was accompanied by
a draft declaration in which James III was made to
renounce his religion and his succession to the throne
as based on divine right. This has not come down to
us, but the advice may be summed up as follows.
James must remember that he has one great advantage
over his competitor in that he was born in England, for
it was urged, the English will never be ruled by a
German who gives them already but too well to understand that he will govern them *in virga ferrea*. He should
leave Lorraine for the reasons already given and also
in order to avoid addresses being made in Parliament
for his removal from that country. He does well to
manage the Scots, but he must never for one moment
imagine that he can ever return to rule over England
through their help, such a conquest is the very worst
method James could adopt to return to England;
only in the last extremity must it be resorted to: he
can only hope to return by winning the love of his
people[1].

With the draft declaration, Gaultier addressed direct
to James III, under the pseudonym of Montgoulin, a
letter repeating this excellent advice.

Do nothing to cause anxiety to the Queen your sister during
her lifetime or to worry her ministers. On all occasions show
the love you have for your fellow countrymen in spite of their
apparent aversion from you. Promise them much, and keep your
word better than did the King your father; praise their behaviour
and manners without affectation; make it clear you will never
attack their religion, their laws or their privileges; manage the
Scots adroitly by making them hope for more than you will grant

[1] *E.H.R.* no. XVII. p. 508.

them, never think of any means of using them for returning to England, for the English will never abide being conquered. Remember you were born an Englishman and consequently have a great advantage over your rival who is a German totally ignorant of the English language, and already makes it only too clear to the good English that he will govern them *in virga ferrea*. You must take good care to receive graciously all those who under pretence of travel will come to see you either from curiosity or to have speech with you. Make much of the pains and sufferings you endure in your exile.

Your patience, wisdom and discretion, the follies and violence of the Whigs and the Princes of the house of Hanover, and the care of your interests taken by your friends will certainly bring you back to your native country.

Do not flatter yourself that you can ever return by force of arms; only the conduct I have here sketched, joined with the love of the people can replace you on the throne of your ancestors. Remember your countrymen are very jealous (though without having much of them) of their religion, their liberty and their property: these three factors caused the ruin of all the plans of the King your father and you ought to use them skilfully to arrive at the goal of your enterprises....Make no difference in public between Whig or Tory. When he is at Montpellier, encourage the Duke of Marlborough to make advances to you, listen and appear to accept his offers. The Earl of Oxford asks this favour of you, and he has private reasons for it[1].

Send word to the Scots to support your interests strongly and to take your side in the coming Parliament when there is any talk about you; your friends will be glad and wish it. Write also to those who have not taken the oaths to take them and to serve the Queen in the next session....

Write to me often and always in English so that I can show Oxford all your letters; always put in something flattering and pleasing to the Queen for I am assured he will show her every-

---

[1] One wonders what knavery underlies this recommendation. Probably the ministers wished to get evidence against Marlborough to use as insurance against their own prosecution, if it should come to that.

thing you send. Never mention Bolingbroke or any other in the letters I shall read to Oxford[1].

Time moreover was short, for the Queen was dying[2].

But the indispensable condition, which was put at the head of this letter, and recurs again and again throughout the correspondence, was that James must dissimulate or entirely change his religion[3]. As a Roman Catholic priest, Gaultier was careful to say that this was not the advice he gave[4], though he put strong material reasons before James in favour of the proposed line of action. Still, when he protested against this proposal he had always, so he told Torcy, received a retort about the example of Henry IV of France, and he himself admitted that it was useless to think of recovering London without having previously abandoned Rome[5].

It was not therefore for lack of good though unscrupulous advice that James III did not return to his native country. Gaultier's letter to him was dated London, February 6: James' reply, a letter to Torcy, was dated from Bar le Duc on February 26, less than three weeks later. It was such as might have been expected from a gentleman of his character. That a man should refuse to change his religion to gain a crown is not sur-

---

[1] *E.H.R.* July, 1915, no. XIX. p. 510. The last paragraph does not mean that James was not to correspond with Bolingbroke, for he is recommended to do so (*ibid.* XXI. p. 511).

[2] *Ibid.* no. XXI. p. 511.

[3] *Ibid.* no. XVII. p. 508; XIX. p. 508; XXII. p. 511; XXIV. p. 512.

[4] *Ibid.* no. XIX. p. 508. "Ce n'est pas moy qui vous donne ce conseil, le caractere que je porte me le deffend et vous ne deuez pas vous attendre qu'aucun Cathe Romain vous le donne, car suiuant ses principes et sa creance il ne peut ny ne doit; cest a vous a vous consulter et a demander au Seigneur qu'il vous fasse connoistre le party que vous devez prendre et ce que vous deuez faire pour sa plus grande gloire, et pour sauuer vne nation qui sans vous ne scauroit jamais être heureuse ni tranquile," Gaultier to James III, Feb. 6, 1714.

[5] *Ibid.* no. XXIV. p. 512.

prising, but his astonishment and disgust at being asked to use the ordinary weapons of statecraft, such as dissimulation and promising more than he could hope or expect to keep, these are indeed points which distinguish a prince or statesman, and raise James III to so high a moral plane that he becomes a curiosity worthy of the school of political projectors in the Academy of Lagado. One can only say that if such was to be his conduct had he ever been restored, his reign would have been short even as his father's.

His letter ran as follows:

Bar le Duc, Feb. 26, 1714.

Gaultier's last letter is so extraordinary and unintelligible that I was not surprised at having received no news of you with it, as I imagined easily the embarassment you are in on what you ought to say about it; meanwhile I cannot answer it without knowing your opinion or receiving your advice, which I ask you to give me with your usual kindness in so delicate a matter. Meanwhile here are my thoughts.

I shall begin with what is called a declaration of which Gaultier does not explain the use to be made, nor the time at which it was to be published: I have had it translated into French so that you may the better judge of it, and when you have read it, I am persuaded you will think the same as I do about it, namely that there are scarcely two lines in it which I could ever use, for it is mainly composed of an abjuration of the faith and a renunciation of my rights. The whole is filled with obscure expressions, some puerile, not one in the style of a document of that nature, and the language is even so bad that it is difficult to believe it was drafted by an Englishman. Can it possibly be that Lord Oxford is the author? and if I were capable of signing it, what would he think of me? I am to renounce my religion (without, it is said, any human intentions, a most obvious lie) which is the greatest obstacle to my restoration, and then I renounce my rights, unless it should please the people to recall me to them: I am to declare that I would never intend to make myself master of Scotland

and that I prefer to wander over the face of the globe to worrying the English. Could so much duplicity, dishonour, and baseness be the means of my restoration? If Oxford seriously proposes these infamous ideas, is there not good reason to fear that it is a trap from which there is no escape? If I refuse, I give him good reason for breaking with me; if I accept, I make myself unworthy to live, still more to reign, and the object of the just scorn of every honest man; for, putting conscience aside, who ever could trust me if I changed my religion for so gross a motive of self interest and temporal advantage?

With regard to the other article, it is true I do not propose to disturb my sister during her lifetime, and moreover that I shall be always ready to sacrifice my comfort and even my life for my country, but to sacrifice for it my honour and my conscience is too much, more than any King has a right to expect from a subject, and I shall never be found capable of doing so. Till my last breath, by the grace of God, I shall preserve my religion, and till then I shall give myself no rest to enter upon my rights, and if I thought otherwise, I am sure that Lord Oxford himself would despise me, for after all, I think him a man of honour and not capable of inspiring sentiments so contrary to it.

As for Gaultier's letter, I do not understand it at all; I send it to you to look at again, praying you to return it to me with the original of the declaration.

Some of the advice I could not follow, such as promising Scotland more than I mean to hold, and forcing my friends to take an oath against their conscience. The article on religion surprises me; dissimulation is so to speak worse than an open abjuration, and thank God, I understand my religion better than to have the face to consult the Lord whether abandoning him is to his glory.

How can I reconcile that former great hatred of the Whigs and the just and reasonable principle of distinguishing my friends from those who are not, with the advice that I must never make distinctions in conversation between Whig and Tory, and the advice given me about Marlborough? Can Lord Oxford make fun of those who talk of my leaving Lorraine in the way shown by the last extract sent me by the Duke of Berwick, and then advise so soon after some travels and a withdrawal to which I can never consent?

Finally, was there ever a more unheard of proceeding than their behaviour towards the Queen and myself? It is well known that the Queen's refusal to recognise the government of England was the sole reason why she has not enjoyed her dowry for five and twenty years, and now they want her to recognise it and at the same time give up her claim to arrears, which the law itself could not refuse her, if after taking a step of that sort she were to demand them in justice.

It is also well known that my religion is the chief obstacle to my restoration, and I am asked to renounce it and at the same time to make my restoration dependent on the will of the people by renouncing my rights rather than disturb their repose.

I leave you to guess what I am to think of all this and how much I feel the need for the arrival of that confidential agent promised so long ago, without whom Lord Oxford and I will never come to an understanding. Pray hurry on his arrival as soon as you can; meanwhile I earnestly ask for the advice of the King of France and your own, for my guidance in so thorny a crisis in which they are certainly taking advantage of me. As I have already said, I will await your answer before writing anything to Gaultier, when that is done I shall follow the Duke of Berwick's advice in not allowing the slightest bitterness to appear. I approve well enough what he proposes I should write, but I do not know how to pass over the declaration in silence, as he advises, without giving rise to false hopes on the two principal points of renouncing my religion and my rights, which I went into thoroughly with Gaultier the last time I saw him, though he seems to have forgotten the greater part of what I said to him on that occasion...[1].

So following Berwick's advice, James wrote letters to Queen Anne, Oxford and Bolingbroke, in which he expressed his willingness that

she remain in quiet possession during her life provided she secure to me the succession after her death....What I once

[1] *E.H.R.* July, 1915, no. xxv. pp. 512–14.

promise, you may rely upon it, I shall religiously perform, and I can say with truth that I heartily abhor all double dealings and dissimulation. All the just securities that can reasonably be asked for your religion, liberties and property I shall be most willing to grant, and all that can be expected from a man of principle and true honour I am ready to comply with, and you have I know too much of both to require more of me....

But on the great questions of his own religion and his divine right to the throne he said not a word[1].

This meant that, though Gaultier continued to urge the renunciation of religion with a zeal which, according to Torcy, ought to earn him the Archbishopric of Canterbury[2], the negociation was practically at an end. The Chevalier took a step further when he issued the circular letter in which he definitely made public his refusal to change his religion[3], and all on the British side, from the Queen downwards, were convinced that James' cause was lost[4]. There was really no exaggeration when Gaultier wrote that the Grand Turk would sooner be King of England than the Chevalier de St Georges so long as he remained a Roman Catholic; indeed Gaultier in his letter says he is quoting Bolingbroke and thirty others[5]. And if Gaultier in May tried to link up once more the negociations with James III on the basis of omitting all mention of religion[6], it was probably done with an eye on party politics, seeing

[1] *E.H.R.* July, 1915, xxvii. pp. 515–16.   [2] *Ibid.* no. xxix. p. 516.
[3] J. Macpherson, *Original Papers*, ii. 525.
[4] *E.H.R.* July, 1915, no. xxx. p. 517. "Cette lettre ne feroit aucune impression sur l'esprit de sa Majesté, et qu'elle n'y repondroit pas ny ne feroit aucune demarche pour luy, tant qu'il ne se conformeroit pas a la Religion etablie par les Loix."
[5] *Ibid.* no. xxxii. p. 517. Even such a compromise as the Chevalier marrying a Protestant while remaining Catholic was ruled out by Bolingbroke as inadmissible (*Aff. Etr. Angl.* vol. 253, fo. 247, Iberville to Louis XIV, Feb. 5, 1714).
[6] *Ibid.* no. xxxiv. p. 518.

that Bolingbroke seems to have been of opinion that Marlborough was in negociations with James on a similar basis[1]. They warned Torcy that such a basis was illusory, but were not prepared to throw away any party advantage that might be gained by using the Chevalier as one of their pawns. So when the Queen died, nothing had been settled, and the Chevalier was left to remain in exile and poverty, and to be hunted from place to place by the anxious rigour of the Hanoverian government.

[1] *E.H.R.* July, 1915, no. XXXII. p. 517. "My lord Bolingbroke est persuadé que le Duc de Marlborough vous trompe, M^r le Duc de Berwick et le Roy d'Angleterre en luy faisant esperer qu'il reuiendra auec sa Religion."

Chapter XII

LAST YEARS AND DEATH

THE treatment meted out to Prior by the government was more than harsh. Gaultier wrote: "Vous méritiez un meilleur traitement après les grands services que vous avez rendus à votre patrie[1]." Stratford in 1720 described his treatment as "unjust and barbarous[2]," and spoke appreciatively of his behaviour under it. Swift, of course, spoke out plainly:

I believe he is the first person in any Christian country that ever was suffered to starve after having been in so many great employments. But amongst the Turks and Chineses it is a very frequent case, and those are the properest precedents for us at this time[3].

During the months of confinement he busied himself with his poem, *Alma, or the progress of the mind*[4]. In 1717 an act of grace was passed, extending an amnesty to political offenders; but such was the fury of the Whigs against Prior, that he was excepted. Why they were so rancorous it is difficult to say. A guess, however, may be hazarded, that the springs of their action may be found in the disappointment Prior had given them in not revealing more of the "Tory plot" to overthrow the Protestant succession. He was a free man, however, by the middle of August, for we find him writing to

[1] Bath Papers, III. 462, Gaultier to Prior, Paris, Oct. 20, 1718.

[2] *Hist. MSS. Comm.* Portland Papers, VII. 281, E. Stratford to Lord Harley, Nov. 2, 1710.

[3] *Ibid.* v. 561, Swift to Lord Harley, Dublin, May 17, 1718.

[4] "A loose and hasty scribble, to relieve the hours of my imprisonment."

L. P.

Swift from Heythrop[1], where he paid a visit to the Duke
of Shrewsbury, who seems to have chivalrously rewarded Prior's services to him in Paris by friendship
in the time of need. But though free, he was penniless.
Lord Harley, Oxford's eldest son, did something for
the poor poet by sending the hat round. Swift, over in
Ireland, collected what he could. "I have sent Mr Prior
all the money which this hedge country would afford,
which for want of a better solicitor is under £200[2]."
Even earlier, steps had been taken to collect money for
the great edition of the *Poems on several occasions* that
was to appear in 1719. A list of subscribers was drawn
up and passed by Prior in 1717[3], and in 1718 he was
busy all the year with printer's proofs:

Dear Sir,

      A pretty kind of amusement I have been engaged in:
commas, semicolons, italics, and capitals, to make nonsense more
pompous, and furbelow bad poetry with good printing. My
friends' letters, in the mean time, have lain unanswered; and
the obligations I have to them, on account of the very book
itself, are unacknowledged. This is not all; I must beg you once
more to transfer to us an entire list of my subscribers, with their
distinct titles, that they may, for my honour, be printed at the
beginning of my book...[4].

    Four weeks later, and we get the same refrain:

I have received yours of the 6th, with the list corrected. I have
two colon and comma men. We correct, and design to publish,
as fast as the nature of this great or sorry work, as you call it, will
bear; but we shall not be out before Christmas, so that our friends
abroad may complete their collection till Michaelmas, and be

---

[1] Swift's *Works*, ed. Walter Scott, Edinburgh, 1814, XVI. 326, Prior
to Swift, Heathrop, August 24, 1717.

[2] *Hist. MSS. Comm.* Portland Papers, v. 561, Swift to Lord Harley,
Dublin, May 17, 1718.

[3] Swift's *Works, ut sup., ibid.*

[4] *Ibid.* 330, Prior to Swift, May 1, 1718.

returned soon enough to have their names printed and their books got ready for them. I thank you most heartily for what you have been pleased to do in this kind. Give yourself no farther trouble; but if any gentleman, between this and Michaelmas, desires to subscribe, do not refuse it. I have received the money of Mr Mitford.

I am going to-morrow morning to the Bath, to meet Lord Harley there. I shall be back in a month.

The Earl of Oxford is still here. He will go into Herefordshire some time in June[1]. He says he will write to you himself. Am I particular enough? Is this prose? And do I distinguish tenses? I have nothing more to tell you, but that you are the happiest man in the world; and if you are once got into *la bagatelle*, you may despise the world. Besides contriving emblems, such as cupids, torches, and hearts for great letters, I am now unbinding two volumes of printed heads, to have them bound together in better order than they were before. Do not you envy me? For the rest, matters continue *sicut olim*. I will not tell you how much I want you, and I cannot tell you how much I love you. Write to me, my dear dean, and give my service to all our friends.

Yours ever,
M. Prior[2].

The reason why matters advanced so slowly was doubtless the magnificence of Prior's ideas about the edition, which were not unworthy of Poseidon Hicks. He evidently intended at first to have it printed on vellum, but was forced to abandon the plan in favour of "paper imperial, and the largest in England[3]." The frontispiece was to be on a scale proportionate to the book.

Morley was with me this morning madder than ever about Fiske the apothecary and his copper-plate. Tonson and Drift

[1] It is characteristic of Oxford's dilatory habits that in September Prior wrote and told Swift that Oxford was still "going into Herefordshire," having been in London all summer.

[2] Swift's *Works, ut sup.* 331, Prior to Swift, May 29, 1718.

[3] Bath Papers, III. 450, Prior to Lord Harley, Duke Street, Nov. 30/ Dec. 11, 1717.

have a little appeased him, and we shall have a plate as big as has been formed since the days of Alexander the Coppersmith[1].

The following letters give us a glimpse of Prior wrestling with those problems of typography which are the price every author has to pay for independence of the printer's devil:

Dear Mr Wanley,   5 April 1718.

       I torment you before my appointed time finding this sheet at home: as soon as you have looked it over it may be carried immediately to the Printer: I will trouble you to-morrow morning for the sheet which you have: it is Comp*li*-ment in the most refined French Dictionaries but I submit it to you as I ought with great reason to do everything concerning Literature.
         Yours ever,
          M. Prior[2].

My good and kind Wanley,

       I send you these sheets as looked over first by Mr Bedford, and then by myself. I have made great letters at *Ye*, *Me* and emphatical words, that this may answer to the tenor of the other poems: But if in the old it be otherwise printed, or you please to alter any thing, you know, and may use your dictatorial power. In a book called *The Custume* [?] *of London*, a folio printed, I think, in Harry the Eighth's time, which I gave our well-beloved Lord Harley, you will find this poem.

  I hope soon to see you at dinner at Mr Black's and am always
       Your obliged and faithful servant
         M. P.[3]

Thursday noon.
11 April 1718.

---

[1] Bath Papers, iii, 450. Prior to Lord Harley, Duke Street, Nov. 30/ Dec. 11, 1717.

[2] B.M. Harl. 3780, fo. 342. He had been in the habit of spelling it Complement, as may be seen from his despatches.

[3] *Ibid.* fo. 344.

Still the work went on, and in September he wrote
to Swift that he had

> now made an end of what you in your haughty manner, have
> called wretched work. My book is quite printed off; and if you
> are as much upon the *bagatelle* as you pretend to be, you will
> find more pleasure in it than you imagine. We are going to print
> the subscribers' names....I cough, but I am otherwise well; and,
> till I cease to cough, *i.e.* to live, I am, [etc.][1]

The book, however, did not appear till early in 1719,
and this third letter to Wanley probably marks the eve
of the publication.

Dear Wanley,

> I must beg the continuance of your care in the
> names of the subscribers, as you have given it to me in the
> printing of the books. I send you my Phiz, pray give my service
> to Mrs Wanley, desiring her to accept it, and assuring her that
> no one loves or esteems her husband and my friend more than

Yours

M. Prior[2].

Jan. 8. 1718/19.

His relations with Lord Harley and his family form
one of the brightest and most pleasing features of his
life. To them he probably owed the re-establishment of
his fortune, so that he could live on a scale not unworthy
of a retired diplomat. He was a great favourite at Wimpole, Lord Harley's seat, where Lord Harley's daughter, later Duchess of Portland, said he "made himself
beloved by every living thing in the house—master,
child and servant, human creature or animal[3]." And
his affection for them shines out clearly from his correspondence. His favourite was obviously the daughter

---

[1] Swift's *Works, ibid.* 335, Prior to Swift, London, Sept. 25, 1718.
[2] B.M. Harl. MS. 3780, fo. 346.
[3] *Works of Alexander Pope*, ed. Elwin and Courthope, VIII. 193 *n.*

whose loving words have just been quoted, to whom he addressed the charming lines:

My noble, lovely, little Peggy
Let this my first epistle beg ye,
At dawn of morn and close of even
To lift your heart and hands to Heaven.
In double beauty say your prayer,
Our Father first, then *notre Pere*,
And, dearest child, along the day,
In everything you do or say,
Obey and please my Lord and Lady,
So God shall love, and angels aid ye.
If to these precepts you attend,
No second letter need I send:
And so I rest your constant friend[1].

At certain times of the year Lord Harley used to send gifts of meat to him. We find him, on Dec. 14/25, 1717, acknowledging

"a great turkey. But," he continues, "if he had brought a letter tied to his leg, to tell whence he came, and how the people did that sent him, he would not have been less welcome. In short, when I asked you for victuals, I did not design your munificence should atone for your want of correspondence; a letter might have served as a kind of table-talk to a turkey. Though *quatenus* man, and subject to hunger, I ought to thank you for your present, *quatenus* friend, and desiring to hear from you, I ought to be a little angry at your silence. Pigeons sent into cities besieged, however they may be good meat in themselves, were always more kindly received when they arrived with any news from friends without doors; and the fish in the Popish legend might claim it as his right to be eat, but had like to have been canonized when the *annulus piscatoris* was found in his belly. And now, my Lord, my resentment shall go no further than to desire you to give my great duty to Lord Oxford, respect to Lady Oxford and Lady Harriette, love to little

1 *Dialogues of the Dead, etc.* ed. Waller, p. 131.

Peggy, good wishes to all your family, and Jonathan's extraordinary sense of your butler's perpetual civility towards him[1]."

At another time it is venison that he acknowledges.
In return he sends Madeira[2]. The affection with which
he was regarded was so great that during the last few
months of his life he spent more and more of his time
at Wimpole[3].

The Harleys visited Cambridge in November, 1719,
and were received in the Library at St John's by the
recitation of verses addressed by Prior to Lady Henrietta. We may imagine that Prior was in high feather,
receiving his grand friends at St John's, and no doubt
felt no small satisfaction in doing so, for the Master
was no doubt made to feel that on this occasion at any
rate, Matthew Prior was as great as the Master.

Besides the Harleys, there were many in the world
of letters with whom he could consort. Swift, indeed,
he never saw again; but his correspondence reveals him
communicating by letter or by visit with many outside
Grubstreet. Atterbury and he were on friendly terms,
until Prior wrote an inexcusable epigram when Atterbury read the funeral service over John, Duke of
Buckingham[4], with whom Prior used to dine in company with other poets—"a sort of *convivium poeticum*
for Pope and Gay are the other two guests[5]." With

[1] Bath Papers, III. 451, Prior to Lord Harley, Westminster, Dec. 14/25,
1717.

[2] *Ibid.* 475, Prior to Lord Harley, Westminster, Dec. 5/16, 1719.
"For domestic news, you have a pipe of Madeira in your cellar."

[3] *Works of Alexander Pope*, ed. W. Elwin and W. G. Courthope,
VIII. 193 *n.* Prior to Chesterfield, Jan. 14, 1721. "For four months past
I have been hid in Cambridgeshire in a place I much love and with a
family I much respect."

[4] For this quarrel with Atterbury, see Dr H. C. Beeching's *Francis
Atterbury*, London, Pitman, 1909, 237–242.

[5] Bath Papers, III. 482, Prior to Lord Harley, Westminster, June 16/27,
1720.

Robert Freind and "Dick" Shelton he naturally remained on intimate terms; with Lord Chesterfield he
kept up a continuous correspondence, while he more
than once refers to meetings of *virtuosi* at his house in
Duke Street;

> I invited the *virtuosi* t'other day; Gibbs[1], Wanley, Wootton[2],
> and Christian: the two first could not come, and the two last
> could not be got away till midnight. Dirty Dibben[3], of Dorset-
> shire, and the Archdeacon of Bath were of the company, as well
> to bless the meat as to drink great share of the claret; Morley
> assisted in tea. It was a conversation about five o'clock, a dis-
> putation towards seven, and a bear-garden about ten. We drank
> your healths over and over, as well in our civil as bacchanalian
> hours[4].

Gibbs, indeed, in 1720 met Prior for business as
well as for pleasure. In 1714 Prior had bought for
£8000 a house named Down Hall, near Harlow, in
Essex. Of the £8000 he paid one-half, and Lord Harley
the other half, and in return for this grant, Lord Harley
was to have the reversion. Prior, and "Squire" John
Morley, who was his factotum in everything that concerned Down Hall, travelled down to view the place.

This visit to Down was celebrated in the most successful of all Prior's longer poems, *Down Hall, a Ballad*,
in which Prior and Morley

> rid Friendly from fine *London*-Town
> Fair *Essex* to see, and a place they call *Down*.

After describing in his own inimitable way the Chariot,
whose "one *Window* was *Canvas*, while t'other was

---

[1] The architect.   [2] The painter.

[3] Thomas Dibben, Fellow of Trinity College, Cambridge, Chaplain
to the Bishop of Bristol at the Congress of Utrecht; precentor of St Paul's
1714; translated Prior's *Carmen Saeculare* into Latin, d. 1741.

[4] Bath Papers, III. 482–3, Prior to Lord Harley, Westminster, June
16/27, 1720.

Glass," the Inn at Hoddesdon, and the accommodation
provided:

> Now hey for *Down-Hall*; for the Guide he was got:
> The *Chariot* was mounted; the *Horses* did trot;
> The Guide he did bring us a Dozen Mile round:
> But O! all in vain; for no *Down* could be found.
>
> *   *   *   *   *
>
> What is this thing, *Morley*, and how can you mean it?
> We have lost our Estate here, before we have seen it.
> Have Patience, soft *Morley* in anger reply'd:
> To find out our way, let us send off our Guide.
>
> O here I spy *Down*: cast your eye to the *West*,
> Where a *wind-mill* so stately stands plainly Confest.
> On the *West* reply'd *Matthew*, no *Wind-mill* I find:
> As well Thou may'st tell me, I see the *West wind*.
>
> Now pardon me, *Morley*, the *Windmill* I spy;
> But faithful *Achates*, no House is there nigh.
> Look again, says mild *Morley*, *Gadzooks* you are blind:
> The *Mill* stands before; and the House lyes behind.
>
> O now a low ruin'd white shed I discern
> Untyl'd and unglaz'd; I believe 'tis a *Barn*,
> A *Barn*? why you rave: 'Tis a *House* for a Squire,
> A Justice of Peace, or a Knight of the Shire.
>
> A House shou'd be Built, or with *Brick*, or with *Stone*,
> Why, 'tis *Plaster* and *Lath*; and I think that's all one.
> And such as it is, it has stood with great Fame,
> Been called a *Hall*, and has given its Name
>   *To* Down, *down, hey derry down.*

In his letters his opinion as to the suitability of the
house as a dwelling did not differ from that expressed
in his song; and in July, 1720, he began to think of
improvements for his estate, which apparently contained a farm and a tenant.

I have been at Down, surveyed the estate, and done everything (as to taking a rent-roll, discoursing my tenant, etc.) that

Morley calls wisdom. It is impossible to tell you how beautiful a situation Down is, and how fine the wood may be made; but for the house, as all the cross unmathematical devils upon earth first put it together, all the thought and contrivance of man cannot make a window to be looked out of, or a door to be shut, in case it were made otherwise habitable: so sooner or later I foresee *destruit domum*; but of this, as the divines say, at another opportunity[1].

In September the designs for the new house were ready[2]; and Gibbs and Prior went over to Down[3]. In January the improvements had been begun: "we have laid out squares, rounds and diagonals, and planted quincunxes at Down. *Chacun a sa marotte*, and that farm will turn my brain[4]." To Chesterfield he wrote at this time: "I have repaired my own farm, am cutting walks through a little wood, and making a fish pond that will hold ten carps, and when I have done this in little, pray tell me what had a Cicero or Pliny to wish, what could a Condé or Chesterfield enjoy more than the same thing in a larger volume[5]?" In the spring and summer the work went on fast, and Prior gave himself up to the delights of a country residence.

"You may laugh at my solitude as much as you please, but I like it infinitely, and shall do more so when the noise of the axes and hammers to the tune of five pound a week grows less tumultuous; but Down in itself considered I love more than Tully did his Tusculum, or Horace his Sabine field, nor would quit it for anything, but to be with you or to serve you[6]." "Wherever

[1] Bath Papers, III. 483, Prior to Lord Harley, Westminster, July 2/13, 1720.

[2] *Ibid*. 488, Prior to Lord Harley, Westminster, Sept. 13/24, 1720. "Gibbs has built me a house, I will bring it over with me."

[3] *Ibid*. 489, Prior to Lord Harley, Westminster, Sept. 17/28, 1720.

[4] *Ibid*. 492, Prior to Lord Harley, Westminster, Dec. 29/Jan. 9, 1720/21.

[5] *Works of Alexander Pope, ut sup.* VIII. 193 *n*.

[6] Bath Papers, III. 504, Prior to Lord Harley, Down, June 8/19, 1721.

that noble youth of Essex [John Morley] is, he may understand
that I am making a stile at the end of Great Hilly Field, where the
cattle got in, and did a power of wrong, to be sure, and putting
brushwood under the old gate, where they plaguy pigs crept
into the pease-close[1]." "I have a great deal to say to my friend
and countryman Morley about sinking a well and splashing a
quickset, by which discourse I may happen to prove I am not so
ignorant of country affairs as some people may imagine[2]."

Thus Prior divided his time mainly between Duke
Street, Down and Wimpole; but the number of places
from which he dates his letters shows that he moved
restlessly about. There is nothing to show that he ever
revisited Wimborne or Godmanstone, though he did,
on one occasion at least, find himself again in Dorset[3].
Soon after being released from custody, he went to
Cambridge, and joined vigorously in the party quarrels
of the University. In November of that year, 1717,
there was an election for the Vice-Chancellorship, and
Prior's side carried it against Bentley. "*Victoria*: for
Gooche 122, against us, 60[4]."

This interest in academic politics was not uncon-
nected with national affairs, in which he was as keen a
politician as ever. Naturally his Toryism had not been
abated by his treatment from 1715 to 1717, and when
Hugh Stanhope invited him to subscribe to the *Memoirs
of the life of James, Earl Stanhope*, he replied that he
wished Hugh Stanhope "would undertake to write a
life that would recompense his pains and gain him more
credit[5]." Prior followed closely the fortunes of such

[1] Bath Papers, iii. 505, Prior to Lord Harley, Down, June 14/25, 1721.
[2] *Ibid.* 506, Prior to Lord Harley, Down, June 22/July 3, 1721.
[3] *Ibid.* 455, Letter to Lord Harley dated at Fontmel [? Magna] near
Shaftesbury.
[4] *Ibid.* 449, Prior to Lord Harley, Cambridge, Nov. 4/15, 1717.
[5] *Ibid.* 501, Hugh Stanhope to Prior, Apr. 6/17, 1721. A very angry
letter.

great measures as the peerage bill of 1719, and in the fortunes of the South Sea Company he had more reason to be interested than was prudent for a man of his slender fortune[1]. "I am tired with politics," he wrote to Swift, "and lost in the South Sea. The roaring of the waves, and the madness of the people, were justly put together[2]." But, apart from his pecuniary interest, he evidently scanned the picture it displayed with rare zest. When the stocks began to fall, he wrote to Harley:

Yesterday the world was in a panic fear, the South Sea ebbed hourly by fifty and sixty down to five hundred; but the apprehension vanished as insensibly as it came on; the stock rose again to above six hundred; the Alley rung with huzzas, and things go on *sicut olim*[3].

Five days later, "South Sea falls, notwithstanding which the merchants are insolent and the Ministry despicable in the city[4]," and a week later

everything was in such confusion, as to the pecuniaries in Change Alley and South Sea, that I did not know what to say; but the confusion still remains, and I must be longer silent—I find—if I stay till I know what to write on that subject: all is floating, all falling, the directors are cursed, the top adventurers broke, four goldsmiths walked off, Walpole and Townshend sent for, that they may settle matters; *sed adhuc sine successu*: and every man with a face as long as a Godolphin's; *vogue la galère*; I must fare like the rest[5].

---

[1] Bath Papers, III. 498, Chesterfield to Prior, March 1/12, 1720/1. "I am concerned to hear of your losses in that national gulf of destruction, the South Sea."

[2] Swift's *Works, ut sup. ibid.* 387, Prior to Swift, Westminster, Feb. 28, 1720/21.

[3] Bath Papers, III. 488, Prior to Lord Harley, Westminster, Sept. 10/21, 1720.

[4] *Ibid.* 489, Prior to Lord Harley, Sept. 15/26, 1720.

[5] *Ibid.* 489–90, Prior to Lord Harley, Sept. 22/Oct. 3, 1720.

He therefore left London, and when he returned to the "Great Bedlam" in January, 1721, he wrote:

Tudway, paragraph by paragraph, is, I own, a good scene; shawms and hautboys with dulcimers and Jews' trumps must need make an agreeable melody, and if tuned to the notes I hear daily of "damn the directors, hang up Aisleby, break Janson and Lambert on the wheel—as in their countries they would have been served"—etc., would make an excellent grand chorus[1].

But although he lived in retirement, it is clear that his political ambitions were not yet dead. He was once more approached to stand for Parliament as representative of his University. He apparently wrote to the Vice-Chancellor accepting the offer[2], for we hear that "Mr Prior is gone down to try his interest at Cambridge[3]." But this venture had even less success than the last. On October 18 one T. W. wrote to Oxford that Prior had no chance of election, adding, "You had better employ your interest for an honest Tory, Mr Annesley, and I think an honest Englishman too[4]." He was treated unhandsomely by the Vice-Chancellor, as is clear from the following letter:

I thank you for sending my letter, for remembering me, for everything. As to my affair here, the divisions multiply so fast, that I think all will end in the Whig interest prevailing. I will tell you the whole matter on Monday, which I long mightily for; the Vice-Chancellor, after many *estocades* against me has produced a letter from the Chancellor that the University choosing me at this time will do a thing that will be a reflection and prejudice to them. I have taken this occasion to get off, for that I never intend to do anything but what should be for their interest, but *que faire?* I think there is an end of my matter, and shall drink on Monday night to the tranquillity of Cambridge and

[1] Bath Papers, III. 493, Prior to Lord Harley, Jan. 3/14, 1721.
[2] *Ibid.* 490, Prior to Lord Harley, Westminster, Sept. 22/Oct. 3, 1720.
[3] *Hist. MSS. Comm.* Portland Papers, v. 603, E. Harley to Oxford, Sept. 27, 1720.   [4] *Ibid.* 605.

the honour of Oxford; my only satisfaction is that these wise
and honourable men have not been able to involve you in this
labyrinth[1].

He very wisely, therefore, threw up the candidature.
He met with some sympathy, but he felt sore about
the matter, as we see from the letter he wrote to Oxford
at the end of the year.

I have stayed here long enough to see the popular folly of our
neighbouring University, though I have not been there since
I last had the honour to write to your Lordship, for where a man
has not been kindly treated, he may easily become troublesome.
The farce acted there had just the same exit which you foretold.
An[nesley] was beaten out of the pit, ill-supported by his new-
acquired friends, and everybody denying that they had had any
hand in bringing him down; my own college, a little ashamed of
the usage they gave their own fellow, whose friendship they have
and may yet have further occasion for, but we pass that....This is
the world, my Lord, and the same tricks are played in courts
and camps, universities and hospitals, and so men act and have
acted, for the proof [of] which your Lordship and your humble
servant need not read much history[2].

From Cambridge he retired to Wimpole, where he
spent four months, and after a visit to Down, to see to
the improvements, he spent the rest of the winter in
London. His health was obviously failing; he wrote to
Swift in February: "I have been ill this winter. Age, I
find, comes on, and the cough does not diminish.

Non sum qualis eram bonae
Sub regno Cynarae—

Pass for that[3]." Two months later he was well enough to

---

[1] Bath Papers, III. 491, Prior to Lord Harley, Cambridge, Oct. 15/26, 1720.
[2] *Hist. MSS. Comm.* Portland Papers, v. 611, Prior to Oxford, Wimpole, Dec. 23, 1720.
[3] Swift's *Works, ut sup. ibid.* 387, Prior to Swift, Westminster,
Feb. 28, 1720/21.

travel to Down before Easter, and return within a few days to London, whence he wrote his last letter to Swift:

To the Reverend Dr Swift   West^r. 25 Apr. 1721.
    Dean of St Patrick in
    Dublin
            Ireland.
Dear Sir,
        I know very well that you can write a good letter if you have a mind to it, but that is not the question, a letter from you sometimes is what I desire, reserve your tropes and periods for those whom you love less, and let me hear how you do, in whatever humour you are, whither lending your money to the Butchers, protecting the weavers, treating the women, or construing *Propria quae maribus* to the country curate; you and I are so established Authors that we may write what we will without fear of censure, and if we have not lived long enough to prefer the Bagatelle to any thing else we deserved to have had our brains knocked out ten year ago: I have received the money punctually of Mr Dan Hayes, have his receipt and hereby return you all the thanks that your friendship in that affair ought to claim and your generosity does contemn; there is one turn for your good. The Man you mentioned in your last has been in the Country these two years, very ill in his health, and has not for many months been out of his Chamber, yet what you observe of him is so true, that his sickness is all counted for policy, that he will not come up till the public distractions force somebody or other (whom God knows) who will oblige somebody else to send for him in *Statu quo prius*: that in the meantime he has foresworn all that has happened, checkmated all the Ministry, and to direct himself at his leisure hours has laid all those lime-twigs for his neighbour Coningsby that keep that precious bird in the cage out of which himself slipped so cunningly and easily.

    Things and the way of men's judging them vary so much here that it is impossible to give you any just account of some of our friends actions; Roffen. is more than suspected to have given up his party as Sancho did his subjects for so much a head, *l'un portant l'autre.* His Cause therefore which is something originally like that of the Lutrin is opposed or neglected by his ancient friends, and openly sustained by the Ministry. He cannot be lower in the opinion of most men than he is; and I wish our friend Har—— were higher than he is.

Our young Harley's vice is no more covetousness than Plainness of Speech is that of his cousin Tom: his Lordship is really *Amabilis*, and Lady Harriette *Adoranda*.

I tell you no news, but that the whole is a complication of mistake in policy, and of knavery in the Execution of it; of the Ministers (I speak) for the most part Ecclesiastical as Civil: this is all the truth I can tell you, except one which I am sure you receive very kindly, that I am ever

Your friend and
Your servant
M. P.

Friend Shelton commonly called Dear Dick is with me. We drink your health. Adieu[1].

At Down, he was busy with Drift "building houses upon paper." On April 14 he sent a present of pigeons to Lady Harriet Harley.

I send your Ladyship eight pigeons, which I hope you will not look upon as ordinary birds, being the first tribute which I have received from Down, and consequently the fairest proof of my great duty to my Lady Harriet Harley. My will and pleasure is that two of them may be roasted immediately for my dear little Lady's private table, the other six for your Ladyship's dinner to-morrow, to be neatly accommodated and incrusted with sweetbreads and "sparagrass" according to the discretion of your cook. Hoping that it may prove an eating-day, and that I may have the honour of assisting at the ceremony of seeing at least half a one of them on your plate, I am [etc.]

Postscript. Squire Morley shall only have some of the crust[2].

[1] B.M. Add. MS. 4291 (not foliated), no. 20. *Endorsed with address* and: "Apr. 25, 1721, Mr Prior's last letter I think."

[2] *Hist. MSS. Comm.* Portland Papers, v. 620, Prior to Lady H. Harley, April 14, 1721.

Save for the visit to town in the middle of April, he seems to have stayed at Down till July. In April he had "a cold and sort of spring ague[1]," and he also suffered from deafness[2], which had troubled him for some time, especially when he had a cold[3]; but his chief danger was undoubtedly from his old enemy the colic or *cholera morbus*, of which he had never been free since his release from custody. In July he moved from Down to Wimpole, where, undeterred by the fiasco of *Solomon*, he busied himself on another quasi-philosophic poem after the same manner. If

> Indeed poor Solomon in rhyme
> Was much too grave to be sublime,

the gloomy subject of this last poem, *Predestination*, makes us glad that it was never finished.

> Apostles teach, and Holy books declare
> That 'tis in God we move, and live and are:

Certainly the first lines are not promising; tediousness, which Johnson in criticising *Solomon*, described as "the most fatal of all faults," gives promise of pervading the poem as soon as the title has been read.

Fate, however, interposed. Arbuthnott said death saved Prior from a terrible fate in his domestic affairs; it saved him certainly from another failure in letters. Before the verses on *Predestination* were worked into an organic whole, his old disease came upon him again.

---

[1] Bath Papers, III. 501, Prior to Lord Harley, Easter Even, 1721.

[2] *Ibid.* 472, Prior to Lord Harley, Nov. 26/Dec. 7, 1719. "I have only seen Brown the surgeon, to whom I have made an *auricular confession*, and from him have received *extreme unction*, and applied it, which may soften the obduracy of my ear, and make it capable of receiving the impression of ten thousand lies which will be poured into it as soon as I shall take my seat at the Smyrna."

[3] Swift's *Works, ut sup. ibid.* 366, Prior to Swift, Westminster, May 4, 1720.

Lord Harley wrote to Wanley describing the course of Prior's illness during these sad days:

On Monday, September 11th

he was taken ill with a violent vomiting; he was something better on Wednesday, and thought his distemper was over; that night it returned with greater violence, he had all the help this country and London could afford, but without effect; so that it pleased God to deliver him from his pain, for yesterday[1] exactly at one o'clock he died. His death is of great trouble to us all here, but I have this satisfaction, that nothing was wanting to preserve his life. We must all submit[2].

His death was a considerable event in the literary world. Swift felt his loss acutely[3], and it called forth a number of poems and memorial verses. He was buried, in accordance with the wish expressed in his will, in Westminster Abbey. Atterbury was too ill to attend, but he wrote to Pope

I would have done it to have shown to his friends that I had forgotten and forgiven what he wrote on me. He is buried as he desired at the foot of Spenser: and I will take care to make good in every respect what I said to him when living, particularly as to the triplet he wrote for his own epitaph, which while we were on good terms I promised him should never appear on his tomb, while I was Dean of Westminster[4].

The verses Atterbury refers to are probably:

> To me 'tis given to die—to you 'tis given
> To live: alas, one moment makes us even—
> Mark how impartial is the will of heaven.

but a very different kind of inscription is on his monument. For this in his will he set aside the sum of £500,

[1] Monday, Sept. 18, 1721.
[2] *Hist. MSS. Comm.* Portland Papers, v. 625, Lord Harley to H. Wanley, Wimpole, Sept. 19, 1721.
[3] Swift's *Works*, Letters.
[4] Dr H. C. Beeching, *Francis Atterbury*, 240–1.

as "a last piece of human vanity," by which a huge erection was set up, with a good bust made according to Hearne at the expense of Louis XIV[1], by Coysevox. As Conyers Place said in after years, when describing the poor condition of Prior's relatives at Godmanstone,

If that last part of human vanity had been mixed with some little regard to this branch of his name and blood, I think Mr Prior would have discharged but a natural duty[2].

"Things change and times change and men change." And Lord Godolphin's platitudinous aphorism will not be disproved in a consideration of Prior's reputation. In Queen Anne's day, and indeed ever since, Prior's fame has rested on his poems. As the writer of fugitive verse he was perhaps second to none amongst his contemporaries of an age when scurrility and grossness were as much sought for in such exercises as poetical feeling. To-day taste has changed to such an extent, that the average British reader finds little to commend in the classical verse of the Augustan age of English literature. While Dryden, Pope and Addison can still be appreciated by the lover of literature, they are too often set aside with a yawn as wearisome or stiff or mechanical or simply "not poetry." If such is the fate of the great fish, no wonder the small fry do not escape, and Prior's more ambitious works have suffered likewise. Not indeed that they have ever been very greatly admired. Few who have been through the experience would disagree with Dr Johnson's remark that having once read Prior's *Solomon*, he had no desire to read it again. The same too applies to the stiff official odes to

[1] *Hearne's Collectanea* (Oxford Historical Society), II. 283.

[2] *Hist. MSS. Comm.* Portland Papers, VI. 34, Conyers Place to Middleton, Dorchester, Dec. 7, 1730. His will, by which he left everything to his mistress, Mrs Elizabeth Cox, caused almost as much stir as his death. From the point of view of his poor relations it was a cruel will, but it was very natural, for they can have been nothing to him.

celebrate a victory or mourn a death. The language is often harsh, and the mixture of contemporaries with classical and mythological heroes is to the last degree forced and unnatural to the modern ear. It is in the shorter poems and epigrams that we must turn for verses which will appeal to the reader of to-day; the lines on Chloe, and the lighter verse such as *Down Hall* or even *Alma*. Yet even here, satiety soon makes itself felt, unless the book is used frankly for "window-reading." The surprise expressed by Venus at the resemblance of Chloe to herself is an idea put forward as the main theme of too many epigrams, while elsewhere the grossness engendered by a dirty mind is often revolting and not always humourous. Yet when all this has been said, it cannot be denied that Prior's lighter verse has a spirit and fire which purge it from the charge of dullness, and make it a lively pastime "in vacant hours." So much for his verses; at the present day, however, a reader would probably find as much entertainment in Prior's prose as in his verse. Swift, who never really pretended to be a poet, in all likelihood influenced Prior's comic verse, and Prior resembles him in excelling in prose. There is the same abundance of spirit and vivacity as in the verse, and there is neither defective prosody nor classical allusions to irritate the reader who does not appreciate the fashion of the time. Whoever was the author of *The Country-mouse and the City-mouse*, to read it requires a special faculty; but the *Dialogues of the Dead*, lately edited by Mr Waller, are in a very different category. They have been justly praised as among the best of their kind, and Prior's correspondence may be included in this class. Leaving aside his official despatches, and making allowance for his ignorance of current events, an ignorance which affects his position as a diplomat rather than as a man of letters,—it is impossible to deny that in spite of or perhaps because of his factiousness, the character sketches and gossip which he retailed in his correspondence put him in the first rank of our letter writers. The spontaneous, unceasing flow of Biblical quotations, the humour which even in days when the prospect seemed darkest, never deserted him, and enabled him to relieve his complaints with a jest, the crisp, vivid sentences, and the clever fantastic ideas such as that of a letter from the donor serving as table-talk to a turkey, all these characteristics, which are found in the *Dialogues* as well as in the letters, serve perhaps to show that Prior's reputation in the world of letters might have been secure, if not as high, had it been founded on his prose rather than on his verse.

It is easy to point out the faults of Prior's character. They have one great merit, that they lie on the surface. Ungrateful, factious, selfish, gross, fond of low company, foul-mouthed and foul-penned, lacking some of the elementary manners and the taste of a gentleman, all this can be charged against him. But the good qualities are also not far to seek. Apart from his wit, which made him one of the foremost men of his time, we know he was not only fond of children, but that he was also beloved by them, a sure sign of redeeming virtue. Nor, though he can be charged with ingratitude, can it be said that he behaved badly by his friends. Without indeed claiming for him that he was a chivalrous friend, we cannot point to any case in which he betrayed the trust of friendship, save in his vote on the impeachment of the framers of the Second Partition treaty. And there the dilemma, as we have seen, was bitter. He had to choose between loyalty to the King and loyalty to one of his earliest friends, and when we remember that Jersey supported the impeachment, we can scarcely blame Prior for his vote. That it cooled the friendship with Halifax is undoubted, but it does not need two to make a rupture. Moreover Prior could approach the Montagus during the days of his prosperity, before the evil days fell upon him, and this releases him from the charge of throwing over the early friendship and then attempting to trade upon it in adversity. His loyalty to Jersey is unassailable, it was based on real affection between the two men, and not on those hopes of gain which spring from the patronage of the great. So too with his friendship with the Harleys. Exasperating as Oxford's procrastinating habits were, and dearly as Prior had to suffer for them when his "extraordinaries" were disallowed by the Whigs, there is no note of resentment in his correspondence, and after Prior's release, there is no dearer or more constant friend than the fallen statesman's son. With Bolingbroke indeed relations were strained after Oxford's dismissal, but here Prior was involved in Bolingbroke's hatred of Oxford even before the revolution in the White Staff. Another long friendship was that of Swift. Though they saw little of each other at the end of Prior's life, they continued to correspond, and Swift was in the forefront of those who worked to relieve Prior's distress after his return to England. Nor was Swift quite the man to make an intimate friend of one whose character was wholly bad merely because of his intellectual attainments: the close friendship between the two, and the undoubted affection that Swift bore Prior are testimony to the fact that Prior's weaknesses lay openly on the surface and that a fund of goodness, which like Swift he may have endeavoured to conceal, lay deep beneath the vicious exterior. It is easy to wish that his moral character had been different; but who knows but that to wish thus, is to wish that he had not possessed those qualities whose complements in his intellect gave us the *Poems*, the *Dialogues of the Dead*, and the letters to Portland and Jersey, to Harley and Bolingbroke?

Appendix A

ON PRIOR'S PARENTAGE AND FAMILY

THERE have been two points of doubt about Prior's origin and forbears, namely the place of his birth and the names of his relatives. In regard to the former, the matter may now be reasonably considered settled in favour of Westminster. The second point concerns his relatives. The *locus classicus* for the family is the letter of Conyers Place to Dr Middleton, written from Dorchester on Dec. 7, 1730 (*Hist. MSS. Comm.* Portland Papers, VI. 33). It runs as follows:

Cousin Middleton, pursuant to your request I send you here an account of Mr Prior's parentage, from his father's brother's son Christopher Prior. Mr Prior's grandfather lived at Godminston, a small village three miles from this town, he had five sons and one daughter called Mary married to one Hunt of Lighe, a village eight miles hence. Thomas and George, two of the brothers, were bound apprentice to carpenters at Fordington joined to this town; whence they removed to Wimborne about eighteen miles hence eastward where Thomas lived and died and where George the father of Mr Prior married, but how long he lived there I cannot find, only his wife, Mr Prior's mother, lies buried at Wimborne or by it, with whom I have heard that Mr Prior desired to be buried before Westminster Abbey was in his eye. That Mr Prior was born at or by Wimborne I find because Christopher said he remembers his cousin Matthew coming over to Godminston when a boy and lying with him. George his father, after his wife's death I suppose, moved to London, encouraged by his brother Arthur who had succeeded in the world and kept the Rummer Tavern by Charing Cross, the great resort of wits in the latter end of King Charles the Second's reign and in my remembrance; who took in his nephew Matthew to wait in the tavern, from which time you know his history. Arthur had much acquaintance in this town whither he used each summer to come down, to see his native country. He had one son named Matthew, I believe, long since dead, and a daughter named Catherine whom her father sent down to this town, where she was a blazing star some time, to secure her virtue from some of his great guests, but it was too late, one Guy of Yorkshire, called then I remember the Great Guy, followed her and attended her here with his coach and six, whence he carried her off.

Christopher says he heard that Catherine married first a French Marquis or Count called Beloe or some such name whom I take to be that cousin Catherine Harrison mentioned in Mr Prior's will, if she is an old woman, otherwise it is likely her daughter. A son of his aunt Hunt made application to Mr Prior, when in his glory, for something to be done for him being a seaman, but Mr Prior put him off with some ready money and some guineas to his aunt; but told him he was not married nor should be, and when he died he would leave what he had amongst his relations.

Christopher, who gives me the greatest part of this account, lives as his father Christopher did before him in the mansion-cottage of the family at Godminston; he is an honest labouring man, had nine children but now only six, within this few months last past it has pleased God to afflict him with the loss of both his eyes sunk quite into his head which has thrown him a charge on the parish. He and his family have much of Mr Prior's face and complexion, large cheek bones, a deep red in their cheeks, for such had Mr Prior when young; this family are now the only relations of the name that I hear of, and if my acquainting my Lord of Oxford with it might prove an occasion to him to exercise some of that generosity for which he is so renowned towards these poor remains of the name and blood, he would through these parts raise living monuments of his regard to Mr Prior's memory at an easy rate, with brasses more to the life than that of Coriveaux; and if that last part of human vanity had been mixed with some little regard to this branch of his name and blood, I think Mr Prior would have discharged but a natural duty.

Now, confusion has taken place because of the name of the brother who kept the Tavern is sometimes mentioned as Arthur and sometimes as Samuel, and because the tavern itself is described sometimes as the Rummer Tavern near Charing Cross, and sometimes as the Rhenish Wine Tavern in Cannon or Channel Row, Whitehall. But Mr Austin Dobson[1], on the authority of James Montague, has shown that the tavern kept by Matthew's uncle was the Rhenish Wine Tavern in Whitehall and not the Rummer at Charing Cross, and I think that Prior's allusions to his friends in Channel Row confirm this view[2]. What has added to the confusion is that the Rummer was kept by *Samuel* Prior in 1688, and though Mr Dobson has noted that James Montague

[1] *Selected Poems of Matthew Prior*, Kegan Paul, 1899, 209 *et seqq.*
[2] See Bath Papers, iii. 38.

spoke of *Arthur* Prior, he has assumed that the substitution of Arthur for Samuel was a "slip of the memory[1]" on the part of Montagu. Now we know that Arthur Prior died in 1687, and this fact taken in conjunction with Conyers Place's circumstantial account makes it tolerably certain that the name of the uncle who kept the Rhenish Wine Tavern was Arthur. Samuel Prior may possibly have been another uncle, but there is very little evidence for this, beyond the existence of a Samuel Prior in 1705 who was a relation of Matthew's.

Consultation of the Godmanstone registers confirms the letter of Conyers Place in certain parts, and its evidence does not anywhere clash with his. The following extracts deal with the Prior family.

Christopher Pryor and Alice Jankins aforesaid did ioyne in Marriage on the 30th day of June 1654. And were then declared Man and wife by Walter Foy.

George Pryor ye Son of Christopher Pryor Labourer was borne the 29th of May 1655.

1674. Widdow Pryor was buried.

1675/6. Laurence ye Son of Christopher Prior was baptized Jan. 18.
Laurence ye Son of Christopher Prior was buried Feb. 4th.

1686. Christopher the son of John Hunt of Leigh and M[ary] his wife was baptized May 7th.

1697. Christopher Prior and Penelope Barret were married July 11th.

1705. Christopher ye Son of Christ: Prior Bapt. Jan: 1st.

1712. Matthias ye Son of Christopher Prior bapt: Aug. 31st.

1715. Thos ye Son of Christopher Prior Bapt: Apr. 17th.

1717. Christopher Prior the son of Christopher Prior was buried October 24.

1744. John ye Son of Thomas Prior and Anne his wife was baptized April ye 12th.

1745. Laurence ye Son of Thomas Prior and Anne his wife was baptized June ye 2nd.

1746. Laurance ye Son of Thomas Prior and Anne his wife was baptized July ye 6th.

1747. Thomas ye Son of Thomas Prior and Anne his wife was baptized February ye 1st.

1749. Christopher ye Son of Thomas Prior and Anne his wife was baptized May ye 7th.

[1] *Op. cit.* 212.

1750. George and Joseph the Sons of Thomas Prior and Anne his wife were baptized Decr. 16th.

1753. August 5th was buried Penelope Prior Affidavit made Aug. 7th.

1754. Ann the daughter of Thomas Prior and Anne his wife was baptized July 7th.

1757. Buried Thomas the son of Tho: Prior September 25.

1758. Buried Christopher Prior November 28.

1784. Mary Daughter of Christopher and Eliz^th Prior, baptised March 28.

1785. Thomas son of Christopher and Eliz^th Prior baptised April 4.

1786. John son of Christopher and Eliz^th Prior baptised Aug. 13.

1788. Joseph son of Christopher and Eliz^th Prior baptised Mar. 9.

1789. Ann daughter of Christopher and Eliz^th Prior baptised Dec. 5.

1792. Eliz^th daughter of Christopher and Eliz^th Prior baptised April 24.

1793. Eliz^th daughter of Christopher and Eliz^th Prior baptised Jan. 9.

1793. Eliz^th daughter of Christopher and Eliz^th Prior buried Feb. 6th.

1794. Eliz^th daughter of Christopher and Eliz^th Prior baptised Jan. 7.

1817. Baptism of James son of George and Elizabeth Prior, June 8.

1818. Marriage of Robert Pashen, labourer, and Ann Prior, Nov. 24.

1821. Marriage of Robert Kiddle and Elizabeth Prior, Jan. 15.

1834. Burial of Christopher Prior, aged 84. Feb. 3.

1840. Burial of George Prior aged 25. Nov. 25.

1842. Baptism of William Henry, son of Martha Prior, widow, October 2.

1850. Baptism of Mary daughter of George and Sarah Prior, May 19.

1851. Baptism of Joseph son of George and Sarah Prior, Dec. 14. [This George Prior was a shepherd who lived at the hamlet of Forston.]

1889. Martha Prior, aged 72, Oct. 11. [Residence Godmanstone.]

If we turn to Arthur Prior, we learn from his will that he had a son Laurence, who may be the same as the Matthew mentioned by Conyers Place, a "sister" named Joane Kellaway, that his brothers Christopher and Thomas were apparently still alive in 1685, when he drew up his will, while George was dead, and Matthew Prior "of the University of Cambridge" is obviously his representative. A daughter named Ann had married one Thompson. Any doubts as to the origin of these Priors will be set at rest by Arthur Prior's statement in the will, which runs as follows:

To the Glory of God's most Holy name do I this   day of September one thousand six hundred and eighty five and in the first year of the reign of James the second, being by the blessing of God in good health of body and of right memory do make and ordain this my last will and testament to be in manner and form following (that is to say) of what personal estate soever the Lord hath blessed me with may be divided unto three shares and that according to the custom of the City of London my wife may have her third part or share, another third part of this estate which is mine own and therefore may dispose of it according to mine own mind and will, and I do therefore out of this part of my estate give and bequeath these legacies following:—

First I give and bequeath unto my cousin Matthew Prior now in the University of Cambridge the sum of one hundred pounds: I give and bequeath to my sister Joan Kellaway the sum of ten pounds: I give and bequeath unto Mary Prior, daughter to Christopher Prior the sum of ten pounds: I give and bequeath unto the other two children of Christopher Prior each of them five pounds: I give and bequeath unto the children of my sister Joan Kellaway to each of them five pounds: I give and bequeath to the poor of the parish where I was born which is Godmanston in the County of Dorset, the sum of five pounds to be bestowed at the discretion of the minister and churchwarden on the poorest sort: I give and bequeath unto the Hospital of Greencoats in Tuttlefields the sum of ten pounds, all which legacies amounts to 160 pounds or thereabouts, which I desire my executor hereafter named to see fulfilled in every particular. And now whereas I have disposed of a good share of the third part of my estate already upon my two daughters to the one upon her marriage, and since to the other, namely my daughter Katherine, I have lately given the five hundred pounds which was due to me out of His Majesty's Exchequer so that I think they ought therewith to be content. And I do will and ordain that my executor hereafter named shall have and enjoy all the rest of my estate whatsoever that shall remain when the legacies beforementioned and my funeral charges are paid and discharged and my will is and I do desire my executor that in case the 500*li* now in His Majesty's Exchequer which I have given to my daughter K. as her portion should at the time of my decease be anyways judged or valued to be less worth than so much money paid her down for her share, in that case my will is that my executor pay her down so much ready money as will make it of the full value of 500*li* five hundred pounds in case she be therewith content and not otherwise. And I do further will and ordaine that my executor pay her one hundred pounds of lawful English money in full of some moneys left her by her grandmother to make her equal with her sister Thompson who has had the like sum paid her already as her share or part of the said money. And I do further desire my executor that in case my two brothers Christopher and Thomas be living (or either of them) at the time of my decease that then he pay to each of them the sum of ten pounds of good English money which I give to them for a legacy. And so I declare this to be my last will and testament as also I do publish and declare my son Laurence Prior to be my sole executor of this my last will and Testament, written with my own hand in one sheet of paper desiring him to see every particular thing herein fulfilled according to my will and desire.

ART. PRIOR.

Signed sealed published and declared to be my last will and testament in the presence of

WM. POWLE.
FRAN. LAKE.
ROBERT GREENWOOD of Grays Inn.

[*Proved*, May 24, 1687.]

Further information as to the family is to be found in Laurence Prior's will, as follows:

In the name of God, Amen. I Lawrence Prior of the City of Westminster do this first day of May in the year of our Lord God one thousand six hundred and ninety and in the second year of the reign of our Sovereign Lord and Lady King William and Queen Mary, I do, I say, being in my perfect senses declare this to be my last will and testament. What estate God has blest me with I do intend to leave as follows, vizt:

I do bequeath unto my coz Matthew Prior the sum of fifty pounds, besides what I have still in my hands of his legacy left by my Father. I do bequeath unto my sister Kathrine the sume of two hundred pounds. The like sum of two hundred pounds I do give to my nephew James Thompson the son of my dearest sister Mrs Ann Thompson deceased. I do give unto Mr John Thompson, Mr Joseph Bagg and Paul Beigen each of them 10li. for mourning and a good Ring each besides. I do give unto Mrs Frances Holmes my gold watch and diamond ring. This I do desire my executrix hereafter named to see performed in all respects, and I do declare my dear mother Mrs Katherine Prior, Widow, to be my sole executrix and to enjoy all the remainder of my estate whatsoever.

LAW. PRIOR.

Witness: JO. BROWNE, THO. VERNON, ROBT. KEYLWAY.

[*Proved*, Feb. 17, 1690 O.S.]

Taking all these pieces of evidence and putting them together we can draw up a conjectural pedigree, somewhat in this way:

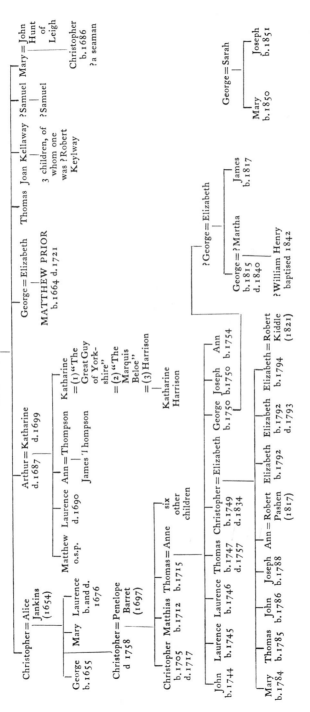

Prior of Godmanstone

Appendix B

LETTERS OF MATTHEW PRIOR PRE-SERVED AT MIDDLETON PARK

THE papers here printed are, for the most part, letters of Prior to Jersey written after Jersey's departure from Paris. They should be dovetailed into the Jersey-Prior correspondence printed in the Bath Papers, vol. III.

No. 1.

Hague 1 May N.S. 1696.

My Lord

      I was never sorry to receive any of your letters till your last, yet I could have wished that that had come a little sooner to my hands, that I might have endeavoured to have found out something else in lieu of what you tell me his Majesty designs for your Lordship. I did not think I should have had so great a Competition for so small a thing. I submit this as I do all my other affairs to his Majesty's kindness and your friendship

I am,

With all respect

No. 4.

[To the Earl of Jersey.]   Paris the 20th May N.S. 1699.

My Lord

      Your letters were all taken care of, St Maurice has his Wine, Butterfield has his, and I enjoy the remainder, I have made your compliments to Lady Salisbury, I have likewise visited Breteuil and find that his man St Martin has left him, and he has another, I believe his Secretaries shave him into the bargain, and since they are so transitory and so little taken notice of by their own Superior, I thought I might save mine the expense of a silver watch; I have it therefore in my hands till I know your further orders, without which since we can save our watch and credit I see no necessity of giving the former. Swager[1] is certainly retiring, he tells Me so himself, and with an air so determined that I dare swear he means it: you know I dare write anything to you, which makes me tell

[1] Portland.

you that I have letters from private people disinterested enough because no way conceived in the matter which say that our friend is insupportable and far from obliging the Nation, the old Gamer and he have had a misunderstanding, and he takes *à droit et à gauche*, and has fellows about him that nobody cares for, for God's sake advise him, as well for everybody's sake that loves him as for his own: I am glad you have had so good weather, God direct all your affairs for the best. I am ever yours.

[Postscript] The *Post Boy* has married me to my Lady Falkland, good, and she thinks it is by my Lady Sandwich's contrivance, good again[1].

No. 6.

Paris the 23rd May 1699.

My Lord

Mr Le Grange tells me that he saw you embark with a fair wind, so I do not question your safe arrival, I have nothing to send you but this account I received from Mr Stanhope of the feats which the Mob have done at Madrid: what becomes of our Count d'Oropeza[2], does he quit or no? I am, ever, my Lord Yours

M. PRIOR.

Renaudot[3] is Renaudot, look in the article of Paris, and see the turn which the dog gives to my Lady's taking leave[4].

Earl of Jersey.

No. 8.

[Addition to letter of May 30.]

The minute these letters were going away I have the honour of your letter of the 15th. I congratulate your new dignity and give you thanks in form for the favour you design me in it. I do assure you, my Lord, I wish with all my soul I were near you now, and at any time when I might ease any of your Embarras and bustles: I shall follow Mr Secretary's directions as to M: L:[5] and give your Lordship an account of my so doing, after I shall have spoken with Mr Torcy, I shall endeavour likewise to obey your commands in relation to the same subject: the post is going away, and gives me only time to tell you that I am perfectly and really my Lord

Your servant

[Postscript] You remember, my Lord, Drift must be Payzant.

---

[1] The reply to this letter is in Bath Papers, III. 345.
[2] The leading minister of the King of Spain.
[3] Editor of the *Gazette de France*.
[4] The reply from Jersey is in Bath Papers, III. 346.
[5] Mark Lynch.

No. 10.

Paris June 6 1699.

My Lord

I have received no commands from you since my last, the English post not being yet come in, and consequently have little to trouble you with this morning.

Renaudot is again the same man as you will observe by the care he has taken to be mighty particular in the circumstances of the Spanish Ambassadors memorial about the Scotch company: his correspondent is d'Herbaut, and these commissioners staying so long in England is not so much to adjust the limits of Hudson's bay as to spy in general how we are in relation to the West Indies, our commissioners of commerce and others that know this best, should be cautioned to let the French gain no advantage from that knowledge in any conferences or discourses. I have heard from the correspondent that d'Herbaut has had some light from the conversation of one of our nation that knows these matters well, and you know the French design lies chiefly that way in case of any change by the King of Spain's death.

Mr Vernon will have told you what Money he has sent me, I have distributed part of it already, and shall give you an account in what manner, either when I may have occasion to send an express, or if I send none when I have the honour to see you, before the end of next quarter which your Lordship will now take care of I shall be with you, according even to the calculation they made of Michaelmas 'tis needless to say how much I desire my separation from you should be short.

I presume the Elephant[1] goes into Holland with his Majesty and that you will be left in the Regence: *ainsi soit il.*

I sent the passport to Guillebert on Thursday. My Lady Sandwich is better, and we hope may live[2].

D'avenant is out of his cage, his father[3] having sent him some money, and being to send him the rest: we have got him a bed in your house, where he is forced to read all day for the money goes to his creditors and I don't give him one penny.

This moment I have Monday's letters, the 22 May V.S.; I hope your having spoken to the Post-masters on that subject will make the arrival of our packets more regular for the future, as I have done I shall continue to press the answer to the demands you made about the piracy and murder at Roagou[4].

My Lord Portland's Entre-Deux is a Jest, and will give him all the

---

[1] Somers.   [2] See Bath Papers, III. 351.
[3] Possibly Charles D'avenant the economist.
[4] The murder of a certain Captain Mansel (see below, pp. 290, 293).

uneasiness of a cast favourite without the quiet of a country gentleman; this method of retiring will lose him even the merit of doing it: he does me the honour to write me a long agreeable letter in which he desires me to be always on his side though he shall never do me any good for my being so. I confess I do not know anything so reasonable as this proposition, and I think I may e'en put Swager amongst the friends I named to you last post.

I wish to God Lord Tankerville had accepted the Commission offered him[1], for he has an active understanding and a good one, I believe Lord Bridgewater is too sedate for such an Employment. I am glad to hear that resolved of which I said I presumed, that the Elephant is to swim to Holland, and that you are to be left in the Regence.

You must give me leave to tell you that there is a tenderness in your care of me which I rather feel than can express: the King is willing I should come home and you permit it, I have said how fully I am satisfied in it, Mr Montagu is my very good friend, and will I dare swear, always continue so: but if things were otherwise, it is a jest to think I'll stay here 3 years longer to carry the Horse[2], except I were commanded to do so by that power which I must not dispute.

I have not one word of our ambassador coming, by which, as much as I can judge of the Gentleman, John and he are a good deal upon the level: without one word relating to the business he desires to know what things I may fancy he shall have occasion for at Paris that are more conveniently brought from London than bought here—but this is not our concern, and I begin to trouble you with impertinences. I am glad you dine with Prince Miramont because I presume A Greater Prince was with you, but I am afraid for your gout; Asses Milk has done wonders, I am very well, I am sorry for poor Lord Westmoreland, but what can one say, he was born and consequently must die[3]. I am ever as I ought to be, yours

No. 11.

Paris the 10th June 1699.

My Lord

I had last night the honour of your letter of the 25th May V.S.[4]: and am surprised to find by it that you had none from me of the post before; in yours of the 17th May, you acknowledged mine of the 20th and 23 May, and since then I have constantly continued to write: my letters are of the 27th, 30th May, 3rd, 6th and now 10th of June, and I hope you will have received these letters in their course, or else there is foul dealing at the post house here, for I have always sent my letters soon enough.

---

[1] The Admiralty.　　　　[2] Manchester.
[3] Died May 19/29.　　　　[4] See Bath Papers, III. 352.

I was yesterday at Versailles where no great matter is stirring, Monsieur de Torcy assured me that they were in search after the 2 persons concerned in the Piracy. I told you what I have done in relation to M: L: the man came to me on Sunday night and has still (or seems to have) the Chimerical design in his head of making out what he proposes in his paper, he is for that reason taking a lodging near the place where he says he shall find Wall, I acquainted Mons[r] de Torcy with this, and am to tell him how L:[1] disposes of himself, as soon as I know; I think they look upon him as something between a knave and a madman, and when they have him I believe his punishment will hardly go further than an *appartement dans la petite maison*[2]. I will get the paper from him though it costs a little money.

I have a letter from my Lord Manchester, he says he has discoursed with your Lordship, but mentions nothing of his coming, only that he designs to send M[r] Stanyan soon away, so I perceive we are not to expect his Excellency very quickly; for Stanyan's coming as they think good, that may do my Lord's private business, but does not relieve me, since I am not to stir till his Excellency comes.

Brown[3] lies with his wife (I think) at Calais, and so does many a man now let her be where she will, he says he waits there for your order, if your Lordship has anything to write to me that may justify sending a messenger, pray send add[l]eheaded Brown from Calais; or if you think good, some soberer Messenger from Whitehall, because I would write a word to you as to what is to be done with the faithful, and how far you would have the Horse and his man acquainted with that matter: and this I would not write by the post, because I must name the persons, and I take it for granted that our letters are broken open. My Lord Portland has written to his friends how that he will be always ready to serve the King when required and that he quits his places not out of any pique but for his honour; I know not what he means, and this Court begin to grow more reasonable upon his subject. Villeroy only thinks England cannot subsist without him, and expects a revolution by the middle of next Week.

I have made your compliments to Vrybergen[4], and have written to Gaugain; I have already told you that I sent the passport to Calais last Wednesday, I can give you no other account of your private commissions than that they are in hand, nor of myself than that I am always and entirely, my Lord, your servant.

[Postscript] I must tell you I am infinitely pleased with the new Admiralty: there is a board of good sailors and honest landsmen tacked together, and I do not doubt but that matters will go well under their

[1] Lynch.
[2] The Bastille.
[3] One of the messengers.
[4] Dutch ambassador in Paris.

administration[1]. Farewell, my Lord, pray believe me truly Yours and get me home as soon as you can.

My Lord Manchester says in his, he is of opinion I should stay as long as I can in France; pray put him off from that opinion, for fear of its delaying me: amongst them all they would have my worship stay here, and I know nobody but your Lordship and myself that would give me the right of a free Englishman, may be, at long run we may be in the right of it; Athanasius and his Man were against the world. I bid you farewell as I use to do of a night, and prate to you half an hour after.

[Endorsed by Jersey] Answered June 10, 1699 [O.S.].

No. 12.

I have written to my Lord D: of Bolton and E. of Berkeley with a saucy humility as if I took it for granted that this alteration in the Commission of Ireland is to make none in the relation I have to it; and desiring to continue in their service, presuming I am already entitled to it.

Mrs Tickett I am afraid will lose her fine head.

[No date.]

No. 13.

Paris the 13th June 1699.
My Lord

The English letters are not yet come in, which is the reason that I have not much to trouble Your Lordship with this morning.

One Wallis a Scotchman is lately gone from hence to England, he has letters with him, and may probably be heard of at the Ship in Westminster, at one Mill's, I know not what can be done upon this advice more than that the man should be watched.

There are some other things of this kind that I will reserve till I have a Messenger or till I have the honour of seeing you; for they are not very pressing, nor do I see well how they can be hindered.

M. L.[2] is to come to me again to-morrow night, as far as I can see subsistence is the greatest part of the man's business, which I shall give him for some time, but I will let his Irish plot go no further than to have him clapped up if he does not give the demonstration he promises.

Rygault has first set a great Pendulum clock upon the table before you, and you pointed at it, by which all the world would have taken you for Tompion the watchmaker. I got this folly changed, and I think the man has now committed one worse; he has put a piece of blue velvet in your hand of above a yard, a kind of mantle, and it really gives the picture a little the air of la rue St Honoré, and as if you were showing your merchandise:

---

[1] The new Admiralty were Bridgewater, Rich, Rooke, Haversham, Mitchel.
[2] Mark Lynch.

I cannot make him alter it and if he does I am afraid it will be for the worse, all that I can say to it is that it is finely painted, and the learned in painting will forgive it very easily, because of the relation it has to the *Ordonnance* of the picture.

I hear my Lord Manchester will not be here these two months. I am ever as I ought to be my Lord, your Lordships most obedient and most humble servant.

M. PRIOR.

Monday's letters are come in, I have none from your Lordship but I do not write this postscript to complain, for I hear from John that you are well and from a better hand that you are a great favourite, which are two satisfactions sufficient for one post: the changes and chances that are made and to be made at Court are I think (as Sir James formerly said) all for the *bêter*. The King is gone for Holland I take for granted, and I hope next post will tell me you are a regent; in which case pray dispatch your ambassador to Paris and send for your subject and servant home. I am yours ever.

No. 14.

Paris the 17th June 1699[1].

My Lord

I am mightily obliged to your Lordship for the kindness of your letter of the 1st June, but more to Mr Yard for his Gazette of the same date, which told me what you had omitted, that you were one of the Lords Justices: so far things go as they should do: 'tis pity one cannot be secretary of state in England and one of the deputies of Ireland at the same time, but since there is a change made in that Commission, I am glad for my own private interest that my poor Lord Dursley (for I shall call him so till he dies) is got into that Government; but, my Lord, this is giving the whole power to Crop[2], and setting up at Dublin as absolute a monarch as him to whom I paid my adorations yesterday.

The King in the 3000 p^{ds} extraordinary has been very kind to your successor, but I find his Excellency[3] will saunter away a month or two. His beau[4] they say setts out this day for France.

M: L:[5] was on Sunday night with me; he says with the greatest assurance imaginable that he has conversed the affair with Wall, and that Wall has not only let him see the Commissions, but has promised to bring him this week to Messieurs Torcy and Pontchartrain. I have given the man money, though I look upon myself at the same time to be his dupe: I have let Monsieur de Torcy know where he is, that he may have an eye upon him, and according to the account M: L: shall give me of his ad-

[1] Cf. Bath Papers, III. 353.   [2] Galway.
[3] Manchester.   [4] Stanyan.   [5] Mark Lynch.

ventures after this conference which he says he is to have, I shall take my measures. The man has the most undaunted impudence and the truest Irish understanding that ever I met with. I gave in another memoir for the liberty of the 7 last Galeriens which you mentioned before you went away, and added to it some others which I have received the names of since your going. I have pleaded the cases of these poor wretches as well as I could, by alleging what their petitions represent, that they were taken prisoners of war, and forced into the French service, for deserting which service, in order to take that of their own country they are condemned. Monsr de Torcy says he will speak of it again to the King; and to say the truth of these things, their denying us this request is injust (*sic*); and, I think, against the articles of peace, though I am not half so fierce for having a war made upon this account, as old Kick was upon that of the fifth mariner.

I see there is nothing done as to the taking up the Pirates; Monsr de Torcy told me he thought there was, but would be able to give me a more positive answer by next Tuesday. My ministry done, I was *convié* (as Monsr Heemskirk calls it) to the Mareschall de Villeroy: his meat was very good, and his questions very simple, so that I ate more than I talked. He drank your health and is extremely on your side since you are Secretary of State.

My Lady Sandwich is out of danger and recovering: I easily conceive all that can be said of the *Impolitesse d'un certain peuple, mais il faut passer par là*. They have not what they should have, but they have one amongst them capable to give it to them provided they follow his example.

Pray don't be angry with me for that stroke of rhetoric, it came in naturally, and one may be allowed to say a fine thing an hour before one goes to dine with Boileau, Fontenelle, l'abbé Regnier, and Monsr D'acier at the Baron's fine house at Charonne.

I have not only written you a letter but drawn you a picture; this letter will find you a little reposed from the fatigue of your Journey. Farewell, my Lord, I am most faithfully and for ever your servant.

[Postscript] Monsr Tomboneau is just come in to me. He will make me say that he is your servant and celuy de la belle my Lady Jersey.

No. 18.
Paris 27th June 1699.

My Lord

I wrote so long a letter to your Lordship last post that I have little to trouble you with this morning: the enclosed billet from Mr Adams tells you that one of the persons accused for the murder of Captain Mansell is taken, I give the interested at St Malos and Morlaix an account of what is done in that affair, though it is (I think) the goods which they have chiefly in mind to. The Court goes to-morrow to Marly, there will be no audience on Tuesday, and so all next week is one continued holiday. The weakness of my eyes with which I am sometimes troubled is fallen upon them, it came I think by too much reading, and must go away again by my not reading at all for some time; which is the way for me to become a very admirable Secretary, but your kindness will make up my defects, external accidents may render me less capable of serving you, but I shall have the will to do it as long as I have life.

I this moment received Monday's letters[1]. John tells me that Mr Stanyan brings me some from my Lord Jersey, which I long to see though I do not expect Mr Stanyan till towards Monday. Lord Manchester talks of being ready in a fortnight after, and says he thinks I shall not stay above a month after he comes: I think so truly, not above a week I hope. Mr Montagu has been very kind to me as to my money matters, and has too much reason to be angry at my coming home. All friends salute you, from Count Marsan to Tomboneau. Farewell, my Lord, I am ever yours.

No. 19.

Paris 1 July N.S. 1699.

My Lord

Mr Stanyan arrived here on Sunday and brought me your Lordship's letter of the 12th [2] which sufficiently instructed me as to the faithful and to which (as to all your orders) I shall pay my best obedience. In a fortnight more we may in all probability expect my Lord Manchester, which is really all I can learn from my successor, this week being Marly I have no news or business to write to you, and it is Marly Croissy, so that I shall not see that Lady till Sunday, in the meantime the ornaments of the Glass. The Glass itself she shall see, being a better Judge than I of the goodness of it. Rygault is finishing the copy of the monarch's picture for you, and takes pains in it: I wish your own may be finished soon enough for me to send over: he has no notion of a picture without all that *embarras* and *fatras* round it, and will make a plain figure leaning upon a table when Madam Gerbois sells her meat unlarded, or the Duke de Gevres wears a plain coat.

Your *seans* Belain has promised shall be Chef-d'œuvres.

Count Marsan is [at] Marly, so I have not sounded him about the sack, but I take it for granted he would be glad of it with all his heart. I shall enter into the matter with Count . . . . . . as soon and as well as I can.

I am equally concerned about Lord Villiers' education: I have written to my two friends about it, I doubt Gaugain is fast: he is trying (if he can)

<hr/>

[1] See Bath Papers, III. 364.   [2] *Ibid.* 357.

to turn over his pupil to Razigade, but I doubt of the success of that endeavour. You will not be against my coming home by way of Holland, when I assure you that there shall not be above 8 days' difference in my stay, in this case Gaugain is at the Hague and I should speak with him, but I do not pretend that this is the reason of my asking you this leave, the true cause is that I may run (though post) through Flanders, make my court and be asked questions about France. But you know, my Lord, that when I ask you anything, it is not to persuade you to consent to what I think good, but to acquiesce in your determination of what really is so. What they expect as to my stay here is, that I conduct his Excellency to his private audience, which audience may be obtained within a week or ten days after his arrival. He hardly can have his public audience till after Fontainebleau. I wish he were come with all my heart.

I received the honour of your letter of the 15th[1] last night, when I am to leave this Court I know not. If I should not have some sort of letter of revocation or order to return, a letter from Your Lordship to Torcy mentioning it to be the King's pleasure that I return will be sufficient I suppose. The reason of my asking you this is that I may have my present assured to me, and as (I have heard) augmented above what is usual to a Secretary: in this you are likewise to be troubled with me.

The volumes of the Stamps are ordered. Clement the library-keeper has taken care that they are very finely bound. I have seen one volume of them at the binder's: I have made your compliment on that account to the Archbishop of Rheims.

Madam Bouillon went from hence last night: you will see her in few days in England: Count d'Evreaux is gone with her, and I think Count de Ronsy.

Little Dick[2] writes me word that he is going to Turin, the King is very well, the young favourite flutters with 8 horses and a gilt coach, and Sr Joseph[3] counterfeits the Gout to stay a little longer at the Hague.

Stepney is out of breath and pants that you are a regent, and secretary of state; What would the world have? and how inordinate are our judgements and desires?

I am going to dine at Hauteoil with Boileau and the *beaux Esprits,* as soon as I have made up my pacquet; 'tis 11 o'clock, beau Stanyan is just up, and sends to me for the news-letter: proud enough that! but he will know in a day or two more that he has to do with one that is twice prouder than himself. I am to my...Lord, the most humble and faithful of his servants, and long for nothing so much as to be near him to receive the honour of his commands for ever.

---

[1] Bath Papers, III. 362.   [2] Shelton.   [3] Williamson.

No. 20.

Paris the 4th July 1699.

My Lord

Our friends Wall and Lynch are safe in the Bastille; I waited yesterday on Monsr de Pomponne, he desired the King should know they were taken, and I accordingly writt a word of it to my Lord Albemarle: advising him that I expected to hear from your Lordship what his Majesty would have done with them. I answered to Monsr de Pomponne that I presumed that His Majesty would leave them to the Justice here; they have not been yet examined, when they are, we shall better know the knave from the dupe; neither of them are conscious that I was any way privy to their being taken.

There are no letters come from England this post, so I have no commands from you, nor advice from my Lord Manchester, and if it had not been for the two apostles mentioned above, I should have had nothing to trouble you with this post but the assurance of my being ever with perfect truth and regard

My Lord
Yours.

No. 21.

Paris July the 8th 1699.

My Lord

We want two posts from England, the letters of Monday was Senight which we ought to have received on Saturday last were (as they say here at the post-house) by mistake put up for Ostend, and those designed for Ostend came to Calais, so we expect the error to be rectified by the Ostend post which is to come in this day at Noon.

I was yesterday at Versailles to introduce my successor, and get my Lord Manchester's passports. They are so far from according his excellency *les droits d'Entrée dans Paris* that they have ordered all his goods to be opened at the Custom-house.

As to L... and W...[1] they are in Statu quo, and are likely to continue so, which is all that I could learn of the ministers about them.

So that not having any commands from your Lordship I need trouble you no longer, for though I did not express it by writing I am persuaded you are satisfied that I am every moment of my life yours.

. [Postscript] The post is come in this moment (1 o'clock). I have the honour of yours of the 22nd[2], I did not say *that Mr Montagu has reason to be angry with me for coming home* [3]in the sense[3] as if I deserved his anger, but I writ thus: Mr Montagu has too much *reason* to be angry, and by it

---

[1] Lynch and Wall.   [2] Bath Papers, III. 364.   [3-3] Repeated in MS.

I meant he has too much *sense*, too much *judgement*, that was what I intended by the word reason, and by no means that he had too much *cause*. I own the word was equivoque and that your critique is extremely just and from this I infer the great necessity of criticising and I take that equivoque in my letter to be a judgement upon me for turning and finding fault with the style of all the world.

I find by Mr Stanyan's letters that Lord Manchester's coming is not yet fixed as to the day: the Horse[1] has lost his young *colt*, but pray saddle him and send him away for all that.

Pray buy Summerhill near Tunbridge, I shall be so glad of it: a good air, a convenient distance from London, Knowles[2] not far off, whores, fiddles, lotteries, waters! what can be desired more?

Madam Mazarine was born; that is enough, she must die[3]. I believe she was the first that ever died of that sex so philosophically; my Lady Sandwich is capable of doing the same. She has been ill again, and I think want of money makes her fever return. Though you see, my Lord, I have nothing to say to you, I have the pleasure of being in haste for the post stays, and it is almost as good as sending an express to write as fast as I do without having time to read it over. I am eternally, my Lord, yours.

[Postscript] My Eyes are well again, and shall write, read or do anything else for your service as long as they have the honour to belong to me.

No. 22.

Paris the 1/11 July 1699.

My Lord
  The post came in last Wednesday so irregularly that I answered yours of the 22nd and had not received that of the 19th[4]. I have taken an extract of the enclosed to you from the post-masters, and sent it with a memorial to Monsr Pomponne. I shall see him (you know) on Tuesday, and consequently be able by next post to send you his answer. I shall likewise speak about Perault and Bedford. The Comtesse de Maillé plagues my heart out likewise about her going to England. The lady is downright a bawd and her husband a gamester, upon which qualifications I do not see that they would starve in any kingdom in Christendom. What she means by a passport is a licence, and that your Lordship should get it for her. I stave her off well enough, and leave her cause to my Lord Manchester.

I send you my sentence pronounced by my Lord Galway[5], and my answer to it[6], which I look upon to be civilly penned, and so much for that matter. King Louis and King Crop[7] are absolute, Fouquet and I

---

[1] Manchester
[2] Knole.
[3] She died June 22/July 2.
[4] Bath Papers, III. 362.
[5] *Ibid.* 358.
[6] See below, No. 23.
[7] Galway.

must obey, if we can defer the evil day till I see you, possibly we might find some method of appeasing Crop's wrath: if not, hang Ireland, 'tis a boggy country, and ruled by a fanatical prince.

I have been much with S^t M[aurice], he says he will write to you; I need not write plainly to you about that thing, but I believe *peu à peu* it will do.

I have a thousand Services to you: President de Mesmes, Tamboneau and Blue-eyes for men of the robe; Villeroy, Count Marsan, Marquis de Gevres amongst the beaux and Courtiers. I am glad everybody loves you, but I never know how perfectly, how much I love you, as when I am from you, but that knowledge is a burden that I do not desire to bear long. I have thought upon that subject a little too tender for a philosopher, —adieu, my Lord, God bless you and yours for ever.

[Postscript] The post is not yet come in. The Marshal de Duras and the Duc de la Meleraye are going to law for pretensions the Marshal has upon the Mazarine family for his daughter's allowance. He has put a seal, [that is an arrest] upon Palais Mazarin.

Forsain a famous merchant of this city and a *nouveau reuni* is put into the Bastile for letting his daughter and a hundred thousand crowns escape to Geneva.

The King of Spain is ill again: these people had an express from Madrid three days since, which told them so.

You see by the enclosed verses that they have damned poetry at St Germains. Adieu, my Lord, I am eternally

Yours.

No. 23.

[To Earl of Galway.]   de Paris ce 11 Juillet 1699.

My Lord

J'apprens par la Lettre que vous m'avez fait écrire du 13/23 Juin[1] que vous destinez l'Employ dont je suis honoré en Irelande à Monsieur May qui en a rempli si dignement les fonctions pendant mon absence. Ainsi dans un bon Deputé Je voy un Rival dangereux, sa diligence sera bien recompensée, mais, hélas! Mon absence ne sera-t-elle punie un peu trop severement? je me suis donné l'honneur Mi Lord, de vous marquer dans ma derniere Lettre que je ne savois pas tout à fait à quoy j'étois destiné a mon retour en Angleterre, que j'ay crû portant que ce seroit pour trauailler sous Mi Lord Jersey, mais je scay bien que sa Majesté a eu la bonté de dispenser de mes Services en Irelande pendant que je continuerois par Ses Ordres en france. j'y suis encore mi Lord et dois étre icy pour quelque temps, car je ne voy pas Mi Lord Manchester se presse extremement à me venir relever; en attendant Mi Lord, vous prierois-je de laisser l'Affaire dans l'Etat ou elle est, et de faire continuer Monsieur

<hr>

[1] Bath Papers, III. 358.

May comme mon Depute jusqu'a ce que la Volonté de Sa Majeste soit sceüe la dessus. Si vous m'accordez ce delay, Mi Lord, ce sera une nouvelle marque de la bonté qui vous avez eüe pour moy, si non, J'obeis à vôtre volonté sans oser examiner sur quelles raisons elle est fondée, c'est mon Malheur, mais non pas ma faute de n'avoir pas été en Irelande j'ay toujours fait ce que les Ordres de Sa Majesté m'ont commandé de faire, et je suis sûr qu'Elle est trop juste de me voir ruiné pour l'avoir fait, ainsi Sa Majesté me demet de ma Charge en Irelande, elle m'en pourvoira de quelque autre, et quand Votre Excellence ne me permettra pas l'honneur d'etre vôtre Secretaire, vous me reserverez toujours celuy d'étre avec un tres profond respect

Mi Lord
Votre tres humble et
tres Obeissant Serviteur.

No. 26.

[To Earl of Jersey.]   Paris the 5/15 July 1699.

My Lord

On Monday night I had the honour of your letter of the 26th[1] and last night I had that of the 29th[2] so that now the posts come sooner. I yesterday discoursed Monsr de Pomponne about the post from England, having 3 days before sent him an abstract of the letter which your Lordship had upon that subject from the post-masters. Monsr Pomponne was I perceived a little surprised at the article which obliges him to have an express ready at Calais, to take the letters the moment they arrive; Pajot who made the treaty has been out of town for 3 or 4 days. Monsr de Pomponne will speak with him and give me his answer on friday when he will be at Paris. He comes hither, the Court going this day to Marly for 10 days.

According to your Lordship's commands of the 29th I made a further application to the ministers in behalf of the English Merchants concerned in the Dunkirk ships taken by Du Bart, and carried to Copenhague: I gave in upon this subject a copy of your memorial of the 9th of February, and to it I added another drawn up from the abstracts I received with your Lordship's letters. Monsr de Torcy will lay the thing before the Council, that upon what we have alleged and the accounts which the French have had from their Ambassador at Copenhague I may have an answer, which Monsr de Torcy will (he says) procure me as soon as possible. I am ever

With great respect
My Lord,
Your Lordships most ob^t
and most humble serv^t
M. Prior.

---

[1] Bath Papers, III. 364.   [2] *Ibid.* 365.

The Spaniards have I hear, had a skirmish with the Scotch Company at Darien, if they go on to act offensively the French will certainly underhand if not openly help the Spaniards. I know not how far we avow the Scotch Enterprize, but if we intend they shall be defended, care should be taken of that business in time.

No. 28.

Paris the 8/18 July 1699.

I just now received your Lordship's letter of the 3rd[1] and shall obey your commands in drawing the money as you order: I have spoken with Madam Croissi about the glass, which I do not see we are likely to have soon enough for me to bring it over: she does not like any glass which has hitherto been made, and the monarch has given order for all the glasses of a considerable bigness to be set by for him as they are made that he may have his choice. She does not like the frame, and will have another ordonnance. She says she waited a year for her own glass, and I think expects we should have as long patience.

I have shown my successor twice at Versailles, they say he is *bien fait, bel homme, ma foy, mais Monsr Prior at-il de l'Esprit?* always follows. The man is well enough truly but he has a quiet lazy genius that will not brille enough at Versailles, nor be feared enough at the Coffee-house amongst the bullies of St Germains.

My Lord Manchester names no day for his coming, I presume he designs to show my Lady Bartholomew-Fair before she leaves London. Patience; I live amongst my savants, and Boileau says I have more genius than all the Academy—good again. So mankind is, and our judgements of other people are commonly founded upon the value they have of us.

I must tell you a story: the abbé de Louvois going out t'other day Doctor of Divinity brought (as the custom is) his thesis to persons of quality his friends, and to the public ministers, which is a civil way of desiring them to be at his act: Excellency was not at home when the abbé came to his house: so the abbé paid Madame a visit, and when he had sat a little while, and saw that the woman put on a stately look and hardly spoke to him, he took his leave. Madame (to show her breeding and generosity) sends a servant after the Abbé, who clapt four new crowns into his hand for his thesis; the abbé thought the fellow mad, and sent him back with the money; the ambassadrice thought that the abbé's refusal proceeded from the money not being enough, and sends back the fellow with 2 crowns more; he overtook the abbé in his coach and offered him the 6 crowns: which the abbé refusing still, Madam let him go like a proud priest as he was: I believe Louvois' son never was so used, nor any secretary ever wrote so foolish a story. Adieu, my Lord, I am perfectly your servant.

[Endorsed by Jersey, Answered July ye 13th [?] 1699.]

[1] Bath Papers, III. 366.

My Lord   Paris the 22^d July 1699.

Having understood that Monsr de Pomponne had referred to the memorial I gave him concerning the posts to Monsr Pajot, I have been with Pajot, Monsr Pomponne not being in town, and Marly being such a time that no man can be found. Pajot says the posts were always upon the foot they now are; and (though he does not deny the strength of the article) he pleads a mutual consent on both sides and that their letters lie as long at Dover, that to have a messenger come away with them after 5 at night would only occasion the letters' arrival here likewise in the night, and consequently (since they would not be given out till next morning) no time would be saved, for that they arrive here at noon now, and are distributed in the afternoon, and all the posts that go forward to Italy and Spain go out at midnight. So far of this is certain that the letters come here about noon and that the Italian and Spanish letters do not go away till midnight, but it is as certain that if the letters did come in the night we might have them soon next morning, which would be some hours gained, and that the letters for some parts of France go out from Paris at noon, so that these letters would evidently get a day: but the question is if the matter of fact be true that their letters are only taken from Dover by the ordinary post and no particular courrier ordered to receive and forward them just at their landing: for if it be not so, Mr Pajot's assertion is extremely impudent, if it be so, our post-masters are in the wrong. This, my Lord, is only what Mr Pajot has said, and is to give an answer to Mr Pomponne, so that when I have it in form (which I think will be on Saturday) I will send it.

Mr Pajot is so far right that on Monday I had your Lordship's letter of Thursday. Pajot says that it shall be regular for the future. For the rest, I am far from taking his protestations for an answer, but when I send it in writing and asserted by Mr Pomponne, the post-masters may best judge of its validity.

I will do what I can for Perault, but I shall scarce get an opportunity to speak with the great Torcy till Tuesday.

Madame le Cocque wrote all the war time to Monsr la Forge here, and the President de Mêsmes had the merit of carrying those letters always to Court; this came from the correspondent who let me know what I wrote to your Lordship last post in cipher.

Madame de Mailli designs to keep a gaming house in England, to say no worse of it, and I think is resolved to begin her voyage soon.

When instead of proroguing your Parliament you dissolve it, I have mighty overtures made me from the University of Cambridge to stand for their representatif, a Prior, a Prior.

Your kindness to me in relation to my Lord Galway's proceedings I must put into the great mass of obligations which I owe you: your letter will have come *bien à propos*, and I shall at least have the pleasure of not falling a fool's sacrifice.

Lord Manchester says he will come in a fortnight (from thursday last). I doubt of it.

St M.[1] dined with me yesterday *en philosophe*, and was much pleased with the boiled mutton and custard. I tire you: I'll write a little about the St Germains rogues in another sheet, and conclude this with my being ever most perfectly your servant.

[Postscript] Durant, Hungate and Hare have been at St Omers, Hungate is dead suddenly after his return, and the other two are privately at St Germains.

O'brien who brought Goodman over is gone to Bruxelles to dun Lord Ailesbury for the reward promised him for that service: if his Majesty's interest with the Elector could get him seized there, it might be of service, I will write to Mr Blathwayt about it. Viner [Sr Robert's son] who is here for his health has been privately at St Germains and with my Lord Middleton.

I have enquired about Arnauld[2]; he is still in the Bastile and likely to continue so: they say of him that he was *un couteau à deux tranchants*, and that it was the people of St Germains who had him put up, for that they employed him at Calais, and he corresponded with us. They do not name with whom, though they know Macky[3] to be the person. I believe his telling what wool was landed at Calais was the great reason of his being imprisoned.

One Clerk a Scotchman called father Cosmo is here: he came from Italy with or soon after the Duke of Berwick, and has a great hand in the distribution of that money which the Pope has sent for the distressed northern catholics, that is for all the assassins and murderers from hence to the isles of Orkney [4]. I believe I shall know in a post or two who are the receivers of this charity at London.

[1] St Maurice.

[2] See Bath Papers, III. 365, 370, 374, 387 for further correspondence about this man.

[3] John Macky, an agent of the Government formerly at Harwich, now at Dover.

[4] Cf. Bath Papers, III. 390, Manchester to Jersey, Paris, Jan. 13, N.S. 1700 (in cipher). "One Clerk a Scots priest who went by the name of Father Cosmo was runaway from hence with some money of the late King's and of several other persons to a [three undeciphered groups] since which I hear he is got to [four undeciphered groups] in Leyden in Holland where I presume it may not be difficult for His Majesty to get him seized...he had a great share of the late King's confidence in several matters." Cf. *ibid.* 392, Manchester to Jersey, Paris, Jan. 15, N.S. 1700. They had that confidence in Cosmos *alias* Clerk that the Duke of Berwick lent him his calesh thinking he would return the same day, but he went with it to Leyden.

K: James and his Lady supped on Thursday at Marly. K: James hunts tomorrow, and will (I doubt not) see all his outlying friends that dare not go directly to St Germains.

They whisper amongst themselves the hopes of a Catholic League, but this is the least 1255 (French King) can 1385 (? do for) them.

Mr Stanhope will I presume have told your Lordship that the French ambassador was selling off his goods and furniture, but upon the King of Spain's relapse and vomiting despatched an express and seemed to resolve to stay longer at Madrid: the answer to that express parted on Saturday from Marly.

Mr Stanhope likewise says that the Council of State had consulted sending a successor to the Elector of Bavaria, that it was resolved the Elector should remove and that the two competitors were the Marquis de Leganez and the Duke of Medina Sidonia: the French are secret in the content of their express if it be so, for nobody here speaks one word of the thing.

No. 31.

Paris the 15/25 July 1699.

Uncipher the 2 next lines yourself, pray, my Lord. 1038 (Lady) 199, 68, 27, 538, (Sandwich) 540 (went) 637 (this) 865 (week) to 1479 (late queen) and 917 (hath had) 774 (audience) of 965 (three) 45 (h) 833 (our) 89 (s)—158 (hi) 42 (g) 44 (g) 483 (in) 89 (s) did 889, (bring) 368, (her) 1038, (lady) 1595 (Middleton) is 454 (com)ing to 1127 (France) with an 1494 (overture) from the 1059 (protes) 439, (an)ts, in 1454 (England) to 1478 (late King) in relation to 1035 (the King) as I hear more particulars I shall write more fully, I have renewed an encouragement in order to be informed: they count mightily about this business.

I have told your Lordship that all the proclamation men have lately been at St Germains, they have received their arrears privately.

I have this morning the honour of your Lordship's letter of the 10th which according to Mr Pajot's promise I ought to have had yesterday. I caught Mr Pomponne on Wednesday night at Paris (he was going the same night to Pomponne) where he stays till tonight: I will not take Pajot's answer (for he is a shuffling fellow) till I have spoken with Mr Pomponne; I will do my best to clear the *affaires à present sur le tapis* against my Lord Manchester's arrival. I thank your Lordship for instructing me in the affair of the Scotch company, I only know that the moment the Scotch are driven out, the 1237 (French) will get in and laugh at us. I shall speak to your Lordship time enough, and be better informed at my arrival in England: and obey you as to talking on that subject here.

It will be impossible but that I shall leave some of your commissions undone, and this does not proceed from my negligence but the impossibility of getting the things done: for instance, the Glace, of which I already wrote you word, the picture it is impossible to make Rygault follow it as closely as he promised. This is all I have to trouble you with this post besides the repetition of my being always with the greatest truth and respect, my Lord,

Your servant.

[Postscript] Fribourg has the small pox, but is pretty well with them.

No. 32.

Paris the 19/29th July 1699.

My Lord

I had your Lordship's letter of the 13th[1] which was Thursday, on Monday as I ought, so that Pajot mends upon it. I send your Lordship enclosed their answer to our postmaster's complaint which answer I had yesterday from Monsr de Pomponne. The accusation that our letters lye at Lyons is founded upon the same Principle: the French allege that they are only obliged to forward our Italian letters by their ordinary posts, which they do, and that we have no reason for a complaint, since their Italian posts have received no change as to their going from Lyons since the treaty was made, but remain just upon the foot they were on at the making that treaty; so that by *all dispatch* in the treaty meant (say they) all dispatch which the ordinary posts ought to make, and nothing else.

As to the affairs *sur le tapis* which I begged Mr de Torcy in your name to get dispatched that my Lord Manchester may begin upon a clear stage, he has promised me to use his endeavours to that end: and to say the truth out, if he determines everything as quick as he did some points yesterday, he may soon finish all. As to the English merchandises seized by John Bart, he says the ships being Dantzickers the merchandise taken on board them is looked upon as good prize. He agrees that these goods are spoiled, but says that our reparation must be upon the Dantzickers: he added, *for otherwise our prize would come to nothing.* I endeavoured to evince that because their prize would come to nothing if these goods were restored, it was not fair that to make it come to something, we that had nothing to do in their quarrel must suffer, and instead of answering me he grew angry. I obtained of him to promise me that I should have a word or two written of positive answer to the memorials given in upon that subject, which I will send as soon as I shall receive it.

The last *galeriens* for whom you asked liberty, and some for whom I likewise have asked, are absolutely denied that grace. He has not had an

---

[1] Bath Papers, III. 372.

answer from Monsr Tallard about Gerard Bedford, so cannot answer for Pierre Perault's liberty.

Nothing more is done as to the pirates that killed Capt. Mansell, than that orders have been long since given out to apprehend them when they can find them and that one of them taken here is in prison. I write to Seward in Bretagne to tell him so, and to see if the persons interested in that affair will prosecute him.

Torcy pretends not to know of Arnold's being in prison, so I could not continue that enquiry: Mr Vernon has written to Mr Stanyan about this man, and I shall tell my Lord Manchester at his arrival the state of that and other matters depending, for I do not see that the young minister is very expeditive in anything but what he refuses. Of the 3 fellows taken at Loo, two of them viz. Pendergarst and Fitzgerard[1] went from St Germains in the winter, as I hear. Pendergarst is a desperate fellow, Herford Hare and Durant (these 3 are proclamation men) are lately gone towards Flanders, this is all I can learn of them: I write it to Mr Blathwayt.

My Lady Middleton is at St Germains: one Scott is come from Scotland with many subscriptions of people of some estates in that kingdom.

The persons to whom the Money for the poor Jacobites in England is remitted are Colbern or Cockbourn a shopkeeper in the round Court, Pate a linen draper in Fleet-Street, and one Clapthorn, a merchant of some note in the City.

Clerk, a Scotch priest, known by the name of Father Cosmo who brought bills for this money from Italy, is recommended by my Lord Melfort as a maître-d'hôtel proper to go to Italy with my Lady Salisbury and the care of her affairs there: rare doings! if one compares this with the 2 lines I wrote in cipher last post.

I will not abuse the liberty you give me of returning by Holland. We say my Lord Manchester setts out to-morrow: I wish him well here, I will do my best in the execution of your commissions, and in every action of my life endeavour to merit your kindness to me. Farewell, my Lord, I am perfectly

Yours.

[Postscript] My Lord Sandwich is returned.

No. 33.

Paris the 1 Aug N.S. 1699.

My Lord

I gave the Baron his seaux yesterday, and he is mightily pleased with them. Your own are pretty well forward, for the Glace *point de*

---

[1] Presumably Henry Fitzgerald mentioned in Bath Papers, III. 374. Blathwayt to Prior, Dieren, Aug. 7, N.S. 1699.

nouvelles, none is yet made that Madam Croissy can like, I make Rygault work and shall perform your other commissions as well as I can.

I told you in my last that I had written to Mr Blathwayt what I heard concerning the 3 persons taken at Loo, I am told since that one of them wrote a letter to his brother here almost in these terms:

"We are now at L— in a short time you will have a noise about your ears concerning me, I doubt our female friend will not prove as she ought to do."

The man who wrote it is Connel, it was dated the 19th of June; the brother[1] has said in discourse here that he did not know what he who wrote the letter meant. I will write this to Mr Blathwayt on Monday.

I have your Lordship's letter of the 17/27th: am mighty glad to think that Lord Manchester is before now parted from London, I never thought I should be so very desirous to see his Excellence as I find I am; but since that desire proceeds from my wishing soon to leave him, *il ne doit pas m'en scavoir gré*. I cannot promise extremely for my successor: I have not a word to trouble you with but that I will speak with Gaugain at the Hague, and do whatever I can for the Master's good and your service. I have a standish made me here, and now I have it, it is too fine for me, I intend to bring it over for you. I am eternally, my Lord, and truly

Yours.

Madam de la force has some pension but how much Tamboneau does not know, I am enquiring amongst the Refugies to be informed of this matter[2].

No. 34.

Paris 5th Aug. N.S. 1699.

My Lord

I had yesterday Monsr de Torcy's answer to the several matters depending here as the enclosed specifies: That relating to the Dantzickers is (your Lordship sees) just what I told you in mine of the 29th past. he had given me. What I could urge to the contrary had little weight with him. I had a great mind at least to have had it in writing, for I think it a very hard sentence, but I could not obtain the favour, and was obliged to be or seem contented with the verbal answer. The other cases need no comment. In my audience with Monsr de Torcy I touched upon the order that strangers should not reside in the French sea ports above

---

[1] The brother would presumably be Richard Connel, lieutenant in the Regiment of Picardy. See Bath Papers, iii. 401, Manchester to Jersey, Paris, Apr. 21, N.S. 1700.

[2] This is an answer to an enquiry of Jersey's dated July 6/16, 1699, "if the Duchesse de la Force, *réfugiée* here is not allowed something from her son by the King's order."

8 or 10 days: the answer is that this order is general to all nations, and not meant against us in particular. I take the answer to be very imperfect, for who can be forbidden the ports of Picardy, Normandy and Bretagne but the English chiefly? and as to the other side, Marseilles to which the Italians chiefly come is excepted from this prohibition, as being a free port.

I enquired about W: and L:[1] Monsr de Torcy said he had not heard that they had been examined and that W: had pestered and swore saying that he had always been faithful to the French interest, by whom he was now punished instead of being recompensed: that during the war we had offered him great sums of money to undertake the burning the French fleets, but that he never could be tempted to it. W: had some papers French and English taken with him about which he makes a great work: all this I think may be written without cipher.

I have the favour of your Lordships letter of Thursday last [the 20/30 July][2]. The Lady I mention has brought over great hopes and encouragement to her party here.

I dined yesterday with the old Mârechal[3], and was catechised after diner alone: he is mighty whimsical, and full of Speculatije of what the Parliament will propose in the winter, how they will cramp the King, how uneasy people are in England, with wise reflexions of our Kingdom's being *le païs des révolutions*. Callières and the newsmongers were all much in the same tone: Adams gave me a touch of it too, and it was plainly the whisper in fashion throughout the whole court. The Court of St Germains supped at Trianon last week, and all this undoubtedly proceeds from reports which they have spread, and which the credulous at St Germains very easily receive.

According to the account that my Lord Manchester set out on Friday we may expect to see his Excellency in a day or two. We have as yet no news from him, but we expect to hear to-day from Calais that he is arrived there. I shall endeavour that he may have his private audience between Saturday and Wednesday next, this Court's journeys being so ordered that he cannot otherwise have it till after Saturday se'nnight. If I can therefore get his private audience over by next week, I will get away as fast as I can after, so that I shall not according to this calculation be here at furthest above 14 or 16 days, as I beg your Lordship to send me by next post your commands in relation to my journey. I should be overjoyed at the hopes of meeting some Company at Loo, *si je voyois jour à cela.*

Count St Maurice is much your servant, but says he cannot forgive the end of your letter *avec respect* and that you laugh at him.

Rygault works: your seaux will be done: I will wait upon Madame de Croissy again to-day about the *Glace.*

---

[1] Wall and Lynch.   [2] Not in Bath Papers, III.   [3] Villeroy.

I am ashamed to trouble you so much about my affairs nor will do it more than to show you what Rogues Crop[1] and his man are, and that the little Duke[2] has done a little trick. I will write again to Loo, and you will act for me with your usual kindness, of which while I am assured, I honour the short haired Monarch with perfect indifference.

I dare not go near Vryberg, his disease being the Smallpox, but I send to him and make your compliments to him. He is very well and will recover in all appearance.

The Duke de Brancar has your letter: Davenant went away yesterday morning: I dare not trust his giddiness with as much as your writing box.

Farewell, my Lord, I am with eternal respect and obedience
Your servant.

No. 35.

Paris the 8th Aug. N.S. 1699.

My Lord

My Lord Manchester arrived here on Wednesday at eleven at night. He has seen St Tot his introductor, and yesterday Monsr de Torcy coming to town I got matters so ordered as that his Excellence paid him his first visit. I waited upon him and took the opportunity of giving Monsr de Torcy your letter: Monsr de Torcy will procure my Lord's audience for the latter end of next week, the Court not returning to Versailles till Wednesday or Thursday, and by the beginning of the week after I shall be moving hence. I will not trouble you with the confusion and bustle I am in with him: he asks ten thousand things and determines nothing: employs everybody, and is afraid all the world designs to cheat him. His maître d'hôtel is a John Trott, his escuyer is one Cole, a strange creature who was with Earl Thomas[3] at the Hague. I have given up my office to the Beau, who is from this day forward to inform Mr Yard, and his master writes to you in form as to his provincial.

Jane complains that his Excellence blows his nose in the napkins, spits in the middle of the room, and laughs so loud and like an ordinary body that she does not think him fit for an ambassador. She is of opinion that another Lord whom she knows is fitter to be a King than he to be a Lord. This I return your Lordship as an equivalent for the news of Mrs Jolly, cy-devant Sarah[4].

Not guilty as to have writ Mr Montagu word that I went by way of Holland. I never said one word of it to him or any man in England. The

---

[1] Galway.   [2] Bolton.   [3] Pembroke.
[4] Cf. Bath Papers, III. 374, Jersey to Prior, Whitehall, July 24/Aug 3, 1699. "Joly is gone to be [Manchester's] gentleman of the horse, and has married Tom's cousin; pray be kind to her and do not call her Sarah but Mrs Joly."

Elephant[1] knew it, I presume, from something that might have been said of it at Loo, and according to his foolish manner, stuffed the great news into letters he wrote into England, at least as far as I can guess from the manner of his writing hither to Mr Stanyan and I. The thing must be so. I am very glad you chid me upon a supposition that this accusation was true, for I would have no action of mine indifferent to you, and, as long as I live, whenever you reprove me, I shall have reason to thank you for taking care of me.

In answer to your Lordship's letter of the 24th July, I mentioned to Monsr Torcy when I waited on my Lord Manchester to him the despatch of Cooper's business, and of everything else that remains undecided. I can say no more as to the Dantzick affair, but that my Lord Manchester, upon fresh orders and reasons which the Merchants must give to invalidate the French answer, must apply himself again by memorial: I think that there is little doubt but that the thing is foul, and the delay as to the answer unkind, for if they would deny to restore the merchandises, they might have given that denial much sooner than in the distance of time from February till August, but they let the goods rot, that when they are rotten the proprietors may be less eager in reclaiming them as thinking it less worth their time and then give us an absolute answer that if they are rotten or no we have no right to reclaim them [at least upon the French] this is what I have argued with Monsr de Torcy, but what signifies reasoning? an eye for an eye and a tooth for a tooth is (whatever Mr Stapleton may think of it) very good sense, and wholesome, though Jewish doctrine.

I will do my best in obedience to all your commands, remaining for ever very perfectly, my Lord, Your servant.

No. 36.

Paris the 12th Aug. 1699.

My Lord

Lady Manchester arrived last Night, garde le cœur! for she is very handsome, she has a sty or little swelling upon her eye, but this does not hinder them from being as fine as any in France. Count Ronssy and Blansac had (before her coming) invited us all to Madam Bouillon's to see the fireworks to-morrow, and have been very obliging to Lord Manchester, which he takes to be upon your account.

My Lord is to have his private audience on Sunday morning of the King, most of his other audiences will (I presume) be deferred till Tuesday, I intend to get away on Thursday or Friday, I wish I may meet those at Loo whom I think you mean.

[1] Somers.

This is all the news I can send you from hence, though if I were with you I could talk till twelve at night and be turned out then without having finished half my story. As to Commissions, Rygault is a hero, I shall have your picture before I leave Paris: he works mightily at it.

Your little writing trunk I have. It is made according to your direction, but the standish I speak of is all silver, to be set upon a table, of a much better *Gout* than yours (which you had in France) but of this more when it shall be unpacked in England. I shall not possibly bring the Glace, but will leave such directions as that it may be safely sent, and (as the Miroitier tells me) before winter. I spoke last night for the two spoons, of which Baleine will take care.

I wrote to the Honourable[1] word of what I could hear of Connel, one Poor or Power went with these people from St Germains, but he is not taken. Connel's brother has said in his drink and to those whom he thought his faithful confidents, that he [Connel] would ruin himself by senseless projects. I have spoken to my Lord Manchester concerning Perault: I shall give you a better account by the next post of the Duchess de la Force's pension.

I cannot enough thank you, my Lord, for your favour to me in my Irish affair. It is a triumph to be able to repress the insolence of the French Vice-monarch's[2] last letter—*n'y pensez pas, Monsieur*. He should have added *Voulons et ordonnons* etc., but your letter will have kept him quiet, and if we have a little time we may possibly teach Mr May that honesty and openness is the best way to make people first secretaries. I have had a thousand considerations of the point we have been long upon, bringing the Lady and the Ox together: this is time if ever, and it should be done. I am for ever most perfectly, my Lord,

Yours.

No. 37.

Paris the 15th Aug. 1699.

My Lord

Pajot keeps his word very ill, for it is 12 o'clock and the post is not come in, so that instead of writing a letter to you I am going to Rygault and Balein who cannot be too often spoken to, nor too much hastened. Lord Manchester has his private audience to-morrow, and I shall bring matters about so as to be able of holding my resolution to get away next friday. Mr Stanyan engages for the newsy part, so that I have only to add that I am ever, my Lord, your servant.

Little Dick[3] tells you what becomes of him. I long to get away and shall be glad to find at Loo what I expect.

[1] James Vernon.   [2] Galway.   [3] Shelton.

Paris the 19th August 1699.

My Lord

The posts come in very irregularly, your letter of the 31st[1] which I ought to have received so as to have been able to acknowledge it by last post I received on Sunday, and Thursday's post which we should have received yesterday is not yet come in: my Lord Manchester must speak of this to Monsr Pomponne: his Excellency sends your Lordship the imperfect answers which this court gave yesterday to the affairs at present *sur le tapis*: will it be always so? your Lordship asks: always, until we answer Count Tallard just as they answer us.

Lord Manchester will tell your Lordship that he had his private audience on Sunday. The King's answer to him was almost in the same terms as he answered to your Lordship, one expression in it was remarkable enough, *qu'il feroit tout avec le Roy d'Angleterre pour la tranquillité de l'Europe, et qu'il iroit même audevant de ce que le roy proposeroit pour cet effêt*: I take this to have a further meaning in it than our ambassador understood, and he does not *voir jour*, I know not if I am right in guessing that something relating to that subject makes the *jour* which you write of.

I use my utmost endeavour in prompting my faithful to enquire into the reasons of those persons' conduct who are imprisoned at Arnheim, I am afraid there was a further mystery of iniquity intended in that business than yet appears. I will be informed the best I can concerning it before I leave Paris, and transmit or carry my informations to the Honourable[2].

I will observe your commands as to my voyage, and in relation to *Swager*[3], who sends me the civillest letters that ever said nothing, I will order matters so as to be going the beginning of next week, I won't pretend *faire l'important icy, mon pauvre Lord Manchester fait de son mieux, mais, ma foy, nous sommes bien neufs*. We shall talk of this at large. *Je voudrois bien qu'il fît jour de demain.*

As to Madam de la force, she solicited that a 1000 crowns a year might be remitted to her, this the Court denied by Monsr de Pontchartrain, so that she has nothing but what her son gives her *sous main* which is not much more than this sum, at least has not been as yet. The money she brought in marriage was above 200,000 livres, and what she could pretend to if not hindered by the excluding edicts was 17,000 or 18,000 livres per annum. I shall know by the next remise of money which will be made her how far her son's charity extends.

W: and L:[4] are *in statu quo*.

[1] Not in Bath Papers, III.
[2] James Vernon.
[3] Portland.
[4] Wall and Lynch.

I am really more angry at Crop[1] for having given you so much trouble than for anything else in that affair: pray don't think I lie in saying so, for it is sincerely true that being perfectly satisfied how great a part you take in what concerns me, I am afraid to abuse of your goodness. This is French, but you know what I mean by it.

The women are all mad this August. You remember the 2 lines I wrote to you in cipher[2]; the woman to whom I made your compliments, when you went away without seeing her, has done the same thing.

I have the kindest letter imaginable from Lord Albemarle, your Lordship has not had the *Démenti*: the King of England has taken our part against the Vice-King of Ireland, and we are safe at least for some time.

I have compliments to you from all the world, having yesterday taken my leave at Versailles. I shall have a letter from Monsr de Torcy for you. Nothing could be so kind as these people when I parted with them, the Grand Monarque said such things to me that if my own King says half as much I shall be satisfied: I am puffed up with the praises that he gave me; but the real honour of being for ever your true and faithful servant will easily wipe off the remembrance of all this imaginary glory I have here. You will see by the incorrectness of this letter that I wrote it surrounded with visits, duns and people sent to me from my Lord Manchester. God bless you and yours, my Lord. Farewell.

No. 39.

My Lord   Paris the 22nd Aug. 1699.

My letter was sent away on Wednesday before the Post that brought us those of Thursday before was come in. Those of Monday arrived more regularly for we had them yesterday. I have therefore these two posts to thank you for [the 3rd[3] and 7th V.S.]. The Court being at Marly there will be no ministerial business done on Tuesday next, or if there were I should not be there, for that morning *Adieu Paris et les beaux yeux*; the baggage stage-coaches it by way of Calais on Monday.

This being the case I could only recommend to his Excellency the affair of the Margaret to be further solicited, and the letter to be got from Mr Pontchartrain to that effect.

As to commissions, I have your seaux, your two spoons, a fork and knife answerable to the porridge spoon, and which Baleine has persuaded me ought to go with them. These 2 last I consented to, though I had not your commission for my so doing, since they are *du gout*, and at last there is nothing lost in them but the fashion.

Your ecritoire I have told you I have.

Your picture wants a days work to be finished, and it sounds like a lie

---

[1] Galway.   [2] See above, No. 31.   [3] Bath Papers, III. 366.

but is really true that Rygault is taken ill of a fever and in bed these 2 days past, but to-morrow if he is better, he goes again to work, and I shall have it, I make little doubt, to send away with the rest of my goods.

I have the princess of Conti from Madame d'Espinois and have packed her up for my Lady.

Lady Sandwich went away yesterday (thursday) morning, the lady I mentioned in my last was a Countess Dowager, brave doings! I was yesterday again with Madame de Croissy, she promises to take care of the Glace, the design, and to embark it so as that you shall have nothing more to do than to give orders for its being taken either from Dieppe or Havre as she shall direct you by letter; but for the time when this shall be done she cannot promise. Since I began my letter Lord Manchester paid his visit privately to Monsr de Pontchartrain: I was with him and took that occasion to take my leave of him and to recommend to him with my Lord Manchester the despatch of such affairs of ours as are under his department. The letter to the Parliament of Bretagne he has promised to write, and we this moment send him a memoir upon it to confound the clamours of Mr Taylor.

There has been I am told a great deal of clamour about the passport I have asked for my goods; the French Commissioners for Trade paid custom last year in England for all their goods and plate. I have said upon that occasion to old St Tot that I only would desire what was usual in these cases, that I was very sensible of the honours and favours I had received from this Court, but that if the King of France did not give me the *Droits*, the King of England repaid me what I should expend, and therefore that I was very easy in the matter, and to Monsr de Torcy I said I desired a passport for your goods, which I thought would not be denied, and I therefore distinguished all yours: that if a passport be denied for my lumber, your goods need not suffer for being in bad company; but as I hear, I have a passport for all I am afraid I cannot have it to-day. Monday and Tuesday are holy-days, and I am afraid the *Grosbagage* must lose their earnest and go off on Friday only, for I would have the picture now unless Rygault dies, and be going myself on Wednesday after having seen the goods put up, for unless I do so, there will be, so far as I can see into the matter, fifty avanies and chicanes, notwithstanding any passport I am likely to have from Court.

I shall write to your Lordship for the last time from hence on Wednesday: I shall find your future letters at Loo, and obey your commands there and everywhere.

The standish is yours and so is everything I have.

I do not question but that Crop[1] is confounded, thank you.

[1] Galway.

I am surrounded with André the tailor, la Haye the upholsterer, Abbés, Duns, Commissions, compliments: oh Lord! oh Lord! as little Dick would have said, what work is here? Farewell, my Lord, I am very sensible of your favours and very perfectly

Your servant.

[For No. 40 see above, p. 104.]

No. 41.

Rotterdam the 3rd Sept. 1699.

My Lord

      I came hither last night, where it is no secret that the yacht is gone to fetch you, so that I may very probably hope to see you at Loo before you receive this letter. I wish at least to have my writing so disappointed. I stay here a day that I may arrive at Loo only when they come home; for else I must be obliged to get out a cock-horse to the review which is made to-day or to-morrow and it is not every secretarie's talent (though it be the Honourables[1]) to ride without boots, and in a long wig. Till I see you, my Lord, I reserve speaking of everything *dans le joli royaume*, and in every country where I shall be till I go into the land of promise (and after too if people mind one another there). I am most perfectly, my Lord, your servant.

No. 42.

Loo the 8th Septr N.S. 1699.

My Lord

      At my arrival here on Saturday I found two letters from your Lordship of the 15th and 22nd August. I need not say how glad I was from the contents of them to find that I should soon see you here, but upon talking with our good friend I perceive my Rotterdam news was not true, that you are not yet ordered to come, but that as soon as the King has an answer from Vienne which is daily expected, you will have an order. I am in the mean time to wait here, and constantly trouble our friend once a day to ask him if the express be come in from Vienne.

I imagine you will not stay long after you are sent for; so soon as the order goes I will get to Rotterdam, that I may talk with you back again to Loo.

I find you are perfectly well here, all for the better, in my little sphere I am so too; whether I owe it to your kindness or my own merit is a difficult question: however it be, I will never stand upon my own legs so long as you please to give me your hand.

[1] Vernon.

The Duke of Zell is here; dogs and horses is the language of the place; the King is in mighty good humour, and our friend is all in all: *tant mieux*. The Elephant[1] is always the same, jocular and ignorant, disguising his want of knowing what is doing by affecting to keep it secret. Everybody else are just as you would fancy them: Ireton and Letems (or L'Etang) deep in the Politics, as Jack Latin is in prayer, and Sir John in the Cellar.

The first thing with which I was saluted at Loo was your triumph over Baldaric-o-Ruvigny reformer of Ireland[2]. I take that affair to be so well retrieved as that I shall gain the point, or have compensation, for I perceive my friends at Loo understand very perfectly my case and my circumstances; what signifies it for all this to be troubling you with *thank you, thank you?* Let Crop[2] write and my Lord Albemarle speak, and I know who will have the better of it.

If I could express how much I long to see you I would go on for another page, but as it is I have only to say that I wish it may be soon. Farewell my Lord, I am perfectly and truly   Your servant.

[No. 43 see above, p. 111.]

No. 45.

Loo September 1/11 1699.

My Lord

      I had this morning a very long and a very gracious audience of his Majesty, of which I shall give you the particularities when I have the honour of seeing you: I am commanded to go away to-morrow morning for The Hague, and to wait there for your coming, and thus I think I have told you my story in two words. I shall obey your counsel in regard to the Swager[3]; the week I have stayed here and the audience this morning have given me a good deal *la cart du païs*, in which whole matter I find myself every day more and more obliged to you.

Mr Blathwayt gives you the news. The King of Denmark being dead is the principal article. Old Boucherat is likewise deceased, the talk is that Pontchartrain is to be Chancellor: if so he will leave his brother-financiers to be squeezed. I should be very glad to see matters come to that pass in France, for it would show their poverty at the same time that it broke their credit; but I fear they will not be so ill-advised in this point as I could wish them, and that my hopes will only end in Speculatije.

My Lord Albemarle is gone yesterday morning to Zutphen; he is expected home to-night: I hope to speak with him before I leave this place. He is not yet come home, 'tis 10 at night and the post is now going. I am ever, my Lord,   Your servant.

[1] Somers.   [2] Galway.   [3] Portland.

[For No. 46, see above, p. 113.]

No. 47.

Hague the 5/15 Sepr 1699.

My Lord

Here I am sauntering since Sunday, how long I must continue to do so, God knows, for I hear not one word of your being sent for. I have dined with my Lord Portland at his retreat, nothing appears so gay and so much a philosopher as he, and (which is yet rarer) he would have all the world of his mind: there is a great deal to be said, and a great deal to be thought (as Sr Joseph[1] used to tell us) upon this subject, which I all reserve till I see you: I have visited the pensioner and little Tallard, which besides my having seen *mes cousines* is the whole of what I have done these 2 days here; I hope in two more to hear that you are sent for. *Je m'ennuye ici comme un chien*, and after the noise and bustle of Paris one had as good live in a tomb as here. Let me have your commands as to what lodgings I shall take for you, as soon as you know when you are designed to come, or what else you would have me do against your coming; which is all I have to trouble you with besides the eternal respect with which I continue for ever, your servant.

No. 48.

Hague the 12/22 Sept. 1699.

My Lord

I divide my time here so equally between the Swager[2] and the Heers on one side, and the French and *mes cousines* on the other side, that I have all the appearances of being a very happy man, but not having heard from England or from Loo since I last wrote to you, I would leave it even to John to judge if I am that happy man or no: to hear Jacquelot dispute and Bougy lie, *bon Dieu! a-t-on été à Paris pour ça?* but I hope to-morrow's post which brings the English letters from Loo will tell me you are sent for, for as an ancient Roman said that a bawdy house taught him to love his own wife, so I assure you, bad company makes me extremely wish for my own master, the 2 French Excellencies Tallard and Bonrepos are very kind to me, *cela va sans dire*, they never miss, you know, in forms, and never hold in things essential, however one sees the best company (which is indifferent enough God knows) at their houses, and it is better dining with them than at the Marechal de Turenne or the Kaysarhoff. You see what stuff I am forced to entertain you with till the courier arrives from Vienne, or the wind changes so that we may have our letters from England. Without one of these I have not one word to add, except

---

[1] Williamson.   [2] Portland.

I entered upon the very large subjects, the obligations I have to you, or the desire I have to be with you (farewell my Lord) if one is most attached to those whom one most desires to see, you have a very despotic power over my soul at present. Ireton passed yesterday morning through the Hague and is gone for England.

No. 50.

Paris Wednesday noon the 4th Novr N.S.

My Lord
        I should have arrived here last night if I had been set on shore at Calais sooner than Monday noon, as it is I came hither just now. My Lord Manchester has put up his letters, so only leaves me to say that you shall hear more from us next post. I am ever,

My Lord,
        Your Lordships most obed^t
        and most humble serv^t
            THOMAS BROWN
        for this is my name at present
        nobody knew me at Calais or on the
        way hither.

No. 51.

Paris the 6th Novr N.S.
nine at night 1699.

My Lord
        By the account my Lord Manchester sends you and which he has done me the honour to impart to me your Lordship sees the present state of our affair, that his Excellency can have no audience till the Court returns from Marli. I think Torcy's way of giving this answer peremptory enough, and I hope at least our way of asking it conformable to His Majesty's orders and neither done with *Empressement* or Negligence. I came hither with all secrecy imaginable, but my being here was soon known after my arrival, I pretend not to be well and take that pretence for not stirring out, so I have seen nobody, nor will till I have done the business for which I was sent. If anything be come from Holland or your Lordship has any further instructions or commands for me, you will be pleased to send them by this messenger. I am a good deal concerned that the affair in which (by your goodness to me) I am intrusted should as yet have no better luck, but *que faire?* I will do my best, and providence must do the rest; the Jacobites are much alarmed at my coming hither: every man has his conjecture and all wrong.
        Since we shall not have the private audience before to-morrow Se'nnight

at soonest and probably not before the Thursday following by which time the affair in Holland may be perfected, may I see Torcy or Tallard in the meantime? and how far may I speak to either of them of it? in this you will order me, and till these orders come I will not go out.

Pray think of the faithful and return me a hundred pound for Braconie and Brocard that I may speak to them with a safe conscience and see how far the latter will deceive the larger sum in question.

I have only to add my being ever with perfect respect

My Lord
Your Lordships most obedient
and most humble servant
M. PRIOR.

No. 52.

Paris the 1/11 Novr 1699.

My Lord

My Lord Manchester makes my writing to you unnecessary: his Excellency giving you an account of his visit yesterday, and with it the unavoidable trouble of deciphering part of his letter. I hope you will find that thus far we have done right: I think we shall get our audience for Saturday, at least we have asked it as fairly as we could. I have not been much abroad; what I have learned as to the public I shall acquaint you with when I have the honour to see you. As to private affairs, I have seen Rygault, and if he keeps his word you shall very soon have the King and the Dauphin. I may tell you, though my letter be broke open in the way that the finance is in a very bad condition and Monsr de Chamillard very uneasy for this is so far from being a secret that all Paris talks of it, and feels it. I cannot really express to you my thoughts of the Obligations I have to you, or the zeal with which I continue for ever

Your servant.

No. 53.

Paris the 14th Novr N.S. 1699[1].

My Lord

On Thursday my Lord Manchester had a letter from Monsr de Torcy intimating that it was impossible for His Excellency to have an audience this evening but giving him his choice either for to-morrow morning or monday both which happen very oddly since he is to make his entry to-morrow and to be in ceremony at the Hôtel des Ambassadeurs on Monday. His Lordship has therefore chosen to-morrow morning, thinking it less proper to lose a day than to have a little bustle extra-

[1] Cf. Bath Papers, III. 379, Manchester to Jersey, Paris, Nov. 21, N.S. 1699.

ordinary; and accordingly we go privately this afternoon to Versailles to have our audience after the Lever to-morrow morning, that we may be back again by eleven, that my Lord may go to Rambouillet to begin the show.

2153 (Count Tallard) was yesterday with 1946 (E. Manchester). Without all doubt 2311 (Torcy) had told 798 (him) what he and 1946 (E. Manchester) had discoursed about the 1961 (particular) 1703 (affair). 2153 (Count Tallard) plainly asked 1946 (E. Manchester) when he 887 (went) to 2320 (Versailles) and when I went back again. As far as I can see 2153 (Count Tallard) is not extremely pleased with the whole matter.

The 1822 (Spanish) 1780 (minister) and 2218 (Emperor's minister) here are lately very well together, and 754 (both) extremely angry with 1917 (his Majesty), *il n'importe.* Calières being of a sudden gone from Paris makes everybody conjecture differently where he should be, some say he is gone to mediate the differences between the Northern Crowns, Palmquist and Meyercroon say not; some say he is gone privately for Holland; one can hardly think that since Bonrepos is upon the place, and another named to succeed him; may be (after all) he is only gone to his own small estate in Normandy.

Our courier is not yet returned from England which makes us think we are to have no new commands from you. I shall regulate my return by the answer we may have to-morrow morning. I wish for nothing more (as to myself) than to return to you, and tell you that I am ever with the greatest truth and respect

Your servant.

No. 57.

[A rough draft with many erasures.]

J'envoye par cet ordinaire au Secretaire Trumbul le traitte pour les 4 m: hommes de Munster, pour faire voir au Roy.

Je vous suis bien obligé de votre souvenir pour Balmier, j'espere qu'il ne sera pas necessaire qu'il passe en Angleterre quand la lieutenance sera vacante au moins que le regiment n'y soit.

J'ay reçu ce matin la vôtre du 12 et une de Milord Godolphin de la même date. Je me rends plus facilement a ses sentiments a l'egard de mon affaire étant tout à fait assuré de votre amitie la dedans. Je ne veux pas vous prescrire ni le tems ni la maniere de la faire. Je laisse tout en entierement à vous ne doutant point que vous ne preniez l'occasion qui sera plus favourable. Je ne pretends pas de vous remercier de ce que vous faites je ne scaurois le reconnoitre autrement qu'en vous aimant à mon ordinaire. Le mariage dont vous parliez m'a fort surpris et d'autant plus qu'il n'y a peu de tems que j'en ay la nouvelle; vous voyez par là que je na'y point eu part la dedans ¹et je n'en aurez jamais dans les affaires semblables. Je souhaite aux interessez beaucoup de bonheur¹—²non plus que dans tout le reste de la vie de cette personne mon sorte pourtant m'a toujours attache a elle et mon inclination m'a toujours fait souhaiter son bonheur. Je le fais dans cette occasion autant que jamais, je suis fasche seulement de n'auoir pas eu la semblable occasion il y a douze ans, mais laissons ce sujet et permettes moy de uous assurer que je uous ayme du fond³ de mon cœur il m'est impossible de uous le dire autant que je le pense².

No. 58.

Faut-il que Je vous demande pardon de ce que je vous ecris sur une affaire qui ne me touche pas autrement qu'en ce qu'elle regarde les interets de Sa Majesté? La dispute entre les Anglois et les Suedois touchant le Pavillon fait beaucoup raisonner aux gens icy, j'espere que le relâchement du vaisseau Suedois dernierement pris fera taire à tout le monde qui est disinteressé, mais il ne satisfera point à ce que J'ay oüi dire au pretensions de Monsʳ de Lilienroet. Vous le connoissez pour un uieux routier de ministre et pendant qu'il semble souhaitter seulement le moindre relâchement du coté de Sa Majesté quand même Sa Majesté ne permettroit que de vive voix que pour l'auenir les navires Anglois ne chercheroient point la rencontre des Suedois (comme le roy Charles 2ᵈ en usa a l'egard des Francois) Mons: Lilienroet se flatteroit qu'une promesse de la sorte une fois donnée pourroit tirer à consequence, si Sa Majesté trouve jamais bon de renouveller ses pretensions il seroit mieux donc selon mon petit avis que tout ce qu'il plaira à Sa Majesté de faire en cette occasion se fisse de son côté sans se communiquer sur ce sujet avec la Suede, et seulement par des ordres secrets donnés aux Anglois. Le Suedois sera satisfait quand il n'y aura plus de dispute, et ne gagnera rien par la maniere dont l'accord se fasse. C'est en ami que Je vous dis tout cecy, vous en userez de même, et en parlerez au Roy si vous trouvez que mes petits sentimens contribuent à son service: mon zèle pour ses Interets doit excuser cette lettre et bien que l'amitié que j'ay pour vous m'engageroit à vous entretenir d'auantage, je fineray en vous assurant que Je suis sincerement à Vous.

M. Keppel.

¹⁻¹ Struck out.   ²⁻² In Jersey's hand.
³ Prior had written here, but it is struck out by Jersey: Monsʳ P— n'ose plus vous importuner mais il m'a prié de vous assurer de sa part de la reconnoissance qu'il a pour les soins que vous auez pour luy.

Appendix C

DIARY AND NOTEBOOKS AT LONGLEAT

BY the kindness of the Marquess of Bath, K.G., I am allowed to print these extracts from the Longleat MS. XXI relating to Prior's work in Paris in the autumn of 1712, and certain sayings which, later in life, he jotted down as reminiscences.

[In Drift's hand]

/Journal relating to the proceedings concerning the Treaty of [fo. 20 Utrecht; Together with other miscellanious remarks. As also Fragments and Bruillons on divers subjects &ca.

/Monsieur de Buys arrived the 18th of October 1711. Was at [fo. 20 b the Secrys Office at the Cockpit and at Lord Treasurers.

22 And was again at the Cockpit with a Committee of Lords.

/October 22nd Monday October the 22nd Monsieur de Buys [fo. 21 had an audience of Her Majesty; The sum of what he said was, that the States Submitted themselves to Her Majesty's Decission, that thô every thing was Stipulated for them that they could desire, which is that a sufficient Barriere should be assured to them, and all the advantages of Commerce, They could yet wish that the Tariff of 1664 had been Stipulated for them and the Barriere named. Her Majesty's Answer was, that as to any Preliminaries, She looked upon them to be Articles of Peace, and therefore to be Stipulated when the Conferences to that end were Opened. She would neither suffer Herself nor Her Allyes to be led into wrong Measures; But thought if a Peace was desired as She hoped she had born such a part of the War as might enable Her to hear what France had to propose, and that She was confident that both Holland and Her other Allies might depend upon it, that She would take care of their Interest as well as that of Her Own People.

October 24th Monsieur de Buys had a Conference with the Cabinet Council Lord Treasurer, Lord Privy Seal, Lord President Duke of Shrewsbury, Lord Keeper, Lord Dartmouth, and Mr Secretary St Johns. /The subject matter of the [fo. 22 Conference was much the same as what Monsieur de Buys hàd before said to Her Majesty. The Lords answered to his Arguments that we could not Stipulate for the particulars of their Barriere, that He [Mr de Buys] himself had not power to do it; That as to the Dutch Tariff of 1664 upon wch he insisted; We conjointly with them would endeavour to obtain it, But that this as other points was referable to a General Treaty. The Lords agreed that, the whole of what Monsr de Buys had said to be referred to Her Majesty for Her Answer, and accordingly Mr Secretary St Johns, went the next morning to Hampton Court.

/October the 26th Mr Secretary St Johns Informed me that he [fo. 23 was to write that Night to my Lord S...d, which letter he would show me. That he was likewise the next Day to write to Monsr de Torcy; Jobson to carry the Express to Calais, from whence the Commandant to take care of it; which Letter he would likewise show me, And that in conformity to the Contents thereof I should immediately desire Monsr G— to write likewise to Monsr de Torcy upon these Heads.

Her Majesty had heard Mon^r de Buys from the States, the points affecting Holland, their Barriere and their Commerce.

Her Majesty was of an Opinion that to facilitate the entring into a Negotiation France should impart to Us the Specification of the Barriere and Tarif (as Monsieur de Torcy's Lre to Monsr Petkum in Feb: 1710 had already done)[1].

As to Savoy more particularly on the side of France that head more explained would bring the Duke of Savoy likewise to be Easier in opening the Negotiation. If we Hollande and Savoy were equally willing to open the Conferences we should find no Obstruction in the course of the Negociation.

That as France can make us more easy in the Begining we shal be more able to assist them mutually in the Carrying on this Affair.

That Monsr de Buys has his final Answer, That Her Majesty has writ to Her Ambassad^r at the Hague, and expects from Him the States Answer as to the place and Time of opening the Conferences.

[1] On fo. 22 b opposite this paragraph are the following words: 22 Art:—Furnes, Menin, Ipres with its dependencies, i.e. Bailleu, Warneton, Comines, Warwick, Popringel [Casel remaining to France] Lille, Doway [remaining] Conde, Maubeuge.

In Monsr Torcy's Lre: Cited—toutes les places denoncées dans l'Article 22^d des Preliminaires, Scavoir, Furnes, Le Fort Knock, Menin, Ipres, Lille, Tournay, Condé et Maubeuge avec les Dependences et aux conditions specifiées par ce meme Article.

Her Majesty Orders her Secretary to impart this to Monsieur de Torcy, and from that the King of France may Judge with what openess and Sincerity Her Majesty endeavours to put this affair in such a Method as She thinks will contribute to the effecting a Safe Lasting and Honourable Peace.

Petkum shows a Letter in Holland from a Minister of France, that we are underhand Treating with that Kingdom, that the P— is to be acknowledged K— of S— at present, and designed Universal Heir to S— neither Her Majesty nor any of Her Ministers imagine that any Minister of France should have been guilty of anything so contradictory to Truth and Reason. But P—m having most certainly showed such a Letter or pretended Lre: Her Majesty Expects that the Ministry/of France shal Disown their Correspond^t [fo. 25 and that Monsieur de T— shal Act herein in such a manner as shal give Her Majesty Satisfaction.

/26 On Tuesday last Mareschal Tallard from Dover [fo. 20 b for Calais.

23
Octob: 1. Sir Robert Beechcroft chosen Lord Mayor.

28 Sworn at Westminster.

My Lord Treasurer being ill at that time and Mr de Buys visiting him, Buys wondered that among the persons who came to his Lordship Mr Prior was not there Lord Treasurer excused it, by saying he intended to present Mr Prior to him —but that his Indisposition continuing he would be sure to tell Mr Prior and did not doubt but that he was very ready to pay him his respects, as also to inform him of every particular step made in the negociation. Mr Prior accordingly waited

31 Octo: on his Excellency (last Wednesday morning).

4 Nov. Sunday 7 in the Evening Mr Buys waited on my Lord Treasurer M^r P being present some of the Discourse was a repetition of what Mr de Buys had already said to the Ministers, and of what he had discussed with Mr P. in the visit aforementioned.

Nov 6. Mr Buys went to hampton Court

7 he paid a visit to Mr Prior with whom he was in conference about [$\frac{1}{2}$] an hour.

/1712   [fo. 26
19 August Dunkirk was already in Our hands. The Preamble of the Suspension of Arms mentions a happy Success to be expected from the Conferences opened at Utrecht. Lord Bolingbroke,

21—2

who Signs the Treaty had Pleinpouvoirs Passeport &c[a].　So
that from the Signing this Suspension the French were no
longer reckoned our Enemies; And at Fontainbleau Lord
Bolingbroke met M[r] Stanhope.

/1712　　　　　　　　　　　　　　　　　　　　　　　[fo. 27

Aug. $\frac{2}{13}$ Saturday, Lord Bolingbroke, M[r] Gautlier, Mons[r] Hare and I,
　　sett out from London, arrived Wednesday following at Paris.
　　$\frac{9}{20}$ Saturday went in M[r] de Torcy's Coach to Fontainbleau.
　　$\frac{11}{22}$ Lord Bolingbroke and M[r] Torcy agreed the Memoire upon
　　which the Suspension of Arms was founded The Suspension
　　being Signed was published at Paris on Tuesday.

[In Prior's Hand]

/1712　　　　　　　　　　　　　　　　　　　　　　　[fo. 75

Aug. 27 NS: I drew vpon my Ld Treasurer 660 p[ds] payable to M[r]
　　Daniel Arthur.　I desired him to let Drift haue 400 p[ds] from
　　Taylour.

Aug. 28 Sunday my L[d] Bolingbroke parted from Paris.

Aug. 29 Munday.　I drew (taking vp) from M[r] Cantillon 2000 liv.

Sep[r] 1: Thursday.　The P. d'Ossune and the Count de Monteleon
　　payed me a long visit.　the substance: that Sicily might not be
　　given to Savoy. that the Q: would find Spain ready to obey
　　her in all things:

Sep. 5: I went to Fountainebleau, having receiued the ratification
　　of the Cessation, wth Ld Dartmouths orders therevpon.

Sept: 6: I exchanged the ratification, and talked wth Mons[r] de Torcy,
　　vpon the heads of my letters from Eng: prepared a letter with
　　his answers [and soon after sent the Proclamation for the
　　Cessation desiring ours Riciprocally, told Lord Dartmouth
　　that I had the Ratification of the Explanatory Clause for Ships
　　beyond the Line—but wanting the Instrum[t] signed by Torcy
　　here, and which should be returned signed by Bol: there, in
　　order to my Exchanging the Ratification] [1].

Sep: 8: I sent Dagley wth letters received from Eng: to wch I added
　　One from my self to E: Peterbrough at Turin.

/Sunday $\frac{25}{14}$ Sepr received by Barlow vpon wch I am to confer [fo. 76
　　wth Mr Torcy and mons[r] Pontchartrain
　　Dans la harangue de la Reine ou Elle dit même que la
　　différence à l'egard de la barriere pour les hollandais n'est que
　　de deux ou tout au plus de trois villes au dessus de ce qui leur
　　soit cedé par le traité de 1709. Sa Maj[té] s'exprime d'vne

[1] Inserted from fo. 28, this passage being in the copy in Drift's hand,
but not in that in Prior's.

maniere que de ne laisser rien à douter que Dunkirk ne fut
cedé aux Anglois, et que l'equivalent pour cette ville ne fut
conclus dans les 2 ou 3 villes dont la reine fit mention voy. haî.
Que les plenipotentiaires de france parlent d'abord en des
termes aussi generaux que la proposition dont il s'agit.
Draught of the Proclamation for the liberty of the Prisoners.
Torcy's letter to Boling⸆:

/Wensday the $\frac{28}{17}$ Septr I dispatched Haywood [fo. 77

Heads

To Ld Bolingbroke.

An account how by his Instructions we had gott off from the Obstacles
wch might have arose to the Renonciation by Henchman's additions: hoping
the orders Ld Lexington had would obviate any New difficulties in Spain.

How We had sett the Conferences again on foot at Utrecht, Torcy
having by the King's order drawn vp instructions to their Plenipotentiaries
by wch Ours may still act conformably to what Her Maj^{ty} declared in her
Speech to the Parliament, and the affair of what towns to be enumerated
for the Barriere may be deferred mons^r Torcy writ a long letter to Lord
Bol: on this subject, and let Me see as well the letter as the Copy of the
Order.

The 1258 [chevalier?] wanted the 1011 (Emp^{rs}) passeport, 2040 (Lorrain) absolutely in the 1011 (Emp^{rs}) interest and holding communication
with our Whiggs at home.

Concerning the 1840 (Bavaria), his behaviour to her Maj^{ty} and his
hopes from thence.

/desired him again as mons^r Torcy had done to sett us right [fo. 77 b
as to our Correspondence.

Thanked him.

Sent after the Courrier: a pacquet to him from Mr Pontchartrain.

Ld Treasurer

A long deduction of the first point with Henchman's addenda and
Torcy's remarks.

Gaue him an account of the manner in wch I had gott the Conferences
renewed referred him on the Subject to w^t I had writ to Ld Bol:

Told him at large the affair of 1258 [chevalier?] & 2040 (Lorrain).

Referred him for all Marchand affairs to what I writ to Ld Dart:

Begged him to take care that the Orders I should receiue from Eng:
might be explicit, and that he would write to Me.

Referred to him the Case of the Griffon.

/Passeports I had of the first Parcell 105 [fo. 78
Received since and sent the 4th 216

Sent to Eng: 480 writ to Ld Dart to send what might make Us even 161 told Him how this Court vsed Us in this behalf.

What we had done in the 2 great points, with a word of observation vpon the D^r.

Sent the Proclamation for the Cessation desiring ours reciprocally Told Him I had the Ratification of the Explañ: clause for Ships beyond the Line, but wanting the Instrument signed by Torcy here and wch should be returned signed by Bol: there, in order to my Exchanging the ratification.

Answered the Merchants Complaints about fish for Newfound: and Corn from Eng: exported for Barcelona or Portugal: they are comprehended as all others in the terms of the Cessation, these Commodities can not be accd Contrebande.

Sent him the Case. of the Griffon Pacquet from Mons͠ Pontchartrain.

/As to Passeports, that they were in the form they had been [fo. 78 b this 100 Year, had the desired effect if respected by the French Ships however should haue been altered but that they were signed by the G: Adm̃: at Rambouillet, and should if desired to be allowed in the next, if any more demanded 2 Ships at Toulon accorded supposing the vsual Ceremonies and Salutes pd to the Port and the Admiralls flagg.

Took notice that in the Proclamation for the Liberty of Prison^{rs} Depar le Roy, the stile as desired was observed, and that I had agreed to the Stile —dans la Grande Bretagne et les Domains y appartenants to comprehend as well Irel. as any or all other her Maj^{ties} Dominions.

/Sept: $\frac{18}{29}$ the Marq: de Monteleon told me he was destined [fo. 79 for Eng: had a Dormant Character wch he would take as her Maj^{ty} might think proper, and that P: intended by his directions to Ld Lexington to let him know that he particularly intended to hon^r the Queen.

Monsr Torcy gaue me the letter from our Com^r in Cheif in Spain wch I sent by way of Dunkirk the next day to Eng:

$\dfrac{\text{22 Sept:}}{\text{3 Oct}^{\text{re}}\text{:}}$ Munday I returned from Versailles, mons^r Torcy having given me the Memoire concerning Wic̃: 1928 (Envoy of Lorraine).

[O. S. 25th. My Plenipotentiary Powers bear Date]¹.

6 Oct^{re}: I drew vpon Ld Treãs 500 pd sterl. value received here of Dr Ri^c Cantillon.

$\dfrac{\text{10 Oct:}}{\text{29 Sep}^{\text{r}}\text{:}}$ Dagley was sent the next Morñ for Eng: my letters bearing date this day

> To Ld Bolingbroke
> Ld Dartmouth

¹ Inserted from fo. 28, where these words appear in the Copy in Drift's hand, but not in Prior's.

Ld Treasurer
Mr Brydges
/Sir J: Stanley   [fo. 79 b
Mr Southwell
Mr Shelton and iñ
Dr Inglis
Capt Jobson at Calais.

Munday the
$\frac{17}{6}$ D: of Argile arrived.
$\frac{18}{7}$ I had an audience of his most Ch: Majty and presented him
my Credential letters: v: my h: his Ans:
$\frac{19}{8}$ I went to Versailles wth D: Argile v. in my letter to Mr T:
his business.

[In Drift's hand]

Monday Comte Monostrolle in a long Visit expounded the hardships
24
under which his Master lay and repeated that he threw himself wholly on
Her Majesty's Goodness and Generosity I repeated the principal to him
upon wch Her Majesty had gone and from which it was impossible to
Deviate. I added fairly to him that I had Letters before me from you
upon which I was going immediately to Versailles the contents of which
showed that the Queen would protect Her Allies in such a manner
/as to get them soon out of the War, and that was the most She [fo. 80
could engage He answered that your Lordp had already a Memll in which
the Elector Specifyed His Desires and beg'd her Majesty's Answer in such
manner as She Should think proper, and repeated the great obligations
that the Elector would have to Her Majesty for the Succours She should
afford to an Afflicted Family. I promised to impart the Substance of his
Discourse to Your Lordship, which I have done, and so leave that Topic.

*That Sicily was promised by France to the Elector for which Sardinia
would be but an unequal Equivalent, and that in the general Stipulation
the Elector hoped that Luxembourg and Namur might be left to him,
with an addition of Limbourg and Hainault which, said he, would be a
little appanage for a Younger Son, and but a little recompence for what
He otherwise Lost. I said, as to my own sense this seemed to me to give
new Ideas, would dismember the Catholique provinces, and was foreign
to ye measures already taken at Utrecht for the Basis of the Peace.

[In Prior's hand]

/Saturday 4 afternoon, set out from Paris, arrived at Winsor [fo. 81
Saturday following, Kist the Queen's hand the next Morning, told the
Subject of my coming and gaue to her Majty the C. King's letter of
Cachette.

$\frac{1}{12}$ Decr I sett out from London, lay at Sittemborn $\frac{2}{13}$ at Dover, heard that D: Marl: was gone from thence for Ostend on Sunday, embarked the Night (tuesday at 12) arrived Wensday the $\frac{3}{14}$ about noon at Calais was mett at my landing by Monsr Molé in his own Coach and carryed to his house, the souldiers vnder their arms and the Drums beating, the Cannon saluted me at my entry and parting from the town. I went from Calais about 4 afternoon and arrived at 10 the Same Night at Boulogne.

Mem^{dum} I took vp 1000 livres ie 50 pistoles of Monsr Pigott.

[Drift's hand resumes]

Proceeded on my Journey the next day—was Escorted to Abbeville.

I met the Duke D'Aumont, was invited to Sup and Ly at Monsr near Clermont.

I arrived at Paris.

Went to Versailles and had a conference with Monsr de Torcy.

/Cop...when we came to what reg[arded the Ele]ctor of Bavaria; [fo. 82 he seemed surprized that no more was Stipulated in that Princes behalf. That this was only just what Lord Bolingbroke had consented to before, nay not even so much for that My Lord Bolingbroke had taken the Electors proposal and ingaged to do what he could in his behalf which now he, Monsieur de Torcy found to be nothing at all. I desired him to consider first that it was all ye Queen could do in relation to the Alliances She is at present engaged. That it cured that Princes fears of his not having Sardinia, and would effectually engage the Dutch to enter into the Queens measures, in hopes they might be quit of such a Neighbour; that it might engage the Elector Palatin to take the same measures in which case the Emperor could not stand out, and consequently the Peace might be universally Signed at the same time. While he urged how hard it was that the Garrisons of those places should be in the hands of the Dutch; He asked me who should pay those Garrisons, I told him I had no Orders upon that head; but that I thought the Dutch should pay their own Garrisons, To this he answered that the Revenue of the country would hardly sustain the Garrisons, and that in this case it was rather a Hardship upon than a favour to the Elector.

As to the Duke of Savoy; He said that the King had heard all that Monsieur Malerade could say, but would not receiue its pretentions. That in one word it would certainly agrandize His R.H. if his Barrier was extended on that side. That everything was /done for him that [fo. 83 could be expected, on the other side, Half a Dutchy and a great Kingdom given to Him, and he begged that matter might be left to the Plenipotentiarys at Utrecht.

The great point, and what is most essential to Us was the Affair of Newfoundland. He insisted that their right of Fishing on the Coast was taken care of by positive and repeated Orders given to Mesnager, and stipulated in the Preliminaries. That the Divisions only as to where they or we should Fish have been disputed and was not yet regulated at Utrecht, But that Cape Breton and the adjacent Islands was given to the French already, and to prove this, He gave me a Draught of what our Plenipotentiaries had proposed to the French in August, whereas the Plan I showed him, was only in April. Upon the whole I promised to compare the 2 plans and to send to Utrecht to know how the Negociation stood there as well as to Peace as to Commerce, as I would likewise do to England; That upon the respective Answers this great point might be determined.

As to a Treaty of Commerce which Mr de Torcy agreed with me ought to be signed as to the principal points of it, at the same time with the Treaty of Peace to the end that as little as could be might be left to Comm^{rs} to be named afterwards, I told him I would draw out the Chief heads of what we might desire, as I would receive likewise those that they might ask, and was ready when they pleased to discourse with the Ministers upon them; And Monsr de Torcy agreed to send away an Express to their Plenipotentiarys at Utrecht by wch I might likewise send to our Plenipotentiarys and know in what State the whole matter Stood and to prepare what I could against the Duke of /Shrewsburys coming. [fo. 84

Dec. $\frac{9}{20}$ Tuesday I had an audience of His Majesty at ten in the Morning Introduced by Monsr de Torcy and gave His Majesty the Queens Letter.

27 Received the King's Passeport for 2 of the Duke of Savoys Grooms to bring home Dogs and Horses from England, The Passeport runs "Librement passer et repasser deux Palfrenieres de notre tres chere et tres ami Frere le Duc de Savoye allant en Engleterre cherchant des Chiens et des Chevaux pour son Service, pour retourner ensuite par notre Royaume a Turin.

Memorandum:

That in the Coasting Trade the Rights and Duties to be paid cannot be appropriated to the Weight and Bulk of the whole Ship, but to the Weight of the Goods thus taken in at one Port, and transported to another.

Memorand^m:

That upon Comm^{rs} to be Named there must be an Article in the Treaty by which what such Comm^{rs} shal agree must be approved and Ratifyed by the respective Soveraigns and take place accordingly as if inserted Word for Word in the Treaty.

[In Prior's hand]

SAYINGS [fo. 137 b

At the Board of trade advising M^r R: Cecil don't sitt next to S^r P: Meadows for He has sold one Elephant already.

*　　　*　　　*　　　*　　　*

To the woman who ask't Me if I would buy the Opera book in the play house No, child, I come to hear w^t they sing but not to mind what they say.

/When at Marly they showed Me the Kings sieges and [fo. 138 conquests painted by Uandermule and amongst others Mons taken in 1691 I asked if they had not the other part of that Picture wch sayd they That I answered in which King William retook that Place in 1695.

/   *   *   *   *   *   [fo. 138 b

To mons^r de Buis who said he had read the English History and observed that it [was] very difficult to find the just balance of our Constitution I replyed it is therefore the more glorious to those who spend their lives in searching.

To C. Iarnac and the french commending the Witt of the present K: of F: then Dauphin, this would not haue had so much Witt, if his brother had not dyed.

To the King of France how I liked the Dauphin? He makes me Melancholy everytime I see Him: why so, S^r; reflecting that the Queen of Eng: has not just such another.

How I liked Madam^selle Charolais if Eng: had a finer lady the Baron Allfeilt: Monsieur on ne peut pas /repondre à cette question: [fo. 139 les Anges n'ont point de païs natal.

To Madam Croissy who asked Me how If the Dut: of Maine did not act Iphigenia in perfection. Ouy, Madame, mais est ce là une merveille? qui, Diautre scauroit representer une Princesse, si non une autre?

To the King to whom Mr de Lione had said that I loved the old Burgundy Wine that His Maj^ty vsed to drink: Monsr Prior sayd the King vous aimez a ce que me dit Lione ce vieux vin, Je croy qu'il n'y a en France que Vous et Moy qui en buvons: vous une flattez agréablement. Point du tout Sire car votre Maj^té prend la liberté de le boire auec de l'eau, mais mons^r Lione me contraint de l'avaler tout pur.

To the King when M^r d'Aumont told him that We blooded the theater too much, and yt he had seen the heads brought in in Titus Andronicus: the K: is this accusation true Monsr Prior. We did it for an extraordinary occasion, to divert the D: of Aumont by the strangeness of the spectacle because he did not understand the beauty of the words.

/Many years ago to Mrs Stepney when I pay'd her a visitt and [fo. 136 b had left her son at Camb: she asking Me how he did, and if he did not drink: I sayd he was very well and drank sometimes moderately. She vrg'd, and desired Me to tell truth, Mr Prior you are constantly w^t him and I can belieue You, did you never see him drunk in yor life. Ans: no indeed Madam, for I was always drunk before him.

To the old E. of Westmorl. at Burleigh He not knowing Me nor I him I was just then come thither to be Govr to the young Lord Burghley. Pray S^r dont you belong to My lord Burghley: Ans: No S^r I haue made but a sorry bargain of it if he does not belong to Me.

BIOGRAPHICAL NOTES

[Names which are to be found in the *Dictionary of National Biography* are shown in the Index by the date of birth or death added to them.]

AGLIONBY, Dr WILLIAM, F.R.S., diplomat, engaged in diplomatic work in Holland, and in 1698 with the postal services between France, Spain and England, sent to Corunna 1701, employed by Queen Anne in Switzerland.

AUMONT, LOUIS MARIE, Duc d', governor of the Boulonnais, ambassador to Great Britain 1712.

AVAUX, CLAUDE DE MESNES, Comte d', French ambassador in United Provinces 1685, to James II in Ireland 1690, at Stockholm 1693, at The Hague 1700–1.

BARROIS, M. DE, Lorraine envoy at Versailles, 1713–4.

BART, JEAN, b. 1651, the celebrated Dunkirk privateer who rose from humble circumstances to commissioned rank, d. 1702.

BAVARIA, MAX EMANUEL, elector of, b. 1662, succeeded 1679, governor of the Spanish Netherlands, expelled by Marlborough and Eugene, restored to his hereditary dominions 1714, d. 1736.

—— JOSEPH FERDINAND, electoral prince of, b. 1693, d. 1699.

BECKAR, BALTHASAR, b. 1634, Dutch theologian, d. 1698.

BEDFORD, GERARD, a prisoner in Newgate whom the French desired released in 1699.

BERRY, CHARLES, Duke of, b. 1686, third son of the Grand Dauphin, married daughter of the Regent Orleans, d. 1714.

BOILEAU-DESPREAUX, NICOLAS, b. 1636, one of the foremost poets of the age of Louis XIV, author of *Le Lutrin* 1674, d. 1711.

BONREPOS, or BONREPAUX, intendant of French navy, sent as envoy to England and Holland 1686–8, to Copenhagen 1691–4, at The Hague 1699, member of the Council of Regency 1715.

BOREAL, JACOBUS, first burgomaster of Amsterdam, plenipotentiary at Ryswick, d. 1697.

BOUCHERAT, LOUIS, b. 1616, lawyer and statesman, chancellor of France 1685, d. 1699.

BOUFFLERS, LOUIS FRANÇOIS, Duc de, b. 1644, marshal of France, especially distinguished by his defence of Lille in 1708, d. 1711.

BOUGY, JEAN JACQUES, Marquis de Reverend de, b. 1655, a Protestant, retired to live abroad.

BOUILLON, DUCHESSE DE, Marie-Anne Mariani, b. 1646, niece of Mazarin, accused of sorcery and murder, exiled and retired to England, d. 1714.

BRANCAS-VILLARS, LOUIS ANTOINE, Duc de, b. 1682, one of the most notorious of the *roués* of the Regency.

BRANDENBURG, FREDERICK, Elector of, b. 1657, succeeded the Great Elector 1688, King of Prussia as Frederick I 1701, d. 1713.

BURGUNDY, LOUIS, Duke of, eldest son of Grand Dauphin, b. 1682, pupil of Fénelon, married, 1696, Marie Adelaide of Savoy (d. 1713), generally blamed for defeat at Oudenarde, d. 1713.

BUYS, WILLERN, Pensionary of Amsterdam 1701, plenipotentiary at the conferences of The Hague and Gertruydenberg, envoy to Great Britain 1711.

CAILLIÈRES, FRANÇOIS DE, b. 1645, engaged on various diplomatic missions, mainly in Holland, plenipotentiary at Ryswick 1697, member of the Academy, d. 1717.

CHAMILLART, MICHEL DE, b. 1651, created controller of finance 1699, his appointment one of Louis XIV's greatest mistakes, d. 1721.

CLEMENT, NICOLAS, b. 1651, *bibliothécaire en second* at Royal Library 1692, d. 1716.

COLOGNE, JOSEPH CLEMENT of Bavaria, Archbishop and Elector of, b. 1671, elected 1688, his election a pretext for the war of that year, d. 1723.

CONTI, MARIE ANNE DE BLOIS, princesse de, daughter of Louis XIV and Louise de La Vallière, b. 1667, married Prince de Conti 1680, abbess of St Cyr 1719.

COYSEVOX, ANTOINE, b. 1640, a prominent sculptor, d. 1720.

CRECY, LOUIS VERJUS, Comte de, b. 1629, French plenipotentiary at Ratisbon 1684, at Ryswick 1697, member of the French Academy, d. 1709.

CRESSET, JAMES, British envoy at Hamburg, later at Zell and Hanover, d. 1710.

CROY, FERDINAND GASTON LAMERALDUS, Duke of, governor of Mons, d. in 1697 of wounds received in action with the Turks.

D'ACIER, ANDRÉ, b. 1651, translator of many classical works, d. 1722.

DESMARETZ, NICOLAS, b. ? 1650, controller of finance in succession to Chamillart 1708–15, d. 1721, father of Marshal Maillebois.

DUGUAY-TROUIN, RENÉ, b. 1673, admiral in the French navy, captured Rio de Janeiro 1711, d. 1736.

DURAS, JACQUES HENRI, Duc de Durfort, marshal of France, b. 1622, d. 1704.

DYCKVELT, EVERARD VAN WEEDE VAN, Dutch envoy and statesman and colleague of Heinsius.

ESPINAY, MADAME D', Marie de Pompadour et de Rochechouart, wife of François d'Espinay, marquis de St Luc, d. 1723.

ESTRÉES, CÉSAR, Cardinal d', b. 1628, engaged by Louis XIV at the time of the great dispute with Rome, d. 1714.

—— VICTOR MARIE, b. 1660, Comte d', marshal, admiral, served by sea at Beachy Head, Teignmouth and Malaga, d. 1737.

EUGENE OF SAVOY, Prince, b. 1663, son of Comte de Soissons and Olympe Mancini, niece of Mazarin, failing to obtain a command from Louis XIV entered the Austrian service, served against the Turks, in conjunction with Marlborough defeated the French 1704–11, wrested the peace of Passarowitz from the Turks 1718, d. 1736.

EXETER, JOHN CECIL, Earl of, b. ? 1648, refused to take the oaths to William III, retired abroad and died at Issy 1700.

FALKLAND, ANTONY CARYE, Viscount, b. 1656, committed to the Tower for peculation in 1694, and died the same year.
—— REBECCA LYTTON, wife of the above, b. 1662, d. 1709.
FONTENELLE, BERNARD LE BOUYER DE, b. 1657, philosopher and poet, d. 1757.
FOUQUET, NICOLAS, Marquis de Belleisle, b. 1615, surintendant des finances, falsified his returns, disgraced and arrested 1661, died in prison 1680. Father of Marshal Belleisle.

GALLAS, ANTON, Count, b. 1669, envoy from the Emperor to Court of Queen Anne, d. 1716.
GAULTIER, ABBÉ FRANÇOIS, chaplain to Lady Jersey and secret agent to Louis XIV, d. 1724.

HARCOURT, HENRI, Duc d', Marshal, b. 1654, soldier and diplomat, ambassador at Madrid 1697–1700, d. 1718.
HARLAY, NICOLAS ANTOINE DE BONNEUIL DE, conseiller d'Etat, plenipotentiary at Ryswick 1697.
HARLEY, MARGARET, later Duchess of Portland, b. 1715, m. 2nd Duke in 1734, d. 1785.
—— THOMAS, cousin of Robert Earl of Oxford, envoy at Hanover 1710, d. 1738.
HEEMSKIRK, Dutch envoy in Paris, 1697–1701.
HEINSIUS, ANTHONY, b. 1641, ambassador to France 1678, threatened by Louvois with the Bastille, grand pensionary and the heart of the opposition to France after the death of William III, d. 1720.
HIGGINS, Sir THOMAS, gentleman usher to James II, secretary of state to James III.
HOORN, ARVID BERNARD, Count, b. 1664, governor of Furnes, d. 1742.
HORNE, Count, Swedish envoy at Vienna 1693, at Warsaw 1704.

IBERVILLE, CHARLES FRANÇOIS DE LA BONDE D', served in Canada and captured Hudson's Bay 1694, overran Newfoundland 1697, ambassador in London 1713–5.

JERSEY, BARBARA CHIFFINCH, Countess of, b. 1663, d. at Paris 1735.

KAUNITZ, DOMINICUS ANDREAS, Count, b. 1655, diplomatist in the Imperial service, d. 1705.
KICK, ABRAHAM, resident in Rotterdam who wished to be made British Consul there in 1694.
KINSKY, FRANZ ULRICH, Count, b. 1634, Austrian statesman and chancellor of Bohemia, d. 1699.

LA FORCE, SUZANNE DE BERINGHEU, Duchesse de, 2nd wife of Henrici Jacques Nompart de Caumont, duc de la Force; a strong Protestant who eventually retired to England.
LA MEILLERAYE, ARMAND CHARLES MAZARIN, Duc de, b. 1632, greatnephew of Richelieu, married Cardinal Mazarin's niece and heiress; an unamiable eccentric, d. 1713.
LEGAÑEZ, MARQUES, governor of Milan 1691–8, imprisoned for conspiracy in Spain 1705, and subsequently in France; d. a prisoner in Paris 1711.

LILIENROEDT, NICOLAS, Swedish ambassador in France, and in Holland 1692 till 1703, d. 1705.

LOUIS, Grand Dauphin, only son of Louis XIV, b. 1661, d. 1711.

LOUVOIS, Abbé CAMILLE LE TELLIER, fourth son of the minister, b. 1675, d. 1718.

LUXEMBOURG, FRANÇOIS HENRY DE MONTMORENCY, Duc de, Marshal, b. 1628, implicated in the Fronde with Condé, one of Louis XIV's greatest soldiers, won Fleurus 1690, Steinkirk 1692, Landen 1693, d. 1695.

MAINE, LOUIS AUGUSTE DE BOURBON, Duc du, legitimatised son of Louis XIV by Mme de Montespan, b. 1670; deprived of the right of succeeding to the Crown under the regency, d. 1736.

MAINTENON, FRANÇOISE D'AUBIGNÉ, Marquise de, b. 1635, wife of Scarron the poet, governess to Mme de Montespan's children, wife of Louis XIV 1683, d. 1719.

MARSIN, FERDINAND, Comte de, Marshal, b. 1656, in command with Tallard at Blenheim 1704, d. of wounds at Turin 1706.

MAZARINE, Madame HORTENSE MANCINI, niece of Mazarin and wife of the Duc de La Meilleraye (see above), b. 1646, separated from her husband, d. 1699.

MEDINA SIDONIA, JUAN CLARO ALFONSO, Duque de, Viceroy of Catalonia, an adherent of Philip V, d. 1713.

MEIERCRON, VON, Danish envoy to the court of France 1683.

MESMES, JEAN ANTOINE DE, b. 1661, President of the Parlement of Paris, one of the chief opponents of *Unigenitus* and of Law's system, d. 1723.

MESNAGER, NICOLAS LE BAILLIF, b. 1658, a prominent commercial lawyer of Rouen, sent to negociate peace at The Hague 1709 and in London 1711, d. 1714.

METZ, HENRI CHARLES DE CAMBOUT DE COISLIN, bishop of, b. 1664, bishop of Metz 1697, d. 1732.

MONSIEUR. *See* ORLEANS.

MONTÉLÉON, ISIDOR CAZADO, Marques de, Spanish ambassador at Utrecht 1713, to England, arrested with despatches of Cellamare conspiracy 1718, ambassador at Venice 1731, d.

MONTPELLIER, CHARLES JOACHIM COLBERT DE CROISSY, b. 1667, bishop of Montpellier 1697, an opponent of the Constitution *Unigenitus*, issued the Montpellier Catechism, d. 1738.

NOAILLES, ANNE JULES, Duc de, Marshal, b. 1650, sent to persecute the Protestants after the Revocation of the Edict of Nantes, d. 1708.

ORLEANS, PHILIP, Duc d', brother of Louis XIV, b. 1640, d. 1701.

—— —— son of the preceding, b. 1674, Regent on the death of Louis XIV, d. 1723.

OROPESA, EMANUEL JOACHIM ALVAREZ DE TOLEDO-PORTUGAL-CORDOVA-MENDEZ-AYALA, Conde de, b. 1642, head of the Austrian party at Madrid 1698, the object of a popular riot 1699, espoused the cause of Charles III and left Spain 1706, d. in the service of Charles at Barcelona 1709.

ORRERY, MARY, natural daughter of 4th Earl of Dorset, Countess of, b. 1648, d. 1710.

Ossuna, Francisco Maria de Paula Tellez Giron, Duque de, b. 1678, Spanish plenipotentiary at Utrecht, d. 1716.

Oxford, Edward Harley, Earl of, b. 1689, succeeded 1724, dissipated his wife's large fortune, collector of the Harleian library, d. 1741.

—— Henrietta Cavendish, Countess of, b. 1693, d. 1735.

Pajot, Léon, Comte d'Ouzenbray, *fermier général des postes* and member of the *Académie des Sciences.*

Palmquist, Swedish ambassador in Paris 1693–1702, later at The Hague.

Paris, Louis Antoine Cardinal de Noailles, Archbishop of, b. 1651, suspected of sympathy with Jansenism, but adhered to the Constitution *Unigenitus*, d. 1729.

Parma, Francesco Farnese, Duke of, stepfather of Elizabeth Farnese, d. 1727.

Pecquet, secretary to Torcy, remaining at the foreign office after his retirement, imprisoned as a friend of Chauvelin 1737.

Perauld, Pierre, a French prisoner whose release the English demanded in exchange for Gerard Bedford.

Pettkum, resident of the Duke of Holstein at The Hague; went to Paris to mediate peace in 1709.

Pomponne, Simon Arnauld, Marquis de, b. 1618, shared Fouquet's disgrace, recalled to be secretary of state for foreign affairs, disgraced again, recalled and became Torcy's guide in 1691, d. 1699.

Pontchartrain, Louis Phelypeaux, Comte de, b. 1643, lawyer; chancellor of France, 1699–1714, d. 1727.

Quiros, Don Francisco Bernardo de, Spanish envoy at Ryswick, espoused the cause of Charles III, whom he served in Brabant, d. 1709.

Reay, George Mackay, Lord, succeeded ? 1680, d. 1748.

Regnier-Desmarais, Abbé François Séraphin, b. 1632, man of letters and grammarian, d. 1713.

Renaudot, Eusèbe, b. 1646, Oratorian, journalist and savant, d. 1720.

Rheims, Charles Maurice le Tellier, Archbishop of, son of the Chancellor Le Tellier, b. 1642, coadjutor archbishop 1668, archbishop 1671, d. 1710.

Ross, General Charles, of Balnagowan; supported the Tories in 1710, M.P. for Ross-shire 1707–32, d. 1732.

Rygault, Hippolyte, b. 1659, the son and grandson of a painter; chiefly a portrait painter, d. 1743.

Salisbury, Frances Bennett, Countess of, wife of the Earl who "turned too soon" in 1688, b. 1670, d. 1713.

Sandwich, Edward Montagu, Earl of, b. ? 1670, d. 1729.

—— Elizabeth Wilmot, Countess of, married the above 1689, d. 1757.

Savoy, Victor Amadeus II, Duke of, b. 1666, succeeded 1675, King of Sicily 1713, exchanged Sicily for Sardinia 1719, abdicated 1730, tried to resume the government 1731, imprisoned, d. 1732.

Saxony, John George IV, b. 1668, Elector 1691, d. 1694, being succeeded by his brother Frederick Augustus, b. 1670, King of Poland as Augustus I 1697, deposed 1704, restored 1709, d. 1733.

SCHMETTAU, WOLFGANG VON, entered the service of the King of Prussia, diplomatist, from 1701 Prussian envoy at The Hague where he d. 1711.

SOMERSET, ELIZABETH THYNNE, Duchess of, formerly Lady Elizabeth Percy, b. 1667?, d. 1722.

STAFFORD, FRANK, gentleman usher to James II at St Germains.

TALLARD, CAMILLE D'HOSTUN, Comte de, Marshal, served in the army and the diplomatic service, ambassador to England 1697–1700, commanded at Blenheim 1704, prisoner of war in England 1704–14, d. 1728.

TENCIN, CLAUDINE ALEXANDRINE GUÉRIN DE, b. 1681, a nun, left her convent and lived a full life; reformed and was the centre of a literary coterie, d. 1749. She was the mother of d'Alembert.

TESSÉ, MANS JEAN BAPTISTE RENÉ DE FROULAY, Comte de, Marshal, b. 1651, d. 1725.

TORCY, JEAN BAPTISTE COLBERT DE CROISSY, Marquis de, b. 1665, secretary of state for foreign affairs 1689–1715, after the death of Louis XIV devoted himself chiefly to letters, d. 1746.

—— CATHERINE FÉLICITÉ DE POMPONNE, Marquise de, daughter of Pomponne the minister.

TOULOUSE, LOUIS ALEXANDRE DE BOURBON, Comte de, b. 1678, son of Louis XIV and Madame de Montespan, commanded the French fleet at Malaga 1704.

VILLARS, CLAUDE LOUIS HECTOR, Duc de, Marshal, b. 1653, the last of Louis XIV's great generals; saved France at Denain 1712, d. on active service at Turin 1734.

VILLEROY, FRANÇOIS DE NEUFVILLE, Duc de, Marshal, b. 1644, captured by the Austrians 1703, released; commanded at Ramillies 1706, d. 1730.

VILLIERS, WILLIAM, Viscount, 2nd Earl of Jersey, b. 1682, a Jacobite, created Earl of Jersey by James III, d. 1721.

—— HENRY, youngest son of the 1st Earl of Jersey, d. s. p. 1743.

VOISIN, DANIEL FRANÇOIS, b. 1654, intendant of Hainault, secretary for war 1709–14, chancellor of France 1714–7, d. 1717.

VRILLIÈRE, BALTHASAR DE PHELYPEAUX, Seigneur de, secretary of state 1661, d. 1700.

ZELL, GEORGE WILLIAM, last Duke, d. 1705.

ZINZENDORF, FRANZ LUDWIG, Count, b. 1661, soldier, councillor and diplomat in the Imperial service, d. 1742.

INDEX